Michigan Cross-Country Skiing Atlas

Third Edition

A Guide to Public and Private Ski Trails

By

Dennis R. Hansen

FIRST EDITION
First Printing—August 1977
Second Printing—December 1977

SECOND EDITION
First Printing—August 1978
Second Printing—January 1979

THIRD EDITION
First Printing—September 1981

MICHIGAN CROSS-COUNTRY SKIING ATLAS 3rd Edition is published by Hansen Publishing Company, PO Box 1723, East Lansing, Michigan 48823-6723

Printed in the United States of America

Library of Congress Catalog Card Number: 80-80212
ISBN: 0-930098-03-X

Graphic Design by Barbara Brown
Cover Photo by Michigan Department of Natural Resources

Dealer Distribution by Holley International Company,
63 Kercheval—Suite 204A, Grosse Pointe Farms,
Michigan 48236 (313) 882-0405

to . . .
Barbara,
Stephanie and Lisa

Preface

This is the 1981 3rd edition of the *Michigan Cross Country Skiing Atlas,* originally published in 1977. The entire book has been revised to provide the latest trail information throughout Michigan and for the first time adjoining border regions of Canada and Wisconsin. Every effort has been made to insure that the information presented is correct. However, because this type of information can readily change, its accuracy can not be guaranteed. With recent funding problems in State government, DNR trails will be subject to some degree of reductions in maintenance and/or closings are possible. I suggest that a phone call be made in advance, to verify critical information in order to insure a pleasurable trip.

Further editions are planned. The author would appreciate and welcome any information of both positive and negative in nature about the trails listed in this book and others that we overlooked. Please send the information to Hansen Publishing Company, PO Box 1723, East Lansing, MI 48823-6723.

This book is intended as an aid for the cross country skier. Skiers should understand that they use the trails and areas depicted herein at their own risk. Therefore, the author, publisher and distributor of the book assume no personal or public liability for accidents or injuries incurred through the use of the *Michigan Cross Country Skiing Atlas*.

To make a success of a project such as this, requires the assistance of countless individuals throughout the region. Without their cooperation, this book could not exist.

Dennis Hansen
East Lansing
1981

Table of Contents

History of Nordic Skiing

by Danforth Holley

Like you, I love skiing, especially Cross Country. I also love our beautiful State of Michigan, which boasts such a vast number of wilderness areas with terrain uniquely suited to Cross Country Skiing that it is fast becoming one of the nation's leading areas for this great ancient sport.

Would you be startled to know that Cross Country Skiing is at least 4,000 years old? On the Island of Rødøy in Northern Norway is a stone-age rock carving depicting a man on skis. This 4,000 year old figure is surrounded by animal figures (not pictured here) which suggests he is a hunter who owes his fame more to his ability to ski than to bag a hearty meal.

Ancient skis have been unearthed in Finland, Sweden and Norway. Ancient Norwegian ski finds include the Øvrebø ski which is about 2,500 years old. The number and quality of workmanship of these various skis is an astounding and fascinating history of man's resourcefulness in an inhospitable environment.

Our first written reference to skis and skiers is found in early Viking sagas from 900 to 1100 A.D., replete with male and female ski gods, hunting, friendly competition, and warfare on skis.

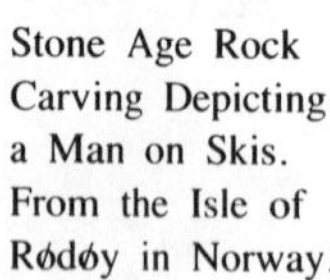

Stone Age Rock Carving Depicting a Man on Skis. From the Isle of Rødøy in Norway.

The earliest skis were made of large animal bones which were smoothed on the joint ends to produce a flat surface that allowed for a swift, gliding motion. These were strapped to the feet with skin or thongs. The world's oldest known skis, made of bone, are displayed at the Djugarden Museum in Stockholm and are at least 4,000 years old.

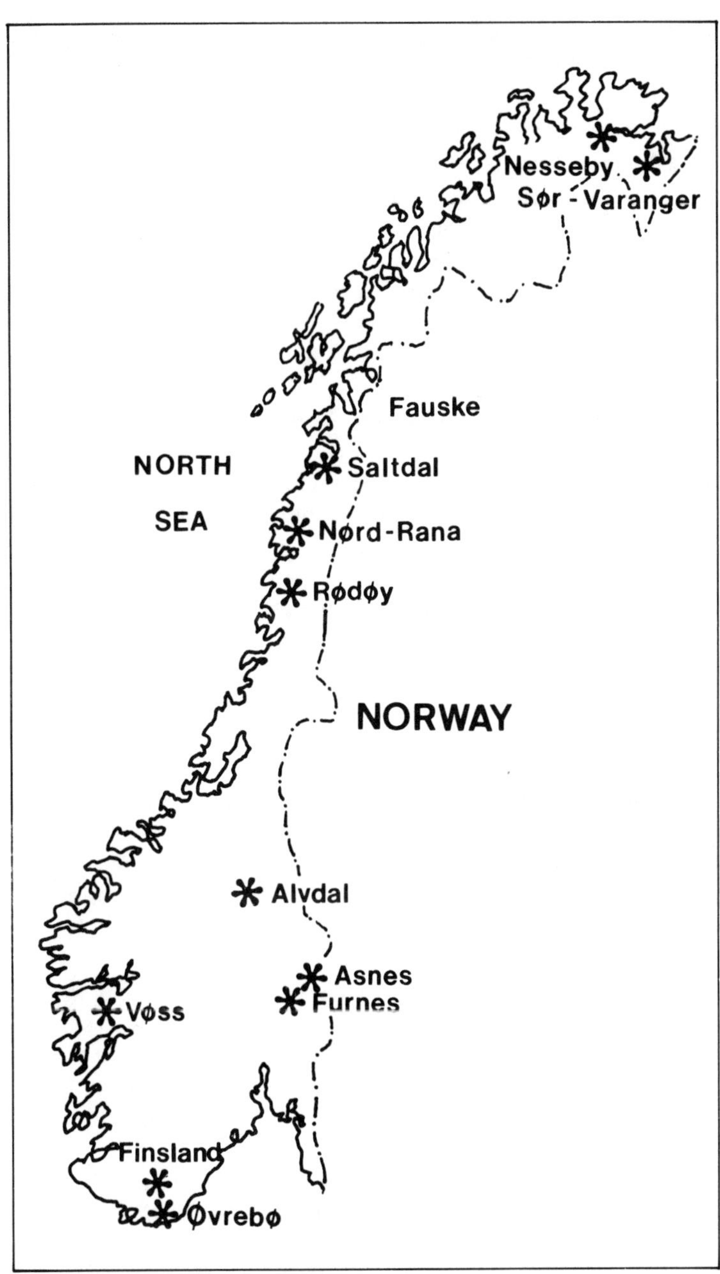

Locations of Ancient Ski Finds in Norway Dating Back from 1,000 to 2,500 Years.

The first historical account of skis used in warfare was during the Battle of Oslo in 1200 A.D. when King Sverre of Sweden sent scouts on skis to spy on the Norwegian enemy camp. Feeling as fiesty as they were fleet on foot, the Swedes continued to use skis in the Wars of 1521, 1576, 1590 and 1610 A.D.

The long tradition of skis in warfare has given birth to great competitive events throughout the world. Here in Michigan the annual North American Vasaloppet Race, of which I am proud to be one of the founders, is patterned after the world's longest ski race (85 kilometers) held each March in Dalecarlia, Sweden, which attracts some of the world's best Cross Country racers. The race honors the Swedish patriot, Gustavus Vasa, who in 1521 skied from Salen to Moran, Sweden, to lead his countrymen against King Christian II of Denmark. The North American Vasaloppet, "Vasa" in recognition of Gustavus Vasa and "loppet" meaning long distance, is a 25 kilometer (16 miles) and a 50 kilometer (32 miles) race, held in Traverse City.

Another race you should know about is the American Birkebeiner Race held each year near Cable, Wisconsin. Initiated in 1973, this 55 kilometer Cross Country back-buster is also patterned after a similar race, this time in Norway, that commemorates a Viking saga about the rescue of a Norwegian child Prince in 1206. "Birkebeiner" means birch legs, referring to the leggings worn by the king's warriors.

The actual sport of skiing, as opposed to its purely practical application in hunting and warfare, began in the Telemark District of Norway in the 1850s when the Norwegian, Sondre Nordheim invented the toe-piece and heel-strap binding which gave proper control of skis for the first time. Impromptu races and jumping contests were held and in the 1850s an annual get-together of ski enthusiasts was held with accompanying one- and two-day festivals. Skiing became fashionable in the 1860s when the Royal Family organized an annual ski-jumping tournament at Holmenkollen, near Oslo, appointed a committee to draft rules, and donated a trophy. This contest soon became the greatest national sports event in Norway and Cross Country and other forms of skiing were added. Today, one can visit the famous Holmenkollen Jump which is still

In the U.S.A., ski teams were sent to the Olympics in the 1930s. In the 1940s and 50s most of the Cross Country Skiing was still done by racers. However, in the 60s, snowbelt families began to get interested in Cross Country Skiing. Early in the decade, there was only one annual open Cross Country Race with less than 100 racers, but by the early 70s, the sport had really caught on.

Here in the U.S.A., two developers have been to modern skiing what Sondre Nordheim was to ancient skiing—Howard Head having pioneered the wood and metal ski and I am credited with the first fiberglass ski, the first L-shaped edge, plastic snow, and Holley Speed Spray, which are all in the Ski Hall of Fame in Ishpeming, Michigan. Ishpeming, which is located in the Upper Peninsula, may sound like an unlikely place for the Hall of Fame, but it is especially appropriate because at the time skiing was becoming a sport, Swedes and Norwegians were coming to Michigan at the onset of the lumber boom. Not only does the museum represent their ardent interest in skiing, but at Ishpeming is the famous "Suicide Hill," one of the most famous ski jumps in the world, and in nearby Ironwood is the "Ski Flying Hill," one of the world's largest jumps.

Cross Country Skiing has also been going on in this area since the Nordic settlers' children first strapped on their home-made skis as their fathers and grandfathers used to do in the Old World.

The history of Cross Country Skiing is full of colorful events and characters and one man whose exploits made him a legend in his own time was John A. "Snow-Shoe" Thompson. A native of the Telemark District of Norway, he was lured to California by gold fever in the 1850s. Learning that mail carriers were hard pressed to make it over the mountains in winter, he set up a route and carried mail on skis across the Sierras. His skill and daring on his hand-carved skis were unmatched, whether in schussing hills at mile-a-minute clips, leaping obstacles 30, 40 and 50 yards, or slaloming down slopes with serpentine grace. He is considered by many to be the Father of American Skiing and has been memorialized since 1946 by an annual Cross Country Ski Race. It is interesting to note he used skis that were 8′9½″ long and one long pole to veer his course from one side to another. One pole was tradition that he brought from Norway.

During World War II the famous American 10th Mounties Division is credited by General Mark Clark as having been a leading factor in winning the war in Italy with their bold Alpine maneuvers for which a special dual purpose binding was utilized for combined Alpine and Cross Country Skiing.

But enough of books and history. It is time to enter the wintery wonders of Michigan, and you will not find yourself alone. The woods are "silent, dark and deep," but also becoming, peopled by those eager to commune with nature without the snarling and fuming intrusion of snowmobiles. Cross Country Skiing equipment is reasonably inexpensive and trail expenses minimal. Skiing with a good rucksack on your back, loaded with good wine, bread and cheese, isn't too dear. For those who love wildlife, photographing beautiful landscapes, deer, elk, rabbits, birds and whomever else you might run across in the wild woods; for those who look for a close-knit family sport which doctors claim is one of the best all around exercises; for those who seek clean air and serenity—there is no better sport.

I believe I have contributed much to the sport of skiing—as a Director of the U.S. Ski Association for 10 years, as a Director of Michigan's oldest Ski Club, Otsego, where I head the Cross Country Ski Program, as a developer and producer of ski waxes and many other products, as a Certified Professional Ski Instructor, plus, I have spent over 50 years skiing throughout this country and

Europe and I have absorbed information that would be helpful to you and that I would be delighted to pass on to you. It is my fervent wish that you take advantage of the years of work and preparation that have gone into the making of this Atlas by going out and exploring the unparalleled beauty of Michigan's Ski Trails.

If I can be of assistance to you, feel free to contact me at 63 Kercheval–Suite #204A, Grosse Pointe Farms, Michigan 48236. Phone (313) 882-0405.

DANFORTH HOLLEY

*The North American Vasaloppet Race has been changed to the North American Vasa Race.

How To Use This Atlas

This guide has been compiled to easily locate any specific trail of interest or to locate trails in any specific part of the state. Therefore, you will find throughout this guide, regional maps of the state to aid you in this task. These regional trail location maps are keyed to both trail descriptions and individual trail maps for easy reference.

The region location map found on the following page divides the state into four regions corresponding to the four main divisions of this book. A regional trail location map is located at the beginning of each of these divisions for that specific area of the state. The key numbers shown on each regional map denotes the specific location of the various trails in the region. For convenience in locating the trails, each map also shows main roads and major cities. It is suggested, especially if you intend to ski some of the more isolated trails, that you acquire the publication *Michigan County Maps and Recreation Guide* from the Michigan United Conservation Clubs, PO Box 30235, Lansing, MI 48909. Cost is $8.00 postpaid. The publication is also available at many bookstores. Following the regional trail location map, written descriptions for each of the numbered trails are given. To locate the trail of interest in the description section, the trail map number found on the trail location map is listed to the far left edge of the left page. The page number for the individual trail map is listed on the far right of the facing page. The trail maps for each region are located immediately after all of the trail descriptions for that individual region.

If you know the name of the trail, there is an index located in the back of the guide that lists the pages on which both the trail map and the trail description can be found.

REGION LOCATION MAP

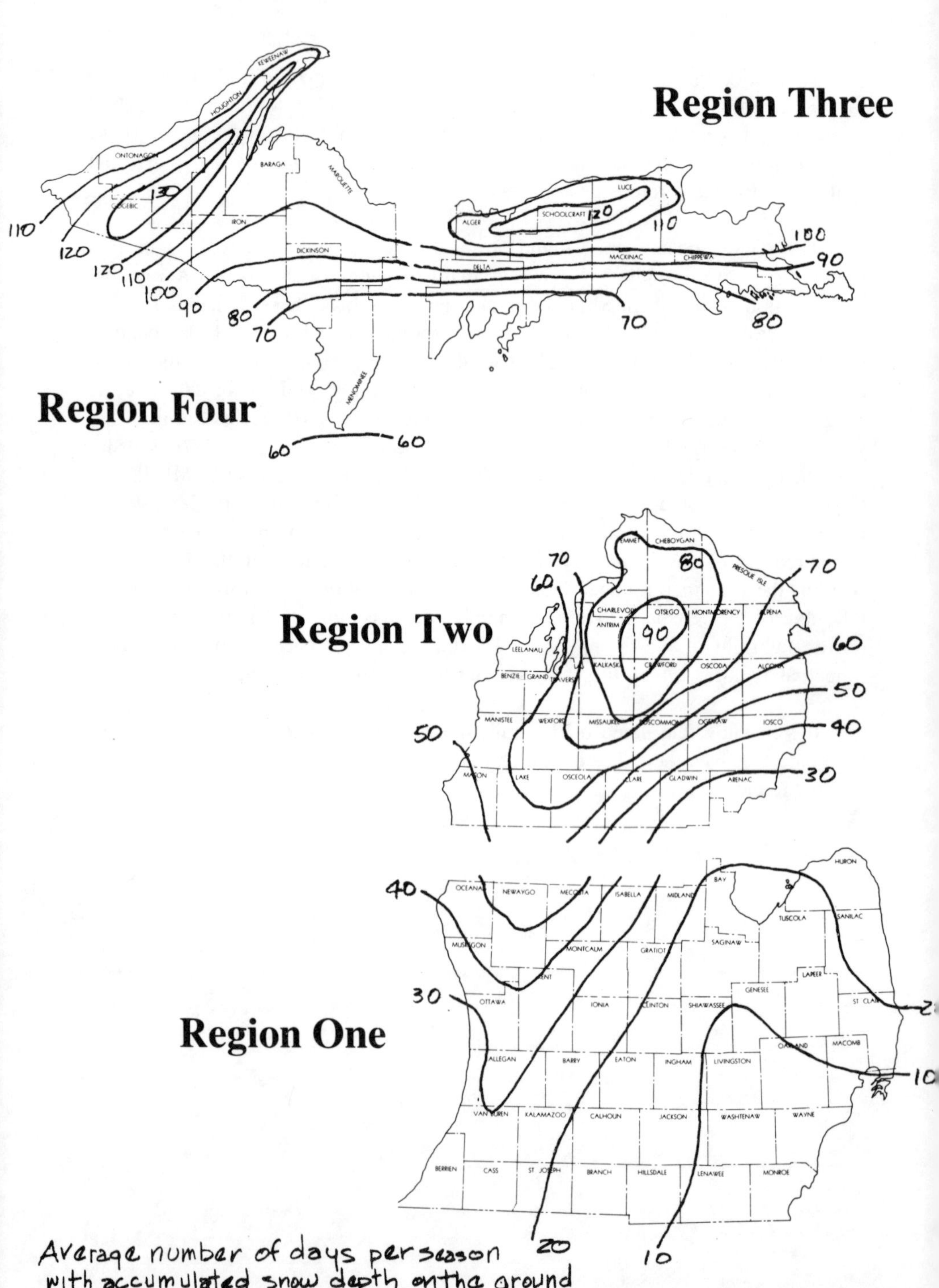

Average number of days per season with accumulated snow depth on the ground of 6' or more. Source: H.S.U. Ag. Ext. Bulletin E-715

Snow Conditions

The lines running through the map on the facing page show the average annual snowfall in inches. Because temperature, elevation and the "lake effect" all play a major part in maintaining good snow conditions, Michigan cross-country skiing opportunities vary greatly throughout the state. Generally acceptable conditions can be found north of Clare most of the winter season. South of this point, skiing conditions can vary greatly from area to area and from year to year. Snow developing from moisture off Lake Michigan plays a major part in this variation in the southwest counties.

On the other extreme, the upper peninsula usually has such a great deal of snowfall that skiing off established trails can be difficult during much of the winter. Only in the beginning of the season when the snow depth is not great or at the end of the winter when the snow has compacted somewhat due to rising temperatures is off trail skiing easy.

Generally the skiing season for the four regions are as follows:

Region One	Late December to Mid February
Region Two	Early December to Late February
Region Three	Late November to Late March
Region Four	Late November to Early April

Legend for Ski Trail Maps

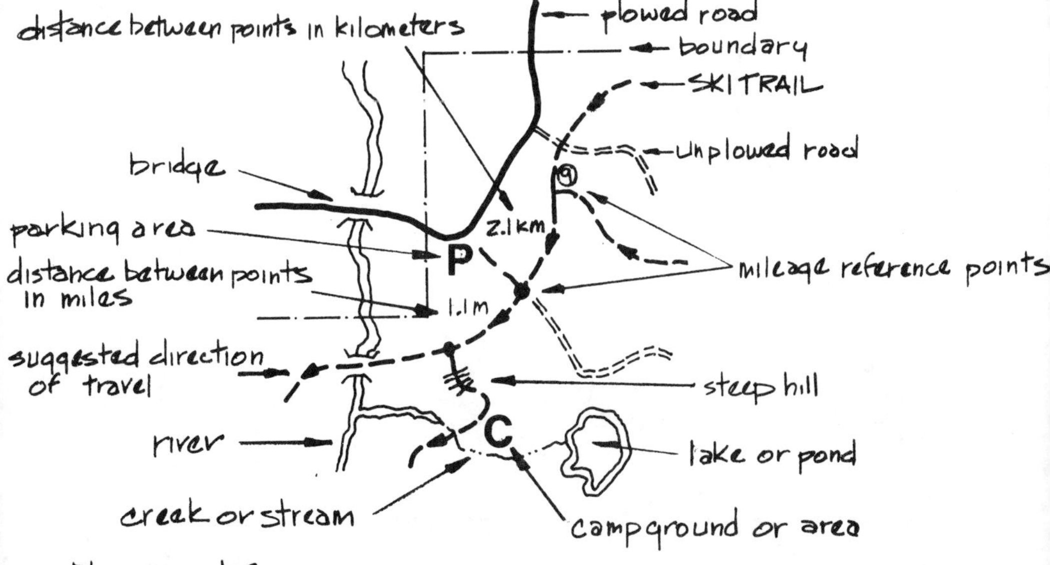

Region One

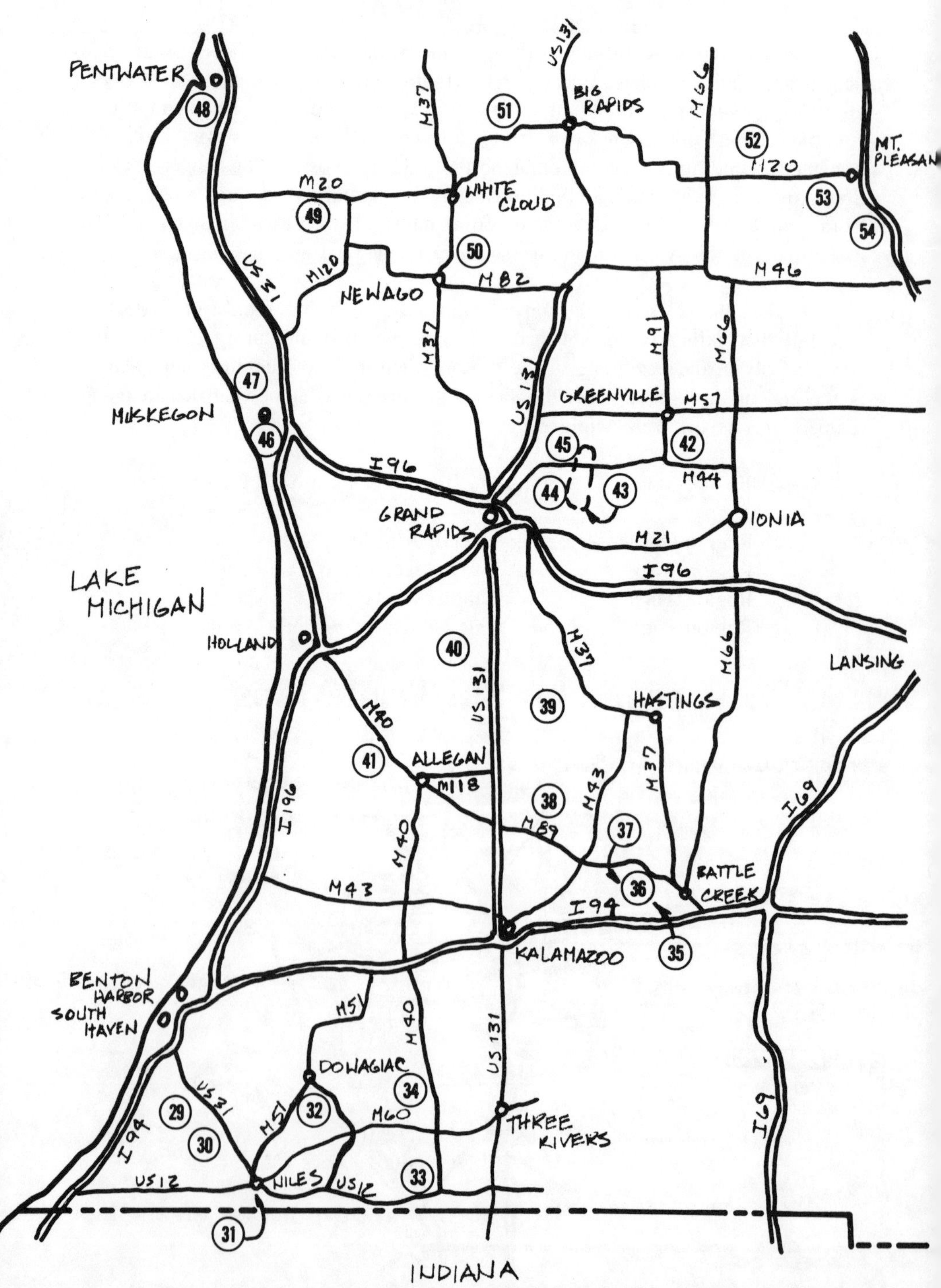

PENTWATER
48
M37
51
US131
BIG RAPIDS
M66
52
MT. PLEASAN
M20
WHITE CLOUD
M20
49
53
54
50
M120
US31
NEWAGO
M82
M46
M91
M66
M37
US131
47
MUSKEGON
GREENVILLE
M57
46
45
42
I96
M44
44
43
GRAND RAPIDS
IONIA
M21
I96
LAKE MICHIGAN
HOLLAND
40
M37
M66
LANSING
US131
39
HASTINGS
M40
41
ALLEGAN
M118
M43
M37
38
I196
M40
M89
37
I69
BATTLE CREEK
36
M43
I94
KALAMAZOO
35
BENTON HARBOR
SOUTH HAVEN
M51
M40
US131
DOWAGIAC
34
US31
29
M51
32
M60
THREE RIVERS
I69
30
I94
US12
NILES
US12
33
31
INDIANA

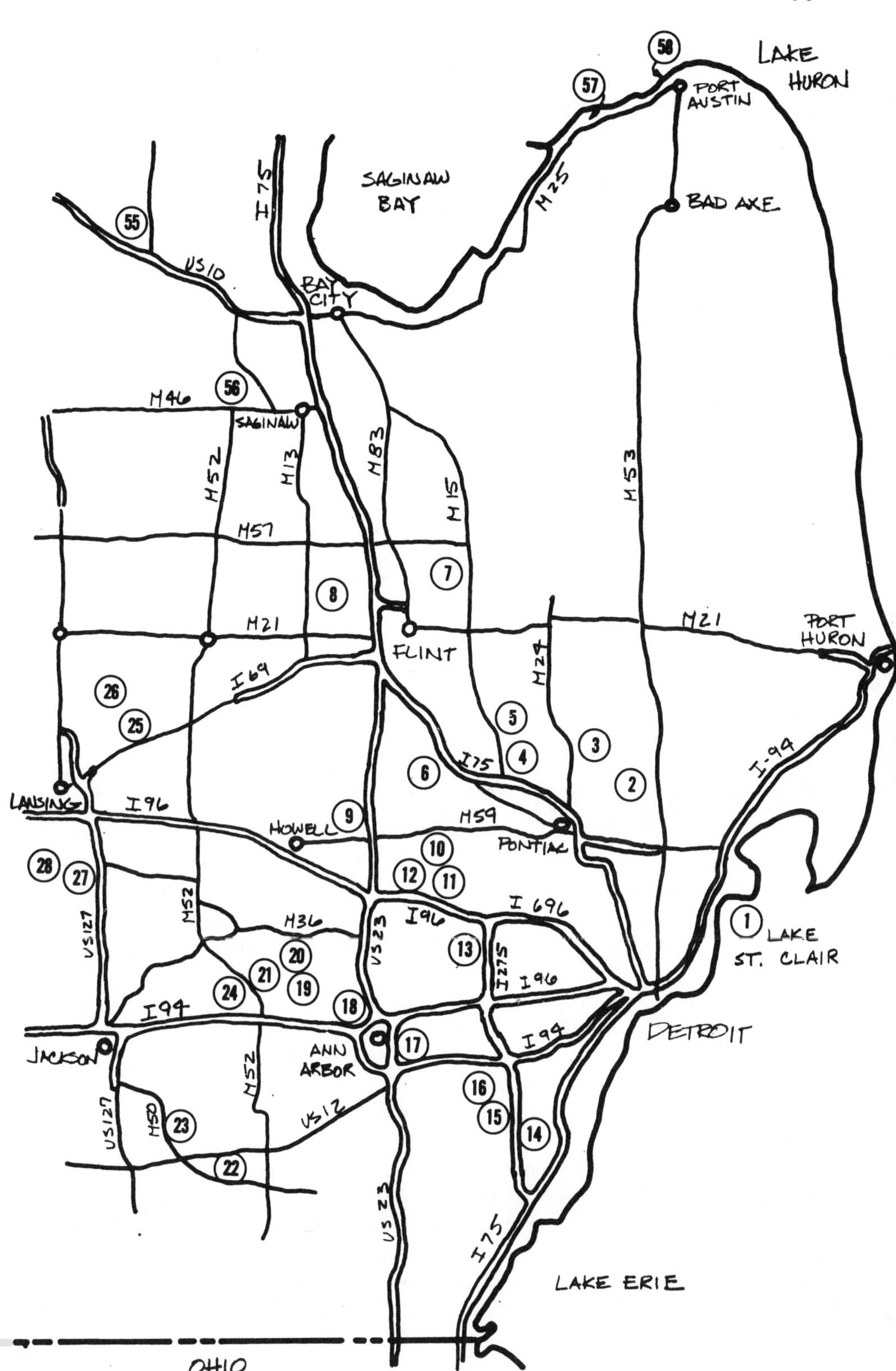
LAKE HURON
PORT AUSTIN
SAGINAW BAY
BAD AXE
M25
I75
US10
BAY CITY
M46
SAGINAW
M52
M13
M83
M15
M53
M57
M21
FLINT
PORT HURON
M24
I69
LANSING
I96
HOWELL
M59
PONTIAC
I-94
I696
LAKE ST. CLAIR
US127
M36
US23
I275
I94
DETROIT
JACKSON
ANN ARBOR
M50
US12
LAKE ERIE
OHIO
1
2
3
4
5
6
7
8
9
10
11
12
13
14
15
16
17
18
19
20
21
22
23
24
25
26
27
28
55
56
57
58

REGION 1 — SOUTH HALF OF THE LOWER PENINSULA

TRAIL MAP NUMBER	Name	Location	Number of Loops Distances (miles)	Total length of System (miles)	Maintained in the Winter	Total Acres
1	Metro Beach Metropark 313-463-4581	3 miles east of I-94 on 16 Mile Rd	NA	NA	NA	200
2	Stoney Creek Metropark 313-781-4242	1.5 miles west of M53 on 26 Mile Rd	4 loops 1.25, 1.75, 1.75, 4.5	9.2	yes	1000
3	Mt Grampian 313-628-2450	2 miles east of Oxford	NA	4.5	NA	NA
4	Independence-Oaks County Park 313-625-0877	2½ miles north of I-75 via Sashabaw Rd	many	20km	yes	830
5	Ortonville Recreation Area 313-627-3828	Two trails— Bloomer No. 3 on State Park Rd; Big Fish Lake on Hadley Rd; both are NE of Ortonville	3 loops	6	no	4000
6	Wathana Ski Touring Center 313-634-4104, 477-8116	8 miles north of M59 on Milford Rd near Holly (just south of I-75)	NA	3	yes	NA

Golf Courses Open for Nordic Skiing in Southeast Michigan

(Key: A-Marked trails, B-Lighted trails, C-Rentals, D-Instruction, E-Food)

Bruce Hills—6771 Taft, Romeo, 752-7244 ABCDE
Maple Lane—14 Mile and Hoover, Sterling Heights, 754-3020 ABCE
Sunny Acres—30750 Little Mack, Roseville, 293-1410 ABE
Rattle Run—7163 St. Clair Hwy., St. Clair, 329-2070 AE
Faulkwood Shores—300 S. Hughes, Howell, 546-4180 ACE
Woodland—7635 W. Grand River, Brighton, 229-9663 ACDE
Ponderosa—6900 E M-59, Howell, 546-7390 ACDE
Oxford Hills—300 E. Drahner, Oxford, 628-2518 E
Dunham Hills—13561 Dunham, Milford, 887-9170 ACE
Springfield Oaks—12450 Andersonville, Davisburg, 625-8133 C
Rochester—655 Michelson, Rochester, 852-4800 ABCDE
White Lake Oaks—991 S. Willims Lake, Pontiac, 698-2700 CE
Pontiac Municipal—800 Golf Drive, Pontiac, 857-7780 E

P —Pro Shop
R —Rentals
W—Warming Area
C —Certified Instruction
S —Snack Bar
D —Dining Room
B —Brown Bag
A —Accommodations

Novice	Intermediate	Expert	Terrain	Trail Use Fee	Campground	Remarks	TRAIL MAP PAGE
√			flat	√		Operated by the Huron-Clinton Metropolitan Authority	none
√	√	√	flat to rolling	√		R,W,C,S,B Operated by the Huron-Clinton Metropolitan Authority with Raupp Campfitters rental shop 781-3000	26
√	√		NA	√		P,R,W,S,D Privately operated alpine ski area	none
√	√	√	flat to hilly	√		W,S Operated by Oakland County Site of race held in January	27
√	√		flat to rolling			Operated by the DNR	28
√			flat to rolling	√		P,R,W,C,S,A Privately operated nordic ski area	none

Golf Courses Open for Nordic Skiing in Southeast Michigan

(Key: A-Marked trails, B-Lighted trails, C-Rentals, D-Instruction, E-Food)

Morey's Golf and Country Club—2280 Union Lake, Union Lake, 363-4101 E
Glen Oaks—30500 W. 13 Mile Rd., Farmington Hills, 851-8356 CDE
Lincoln Hills—2666 W. 14 Mile Rd., Birmingham, 647-4159 CDE
Red Oaks—John R and 12 Mile Rd., Madison Heights, 588-1200 D
Beechwoods—22200 Beech, Southfield, 354-4786 CDE
William Rogell—18601 Berg, Detroit, 928-5316/685-2379 ACDE
Riverview—15015 Sibley, Riverview, 479-4333 ACDE
Hawthorne Valley—31002 W. Warren, Westland, 422-3440 E
Whispering Willows—20690 Newburg, Livonia, 476-4493 A
Lower Huron—17845 Savage, Detroit, 697-9181
Water's Edge—25215 W. Grand River, Grosse Ile, 675-0777 ACDE
Raisin River—1500 N. Dixie Hwy., Monroe, 423-2050 ABE

REGION 1 SOUTH HALF OF THE LOWER PENINSULA

TRAIL MAP NUMBER	Name	Location	Number of Loops Distances (miles)	Total length of System (miles)	Maintained in the Winter	Total Acres
7	Holloway Reservoir Regional Park 313-736-7100	NE of Flint. Exit I-69 at Elba Rd, north on Elba Rd to Coldwater Rd, then west on Coldwater Rd to entrance	1 loop	2.8	no	800
8	Flushing County Park 313-736-7100	North of the Village of Flushing on McKinley Rd	1 loop	1.2	no	110
9	Waldenwoods 313-632-7304	1.25 miles north of M59 on west service drive for US23	6 loops .25,.25 1,1.25 3,5	10	no	1400
10	Highland Recreation Area 313-887-5135	12 miles west of Pontiac via M59	3 loops 3,4,5	12	no	5400
11	Proud Lake Recreation Area 313-685-2379	Between Milford and Commerce, 4 miles north of I-96 via Wixom Rd	several	20	no	2200
12	Kensington Metropark 313-685-1561	4.5 miles east of Brighton via I-96	6 loops .9,1.7,2 6.4,4.1, 7.1km	23	yes	3000
13	Maybury State Park 313-349-8390	4 miles west of I-275 via 8 Mile Rd	many	18	no	940
14	Oakwoods Metropark 313-782-1255	1 mile east of I-275 off Willow Rd on the Huron River near Flat Rock	NA	NA	NA	1300
15	Willow Metropark 313-782-1255	Adjacent to I-275 off Willow Rd on the Huron River near Flat Rock	NA	NA	NA	1500
16	Lower Huron Metropark 313-697-9181	1 mile south of I-94 at Haggerty Rd exit, then east 1 mile to Hannan Rd, then south ½ mile to entrance	NA	NA	NA	1200

P —Pro Shop S —Snack Bar
R —Rentals D —Dining Room
W—Warming Area B —Brown Bag
C —Certified Instruction A —Accommodations

Novice	Intermediate	Expert	Terrain	Trail Use Fee	Campground	Remarks	TRAIL MAP PAGE
	√		rolling			Operated by the Genesee County Parks and Recreation Commission	**none**
√			flat			Operated by the Genesee County Parks and Recreation Commission	**none**
√	√	√	flat to hilly	√	√	W,S,B,A Privately operated resort and conference center Campground on property Several wooded trails	**29**
√	√		rolling to hilly			R,W Heavner Ski Center, 313-685-2379	**30**
√	√		flat to rolling	√		P,R,W at Heavner Ski Center located on Garden Rd, ¼ mile west of Wixom Rd, 313-685-2379 Moonlight ski tour each week from ski center	**31**
√	√		flat to rolling and hilly	√		R,W,C,S,B Operated by the Huron-Clinton Metropolitan Authority with Raupp Campfitters rental shop 685-1408 Some trails on the golf course	**32**
√			flat to gently rolling	√		P,R,W,C,S by private concessionnaire Ski trails utilize horse, bicycle and hiking trails	**33**
√			flat			R,W,S,B Operated by the Huron-Clinton Metropolitan Authority with Raupp Campfitters rental shop	**34**
√			flat			R,W,S,B Operated by the Huron-Clinton Metropolitan Authority with Raupp Campfitters rental shop	**35**
√			flat			Operated by the Huron-Clinton Metropolitan Authority Next to Willow Metropark	**36**

REGION SOUTH HALF OF THE LOWER PENINSULA

TRAIL MAP NUMBER	Name	Location	Number of Loops Distances (miles)	Total length of System (miles)	Maintained in the Winter	Total Acres
17	County Farm Ski Trail 313-994-2575	1 mile west of US23 on Washtenaw Ave. Parking lot off Manchester on Medford	1 loop	1.5	no	NA
18	Washtenaw County	Various	NA	NA	NA	NA
19	Hudson Mills Metropark 313-426-8211	12 miles NW of Ann Arbor on the Huron River off N. Territorial Rd at Hudson Mills	1 loop	NA	NA	935
20	Pinckney Recreation Area 313-426-4913	Trail starts at Silver Lake Beach across Silver Hill Rd from area headquarters, 5 miles SW of Pinckney via Toma and Tiplady Roads	3 loops 2,5,17	21	no	9600
21	Park Lyndon North Ski Trail 313-994-2575	1 mile east of M52 on North Territorial Rd	1 loop	1.1	no	NA
22	Shamrock Valley 517-467-2137	In the Irish Hills, one block south of the Irish Hills Twin Towers on US12	NA	2	no	20
23	Sauk Valley Farms 517-467-2061	Brooklyn	NA	10km	no	500
24	Waterloo Recreation Area 313-475-8307	3 miles NW of Chelsea via Sibley, Conway and Bush Rds	several	4	no	17000
25	Rose Lake Wildlife Research Area 517-339-2550	12 miles NE of Lansing via M78 and Upton, Peacock or Woodbury Rds	many	10	no	3300
26	Sleepy Hollow State Park 517-651-6217	North of Lansing, 6 miles east of US27 on Price Rd	3 loops	5	no	2670

P —Pro Shop
R —Rentals
W—Warming Area
C —Certified Instruction
S —Snack Bar
D —Dining Room
B —Brown Bag
A —Accommodations

Novice	Intermediate	Expert	Terrain	Trail Use Fee	Campground	Remarks	TRAIL MAP PAGE
√			rolling			Operated by Washtenaw County Parks and Recreation Excellent beginner area	**37**
			varies			Write Washtenaw County Parks and Recreation Commission, 2355 W. Stadium, Ann Arbor 48107, for booklet on area trails	**none**
√			flat			Operated by the Huron-Clinton Metropolitan Authority	**38**
√	√	√	rolling to hilly		√	3 campgrounds, one is plowed at Bruin Lake Excellent trails for cross country skiing	**39**
	√		hilly			Heavily wooded Write Washtenaw County Parks and Recreation Commission, PO Box 8645, Ann Arbor, MI 48107 for booklet on other area trails	**40**
√			rolling	√		P,R,W,S Privately operated alpine ski area Trails groomed daily Trail ticket allows use of all ski tows	**none**
	√	√	hilly		√	P,R,W,S,A Privately operated camp and conference center	**none**
√			flat to rolling	√		Campground at Big Portage Lake	**41**
√	√		flat with some hills			Very heavily used, best time is very early in the morning YOU are the guest of the hunter in this area, remember it!	**42**
√	√	√	flat to hilly	√			**43**

REGION 1 SOUTH HALF OF THE LOWER PENINSULA

TRAIL MAP NUMBER	Name	Location	Number of Loops Distances (miles)	Total length of System (miles)	Maintained in the Winter	Total Acres
27	VeeVay Valley Golf and Ski Club 517-676-5366	1 mile south of Mason via US127 exit at Kipp Rd, west to Jewett Rd, east on Tomlinson Rd .25 mile to entrance	2 loops 7,8km	15km	no	150
28	Riverbend Natural Area 517-676-2233	7 miles west of Mason at Grovenburg and Nichols Rd	5 loops	8km	yes	250
29	Tabor Hill Vineyard 616-422-1161	7 miles east of Bridgeman	3 loops 3,4 & 8km	15km	yes	85
30	Royal Valley Ski Resort 616-695-3847	Just north of Buchanan on Main St. Road	NA	5	NA	NA
31	Niles Township Community Park 616-683-8716	One mile north of US12 off Bond St on the south side of Niles	NA	NA	no	NA
32	Southwestern Michigan College 616-782-5113	2 miles SE of Dowagiac off Dailey Rd. Parking available at the gym parking lot	several	10	NA	NA
33	Camp Bellowood 616-295-6915	1.5 miles east of Union on US12	many	10	no	250
34	Sha Ro Co Farm 616-476-2464	10 miles west of Three Rivers north of M60	many	10	yes	80
35	Fort Custer Recreation Area 616-731-4200	1 mile east of Augusta on M96	NA	NA	NA	3000
36	Turskiree Trails 616-731-5266	5 miles west of Battle Creek on M89 at 46th St	many	30km	yes	250

P —Pro Shop
R —Rentals
W—Warming Area
C —Certified Instruction
S —Snack Bar
D —Dining Room
B —Brown Bag
A —Accommodations

Novice	Intermediate	Expert	Terrain	Trail Use Fee	Campground	Remarks	TRAIL MAP PAGE
√			flat to rolling most trails in wooded area			P,R,W,C,S,D Privately operated nordic ski area on a golf course Night skiing	**none**
√	√		rolling to hilly			R,W,C,S Managed by Ingham County Parks Trail groomed as needed	**44**
√	√		rolling			R,W,S Ski trails through vineyard. Wine tasting room at trailhead Ski rentals by appointment only	**none**
√	√		NA	√		P,R,W,S Privately operated alpine ski area	**none**
√			NA				**none**
			NA				**none**
			flat to rolling	√		Operated by Elkhart County YMCA, 200 E. Jackson, Elkhart, IN 46514 Lake on property	**45**
√	√	√	rolling to hilly	√		P,R,W,S,D,B Privately operated nordic ski area Many special programs and group rates available Instruction available Open daily 10-5	**none**
√			flat to rolling			Under development	**46**
√	√	√	flat to hilly	√		R,W,S,B Privately operated nordic ski area Trails set in a beautiful rolling, wooded steam valley Trails are double wide and groomed weekly Open weekends and holidays	**47**

REGION 1 — SOUTH HALF OF THE LOWER PENINSULA

TRAIL MAP NUMBER	Name	Location	Number of Loops Distances (miles)	Total length of System (miles)	Maintained in the Winter	Total Acres
37	Kellogg Forest 616-731-4597	At M89 and 42nd St north of Augusta	many	6+	no	590
38	Lake Doster Resort 616-685-5380	Three miles east of Plainwell on M89, 8 miles north of Kalamazoo	5 loops 2,3.5, 4.5,6,7	22	yes	1300
39	Yankee Springs Recreation Area Barry State Game Area 616-795-9081 616-795-3280	9 miles west of Hastings via Gunn Lake Rd	6 loops 2 to 6	23	no	unlimited
40	Lake Monterey Ski Touring 616-896-8118	16 miles south of Grand Rapids via US131, then west on 142nd Ave (Dorr exit)	3 loops 1,2,4	7	yes	NA
41	Allegan State Game Area 616-673-2430	8 miles west of Allegan on 118th Ave via M40/89, Monroe Rd, then left on 118th Ave	6 loops 2 to 13	23	no	6000
42	Candlestone Inn 616-794-1580	One mile north of M44 on M91 west of Belding	3 loops 2,4,4km	10km	yes	260
43	Egypt Valley Trail	8 miles NE of Grand Rapids via Knapp St and Honey Creek Ave	1 loop	12	no	NA
44	Cannonsburg State Game Area 616-456-5071	18 miles NE of Grand Rapids via Knapp St and Egypt Valley Rd	3 loops	11	no	2000
45	Cannonsburg Ski Resort 616-874-6711	5 miles NE of Grand Rapids, 3.5 miles east of M44 on Cannonsburg Rd (West River Dr) or 2.5 miles south of M44 via Valley Ave, then west on Cannonsburg Rd	6 loops .5,1,1.5, 2,3,5km	10 km	yes	365

P —Pro Shop
R —Rentals
W—Warming Area
C —Certified Instruction
S —Snack Bar
D —Dining Room
B —Brown Bag
A —Accommodations

Novice	Intermediate	Expert	Terrain	Trail Use Fee	Campground	Remarks	TRAIL MAP PAGE
√	√		rolling to hilly			Owned by Michigan State University as a forestry research area 2 miles from Turskiree Trails	**48**
√	√	√	rolling to steep hills	√		P,R,C,S,D Privately operated resort All trails groomed with a track setter	**none**
√	√		rolling		√	Horse trail in game area is a good bet	**49**
√			flat to slightly rolling some trails on golf course	√		P,R,W,C,S Privately operated nordic ski area at Sandy Pines Resort	**none**
√	√	√	flat to rolling		√	Trails north of 118th Ave are flat Campground may not be plowed Sign in at headquarters before using trails Skiing prohibited until January 1st	**50**
√			flat to rolling			R,W,S,D,A Privately operated resort Most trails on the golf course Flat River State Game Area nearby All trails groomed with a track setter	**none**
√	√		rolling			Trail crosses some private land to connect Cannonsburg State Game Area with two county parks Cooperative effort of the Kent County Road Commission, Sierra Club, Michigan Trail-finders, Fountain Street Ski Club, Explorer Scouts and the DNR	**51**
√	√		rolling with some steep hills			Part of Egypt Valley Trail	**52**
√	√	√	rolling wooded hills	√	√	P,R,W,C,S,D Privately operated alpine ski area All trails groomed with a track setter Campground nearby	**none**

REGION 1 — SOUTH HALF OF THE LOWER PENINSULA

TRAIL MAP NUMBER	Name	Location	Number of Loops Distances (miles)	Total length of System (miles)	Maintained in the Winter	Total Acres
46	Hoffmaster State Park 616-798-3711	5 miles north of Grand Haven west of US31	1 loop	3.5	no	1000
47	Muskegon State Park 616-744-3480	3 miles north of Muskegon on Lake Michigan	NA	NA	NA	1200
48	Pentwater Ski Trails 616-864-6811	Pentwater area along Lake Michigan	many	31km	yes	many
49	White River Trail 616-689-6696	7.5 miles SW of Hesperia, at Pines Point Campground. Take M82 south 1 mile from Hesperia, west on Garfield Rd 5 miles, south on USFS 5118 1½ miles to campground on USFS 5637	3 loops	4.5	no	700
50	Woods & Waters Camping and Recreation 616-689-6701	5 miles north Newaygo, 1.5 miles east on 40th St, ½ mile south on Spruce St	4 loops 3,3,4, 10km	20km	no	unlimited
51	Hungerford Ski Trail 616-689-6696	SW of Big Rapids. 7 miles west of US131 via M20, then turn north where M20 turns south, parking lot will be a little over a mile ahead	4 loops	16.5km	no	4000
52	Lake Isabella 517-644-2300	9 miles west of Mt. Pleasant via M20, then 3 miles north on Coldwater Rd	NA	15	yes	5000
53	Riverwood 517-772-5726	3 miles SW of Mt. Pleasant via Mission St and East Broomfield Rd	NA	NA	yes	250

P —Pro Shop S —Snack Bar
R —Rentals D —Dining Room
W—Warming Area B —Brown Bag
C —Certified Instruction A —Accommodations

Novice	Intermediate	Expert	Terrain	Trail Use Fee	Campground	Remarks	TRAIL MAP PAGE
√	√		flat to hilly		√	Trails overlook Lake Michigan	53
√	√		flat to rolling on sand dunes and surrounding area	√	√	Established trails in 600 acre quiet area	54
√	√	√	flat to hilly			P,R at Rek-N-Reef Ltd, 347 S Hancock in Pentwater W,S,D,A in Pentwater Rek-N-Reef provides trail maps of area trails as well as many other services	none
√	√		flat to rolling		√	Managed by USFS White Cloud District	55
√	√	√	flat to rolling		√	P,R,W,S,B,A Privately operated lodge campground and nordic ski area in Manistee National Forest Wooded trails Lodge has indoor heated pool, whirlpool and saunas	none
√	√		rolling to hilly			Managed by the USFS White Cloud District	56
√	√		flat to rolling	√		R,W,S Privately operated trail system by The Cumberland Gap of Mt. Pleasant 517-773-6103	none
√			flat to rolling	√		R,W,S Privately operated trail system by The Cumberland Gap of Mt. Pleasant 517-773-6103 Open weekends only Trails on golf course	none

REGION 1 SOUTH HALF OF THE LOWER PENINSULA

TRAIL MAP NUMBER	Name	Location	Number of Loops Distances (miles)	Total length of System (miles)	Maintained in the Winter	Total Acres
54	Valley View 517-828-6618	½ mile SE of Shepherd at Blanchard Rd and US27	NA	NA	yes	NA
55	Pine Haven Recreation Area 517-631-6502	2 miles west of the US10-West River Rd interchange on Maynard Rd near the Village of Sanford	4 loops .2,.8,1.2, 2.8	5	no	325
56	Bintz Apple Mountain 517-781-2550	1 mile west of Saginaw on M46, then 6 miles north on North River Rd	many	6	yes	360
57	Sleeper State Park 517-856-4411	3 miles NE of Caseville on M25	NA	1.5	no	1000
58	Port Crescent State Park 517-738-8663	9 miles NE of Caseville on M25	2 loops 1.1,1.2	2.3	no	655

Novice	Intermediate	Expert	Terrain	Trail Use Fee	Campground	P —Pro Shop, R —Rentals, W—Warming Area, C —Certified Instruction, S —Snack Bar, D —Dining Room, B —Brown Bag, A —Accommodations Remarks	TRAIL MAP PAGE
√			flat to rolling	√		R,W,S Privately operated trail system by The Cumberland Gap of Mt. Pleasant 517-773-6103 Trails on golf course	**none**
√	√	√	flat to hilly			Operated by the Midland County Parks and Recreation Commission, 1270 James Savage Rd, Midland, MI 48640 Expansion of trails and facilities planned	**none**
√			flat to rolling	√		P,R,W,S,D Privately operated alpine ski area Some trails lighted Some trails groomed with a track setter	**57**
√			flat	√		On Lake Huron	**none**
√			flat	√		On Lake Huron	**58**

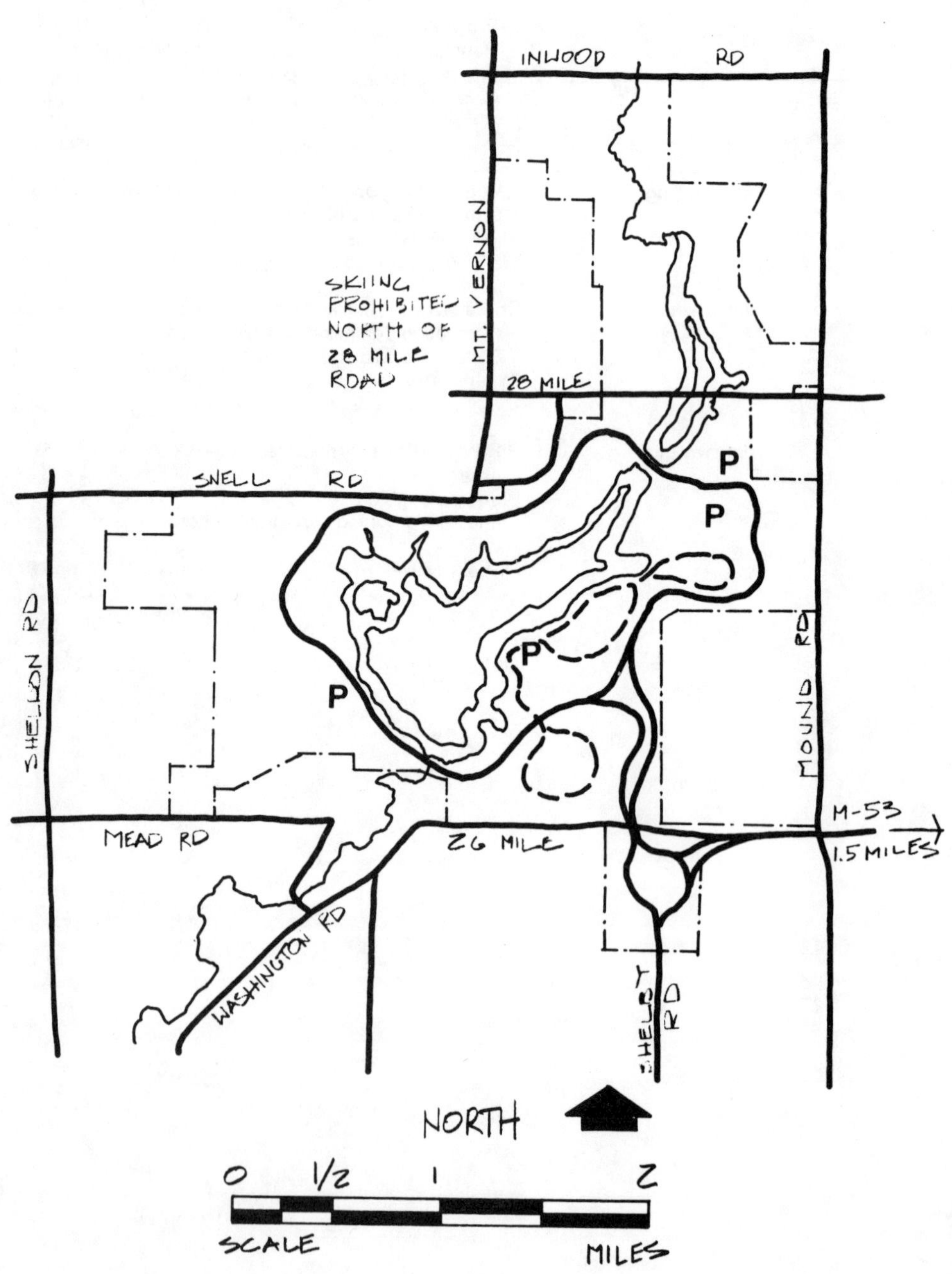

STONEY CREEK METRO PARK

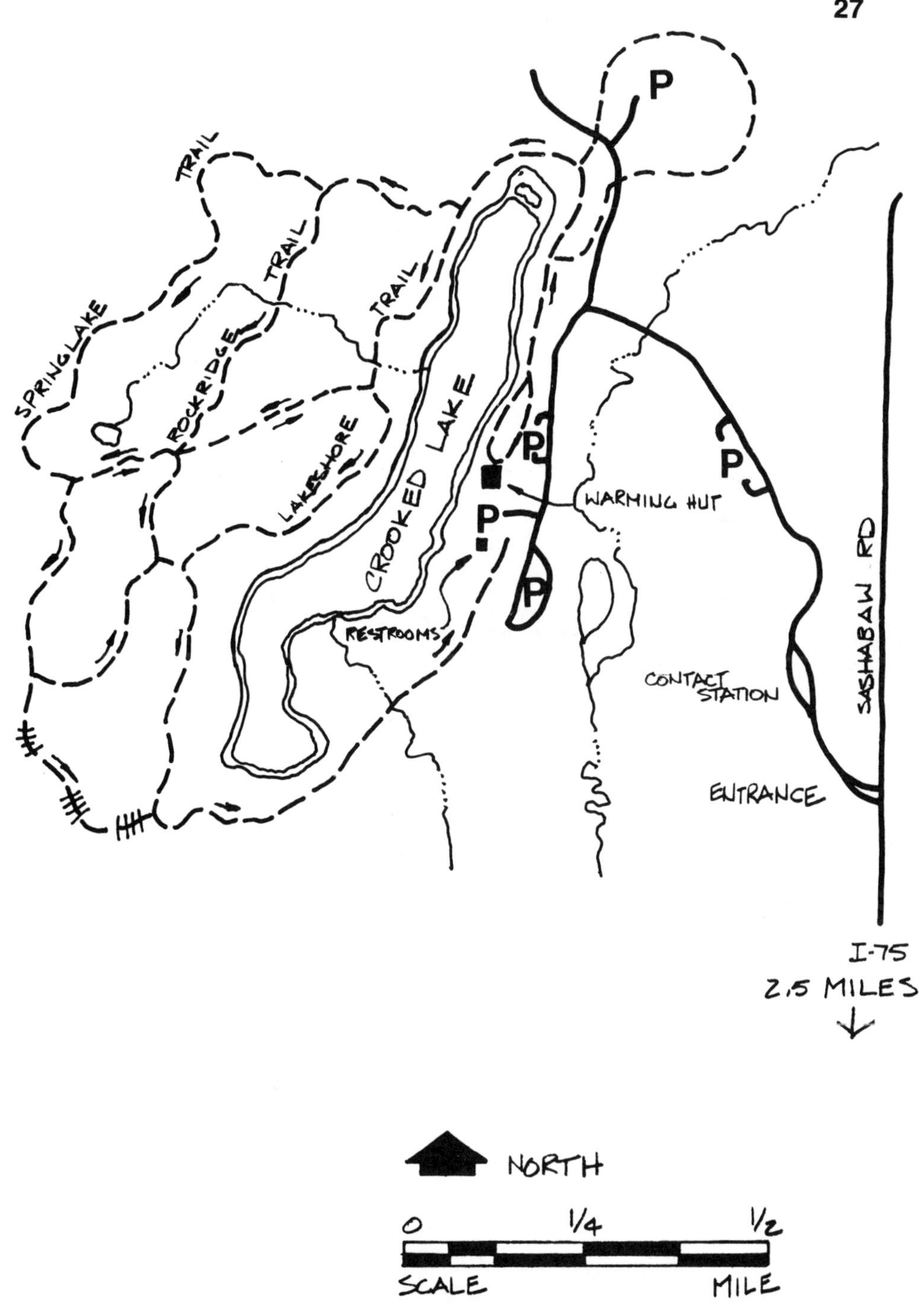

INDEPENDENCE OAKS COUNTY PARK

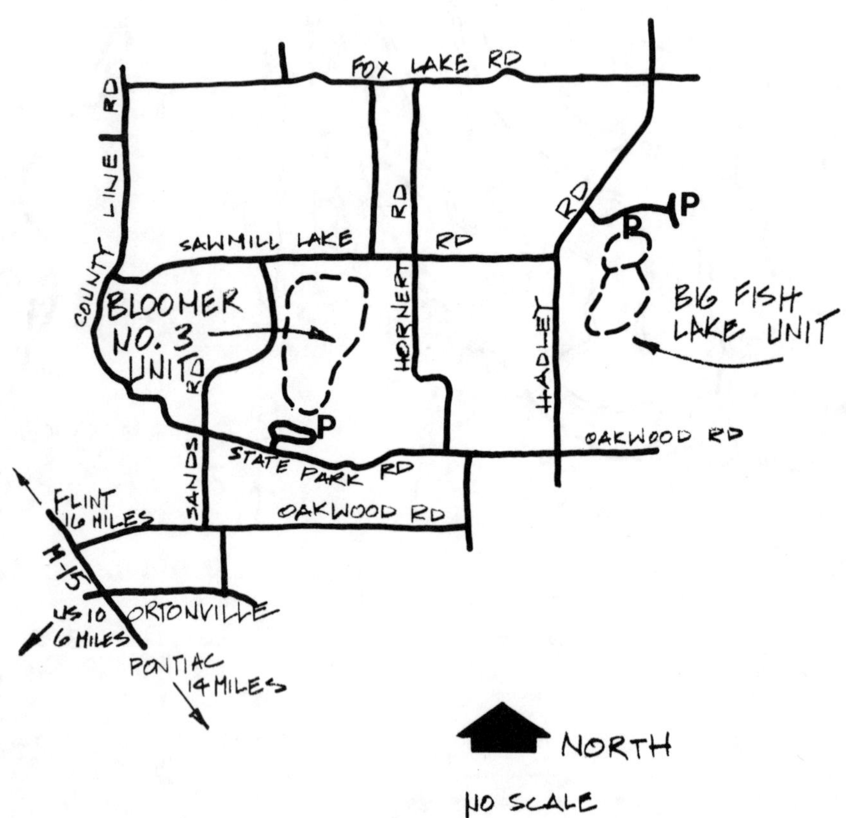

ORTONVILLE RECREATION AREA

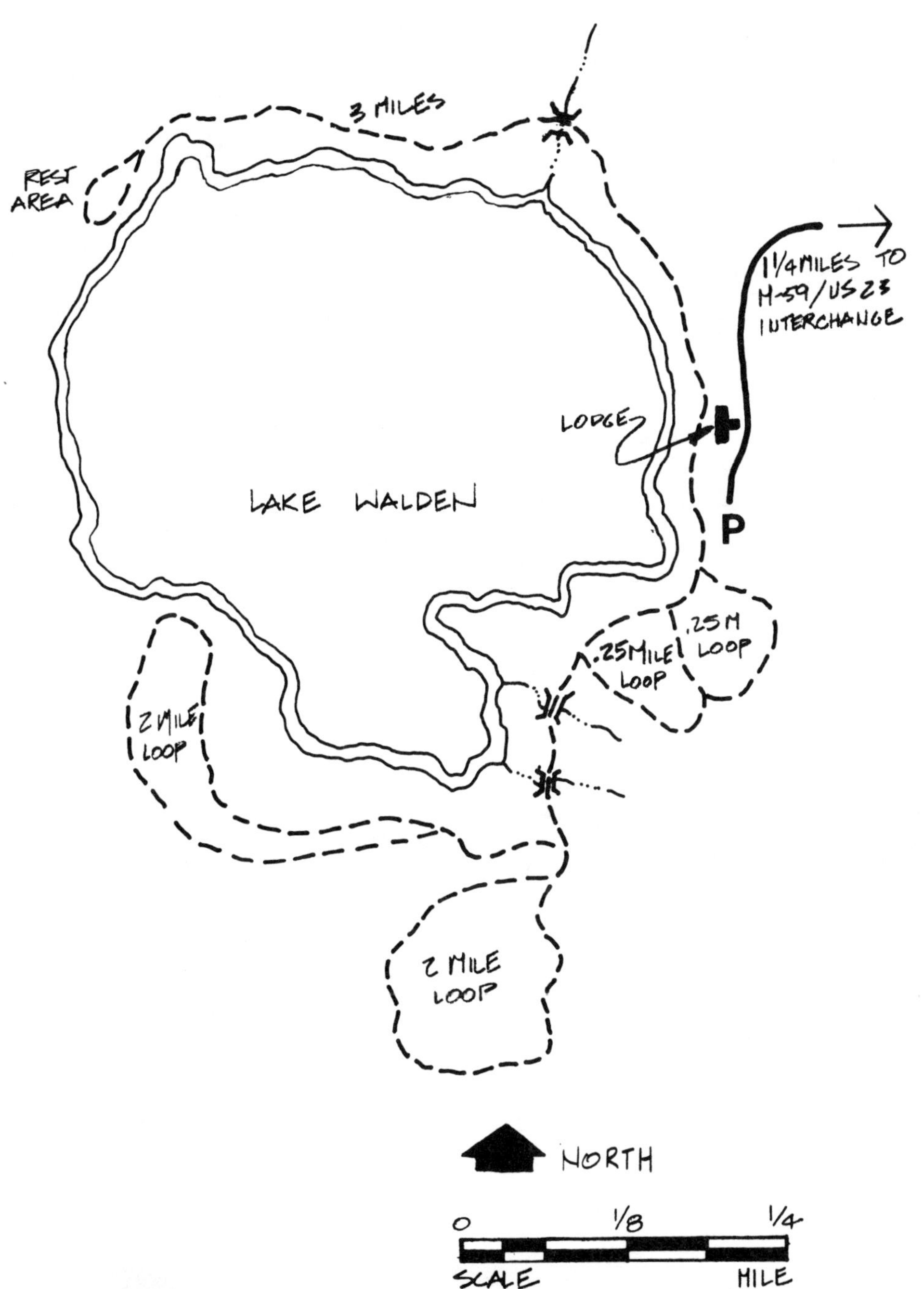

WALDENWOODS

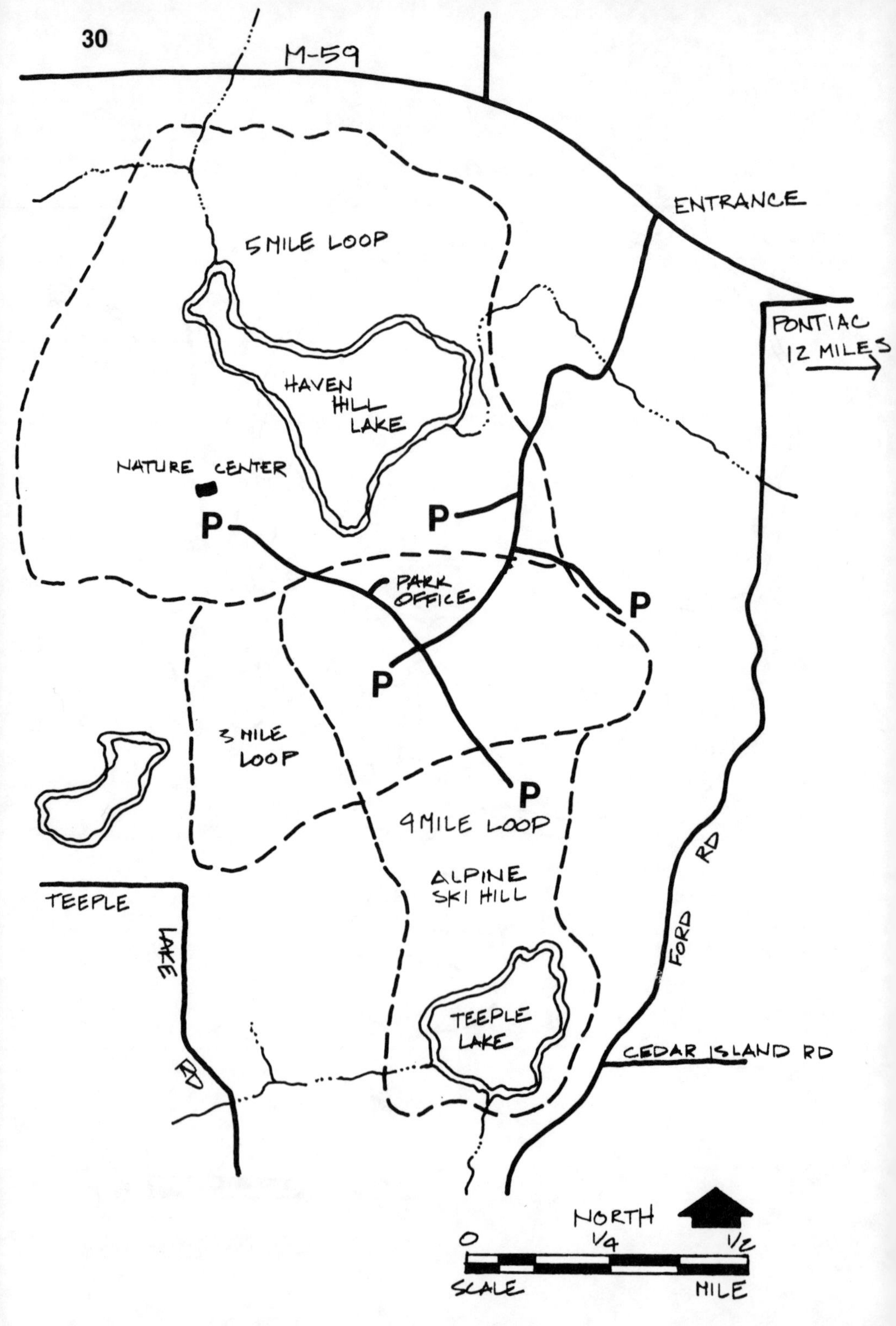

HIGHLAND RECREATION AREA

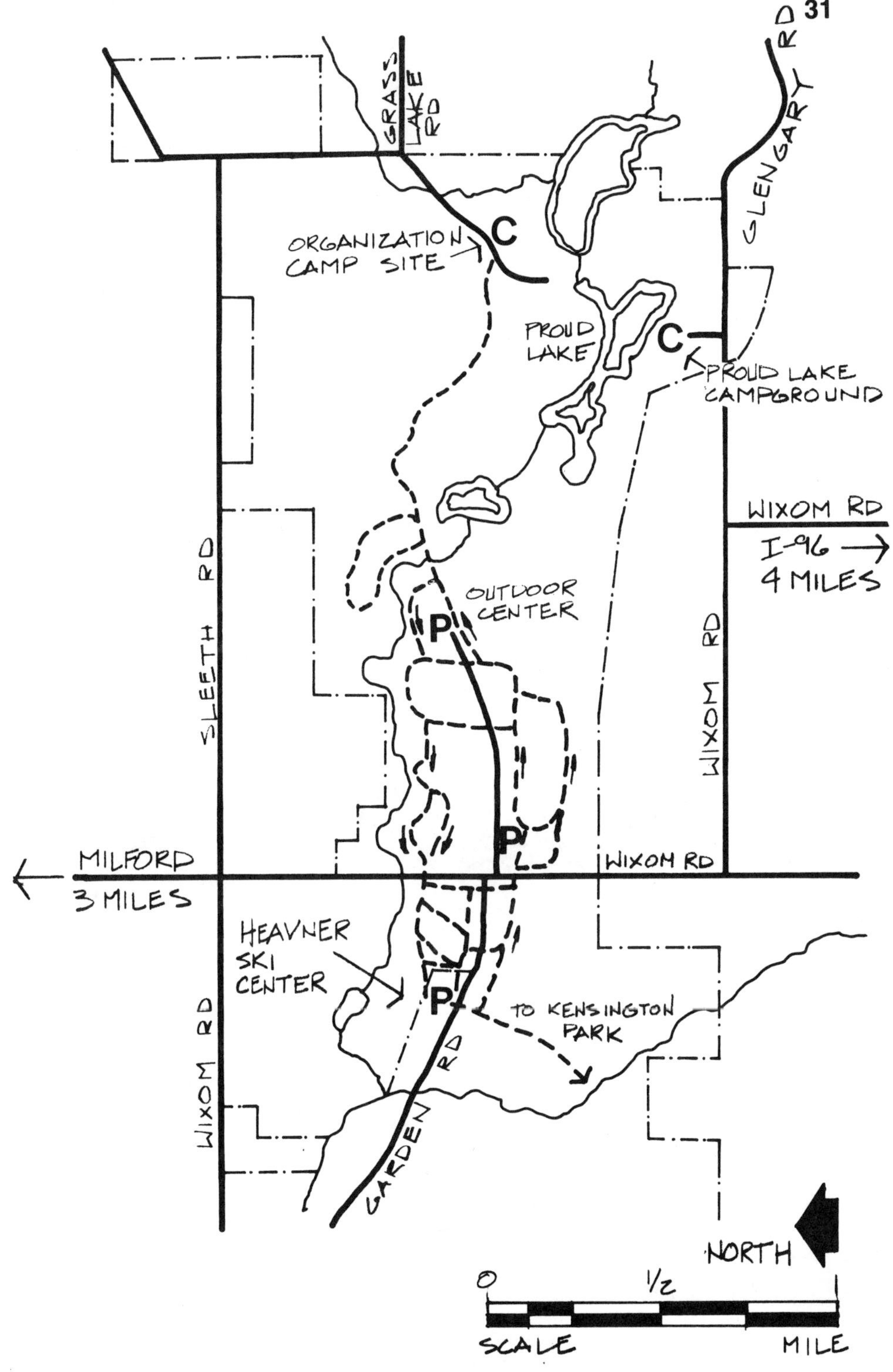

PROUD LAKE RECREATION AREA

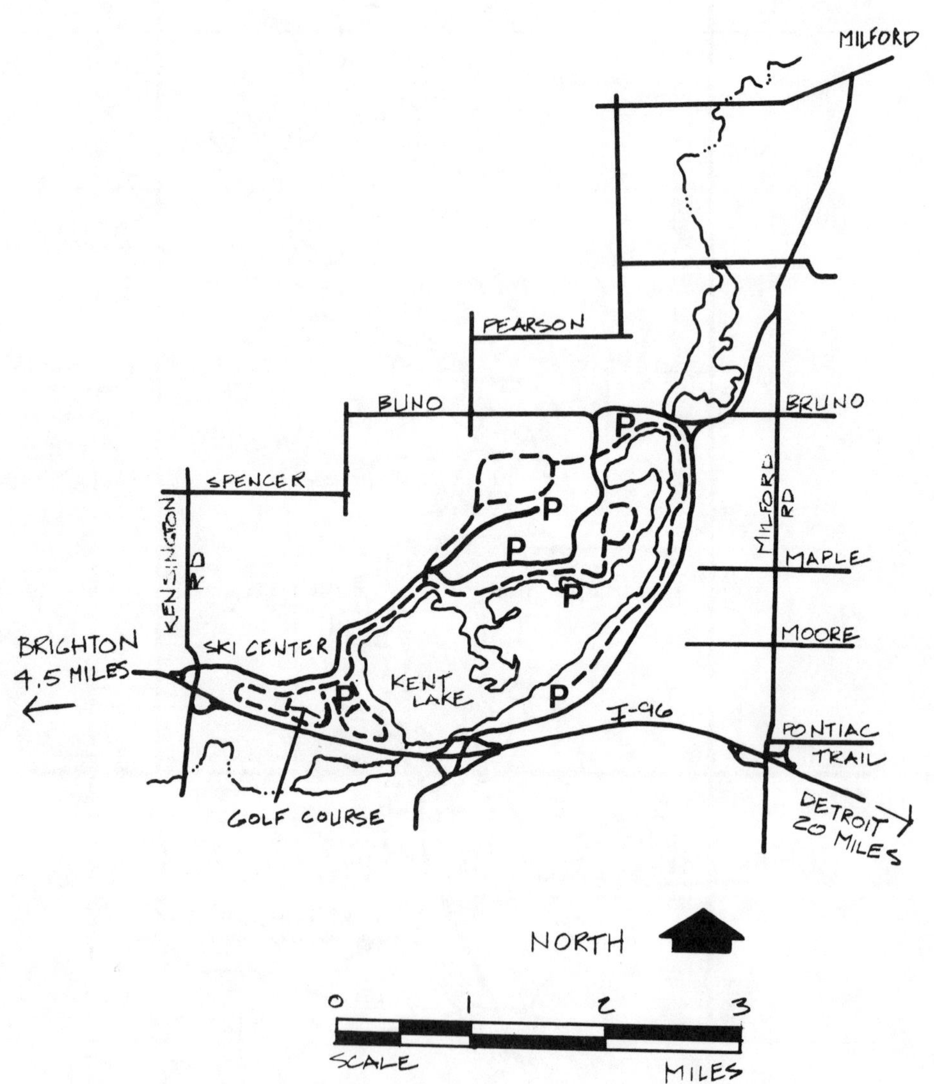

KENSINGTON METRO PARK

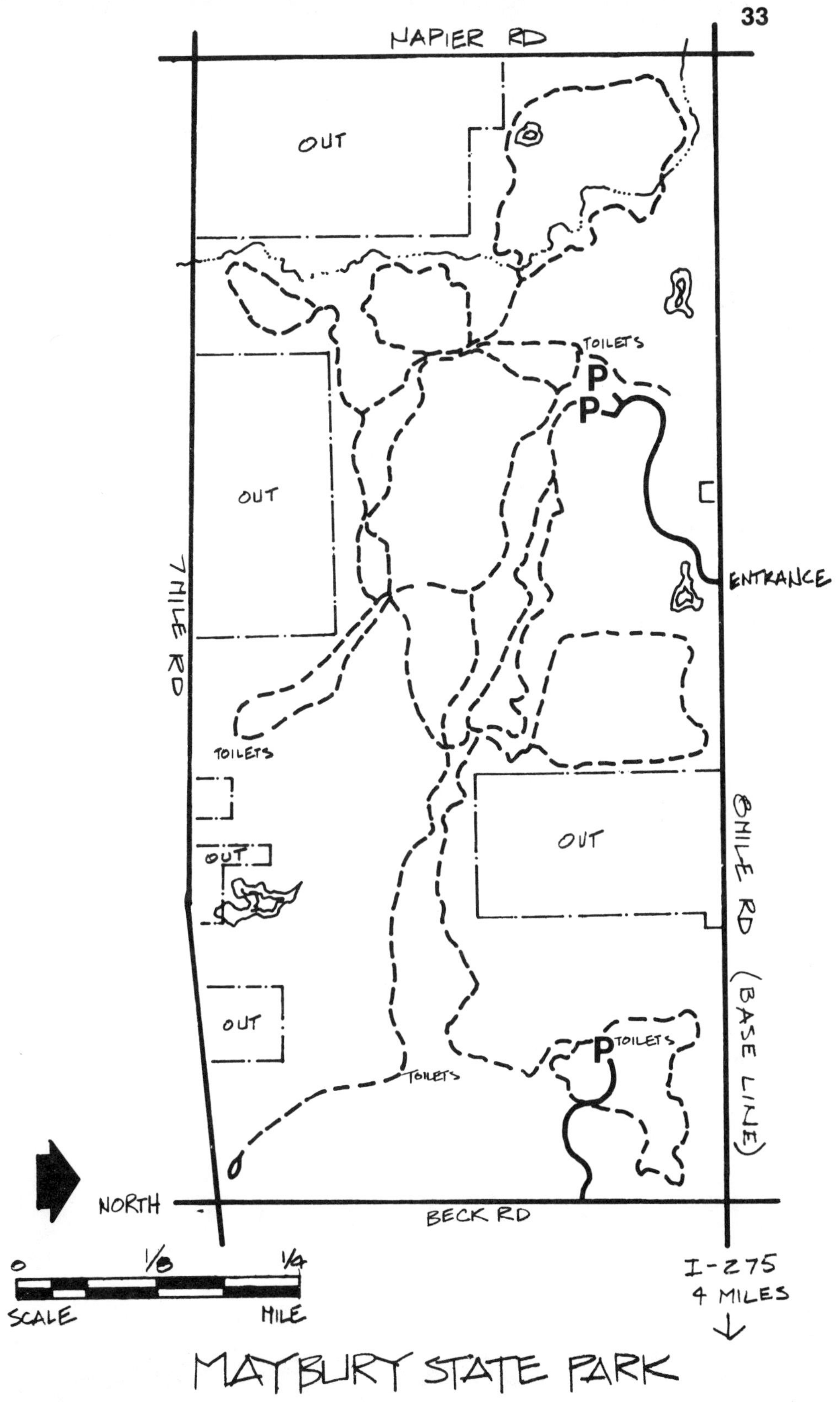

MAYBURY STATE PARK

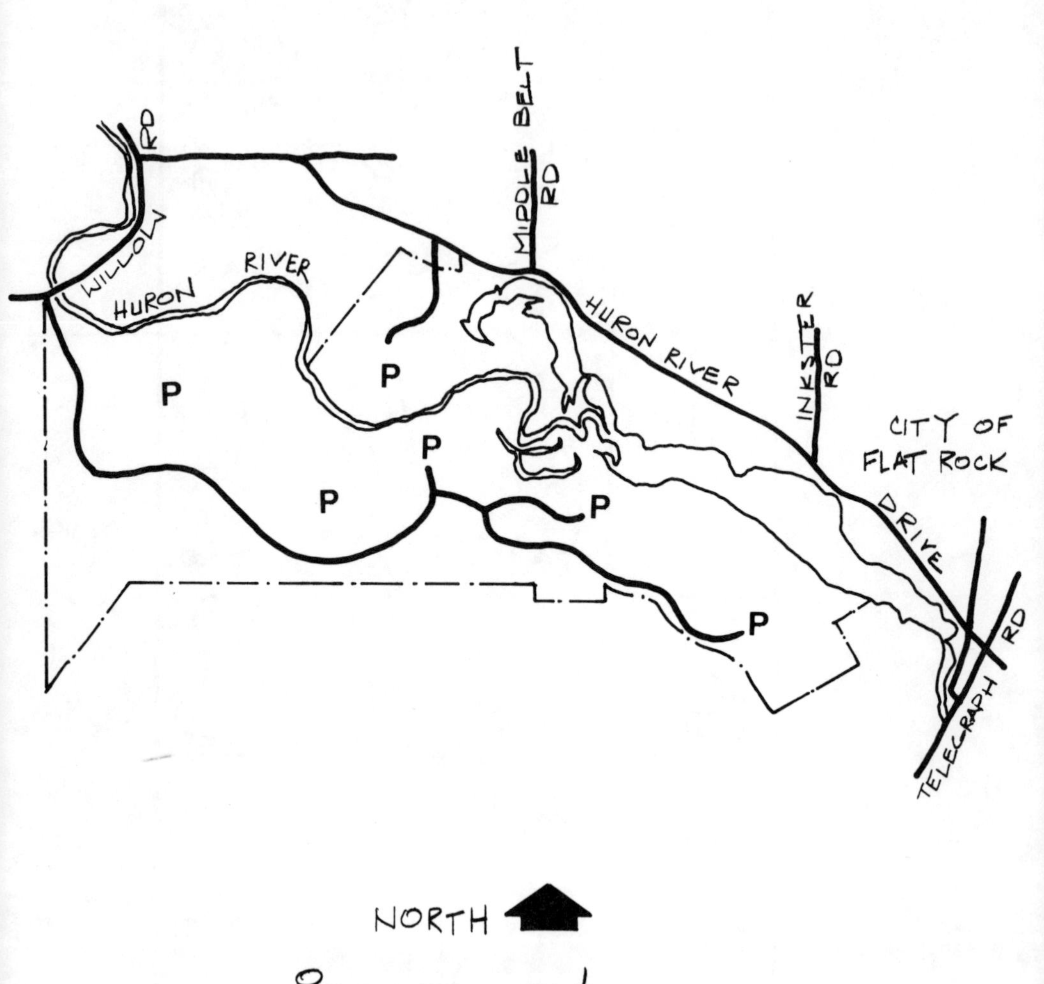

OAKWOODS METRO PARK

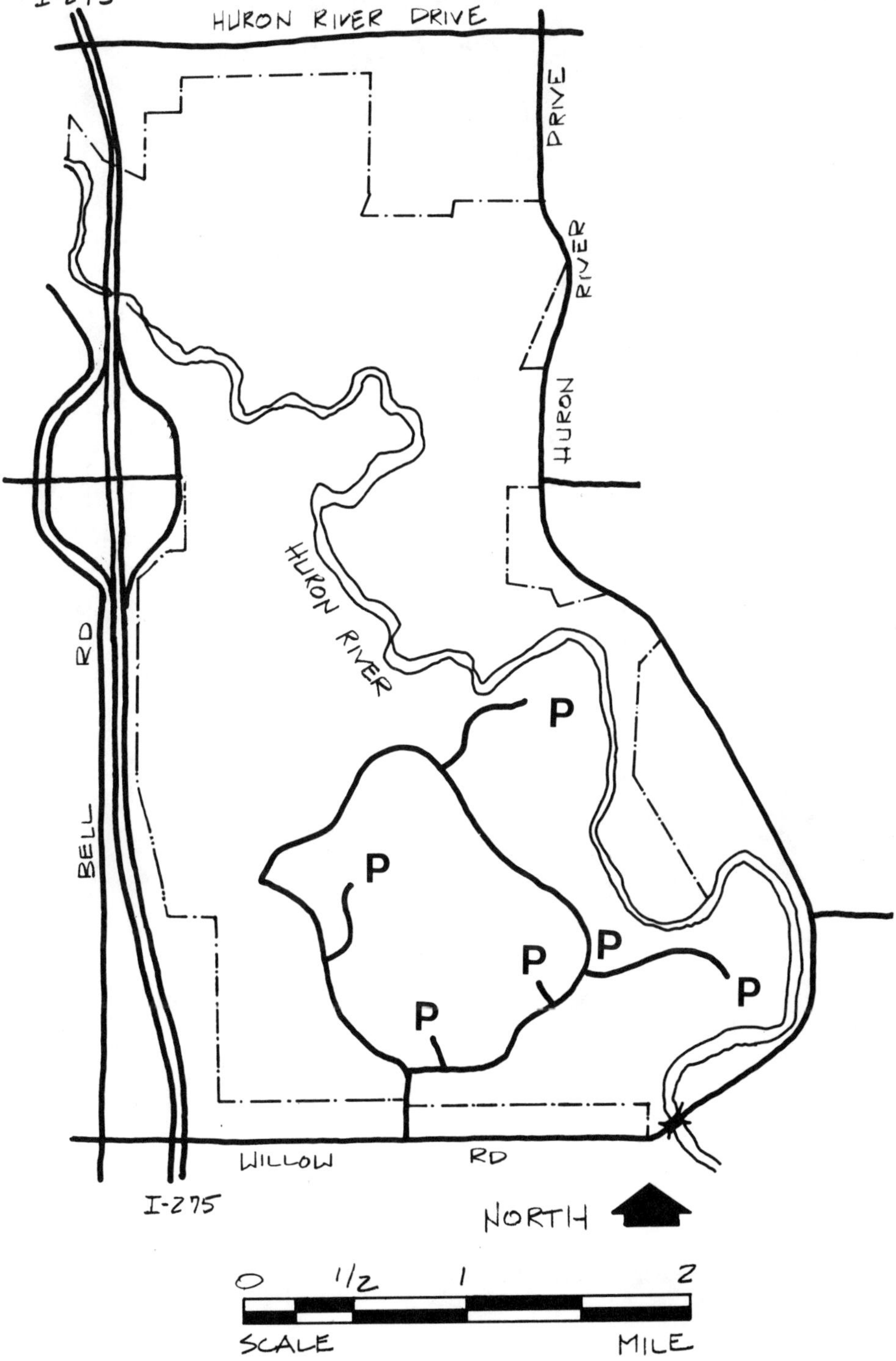

I-275

HURON RIVER DRIVE

HURON RIVER DRIVE

HURON RIVER

BELL RD

P

P

P

P

P

P

WILLOW RD

I-275

NORTH

0 1/2 1 2

SCALE MILE

WILLOW METRO PARK

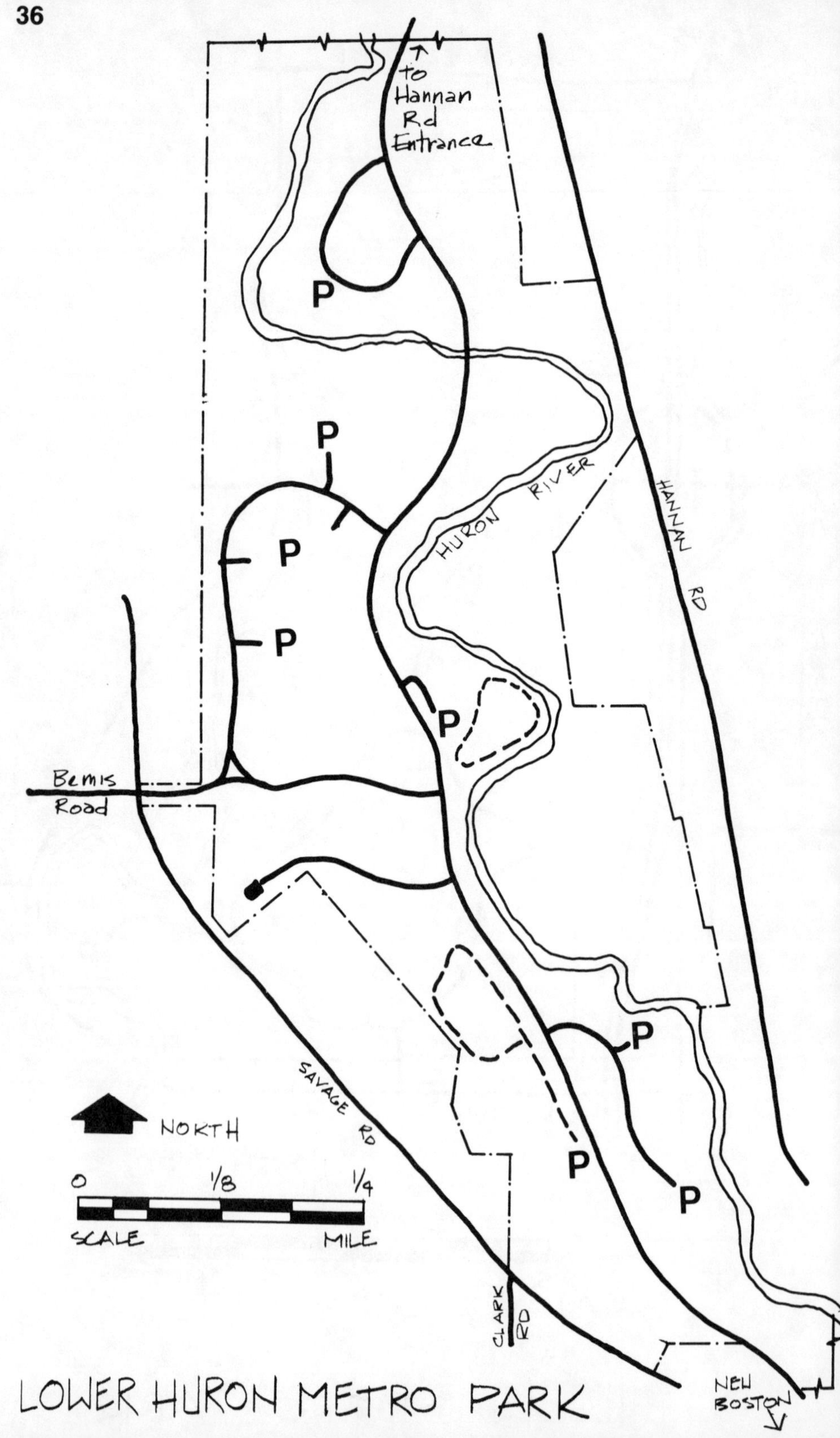

LOWER HURON METRO PARK

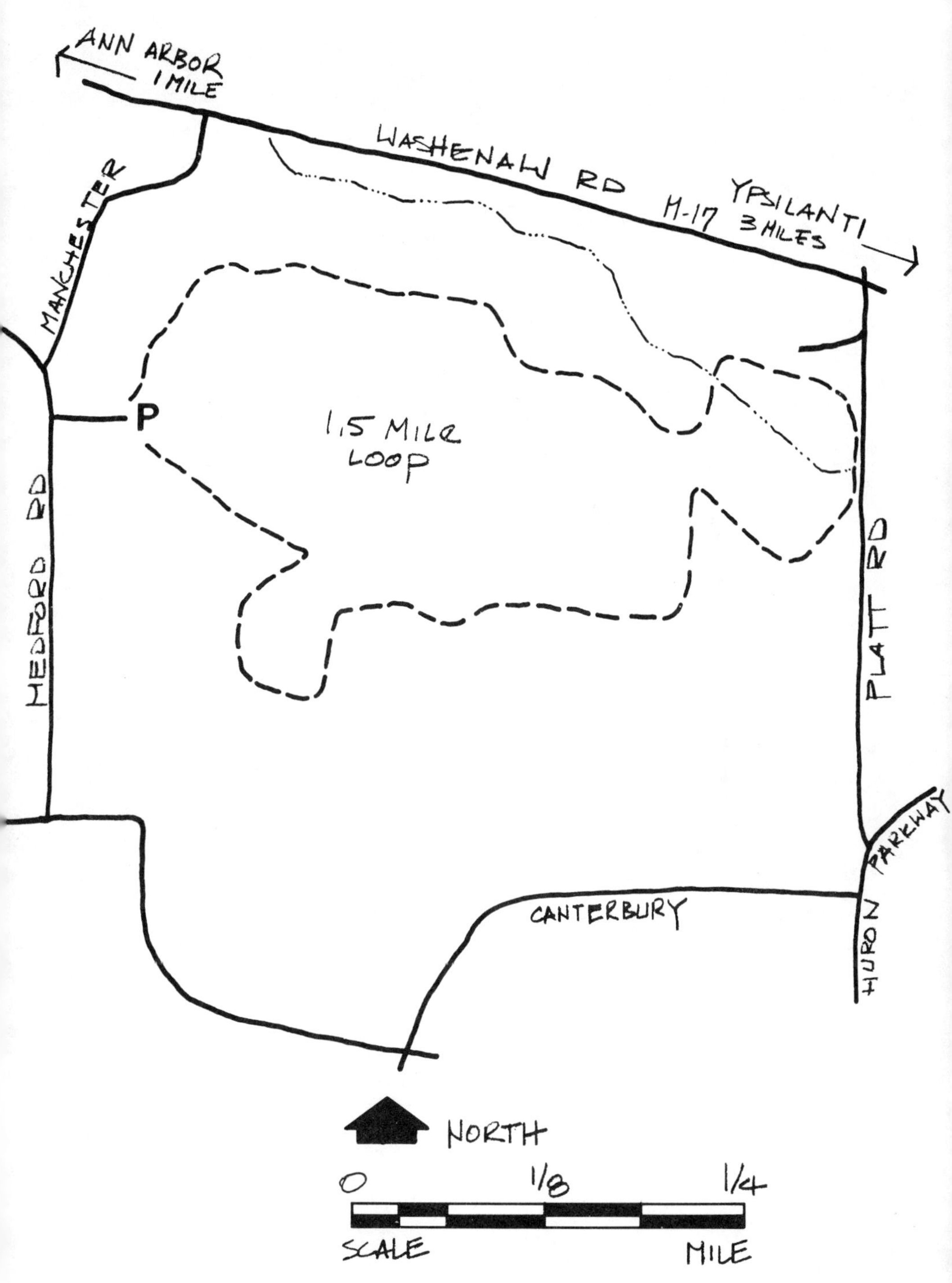

COUNTY FARM SKI TRAIL

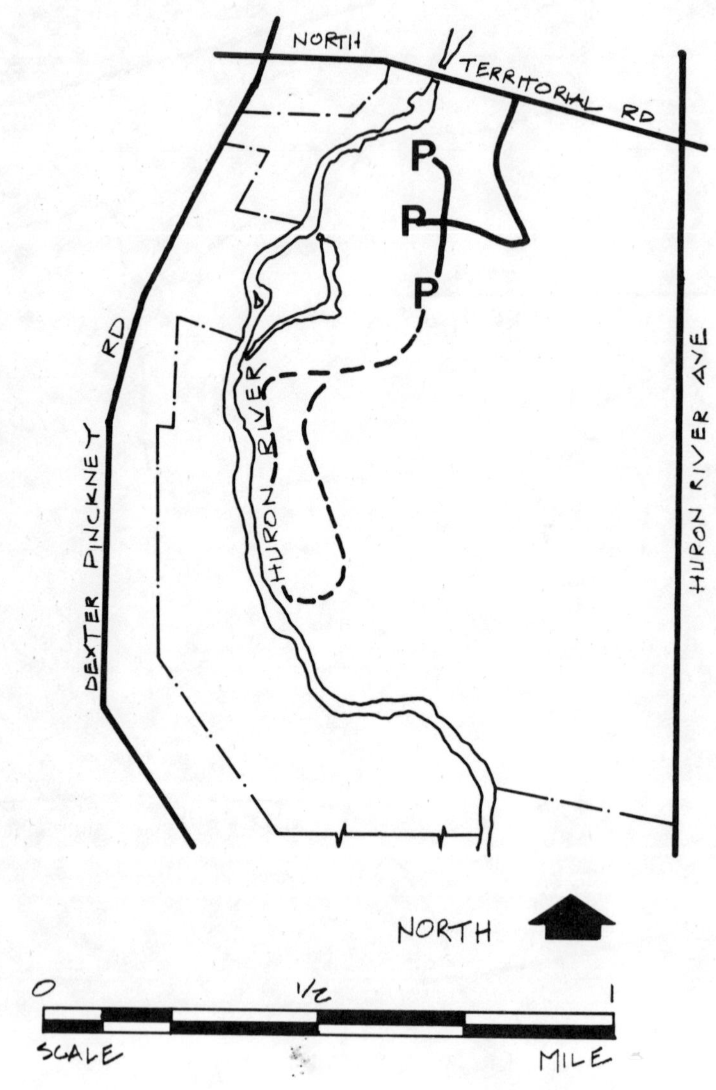

HUDSON MILLS METRO PARK

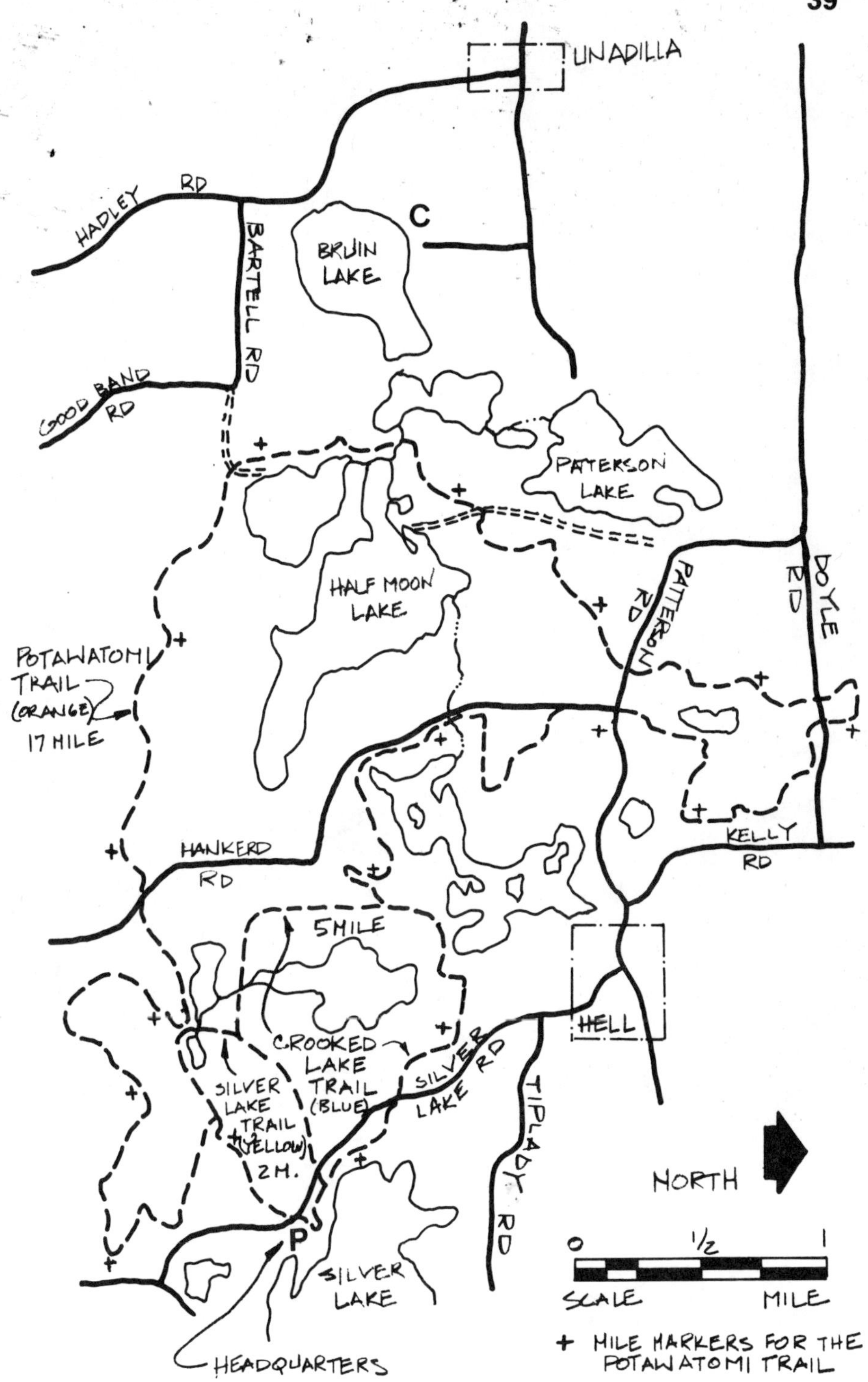

PINCKNEY RECREATION AREA

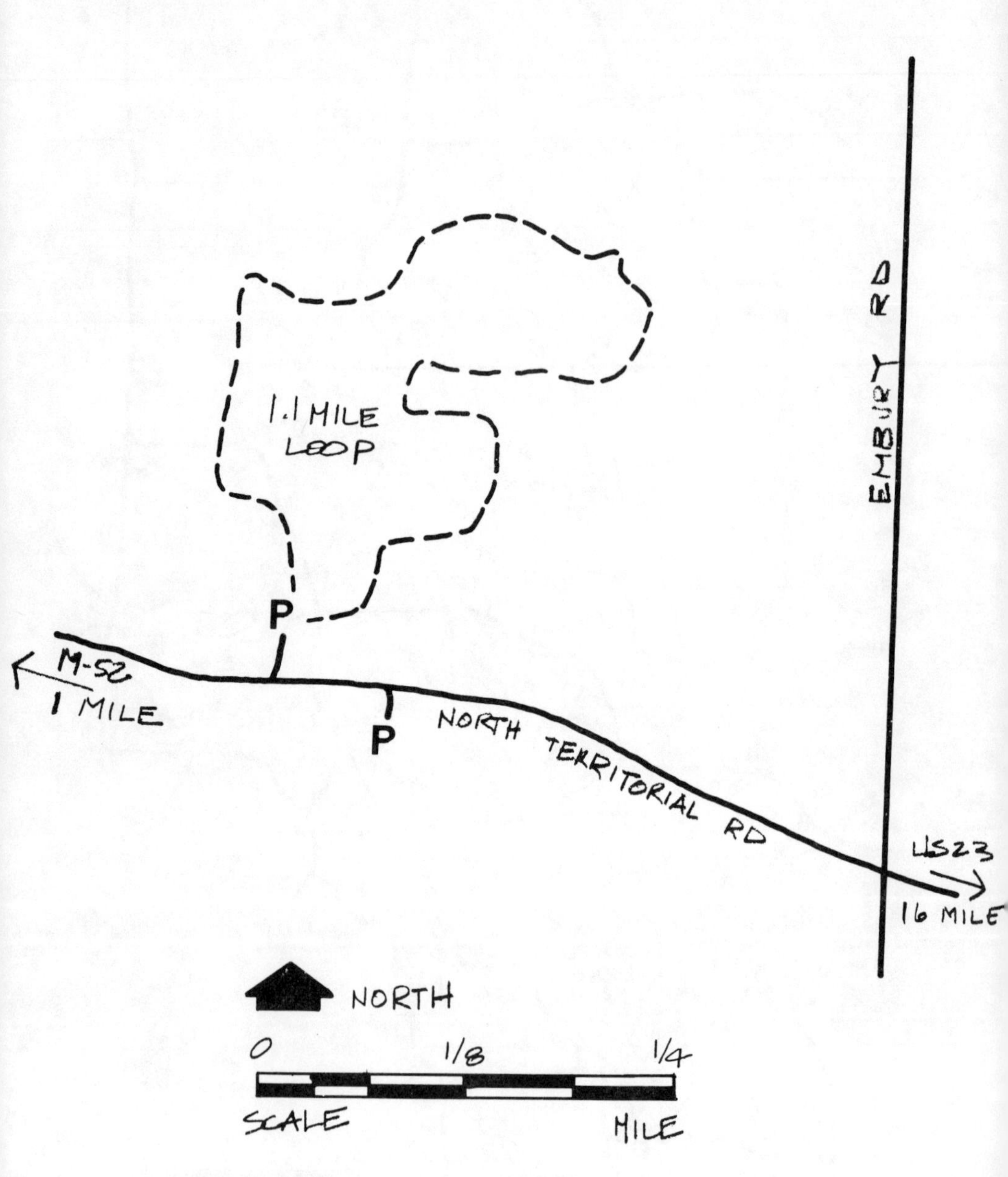

PARK LYNDON NORTH SKI TRAIL

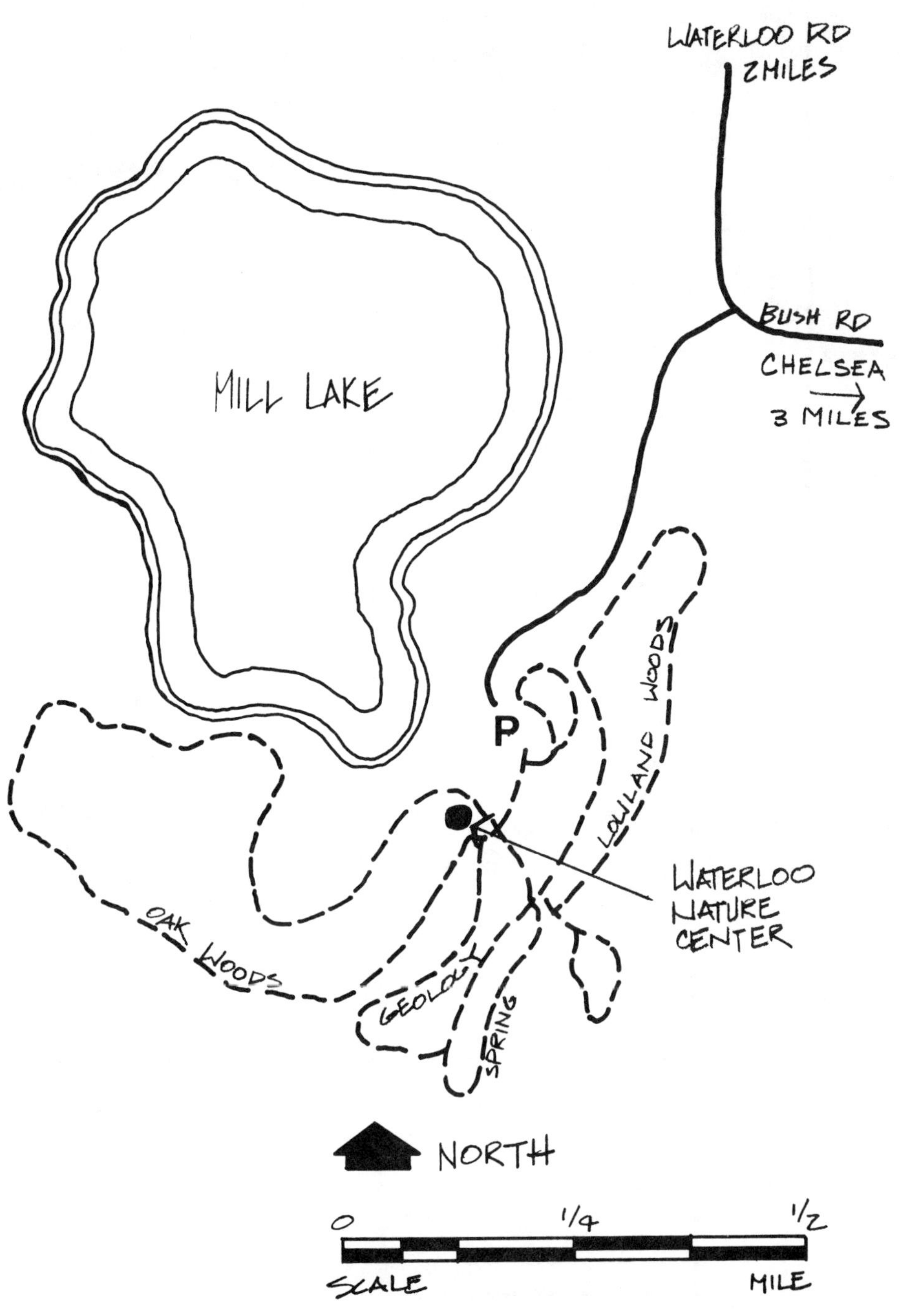

WATERLOO RECREATION AREA

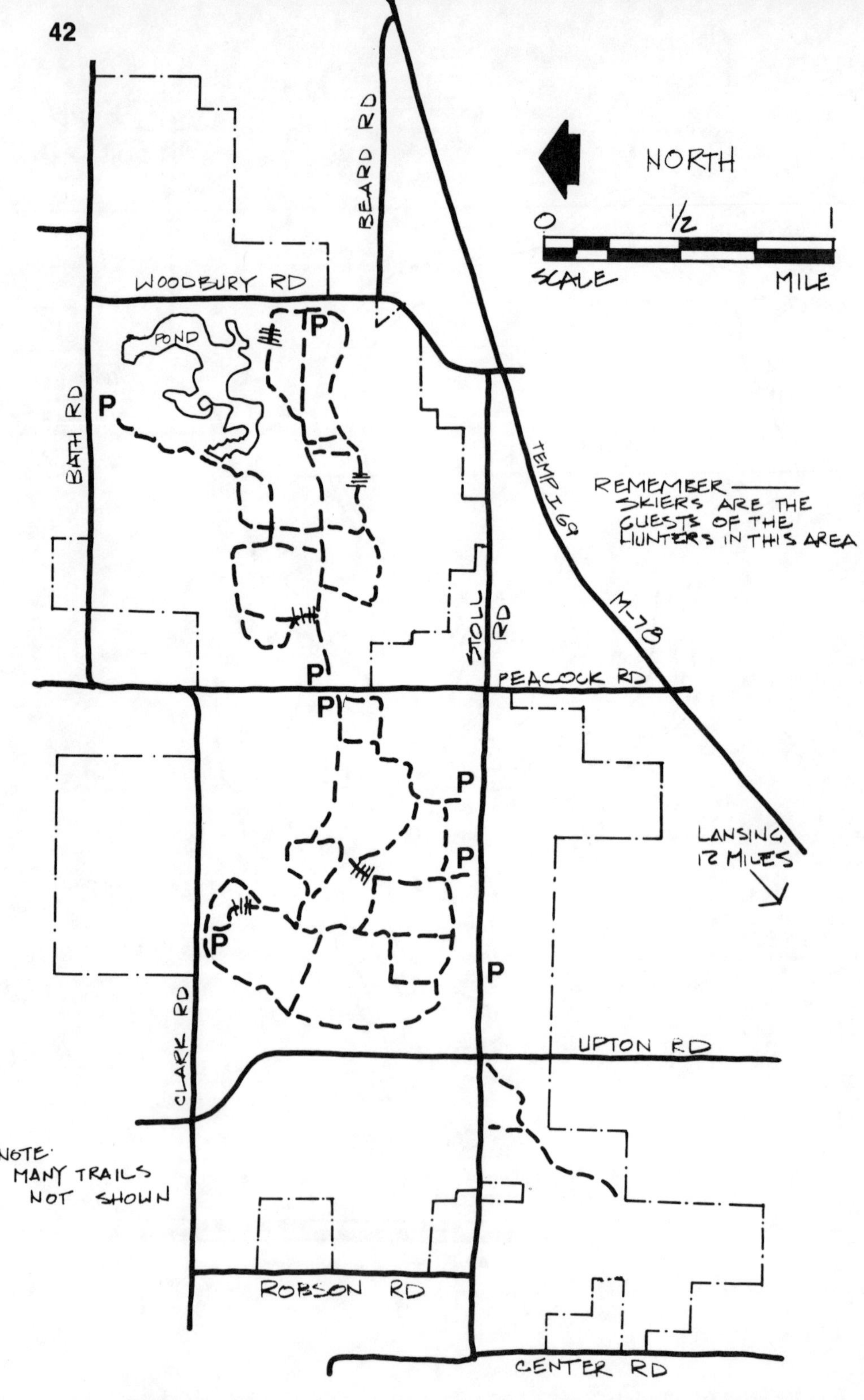

ROSE LAKE WILDLIFE RESEARCH AREA

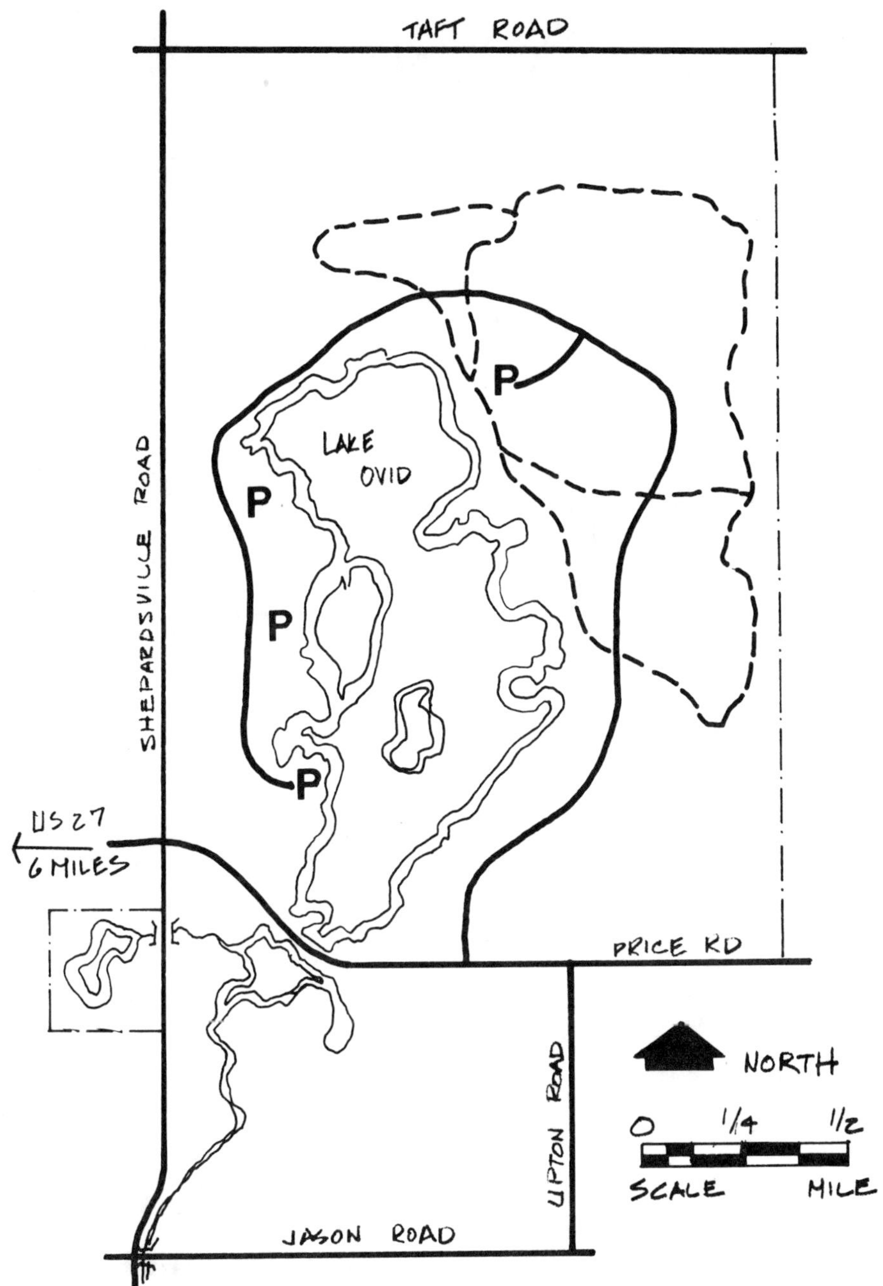

SLEEPY HOLLOW STATE PARK

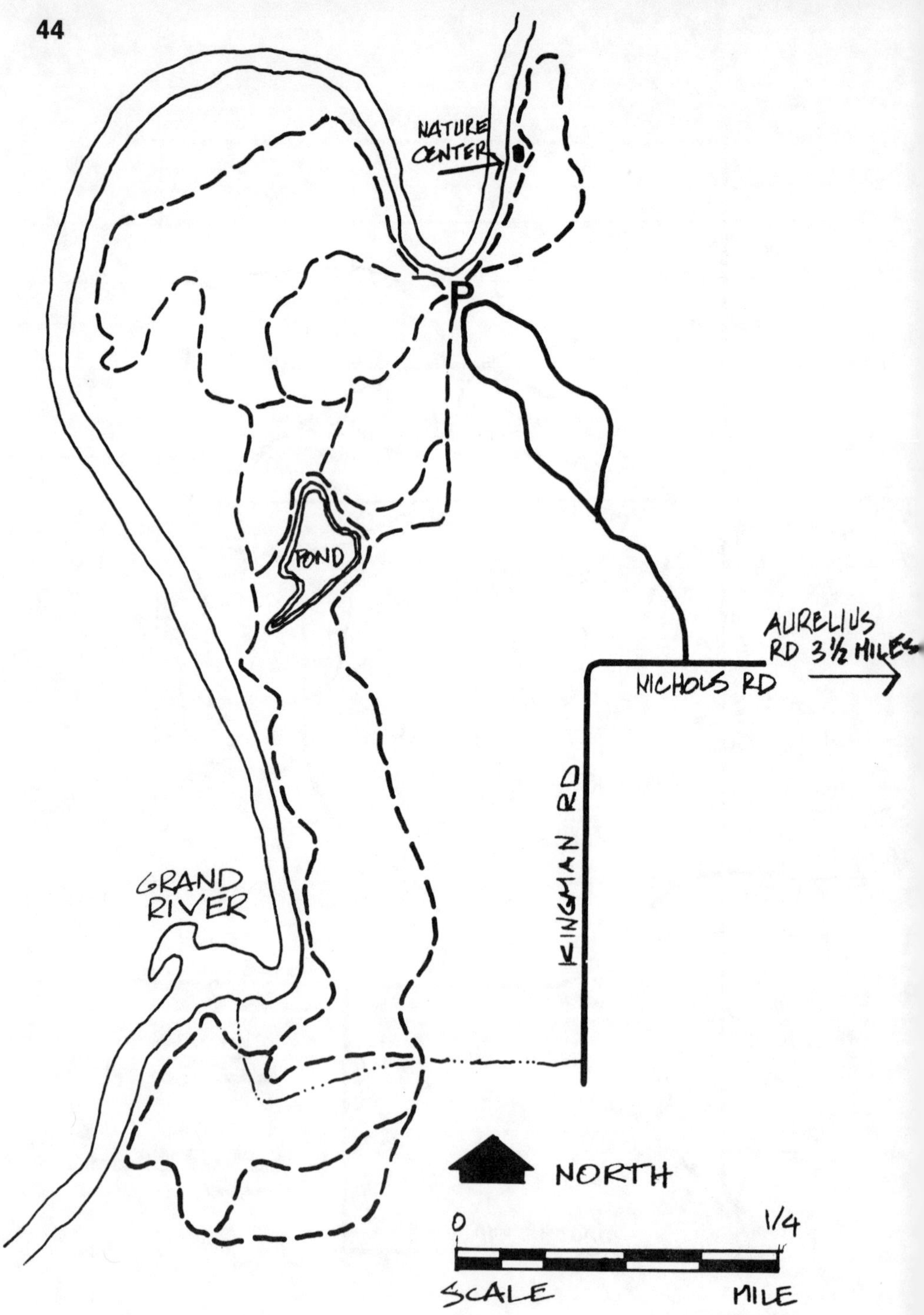

RIVERBEND NATURAL AREA

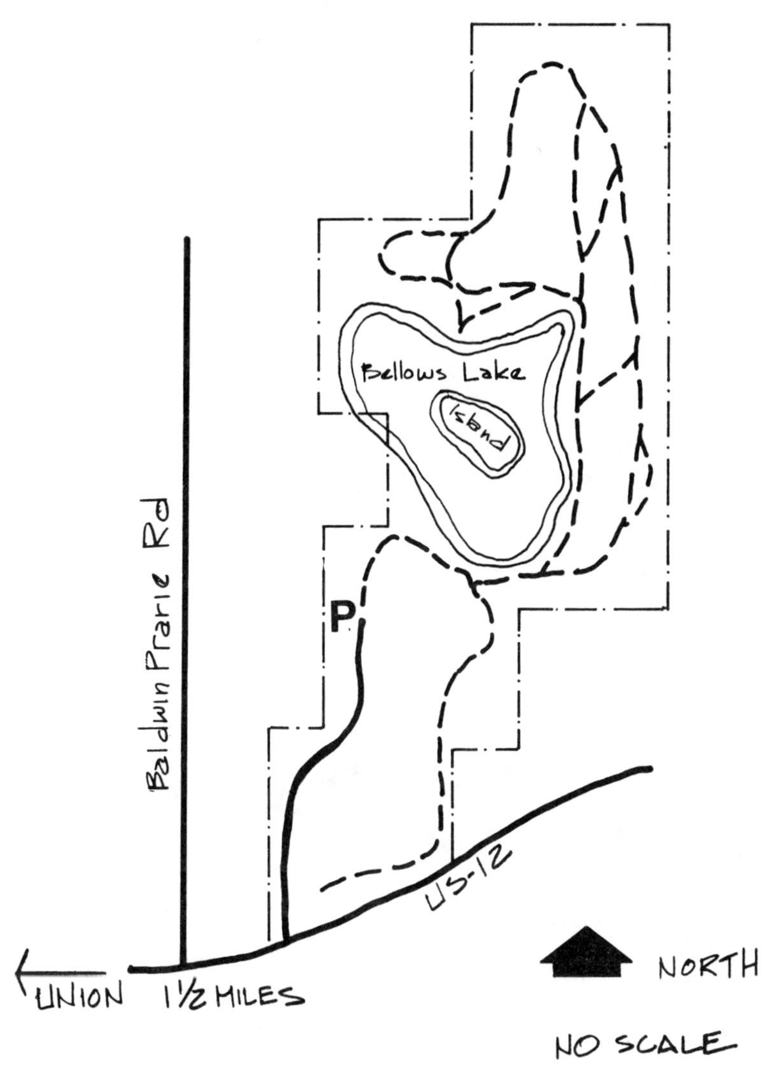

CAMP BELLOWOOD

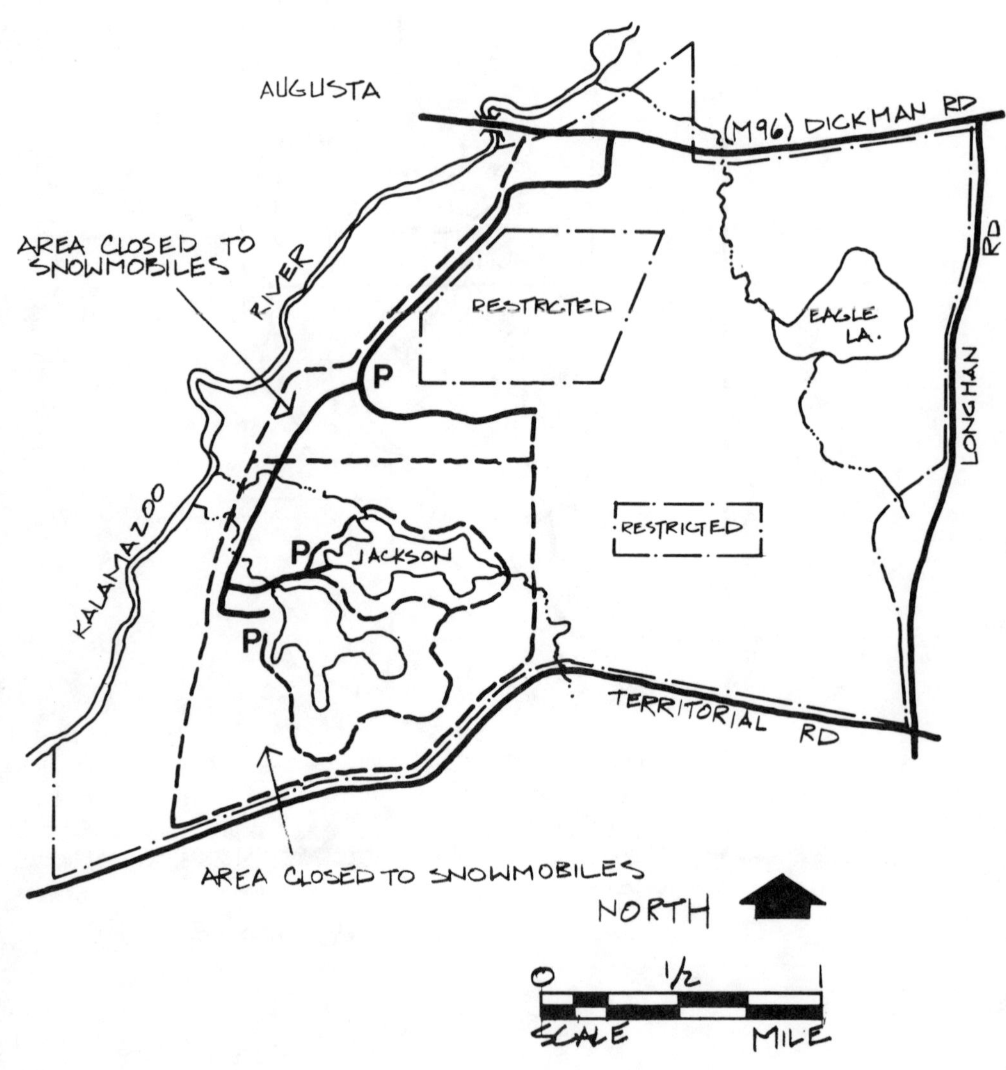

FORT CUSTER RECREATION AREA

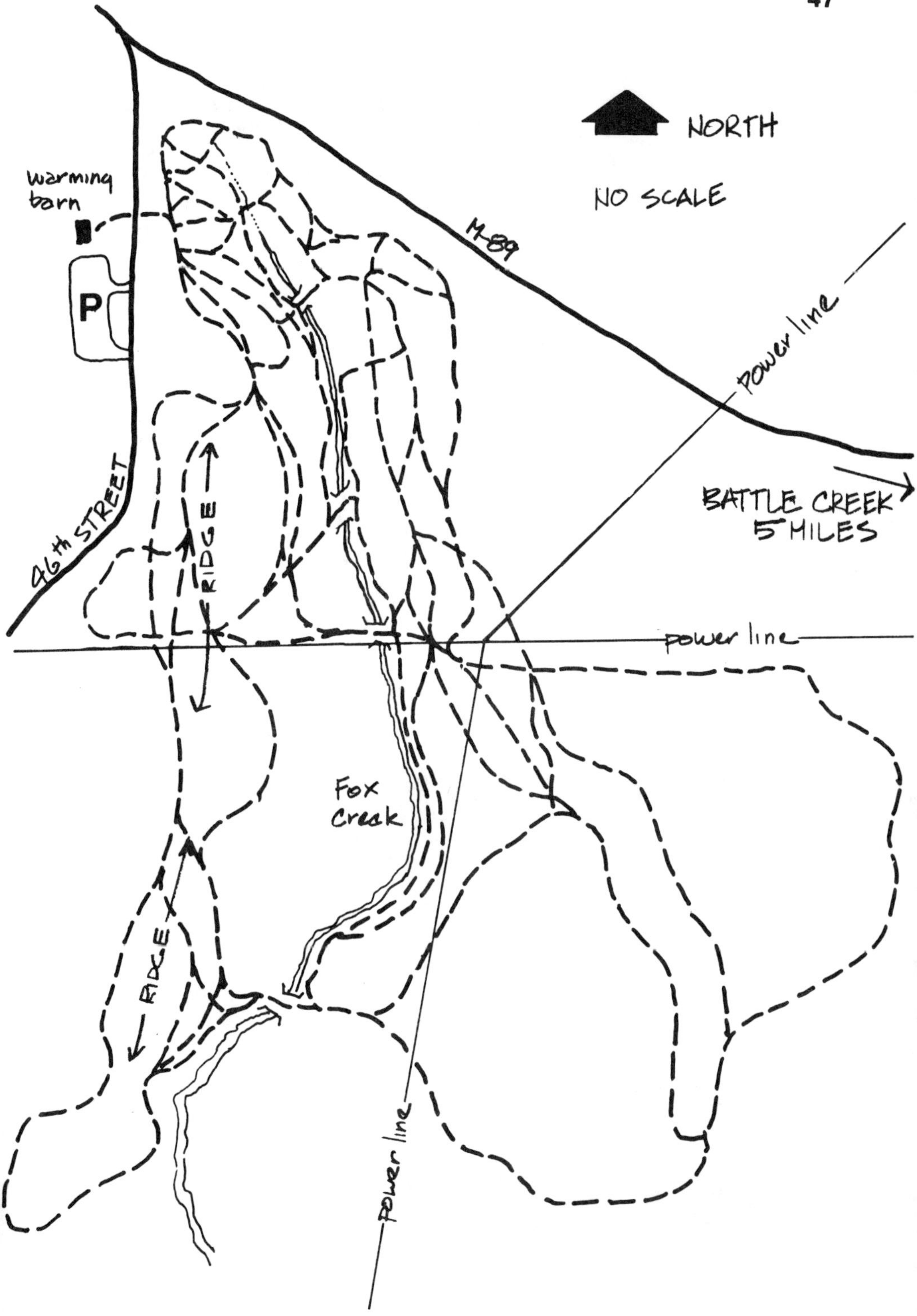

NORTH

NO SCALE

M-89

warming barn

P

46th STREET

RIDGE

power line

power line

BATTLE CREEK
5 MILES

Fox Creek

RIDGE

power line

TURSKIREE TRAILS

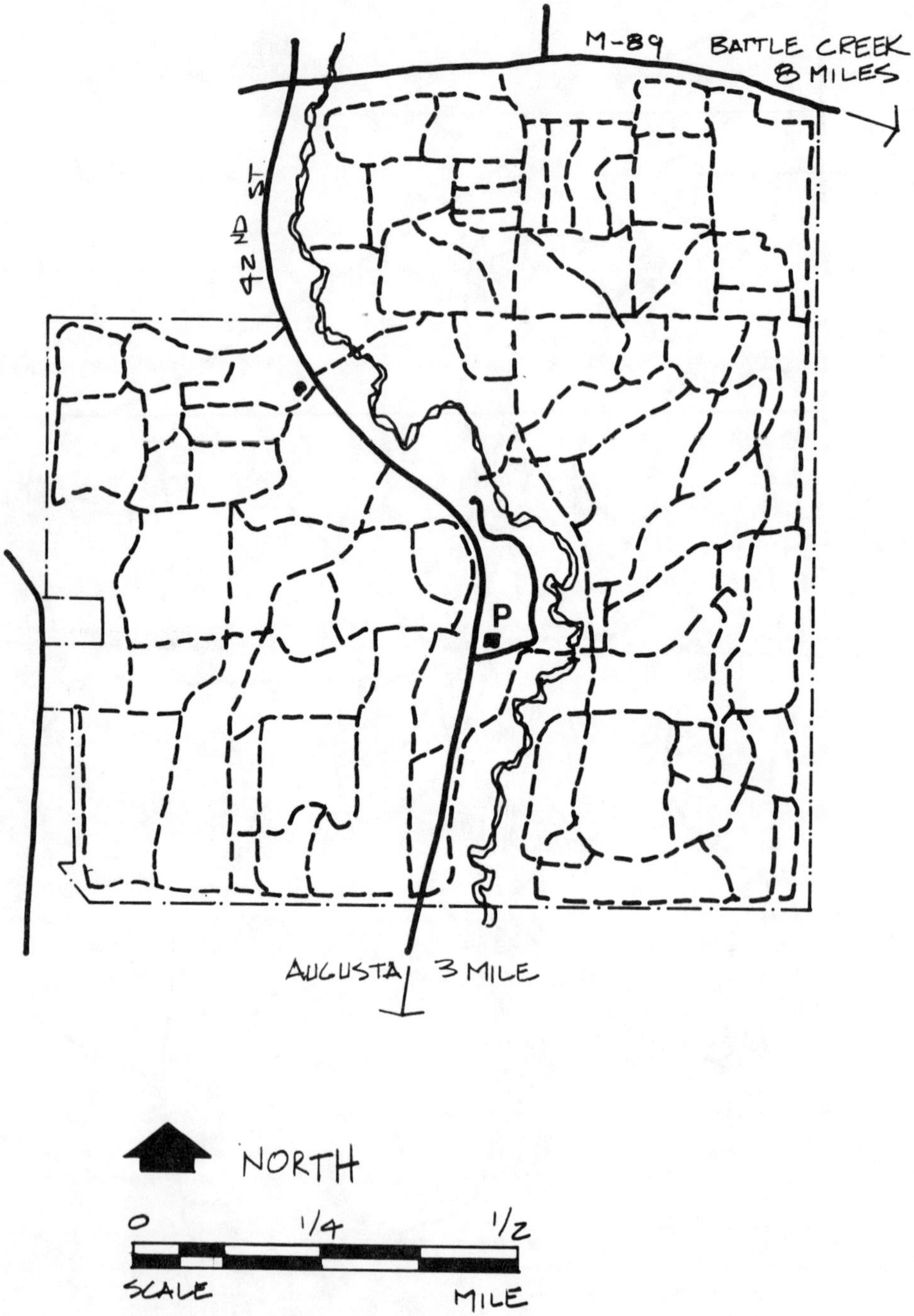

M-89
BATTLE CREEK
8 MILES
42 ND ST
P
AUGUSTA 3 MILE
NORTH
0
1/4
1/2
SCALE
MILE

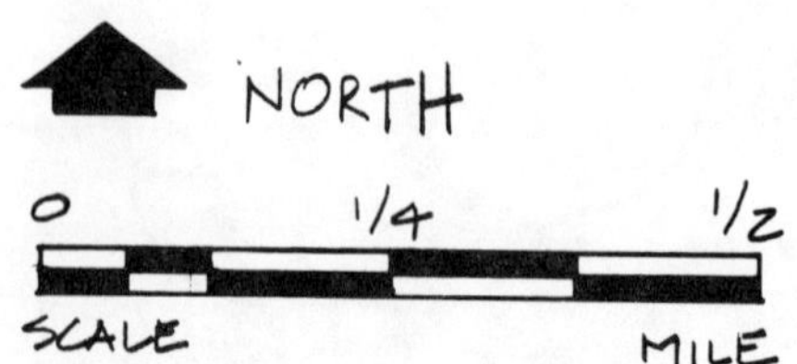

KELLOGG FOREST

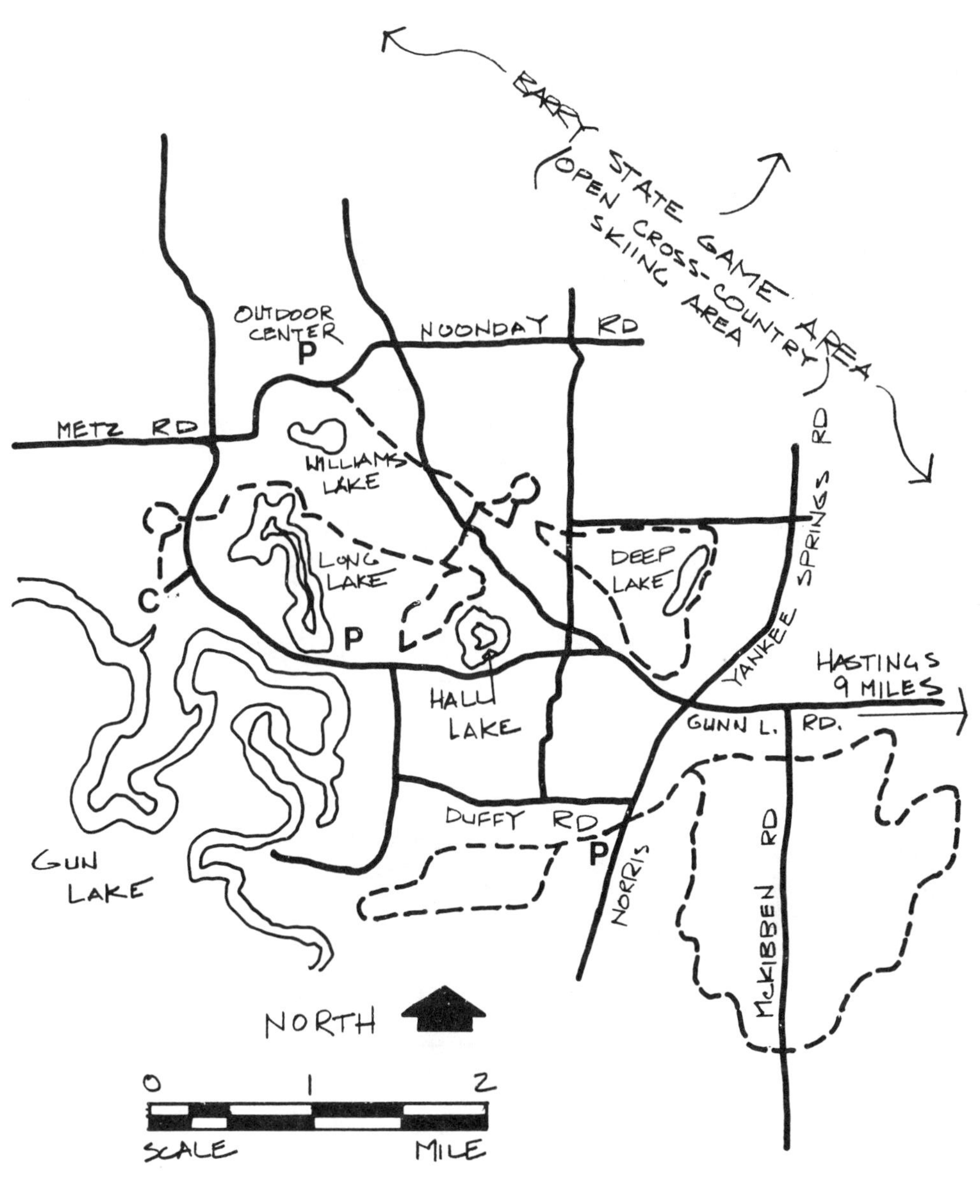

YANKEE SPRINGS RECREATION AREA

BARRY STATE GAME AREA

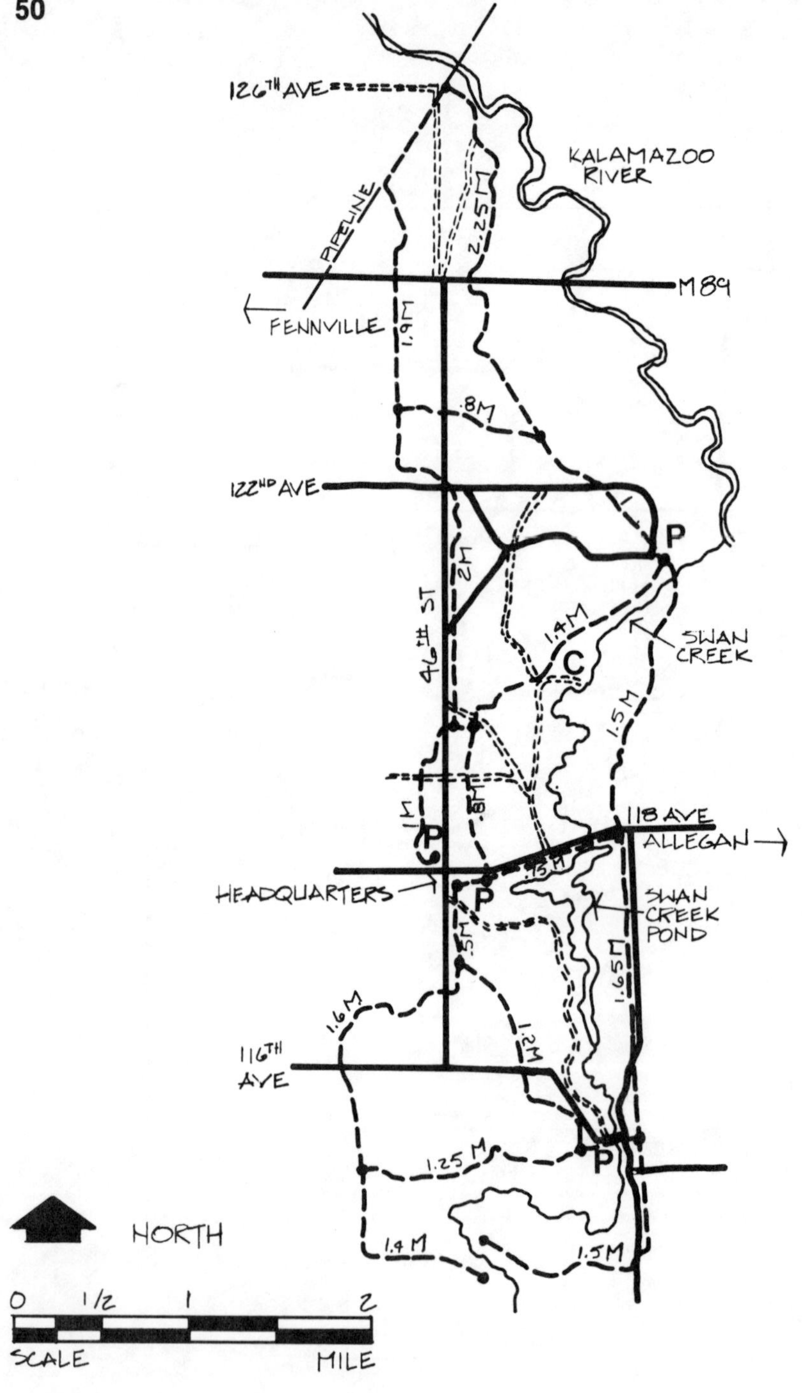

ALLEGAN STATE GAME AREA

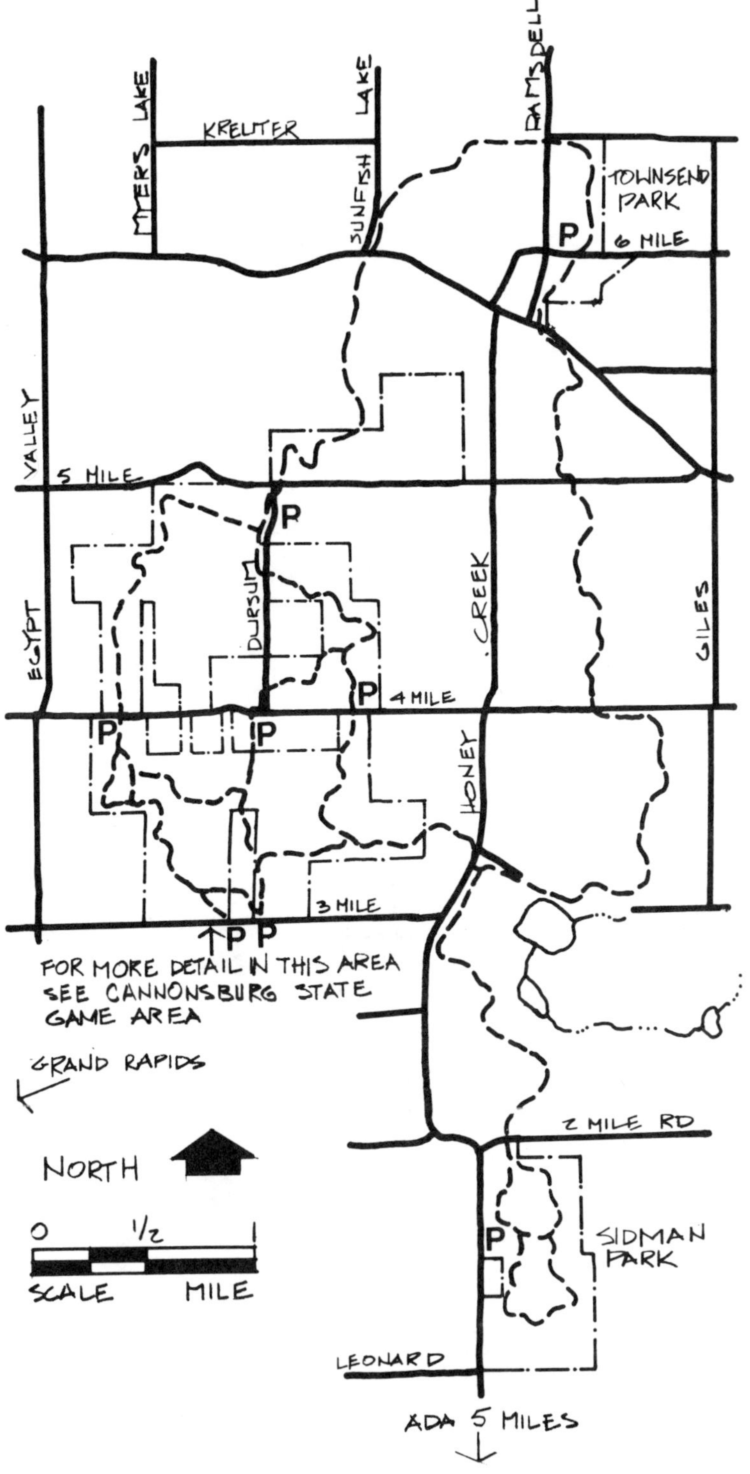

EGYPT VALLEY TRAIL

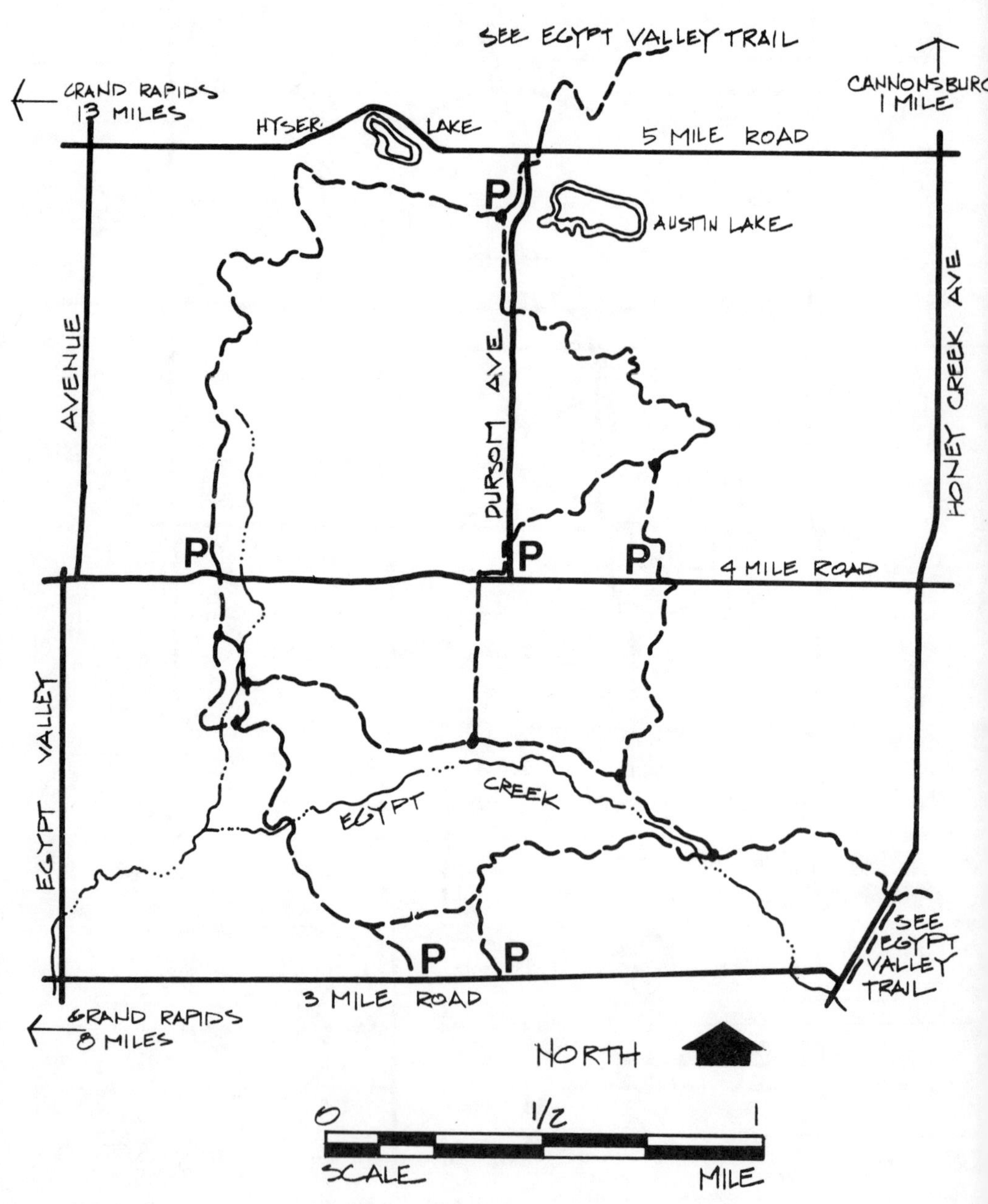

CANNONSBURG STATE GAME AREA

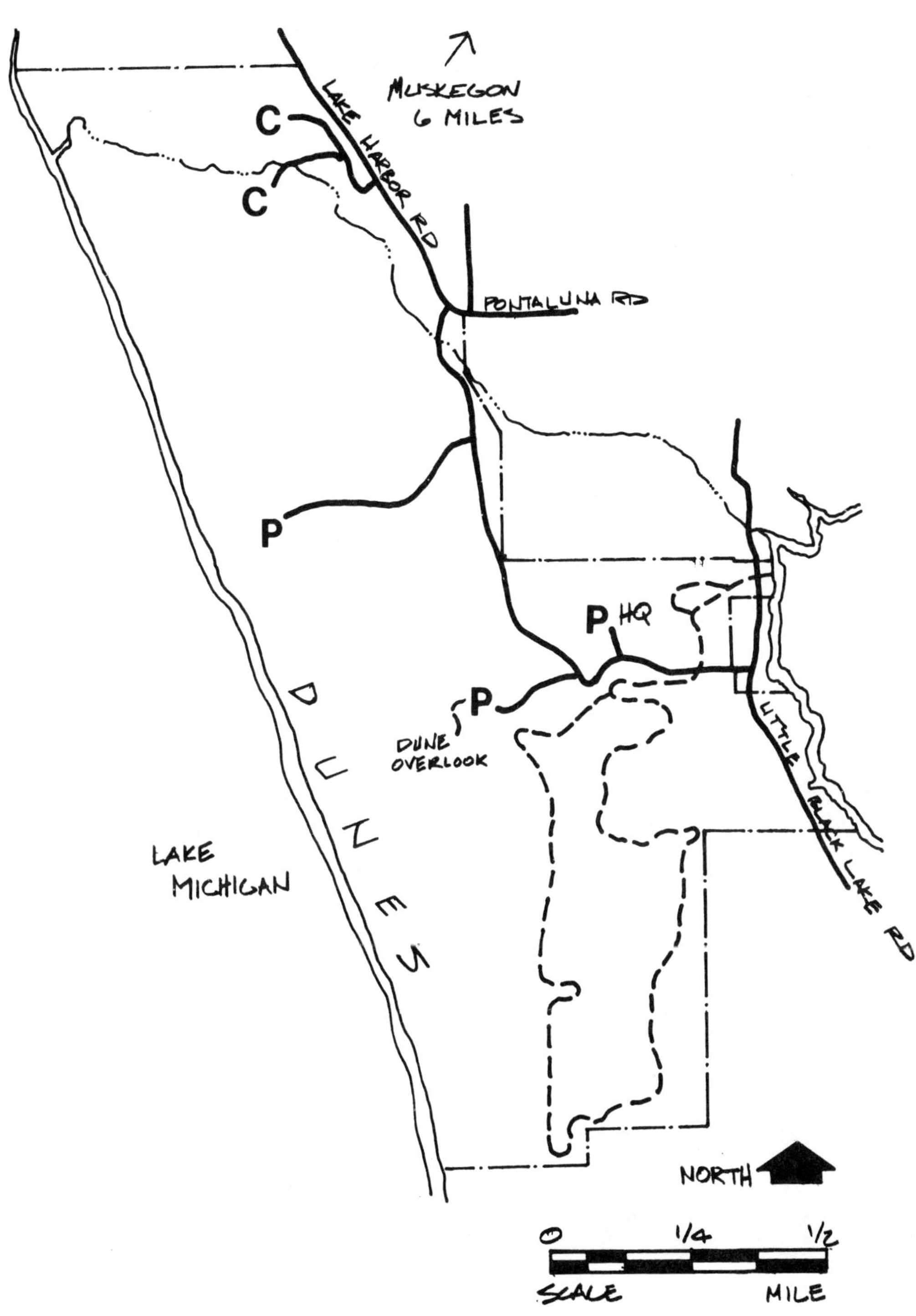

HOFFMASTER STATE PARK

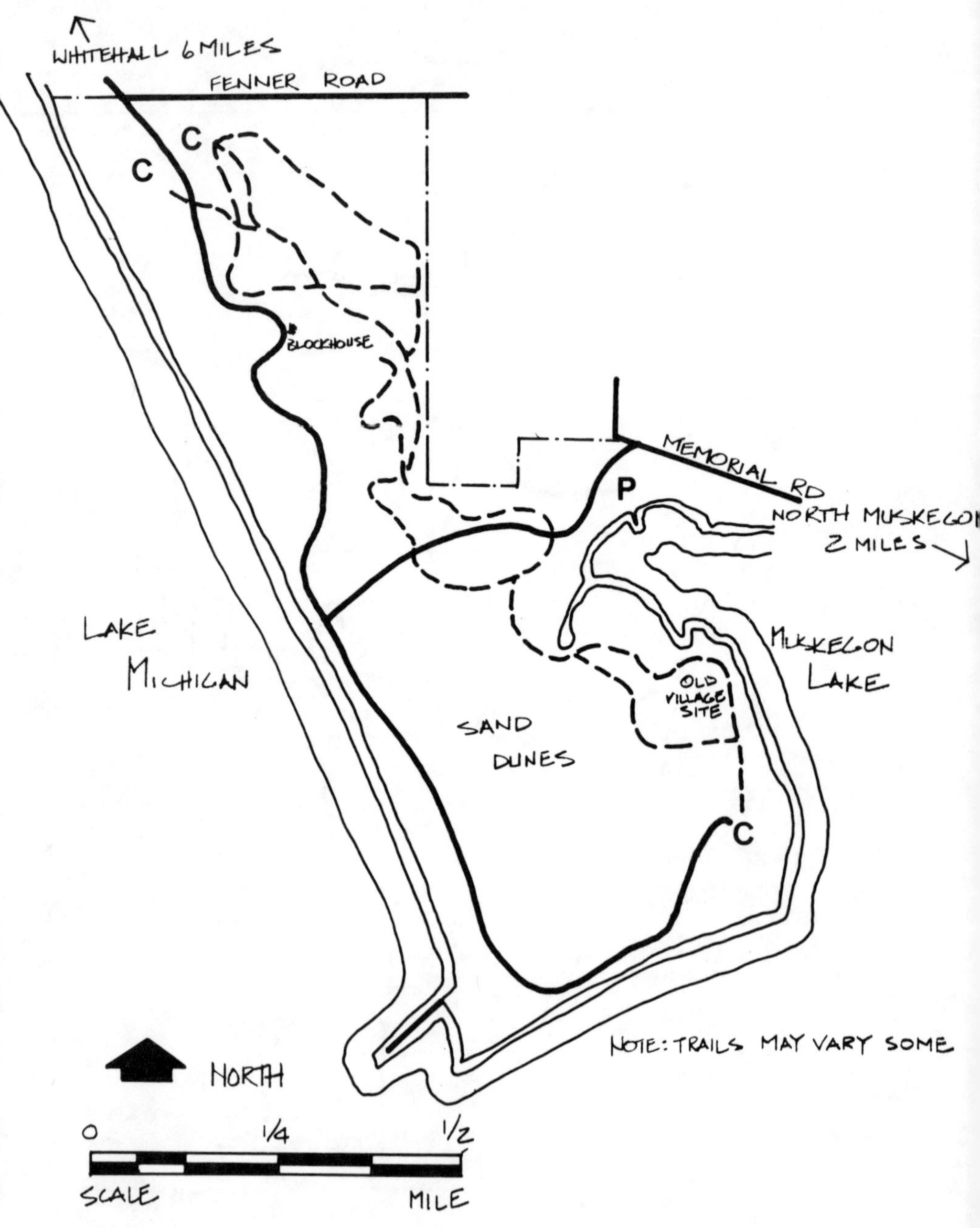

MUSKEGON STATE PARK

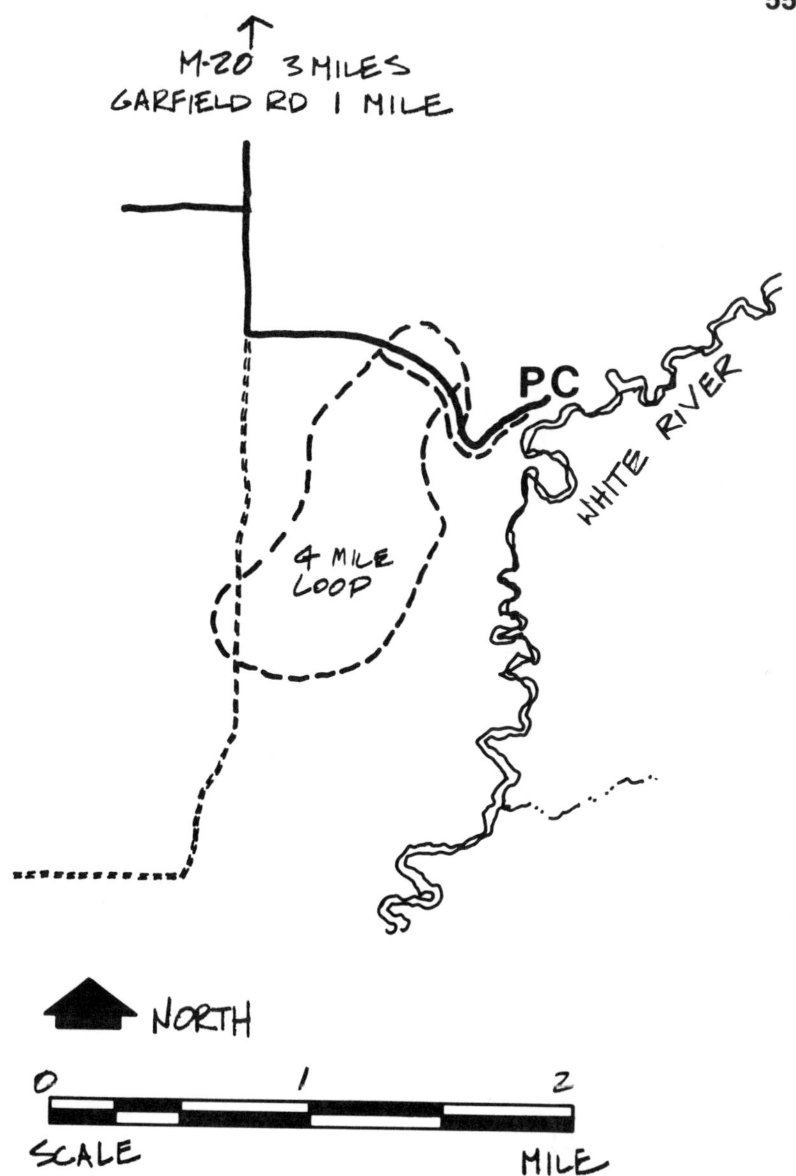

WHITE RIVER TRAIL

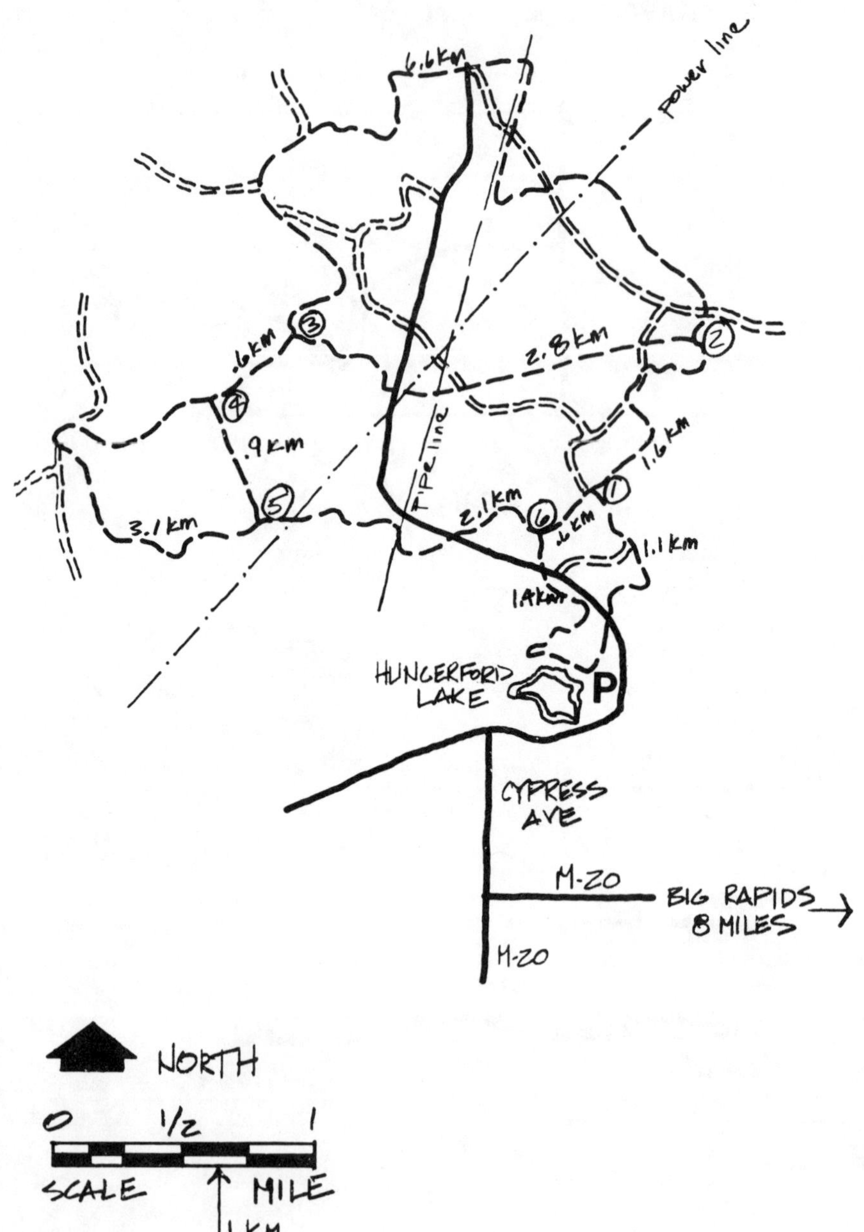

HUNGERFORD SKI TRAIL

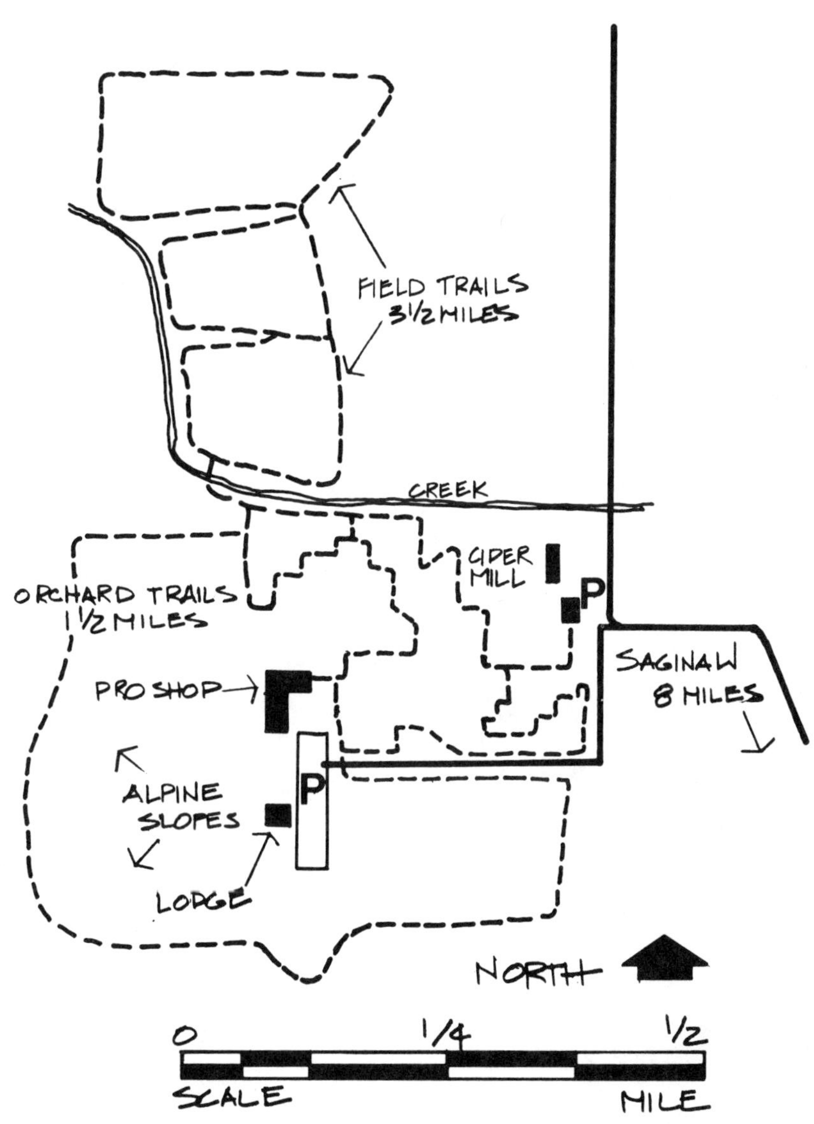

BINTZ APPLE MOUNTAIN

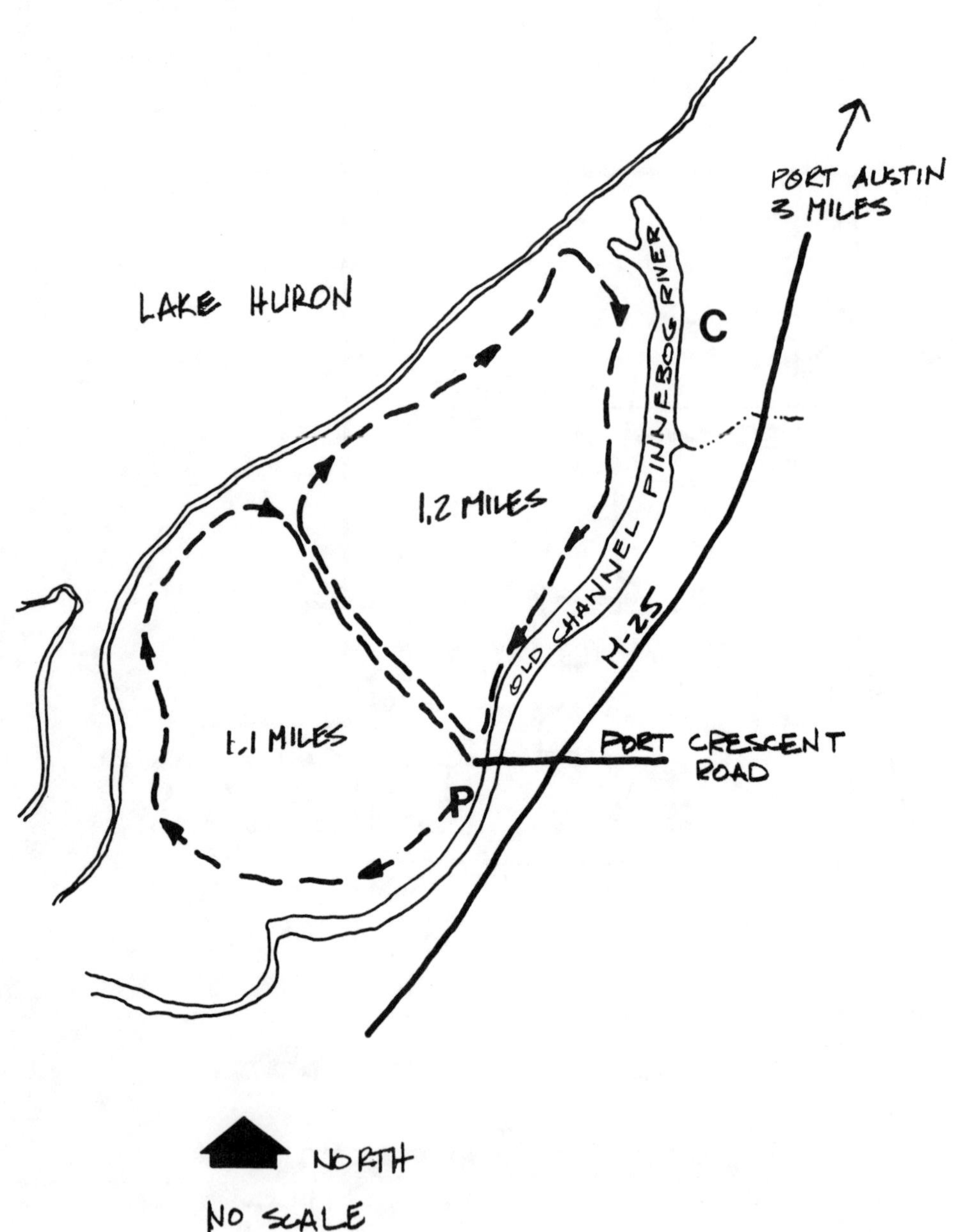

PORT CRESCENT STATE PARK

SKI TOUR'S PLEDGE

I will protect the land and natural resources of the land on which I ski.

I will make it my personal business to leave the land in such a condition that except for the tracks of my skis upon the snow, no one will ever know that I was there.

I will always treat the land gently so that I may return in the future and be welcomed as an old friend.

Region Two

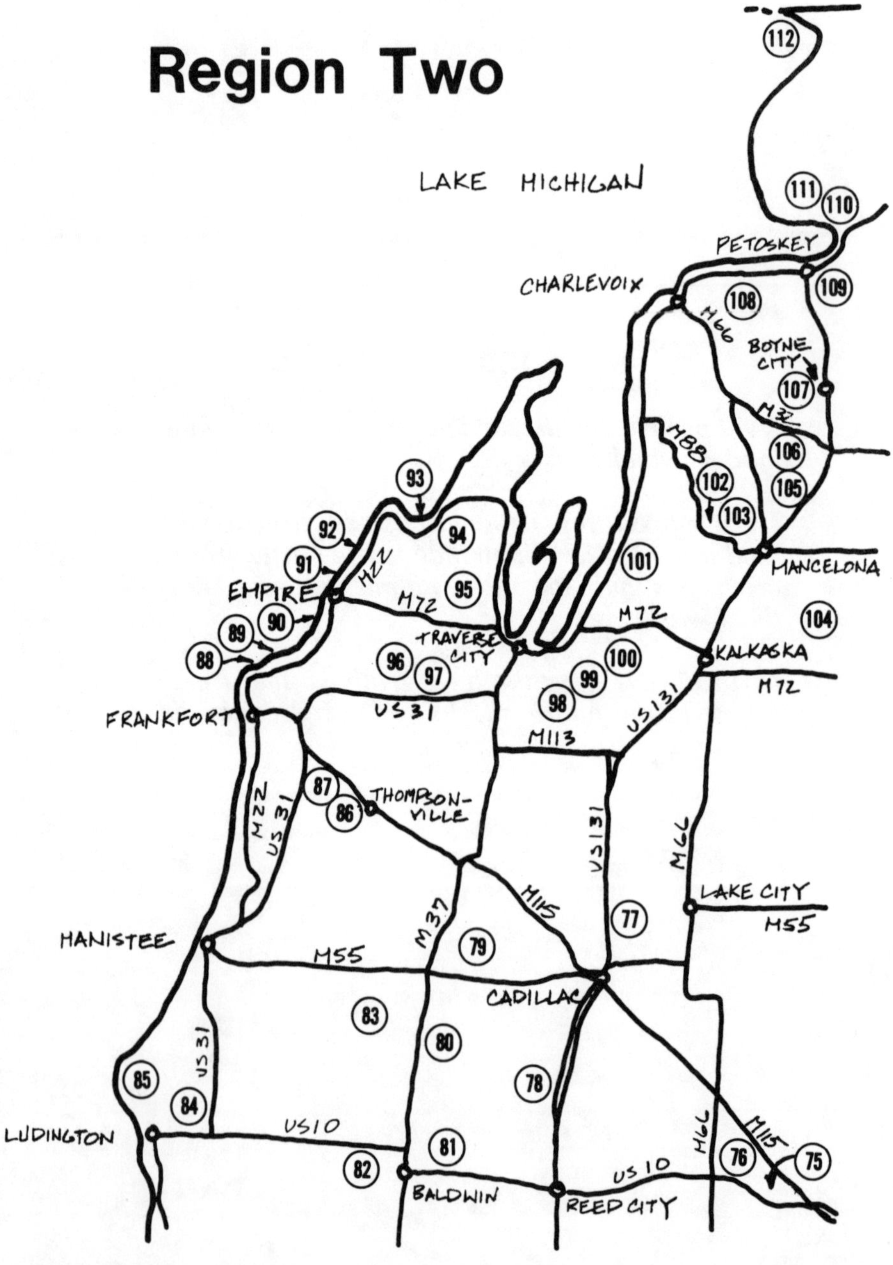
LAKE MICHIGAN
112
111
110
PETOSKEY
109
CHARLEVOIX
108
M66
BOYNE CITY
107
M32
M88
106
105
102
103
93
92
94
MANCELONA
91
M22
101
EMPIRE
95
M72
90
M72
104
89
TRAVERSE CITY
100
88
96
97
99
KALKASKA
M72
98
FRANKFORT
US31
M113
US131
87
THOMPSONVILLE
86
M22
US31
US131
M66
LAKE CITY
M115
77
M55
MANISTEE
M37
79
M55
CADILLAC
83
80
US31
78
85
84
LUDINGTON
US10
M66
M115
81
76
75
82
US 10
BALDWIN
REED CITY

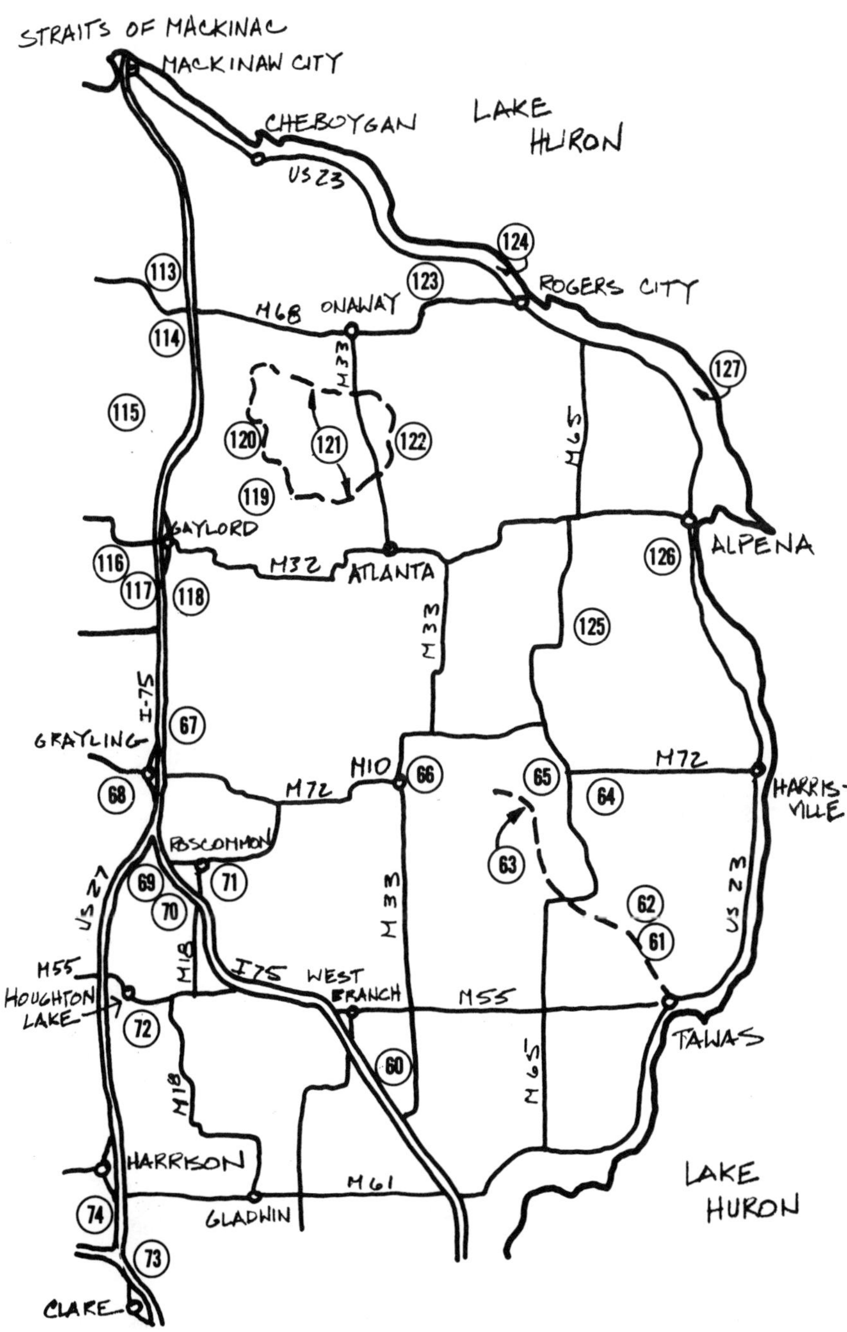
STRAITS OF MACKINAC
MACKINAW CITY
CHEBOYGAN
LAKE HURON
US23
124
113
123
ROGERS CITY
M68
ONAWAY
114
M33
127
115
M65
120
121
122
119
GAYLORD
ALPENA
116
M32
ATLANTA
126
117
118
M33
125
I-75
67
GRAYLING
M10
M72
68
M72
66
65
64
HARRIS-VILLE
ROSCOMMON
63
71
69
US27
70
M33
62
US23
61
M55
I75
WEST BRANCH
M55
HOUGHTON LAKE
M18
72
TAWAS
60
M18
M65
HARRISON
LAKE HURON
M61
GLADWIN
74
73
CLARE

REGION 2 NORTH HALF OF THE LOWER PENINSULA

TRAIL MAP NUMBER	Name	Location	Number of Loops Distances (miles)	Total length of System (miles)	Maintained in the Winter	Total Acres
60	Greenwood Campground 517-345-2778	I-75 to 202 mile exit, north on M33 4 miles, then west on Greenwood Rd 1¼ miles	4 loops	6	yes	unlimited
61	Corsair Ski Trail 517-362-4477	8.5 miles NW of Tawas on Monument Rd	many	35km	yes	unlimited
62	Highbanks Ski Trail 517-362-8643	12 miles NW of Tawas via Monument Rd, River Rd and Cooke Dam Rd	point to point	10km	yes	350
63	Shore to Shore Trail 517-362-4477/78 517-724-6471/ 5431	Trail extends from Tawas to the west county line of Alcona County crossing Monument Rd and M65	point to point	45	no	unlimited
64	Reid Lake Foot Travel Area 517-724-5431	19 miles west of Harrisville on M72	4 loops 1,2,2, 3.25	7.25	no	2400
65	Hoist Lakes Foot Travel Area 517-724-6471/ 5431 616-775-2421	About 22 miles west of Harrisville at the junc- of M72 and M65	4 loops	32.2km	no	10000
66	Hinchman Acres Resort 517-826-3991	4 blocks north of the blinker light in Mio on the AuSable River	5 loops 1.5,4,6, 7,8km	25km	yes	unlimited
67	Hartwick Pines State Park 517-348-7068	1.5 miles north of I-75 on M93 near Grayling	many	10	no	9200
68	Hanson Recreation Area 616-348-9266	2 miles west of Grayling via M72 and M93, follow signs to ski area	8 loops 1 to 7	24	no	900

P —Pro Shop
R —Rentals
W—Warming Area
C —Certified Instruction
S —Snack Bar
D —Dining Room
B —Brown Bag
A —Accommodations

Novice	Intermediate	Expert	Terrain	Trail Use Fee	Campground	Remarks	TRAIL MAP PAGE
√	√		flat to rolling	√	√	P,R,W,S Privately operated year-round campground	78
√	√	√	rolling to hilly			Managed by the USFS Tawas District For complete ski shop services contact Nordic Sports in East Tawas 517-362-2001 Trail groomed twice weekly One of the best recreational trail systems in the state	79
√	√		rolling			Trail follows AuSable River highbanks Very scenic trail Trail groomed weekly For complete ski shop services, contact Nordic Sports in East Tawas 517-362-2001	80
√	√		flat to rolling		√	Very scenic sections along AuSable River at Rollway Rd and M65 See map for access points and campgrounds Contact Nordic Sports in East Tawas for complete pro shop service 517-362-2001 Managed by USFS Tawas and Harrisville Districts	81
√	√		rolling to hilly		√	Managed by USFS Harrisville District	82
√	√	√	rolling to hilly		√	The largest "quiet area" (closed to motorized vehicles) in the state The extensive trail system allows many different combinations of tours Contact the USFS offices at Cadillac or Harrisville for the most up-to-date maps and information	83
√	√		flat	√	√	R,W,S,B,A Privately operated resort on the AuSable River Majority of trails on USFS land but developed and maintained by the resort Ice skating rink on property Excellent "family oriented" facility	84
√	√		flat to rolling with some steep hills	√	√	Beautiful scenery along trail	85
√	√	√	flat to steep			R,W,S,B Trails start at alpine ski area	86

REGION 2 NORTH HALF OF THE LOWER PENINSULA

TRAIL MAP NUMBER	Name	Location	Number of Loops Distances (miles)	Total length of System (miles)	Maintained in the Winter	Total Acres
69	North Higgins Lake State Park 517-821-6125	One mile east of US27 and the Military Rd exit	3 loops 1,3,5	8	no	NA
70	Cross Country Ski Headquarters 517-821-5868	3.5 miles north of South Higgins Lake State Park on Co Rd 100 (east side of Higgins Lake)	5 loops	16km	yes	480
71	Tisdale Triangle Pathway 517-422-5522	East village limits of Roscommon at the end of Main St or Tisdale Rd	5 loops 2.4,4,6.1, 3.6,4.4	10	no	1000
72	Nokomis Pathway 517-422-5191	SW of Prudenville via M55 and 3.5 miles south on Reserve Rd (Co Rd 400/401)	2 loops .75,1.5	1.8	no	unlimited
73	Chalet Cross Country 517-386-9697	5 miles north of Clare on Old 27	3 loops	20km	yes	270
74	Snowsnake Mountain 517-539-6583/7793	9 miles north of Clare on US27 at Lake George exit (Mannsiding Rd)	NA	5	no	270
75	Neithercut Woodland 616-774-3412	4.5 miles west of Farwell on M115	2 loops	2.5	no	252
76	Green Pine Lake Pathway 616-832-2281	14 miles NW of Clare on M115 at Pine Lake State Forest Campground	3 loops 1,2.5,5	8.75	no	unlimited
77	Cadillac Pathway 616-775-9727	4.5 miles NE of Cadillac via US131 then east on Boon Rd (34 Mile Rd)	4 loops 1.3 to 11	8.35	no	NA
78	Cool Cross Country Ski Touring Center 616-768-4624	11.5 miles north of Reed City on US131, then west ½ mile on LeRoy Rd, then north 1 mile on Reed Rd	many	50km	yes	600

P —Pro Shop; R —Rentals; W—Warming Area; C —Certified Instruction; S —Snack Bar; D —Dining Room; B —Brown Bag; A —Accommodations

Novice	Intermediate	Expert	Terrain	Trail Use Fee	Campground	Remarks	TRAIL MAP PAGE
√	√		flat to rolling	√		North side of Higgins Lake	**87**
√	√		flat to rolling			P,R,W,B Trails adjacent to ski shop Trails groomed bi-weekly Instruction available for beginners	**88**
√	√		flat to rolling			Heavily wooded Popular trail for local skiers	**89**
√			rolling				**90**
√	√	√	flat to hilly	√		P,R,W,S,B Privately operated nordic ski area All trails are groomed Most trails for intermediate to expert skiers	**91**
√	√		rolling hills	√		R,W,S Privately operated alpine ski area	**none**
√	√		rolling	√		W A conservation education environmental interpretation facility operated by Central Michigan University	**92**
√			flat to slightly rolling		√	Trail connects to Mud Lake State Forest Campground	**93**
√	√		flat to rolling			One section of the trail follows the Clam River Trail expansion planned	**94**
√	√	√	flat to hilly	√		P,R,W,C,S,B,A Privately operated nordic ski area Trails groomed as necessary Site of Cool X-C Leroy Loppet, Cool X-C 15 Kilo and Cool X-C Michigan Relay races Heated waxing area Excellent trail system	**95**

REGION 2 NORTH HALF OF THE LOWER PENINSULA

TRAIL MAP NUMBER	Name	Location	Number of Loops Distances (miles)	Total length of System (miles)	Maintained in the Winter	Total Acres
79	MacKenzie National Recreation Trail 616-775-8539	At Caberfae Winter Sports Area, 12 miles west of Cadillac via M55	many	24km	no	unlimited
80	Pine Valleys Pathway 616-745-4651	13 miles north of Baldwin via M37 at the Little Manistee River	4 loops	7.3	no	1000
81	Sheep Ranch Pathway 616-745-4651	2 miles east of Baldwin via M37 and north on Mud Trail	2 loops 2,4.5	5	no	360+
82	Bowman Lake Foot Travel Area 616-745-4631	6 miles west of Baldwin on 56th St	several	4	no	1000
83	Timberlane Ski Touring Lodge 616-266-5376	Between Manistee and M37 8 miles SW of Wellston via Bosschew Rd (USFS 5192 or Co Rd 669)	3 loops 4,5,7km	16km	yes	400
84	West Shore Community College 616-845-6211	NE of Ludington, 5 miles east of Ludington via US31/10, then north on Stiles Rd 3.5 miles	1 loop	1	no	10
85	Ludington State Park 616-843-8671	6 miles north of Ludington on M116	many	15	no	4000
86	Crystal Mountain 616-378-2911	2 miles west of Thompsonville on M115	4 loops 1,1.6,1.6, 4.2km	8.4km	no	NA
87	Betsie River Pathway 616-775-9728	5 miles NW of Thompsonville via M115, King Rd and Longstreet Rd	5 loops 1.9,2.1, 5.6,6.5, 7.4	8.9	no	unlimited

P —Pro Shop
R —Rentals
W—Warming Area
C —Certified Instruction
S —Snack Bar
D —Dining Room
B —Brown Bag
A —Accommodations

Novice	Intermediate	Expert	Terrain	Trail Use Fee	Campground	Remarks	TRAIL MAP PAGE
√	√	√	flat to hilly			P,R,W,S,D,A Privately operated alpine ski area under permit from USFS Trail on USFS property and managed by the Cadillac District Trail starts at south (far end) side of parking lot	**96**
√	√		rolling to hilly				**97**
√			flat to rolling		√	Scenic area Campground road not plowed, ski in only Expansion planned to add 11 miles	**98**
√	√		rolling to steep		√	Managed by USFS Baldwin District	**99**
√	√	√	flat to rolling	√		R,W,C,D,A Privately operated nordic ski area Adjacent to the Manistee National Forest Trails always groomed Facility primarily set up for complete weekend packages including room, board, instruction, guided tours and entertainment. Write for brochure. Mailing address Irons, 49644 Food available on weekends only	**none**
√			rolling hills			W,S in the community college buildings	**none**
√	√	√	rolling to hilly	√	√	Trails used for skiing are hiking trails so the appropriate degree of caution when skiing them should be exercised	**100**
√	√	√	NA	√		P,R,W,C,S,D,A Privately operated alpine ski area Trail connects with Betsie River Pathway	**101**
√			flat to rolling			Trail connects to Crystal Mountain nordic trail system	**102**

REGION 2 NORTH HALF OF THE LOWER PENINSULA

TRAIL MAP NUMBER	Name	Location	Number of Loops Distances (miles)	Total length of System (miles)	Maintained in the Winter	Total Acres
88	Old Indian Cross Country Ski Trail 616-352-9611	Trailhead is just east of the M22 and Sutter Rd intersection on the north side of Crystal Lake	2 loops 2.2,2.25	3.6	no	NA
89	Platte Plains Cross Country Ski Trail 616-352-9611	At Platte River Campground 14 miles south of Empire on M22	3 loops 2.8,7.6, 9	12.3	no	NA
90	Empire Bluff Cross Country Ski Trail 616-352-9611	One mile south of Empire on Wilco Rd, just west of the USAF radar station	not looped	1.5	no	NA
91	Schauger Hill and Windy Moraine Cross Country Ski Trails 616-352-9611	3.5 miles north of Empire on M-109	3 loops 1.5,2.4, 2.5	6	no	NA
92	Alligator Hill Cross Country Ski Trail 616-352-9611	1.5 miles west of Glen Arbor via M109, on Day Forest Rd	3 loops 2.5,2.5, 2.7	7	no	NA
93	Good Harbor Bay Cross Country Ski Trail 616-352-9611	North of Glen Arbor on Lake Michigan via M72 and Co Rd 669 at picnic area	1 loop	2.8	no	NA
94	Sugar Loaf Mountain Resort 616-228-5461	NW of Traverse City between Cedar and M22 near Lake Michigan	3 loops 2.8,4,8 km	15km	yes	500
95	Timberlee Ski Area 616-946-4444	9 miles NW of Traverse City via M22, Co Rd 633 and Co Rd 614	2 loops	NA	NA	NA
96	Chain-O-Lakes Pathway 616-325-4611	Trail starts at Lake Ann State Forest Campground, 2 miles SW of the Village of Lake Ann via Almira and Reynolds Rds	2 loops 1.25,2	2.5	no	NA

P —Pro Shop
R —Rentals
W—Warming Area
C —Certified Instruction
S —Snack Bar
D —Dining Room
B —Brown Bag
A —Accommodations

Novice	Intermediate	Expert	Terrain	Trail Use Fee	Campground	Remarks	TRAIL MAP PAGE
√	√		flat to rolling		√	Trail overlooks Lake Michigan at one point Southern most trail in Sleeping Bear Dunes National Lakeshore	103
√	√		flat to rolling		√	Trail passes partially through dunes Excellent trail system Managed by the Sleeping Bear Dunes National Lakeshore	104
		√	hilly			Overlooks Empire and Lake Michigan Managed by the Sleeping Bear Dunes National Lakeshore	105
√	√	√	flat to hilly		√	Trail overlooks Lake Michigan Visitor center at trail head is open weekends Managed by the Sleeping Bear Dunes National Lakeshore Excellent trail system	106
√	√	√	rolling to hilly		√	Scenic lookouts along trail D.H. Day campground is ½ mile from trail Visitor center is located on M109 south of Glen Lake Managed by Sleeping Bear Dunes National Lakeshore	107
√			flat			Managed by Sleeping Bear Dunes National Lakeshore	108
√	√	√	flat to rolling with some hilly sections			P,R,W,C,S,D,A Privately operated alpine ski resort	none
√	√	√	flat to hilly	√		P,R,W,S,A Privately operated alpine ski area	none
		√	rolling to hilly		√		109

REGION 2 NORTH HALF OF THE LOWER PENINSULA

TRAIL MAP NUMBER	Name	Location	Number of Loops Distances (miles)	Total length of System (miles)	Maintained in the Winter	Total Acres
97	Lost Lake Nature Pathway 616-946-4920	2.5 miles NW of Interlochen Corners via US31 and Wildwood Rd	3 loops 2.5,4.5, 5.5	6	no	2500
98	Ranch Rudolf 616-946-5410	15 miles SE of Traverse City on the Boardman River via Garfield Rd, Hobbs Hwy, Ranch Rudolf Rd and Brownbridge Rds	3 loops 1.5,3,4	9	yes	240
99	Muncie Lake Pathway 616-946-4920	14 miles SE of Traverse City via Garfield Rd, Hobbs Hwy and Ranch Rudolf Rd. Just west of Ranch Rudolf	6 loops 1.85,4, 5.45,6.5, 7.7,8.55	10	yes	unlimited
100	Sand Lakes Quiet Area 616-946-4920	5 miles SSE of Williamsburg via M72 and Broomhead Rd	many	13	no	2800
101	Maplehurst Ski Area 616-264-9675	Proceed north on US31 out of Elk Rapids for 3.2 miles, turn east on Winters Rd for 2.3 miles to the ski area	several	7.5	yes	800
102	Hilton-Shanty Creek Touring Center 616-533-8621/ 800-632-7118	2 miles SE of Bellaire and 10 miles NW of Mancelona on M88	many	28km	yes	2000
103	Schuss Mountain 616-587-9162	5 miles west of Mancelona on M88	NA	15km	no	1400
104	Blue Lake Ski Area 616-587-8298	Between Kalkaska and Frederic via Co Rd 612 and Blue Lake Rd	many	13	yes	NA

P —Pro Shop
R —Rentals
W—Warming Area
C —Certified Instruction
S —Snack Bar
D —Dining Room
B —Brown Bag
A —Accommodations

Novice	Intermediate	Expert	Terrain	Trail Use Fee	Campground	Remarks	TRAIL MAP PAGE
√	√		flat to slightly rolling		√	Campground on trail not plowed	110
√	√	√	flat to hilly			P,R,W,C,D,S Privately operated resort Citizen and USSA races held often throughout the season Some trails follow the Boardman River and nearby creeks Trail connects to Muncie Lake Pathway	111
√	√		rolling to hilly			Very scenic trail in Boardman River valley Very heavy usage	112
√	√	√	flat to very steep		√	Ski-in campsites only Beautiful area for skiing	113
√	√	√	rolling to steep hills	√	√	P,R,W,S,D,A Privately operated alpine ski area All trails maintained with a track setter Spectacular views of Grand Traverse Bay and Torch Lake	114
√	√	√	flat to very hilly	√	√	P,R,W,C,S,D,A Connected with the Hilton-Shanty Creek Lodge alpine ski resort All trails are groomed and maintained with a double track setter Trails to Schuss Mt. Nastar cross country races held twice weekly	115
√	√	√	flat to hilly	√	√	P,R,W,C,S,D,A Privately operated alpine ski area Some trails on the golf course KOA campground nearby Trail to Hilton Shanty Creek Lodge	116
√	√	√	rolling to hilly			R,W,D,A for AYH members Trails adjacent to Blue Lake Youth Hostel Trails are on state land and are open to the public at no charge Additional trails in the area are not marked	117

REGION 2 NORTH HALF OF THE LOWER PENINSULA

TRAIL MAP NUMBER	Name	Location	Number of Loops Distances (miles)	Total length of System (miles)	Maintained in the Winter	Total Acres
105	Jordan River Pathway 616-582-6681	In the Jordan River State Forest south of M32 and west of US131 Trail pickup points at Deadmans Hill Historic Site or the federal fish hatchery both of which are off US131	2 loops 3,18	19	no	unlimited
106	Warner Creek Pathway 616-582-6681	South of M32 1½ miles west of US131	1 loop	3.8	no	440
107	Boyne Nordican 616-549-2441/ 800-632-7174	3 miles west of Boyne Falls on Deer Lake Rd west side of Boyne Mountain	6 loops 5,5,7.5, 7.5,10km	42km	yes	NA
108	Windmill Farm Cross Country Ski Area 616-547-2746/ 6821	6 miles east of Charlevoix on Boyne City Rd (C56) on the north side of Lake Charlevoix	5 loops 3,4,6,8, 10km	20km	yes	500
109	North Central Michigan College Ski Trails 616-347-3973	½ mile south of Petoskey on Howard St	3 loops 2,2.5,3	10	no	200
110	Nub's Nob 616-526-2131	3 miles north of Harbor Springs via US131 and Pleasantview Rd	1 loop	8 km	no	NA
111	Boyne Highlands 616-526-2171	8 miles west of Petoskey via US131	1 loops 3.5,5	8	yes	500
112	Wilderness State Park 616-436-5381	9 miles west of Mackinaw City on Lake Michigan	many	35	no	7200
113	Burt Lake State Park 616-238-9392	½ mile west of Indian River on M27	2 loops	1	no	400
114	Wildwood Hills Pathway 616-238-9313	3 miles west of US27 on Wildwood Rd between Indian River and Wolverine	3 loops 4,6.5, 9.5	10.5	no	2000

P —Pro Shop
R —Rentals
W—Warming Area
C —Certified Instruction
S —Snack Bar
D —Dining Room
B —Brown Bag
A —Accommodations

Novice	Intermediate	Expert	Terrain	Trail Use Fee	Campground	Remarks	TRAIL MAP PAGE
	√	√	rolling to very steep		√	Trail not specifically designed for skiing, may require removal of skis at some points Very scenic trail in Jordan River valley	**118**
√			flat to rolling			Trail passes through hardwood forest	**119**
√	√	√	rolling to hilly	√		P,R,W,C,D,A Privately operated nordic ski area Separate trails for racing and touring	**120**
√	√	√	rolling to hilly	√		P,R,W,C,S,B Privately operated nordic ski area 1 km lighted practice loop Trails groomed every other day	**121**
√	√		rolling			W,S,B Trails maintained by NCMC	**122**
√	√		rolling to hilly	√		P,R,W,S,D,B,A Privately operated alpine ski area	**none**
√	√		flat to hilly	√		P,R,W,C,S,D,A Privately operated alpine ski area	**none**
√	√	√	flat to hilly	√	√	Ski in cabins available Very beautiful area	**123**
√			flat	√	√	Trail through campground	**124**
√	√		rolling to hilly			Excellent trail system	**125**

REGION 2 NORTH HALF OF THE LOWER PENINSULA

TRAIL MAP NUMBER	Name	Location	Number of Loops Distances (miles)	Total length of System (miles)	Maintained in the Winter	Total Acres
115	Spring Brook Pathway 616-582-6681	NE of Boyne Falls on Co Rd 626, then north on Slashing Rd 2.5 miles. Just north of Thunder Mountain ski area	2 loops 4,5	5	no	500
116	Pine Baron Pathway 517-732-5128	6 miles west of Gaylord via Old Alba and Lone Pine Rds	5 loops 2,2,2.5, 2.5,6.25	7	no	1000
117	Ken Mar on the Hill 517-732-4950	4 miles south of Gaylord on Old 27	9 loops 1.2 to 6.4km	26km	yes	115
118	Michaywe 517-939-8910/ 8800	5 miles south of Gaylord via Old 27 and east on Charles Brink Rd	NA	12	no	2800
119	Tyrolean Ski Resort 517-732-2743	12 miles NE of Gaylord via M32, F44 and Sawyer Rd	many	20	no	200
120	Shingle Mill Pathway 517-983-4101	11 miles east of Vanderbilt on Sturgeon Valley Rd at the Pigeon River Bridge State Forest Campground	5 loops .75,1.25, 6,10,11	16	no	unlimited
121	High Country Pathway 517-983-4101	In Black Lake, Thunder Bay and Pigeon River Country State Forests. Access from M33 north of Atlanta at Clear Lake State Park or Shingle Mill Pathway	1 loop	80+	no	unlimited
122	Sinkholes Area 517-983-4101	16 miles north of Atlanta via M33 and east on Tomahawk Lake Highway to Shoepac Lake SFG	2 loops .75,1.5	2	no	unlimited

P —Pro Shop
R —Rentals
W—Warming Area
C —Certified Instruction

S —Snack Bar
D —Dining Room
B —Brown Bag
A —Accommodations

Novice	Intermediate	Expert	Terrain	Trail Use Fee	Campground	Remarks	TRAIL MAP PAGE
√	√		flat to rolling			Varied forest cover	126
√	√		flat to gently rolling		√	Campground at Otsego Lake State Park	127
√	√	√	flat to very hilly	√		R,W,C,S,B,A Privately operated nordic ski area Free instruction and daily clinics Night skiing W,F,S nights on a 2.5km lighted trail Site of the Ken-Mar Classic citizen race held in February Some trails groomed with a track setter	128
√	√		flat to rolling with steep hills			R,W,C,D Privately operated resort with alpine ski area 5 miles of the trail system is maintained in the winter	129
√	√		flat to rolling	√		P,R,W,C,S,D,B,A Privately operated alpine ski area Complete lodge facilities with indoor heated pool Trails groomed weekly	none
√	√	√	rolling to very steep		√	Plowed campsites at Pigeon River Bridge only Water is available at field office Very scenic trail	130
	√	√	rolling to hilly		√	Not specifically designed for skiing Should only be used by experienced skiers with winter camping skills Many campgrounds along trail, only Clear Lake State Park and Pigeon River Bridge State Forest Campgrounds are plowed	131
√			flat to rolling		√	Trail circles several sinkholes Area closed to motorized vehicles	132

REGION 2 NORTH HALF OF THE LOWER PENINSULA

TRAIL MAP NUMBER	Name	Location	Number of Loops Distances (miles)	Total length of System (miles)	Maintained in the Winter	Total Acres
123	Ocqueoc Falls Bicentennial Pathway 517-733-8722	11 miles east of Onaway via M68 and Ocqueoc Falls Rd	3 loops 3,4,6.5	7	no	1200
124	Hoeft State Park 517-734-2543	4 miles north of Rogers City on US23	3 loops	2	no	300
125	Chippewa Hills Pathway 517-354-2209	SW of Alpena, 11 miles west of US23 at South Ossineke via Nicholson Hill Rd	4 loops .5,1.3, 2.5,4.5	7.5	no	640
126	Norway Ridge Pathway 517-354-2209	4.5 miles SW of Alpena on Werth Rd	4 loops	7	yes	800
127	Besser Natural Area 517-354-2209	North of Alpena on US23 then north on Co Rd 405 at Lakewood for 3 miles	1 loop	1	no	100

P —Pro Shop S —Snack Bar
R —Rentals D —Dining Room
W—Warming Area B —Brown Bag
C —Certified Instruction A —Accommodations

Novice	Intermediate	Expert	Terrain	Trail Use Fee	Campground	Remarks	TRAIL MAP PAGE
	√		rolling with one steep hill			Ocqueoc Falls is along the trail	**133**
√			flat	√		Trail along Lake Huron	**134**
√	√	√	rolling to hilly			The shorter loops have the more difficult slopes	**135**
√			flat to rolling			Heavily used trail by local skiers	**136**
√			flat			Nature trail	**none**

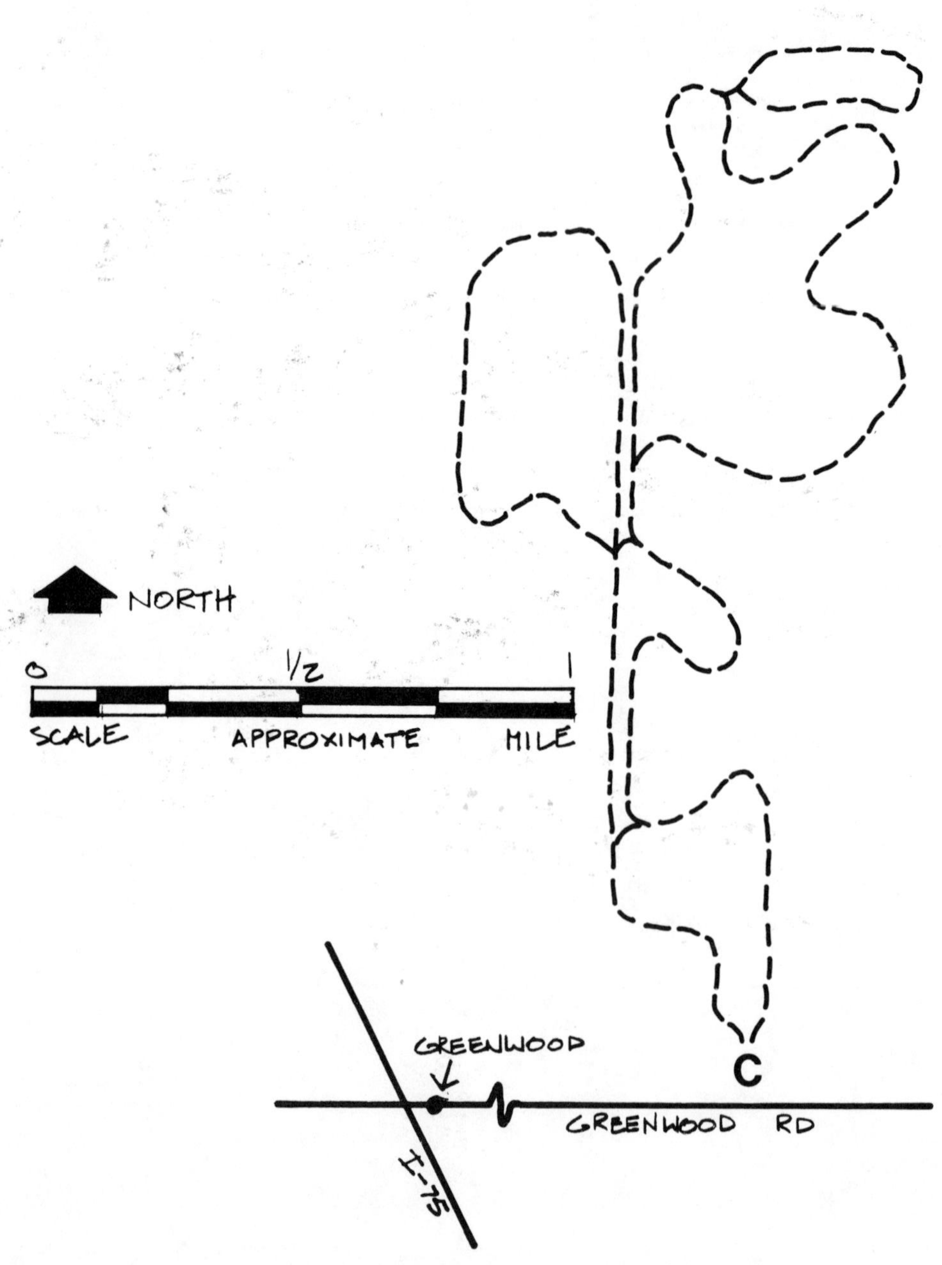

GREENWOOD CAMPGROUND

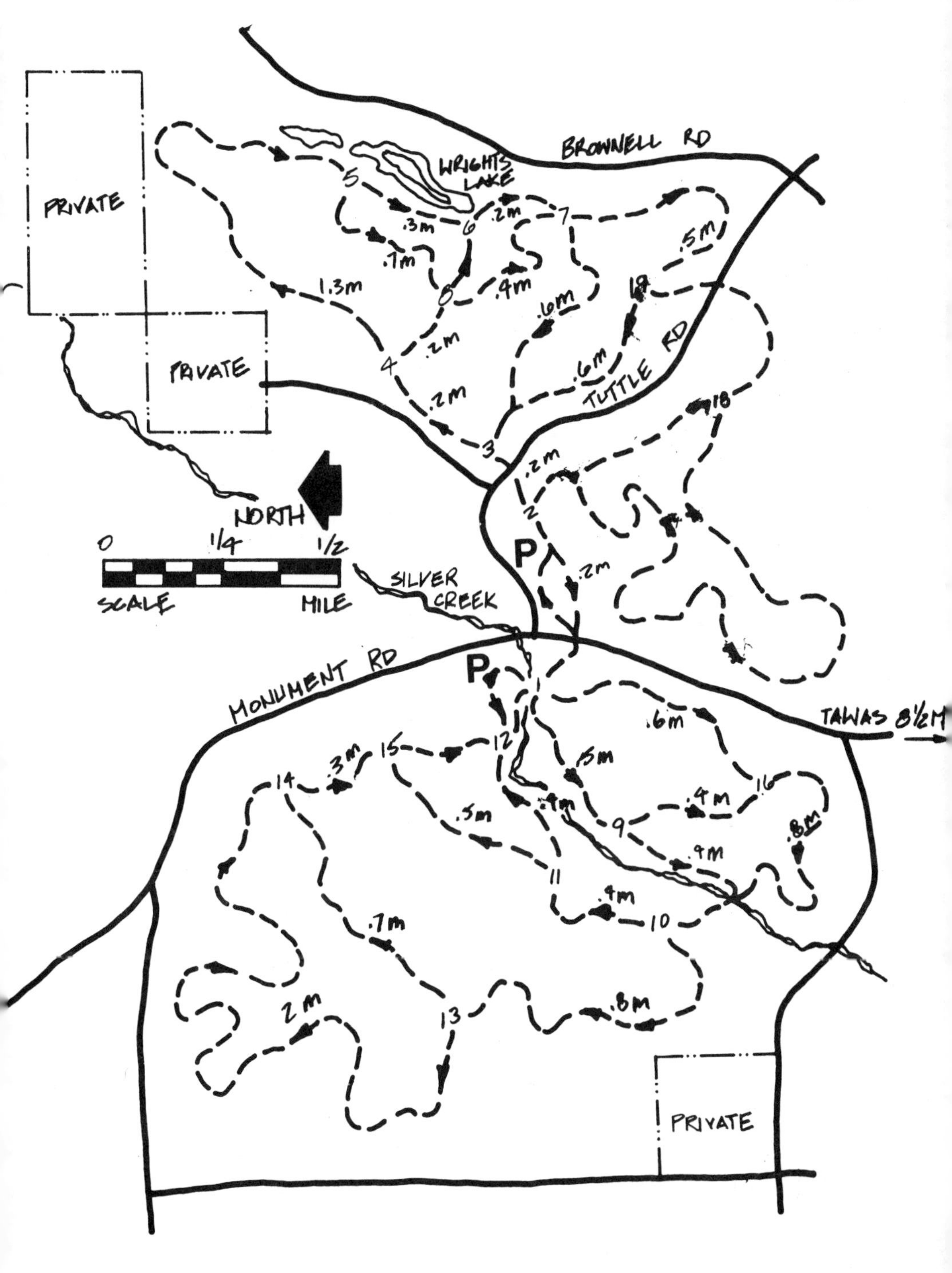

CORSAIR SKI TRAIL

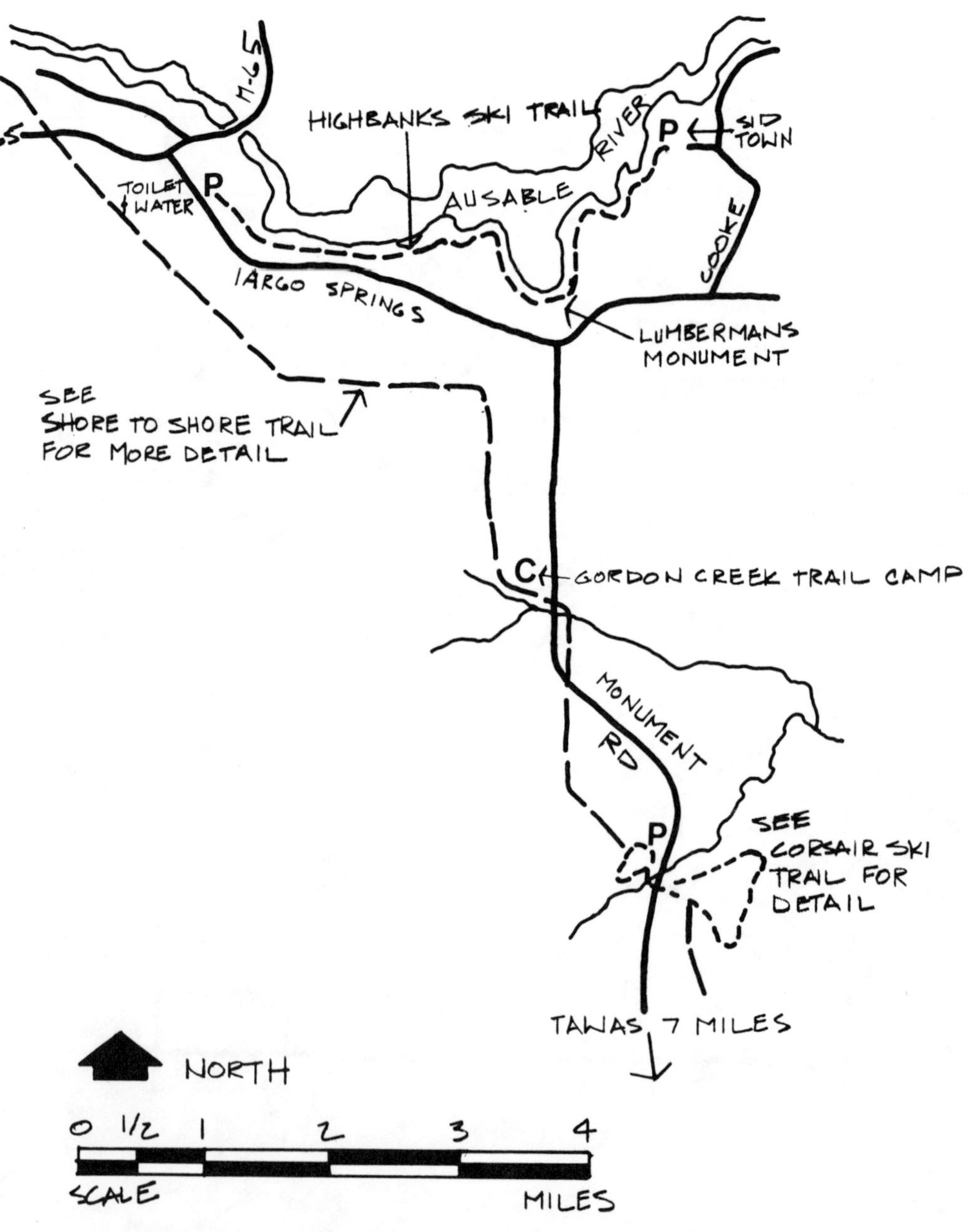

HIGHBANKS SKI TRAIL

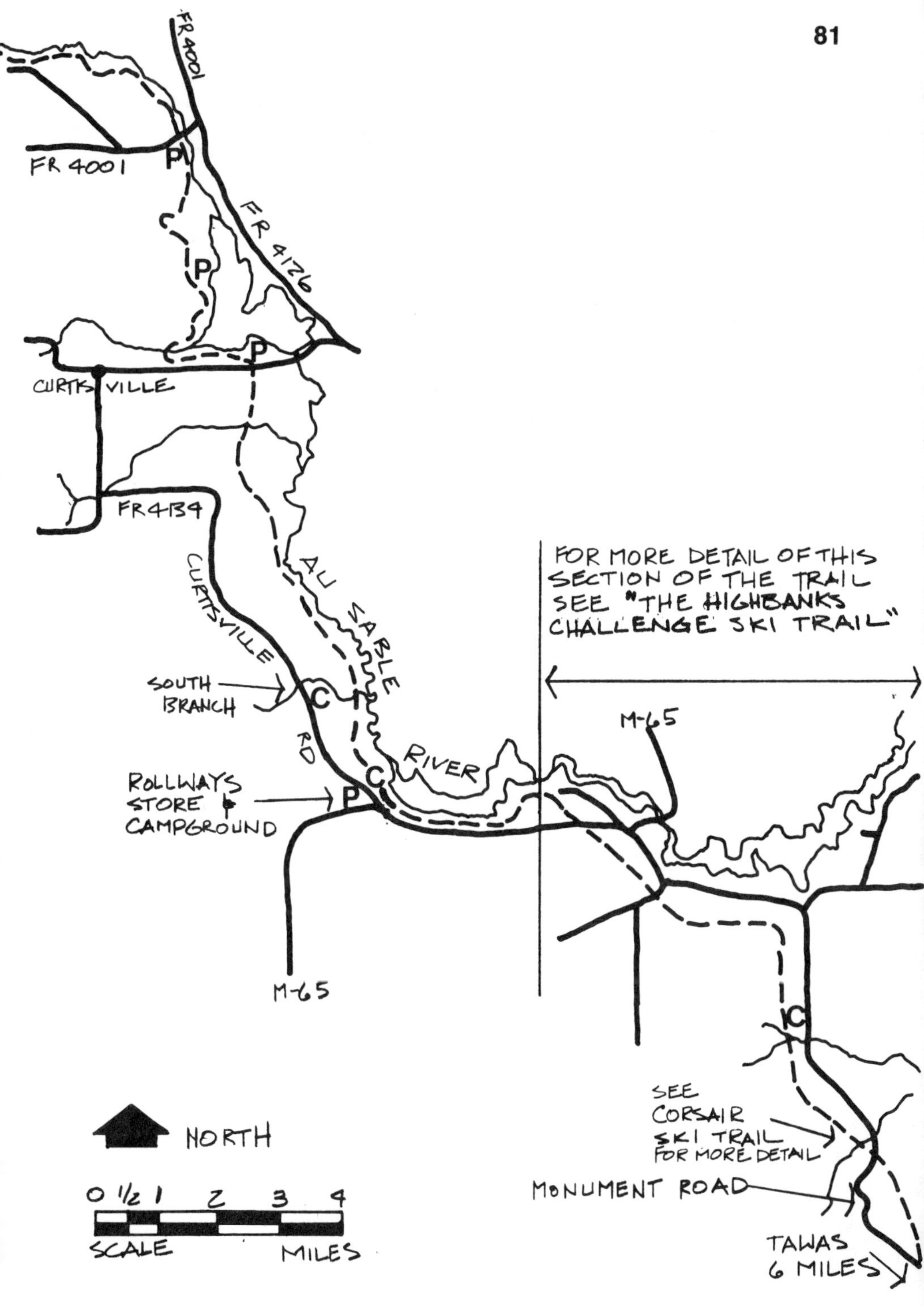

SHORE TO SHORE TRAIL

TAWAS & HARRISVILLE RANGER DISTRICT - U.S.F.S.

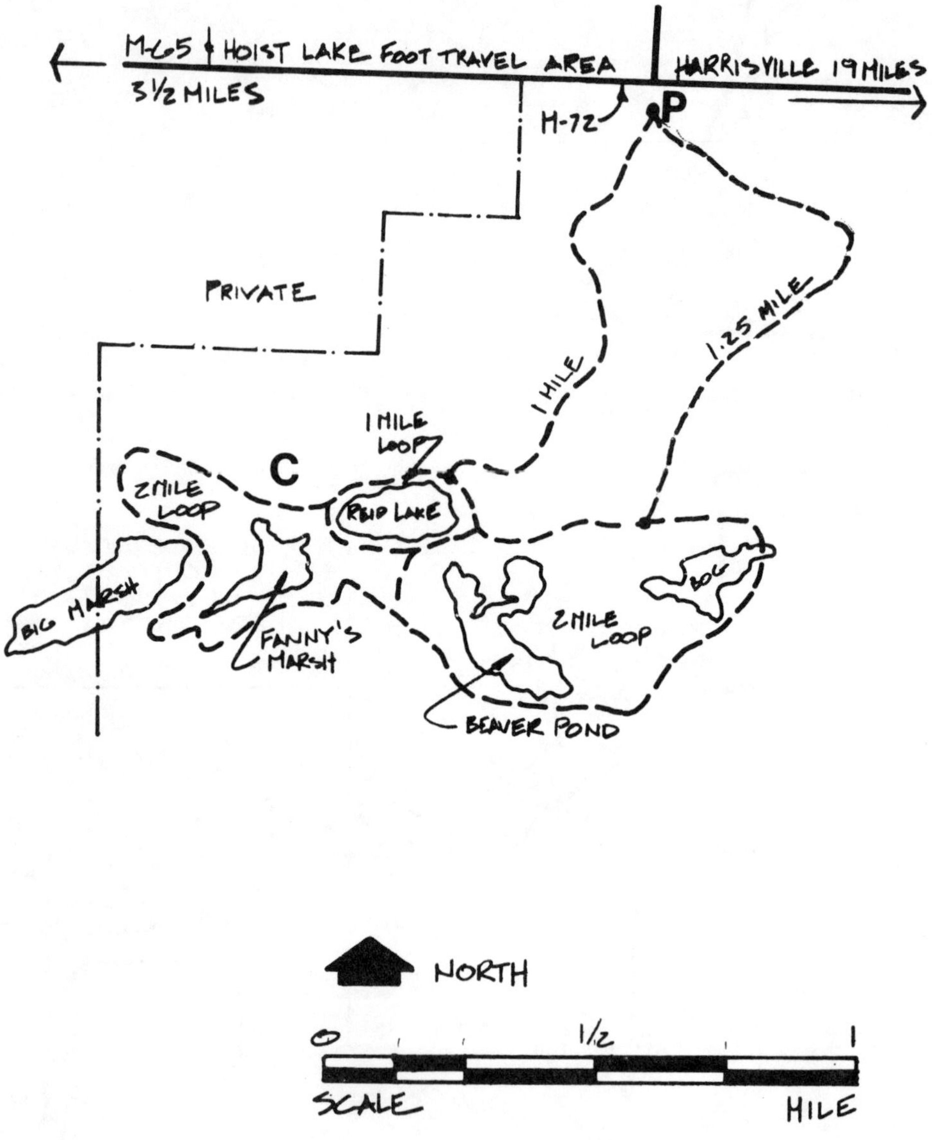

M-65
HOIST LAKE FOOT TRAVEL AREA
3½ MILES
HARRISVILLE 19 MILES
M-72
P
PRIVATE
1.25 MILE
1 MILE
1 MILE LOOP
C
2 MILE LOOP
REID LAKE
BIG MARSH
FANNY'S MARSH
2 MILE LOOP
BOG
BEAVER POND
NORTH
0
1/2
1
SCALE
MILE

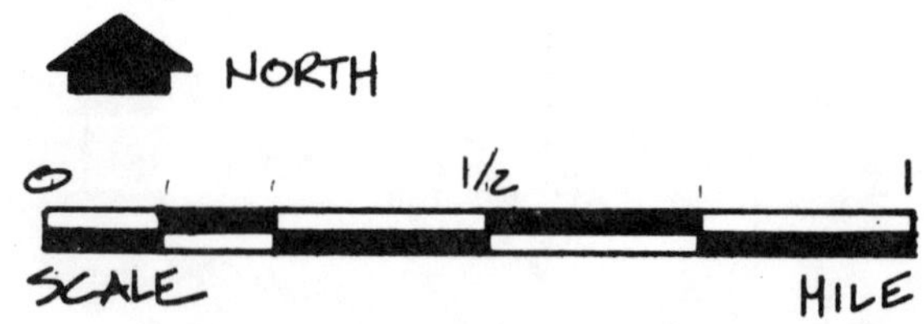

REID LAKE FOOT TRAVEL AREA

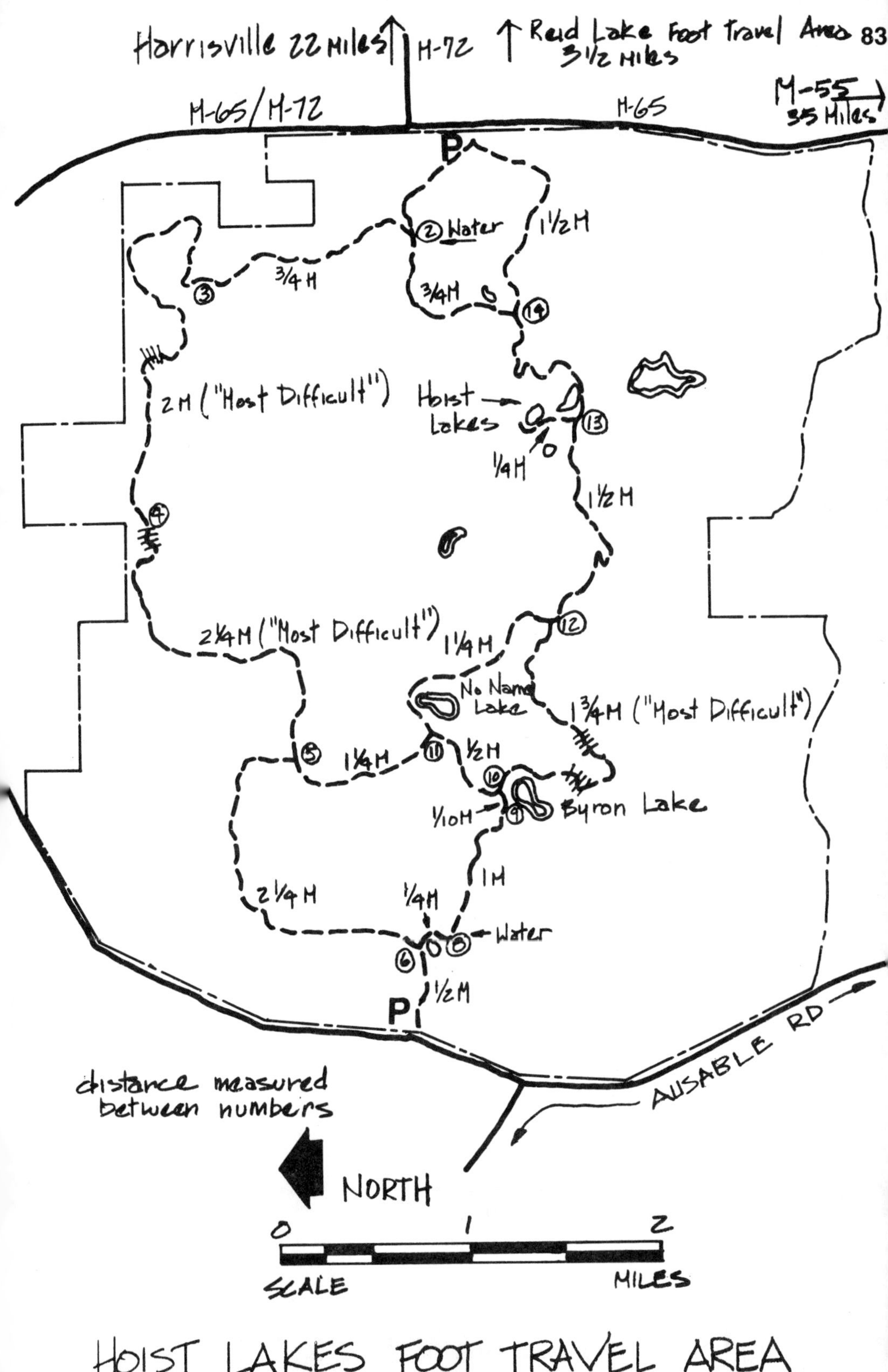

HOIST LAKES FOOT TRAVEL AREA

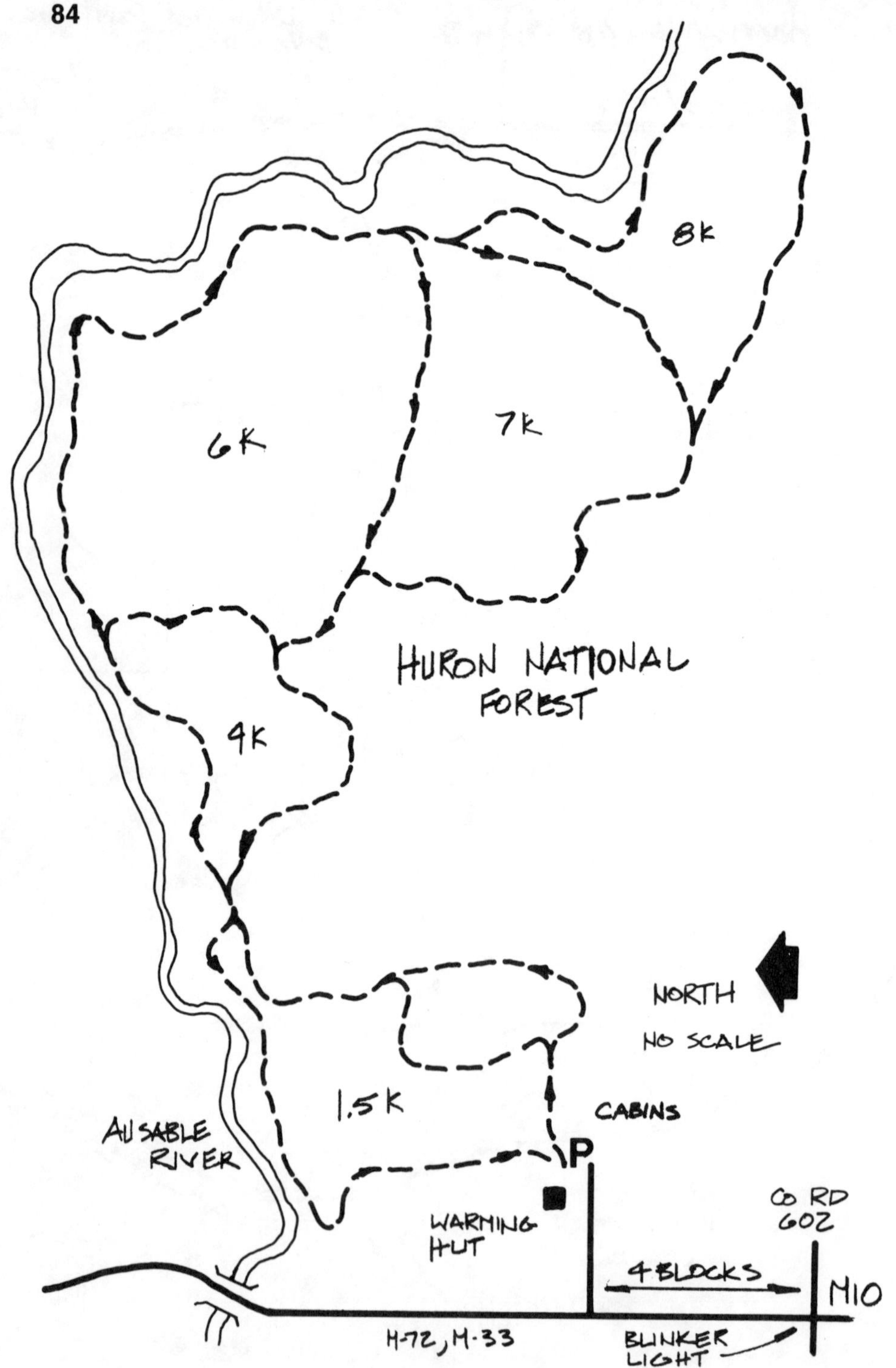

HINCHMAN ACRES RESORT

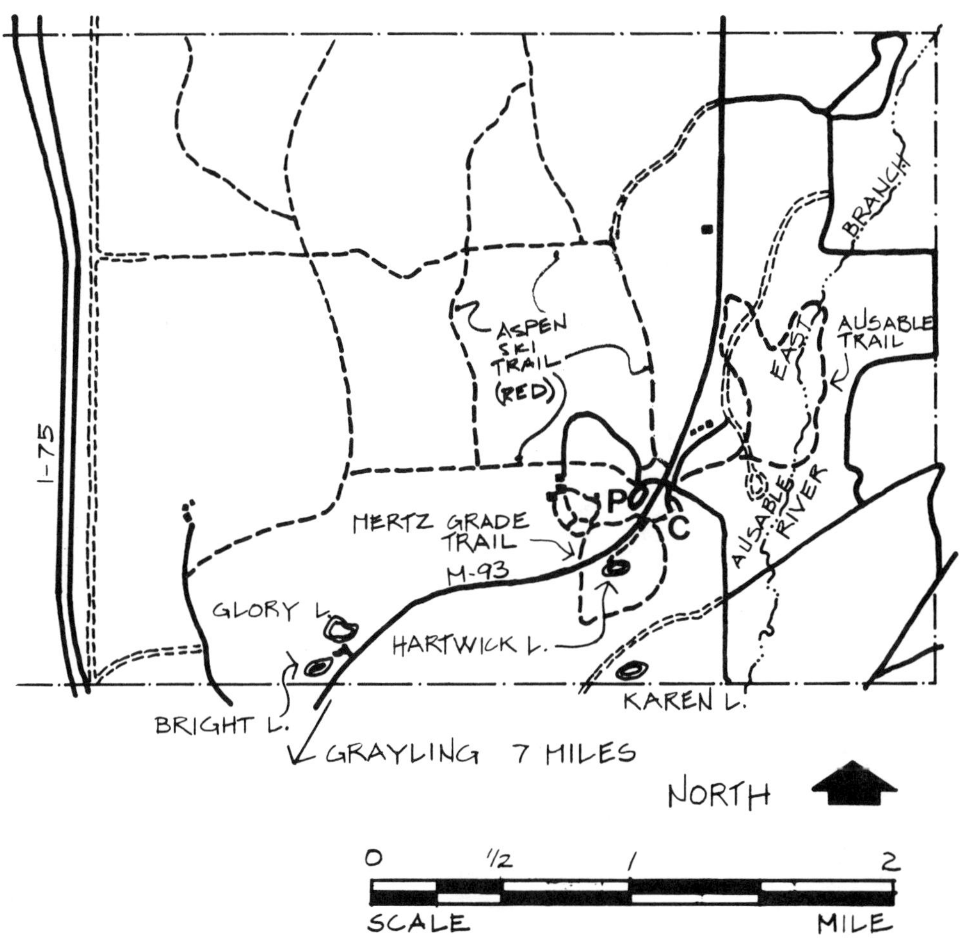

HARTWICK PINES STATE PARK

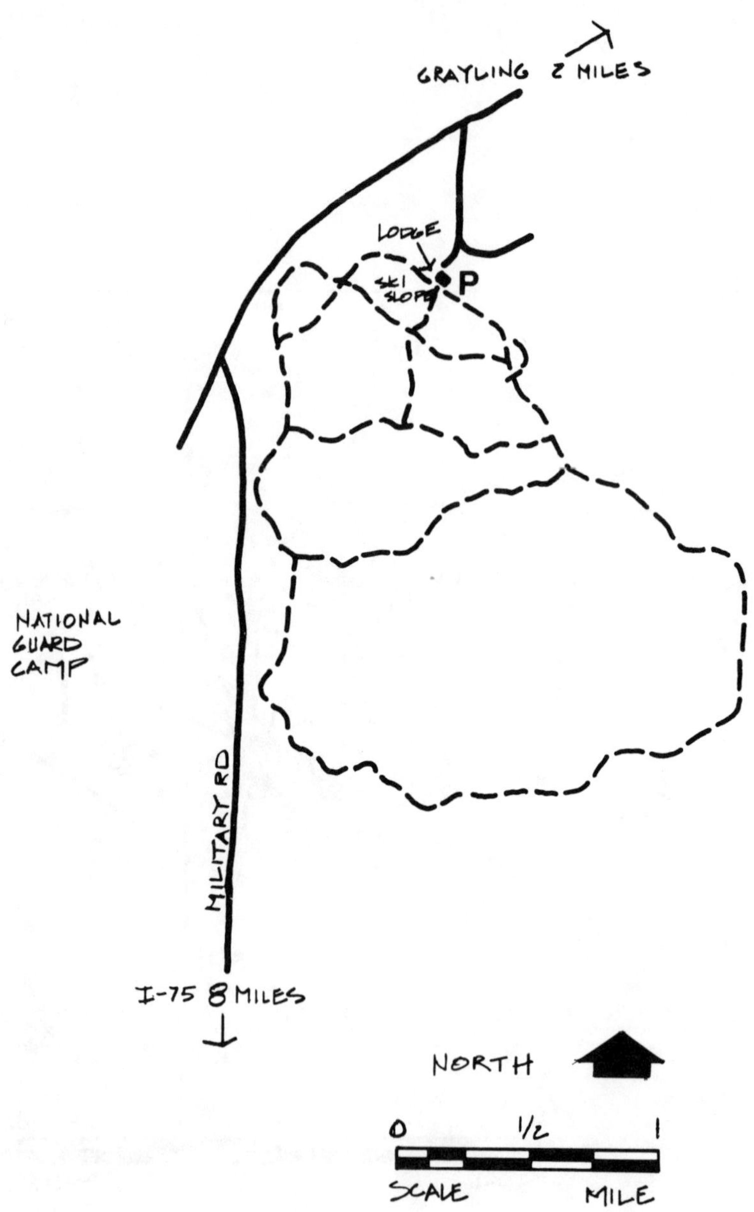

HANSON RECREATION AREA

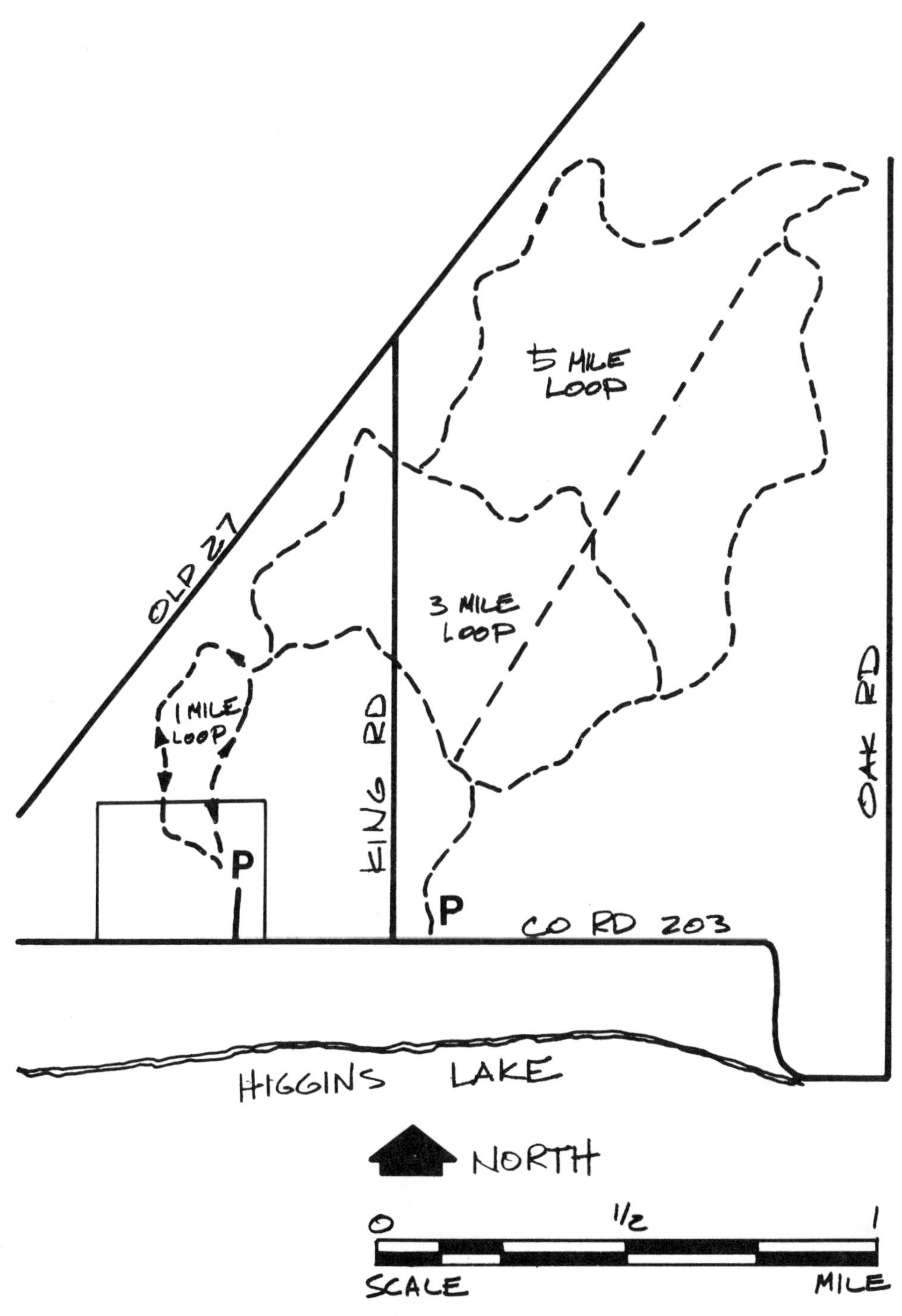

NORTH HIGGINS LAKE STATE PARK

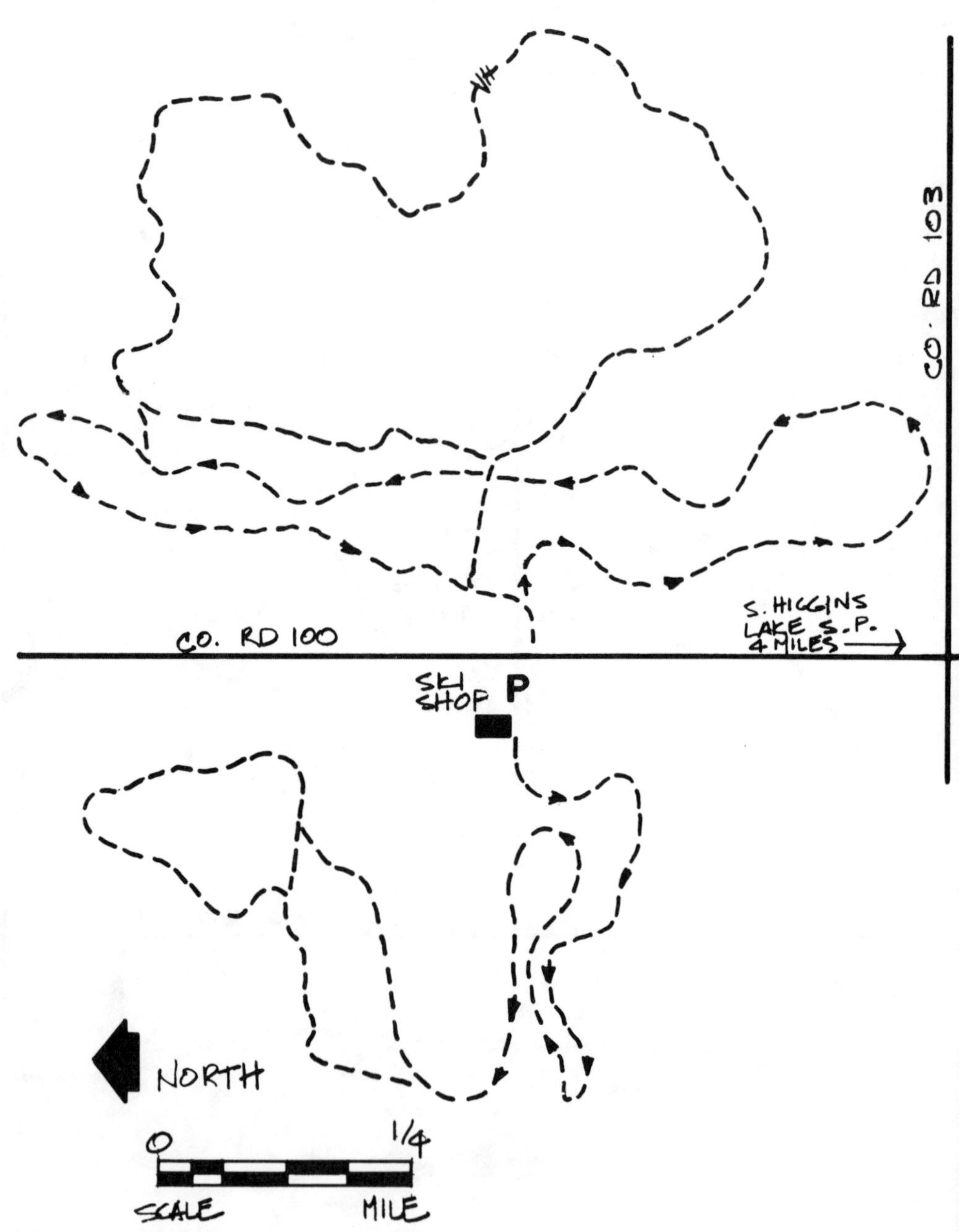

CROSS COUNTRY SKI HEADQUARTERS

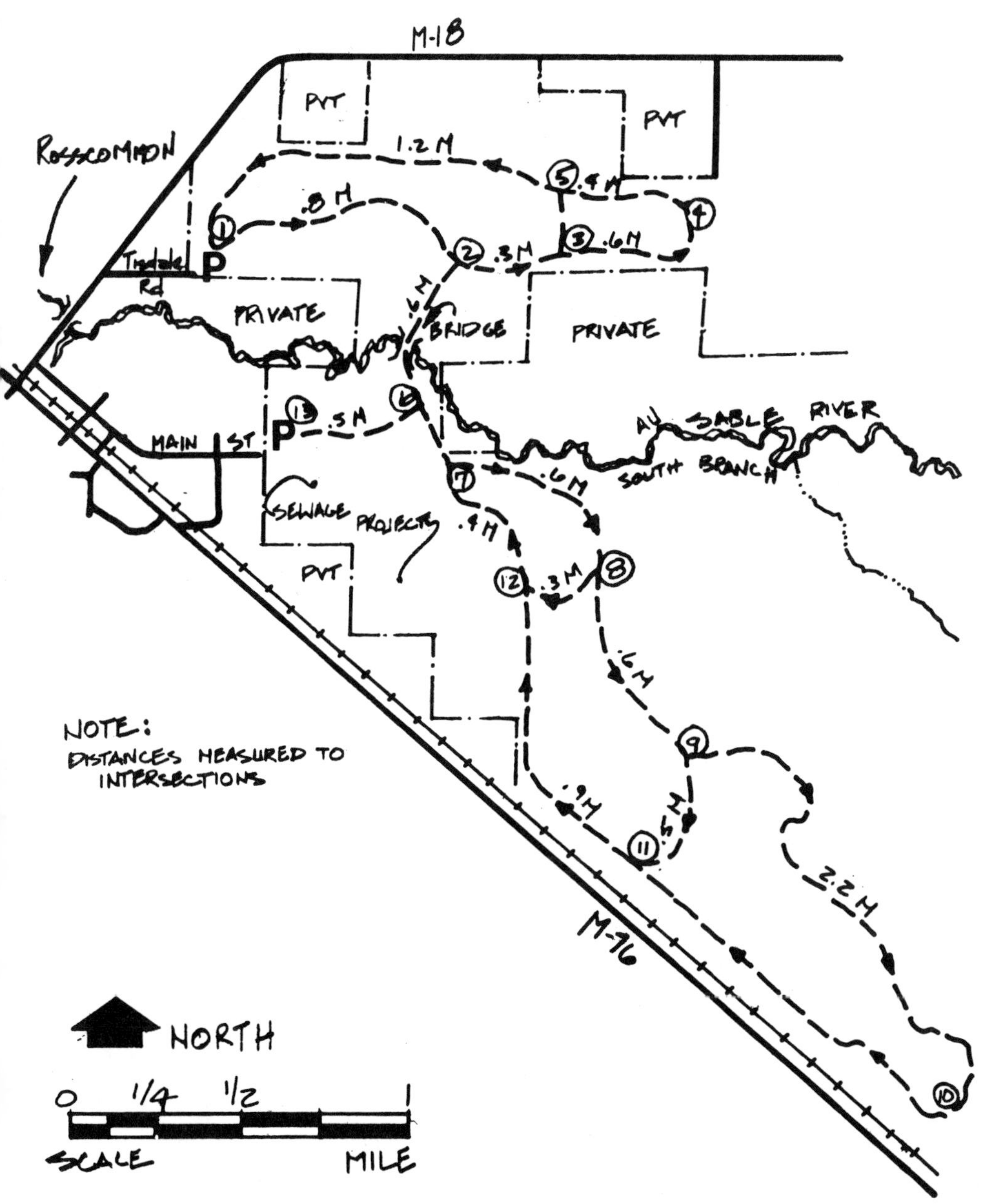

TISDALE TRIANGLE PATHWAY

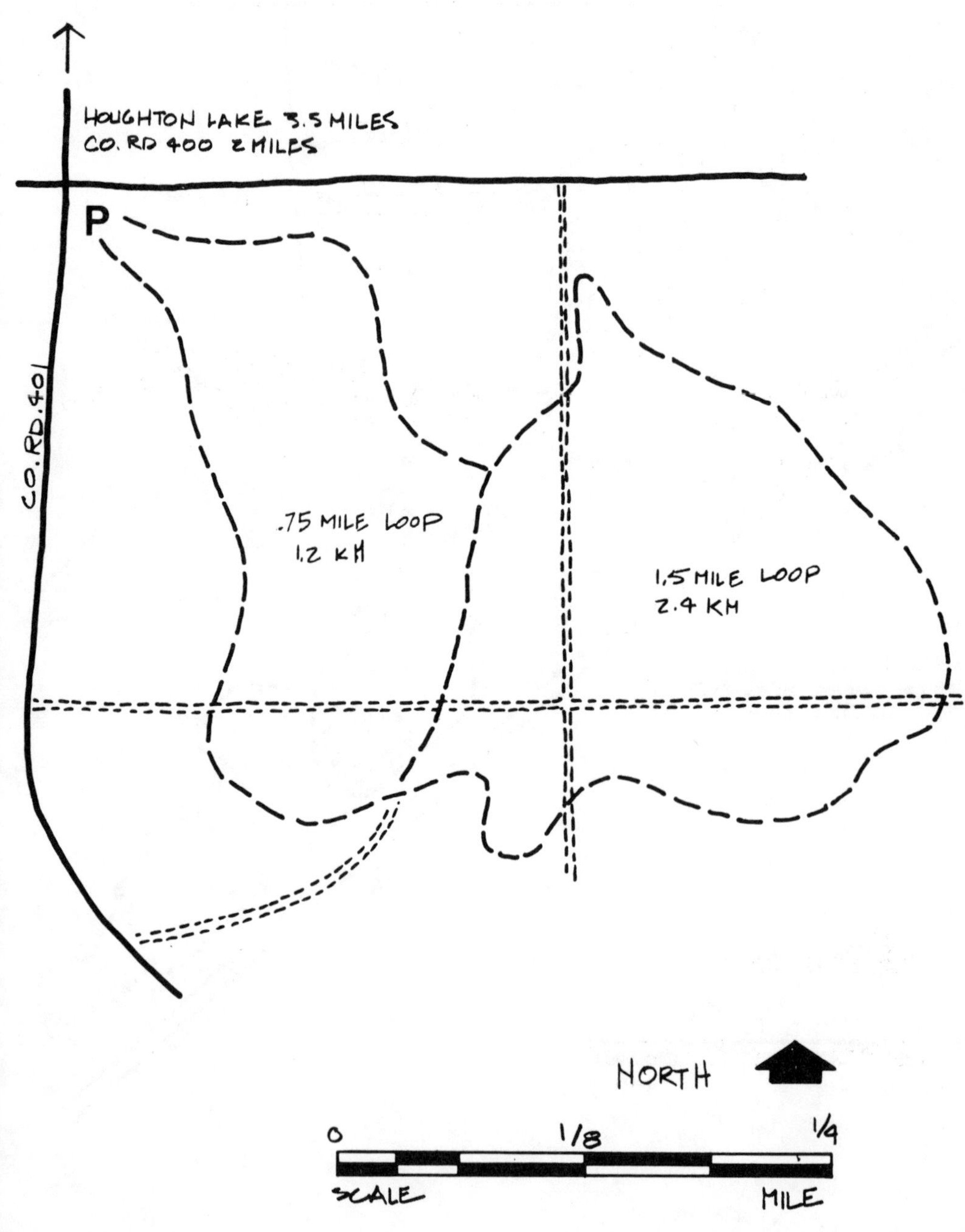

NOKOMIS PATHWAY

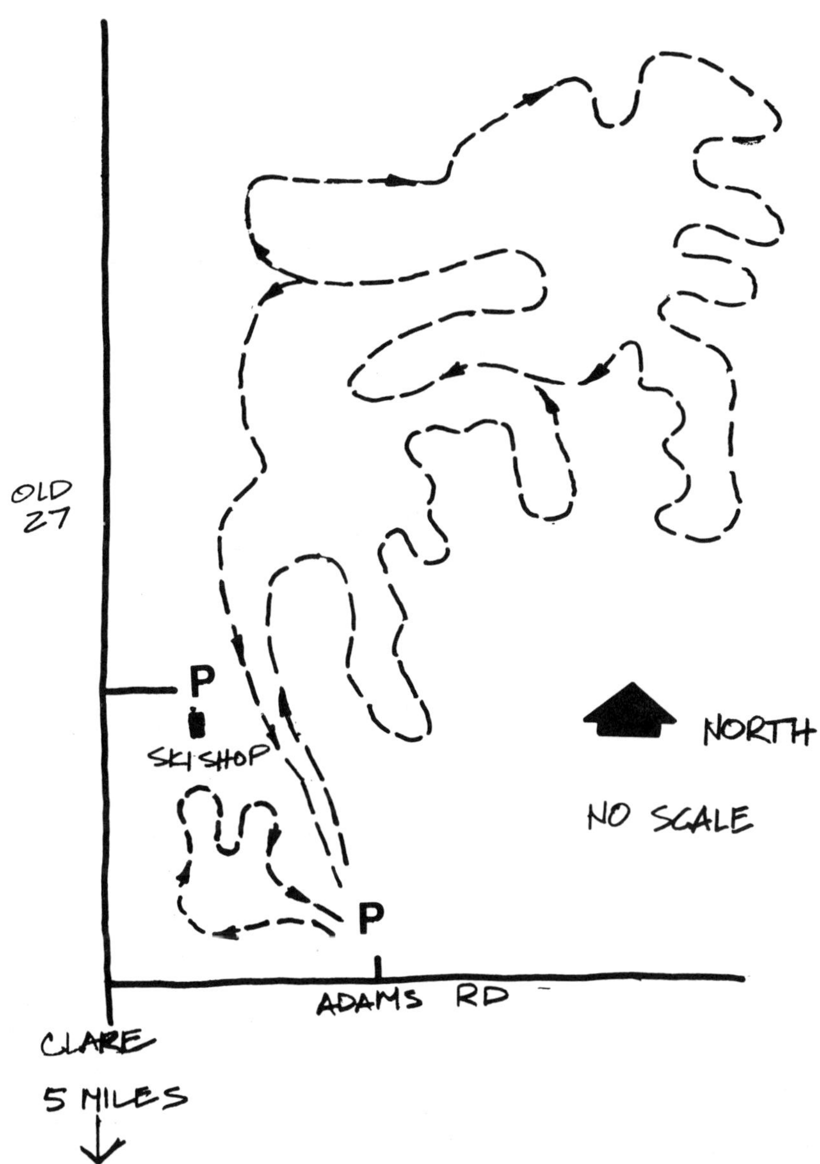

CHALET SKI TRAILS

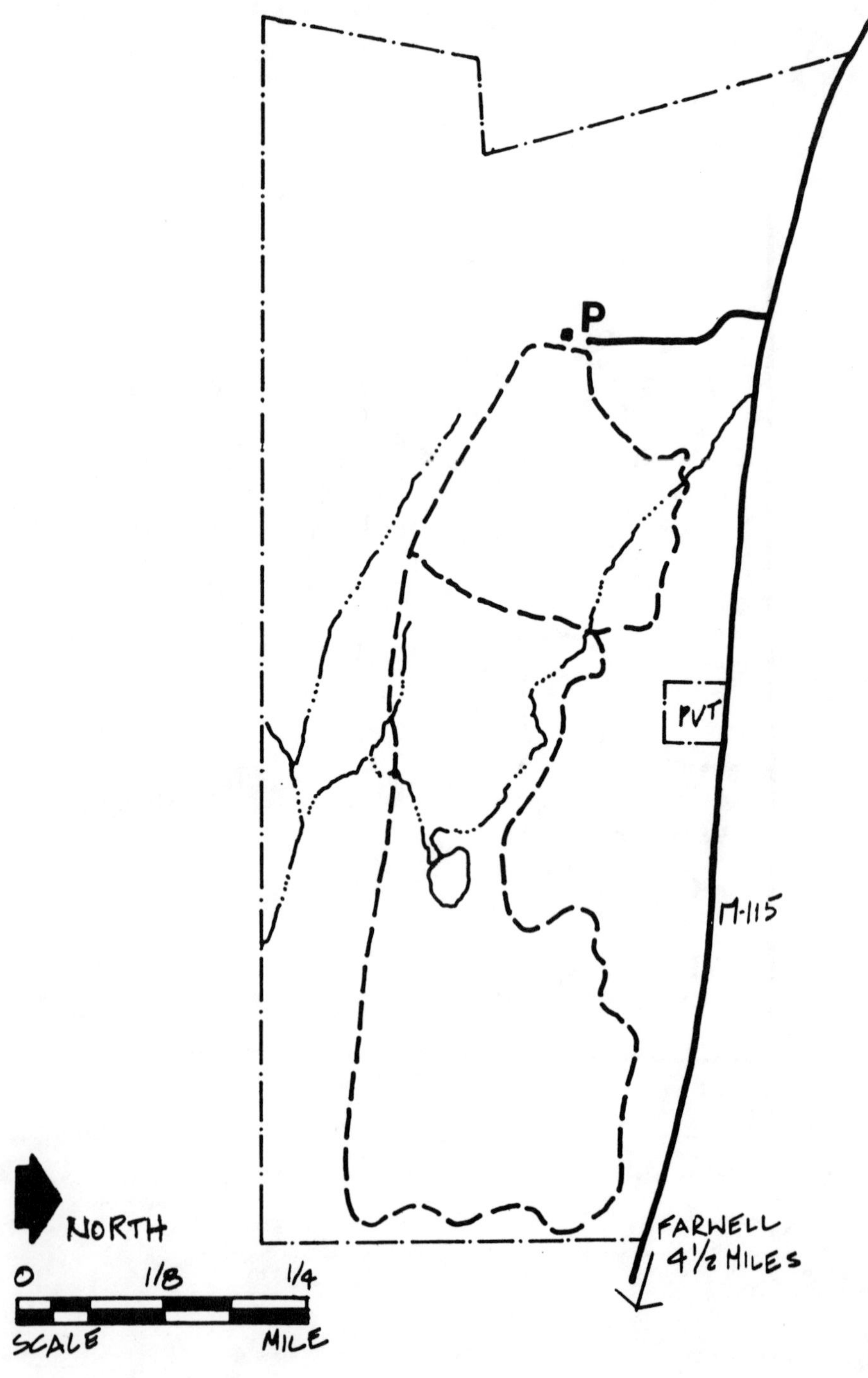

NEITHERCUT WOODLAND

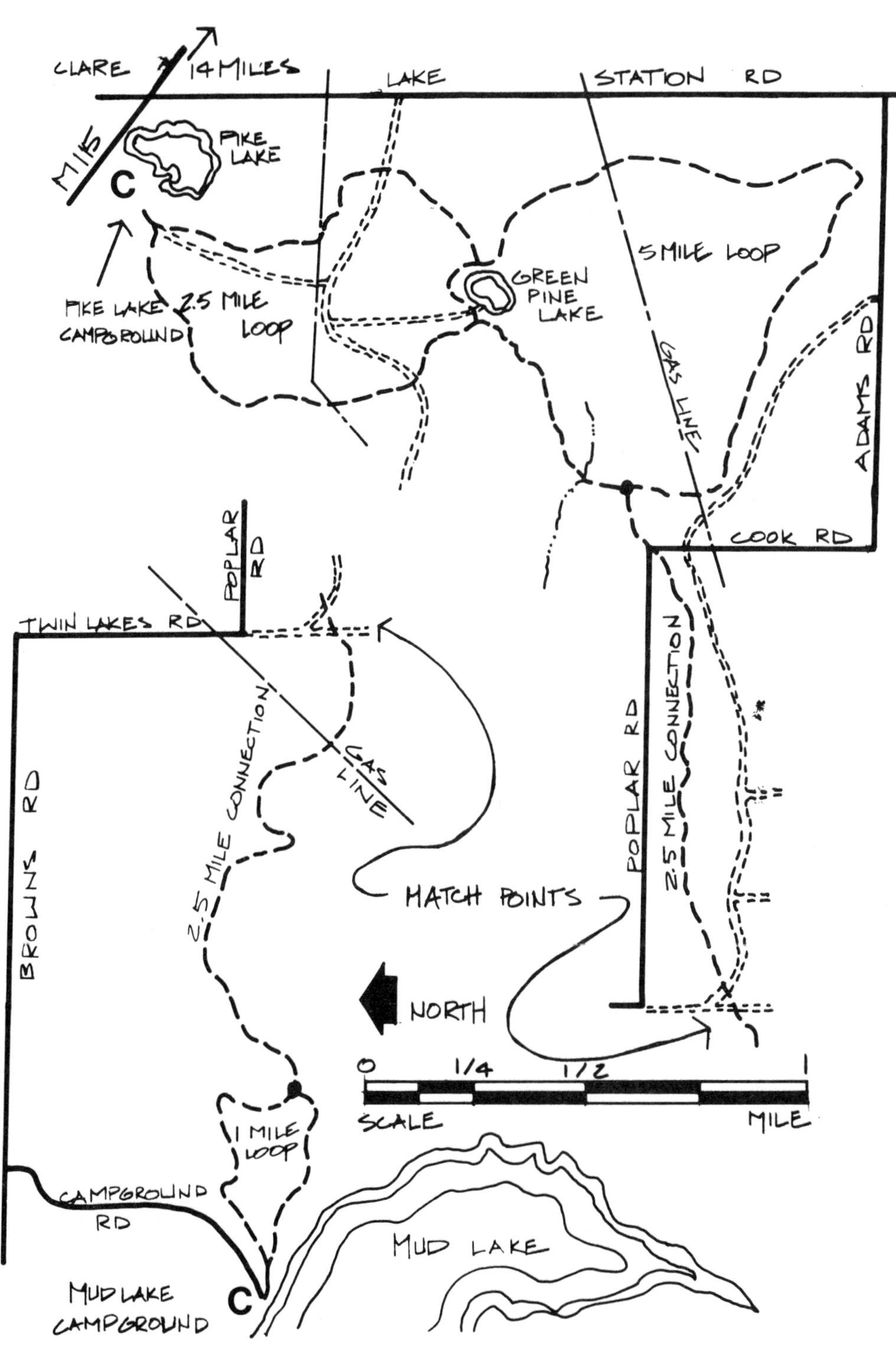

GREEN PINE LAKE PATHWAY

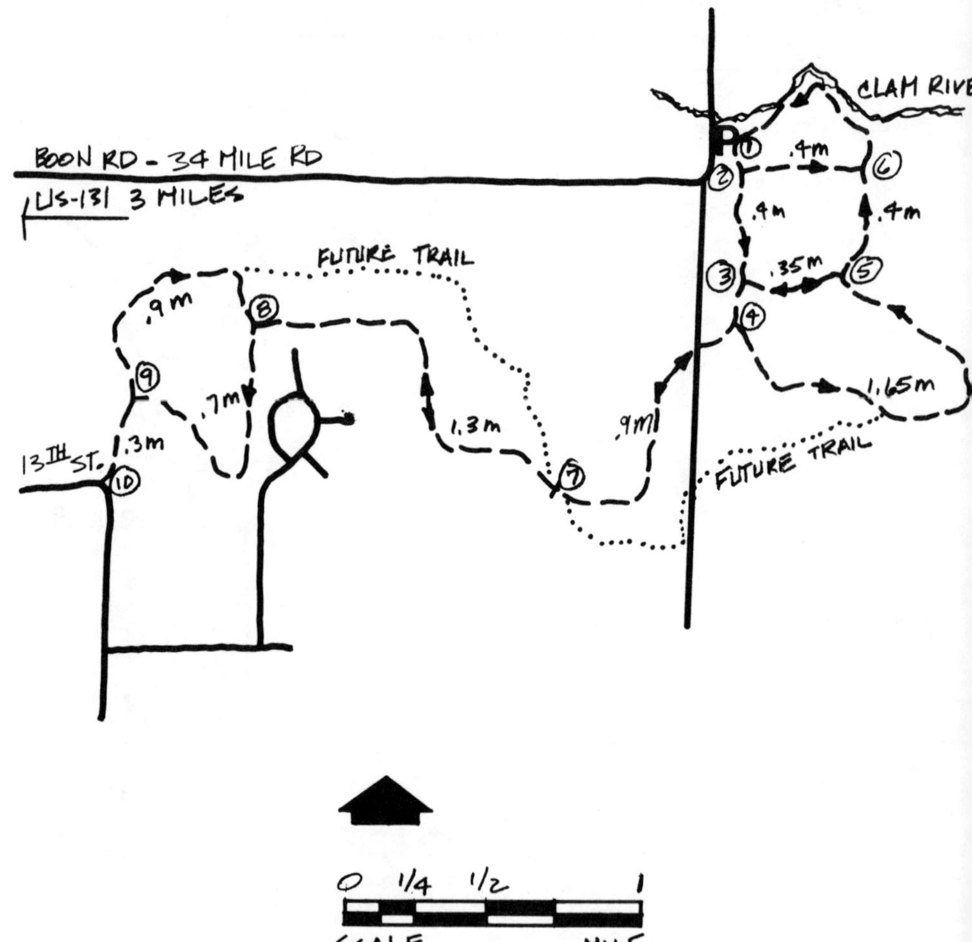

CADILLAC PATHWAY

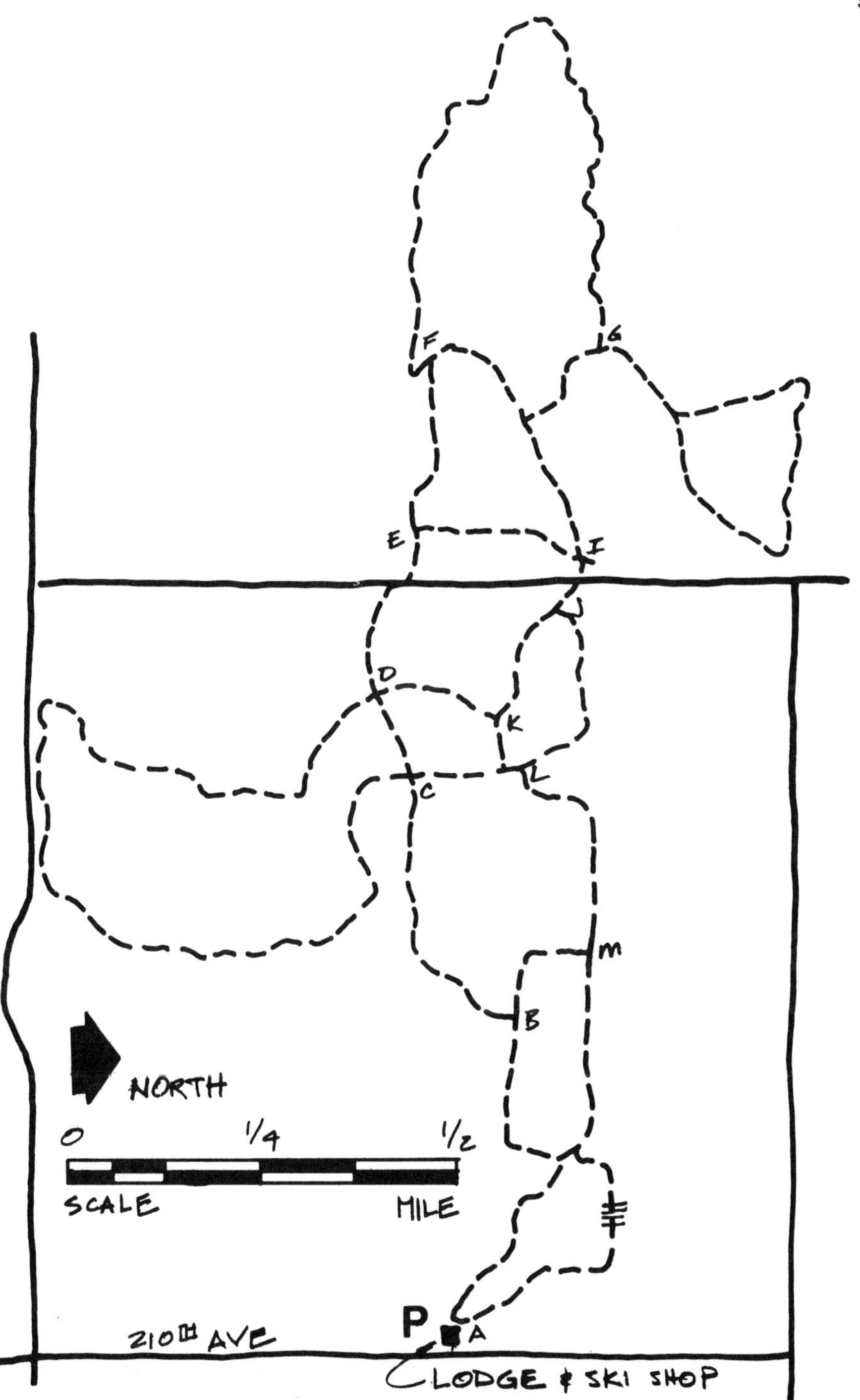

COOL CROSS COUNTRY SKI TOURING CENTER

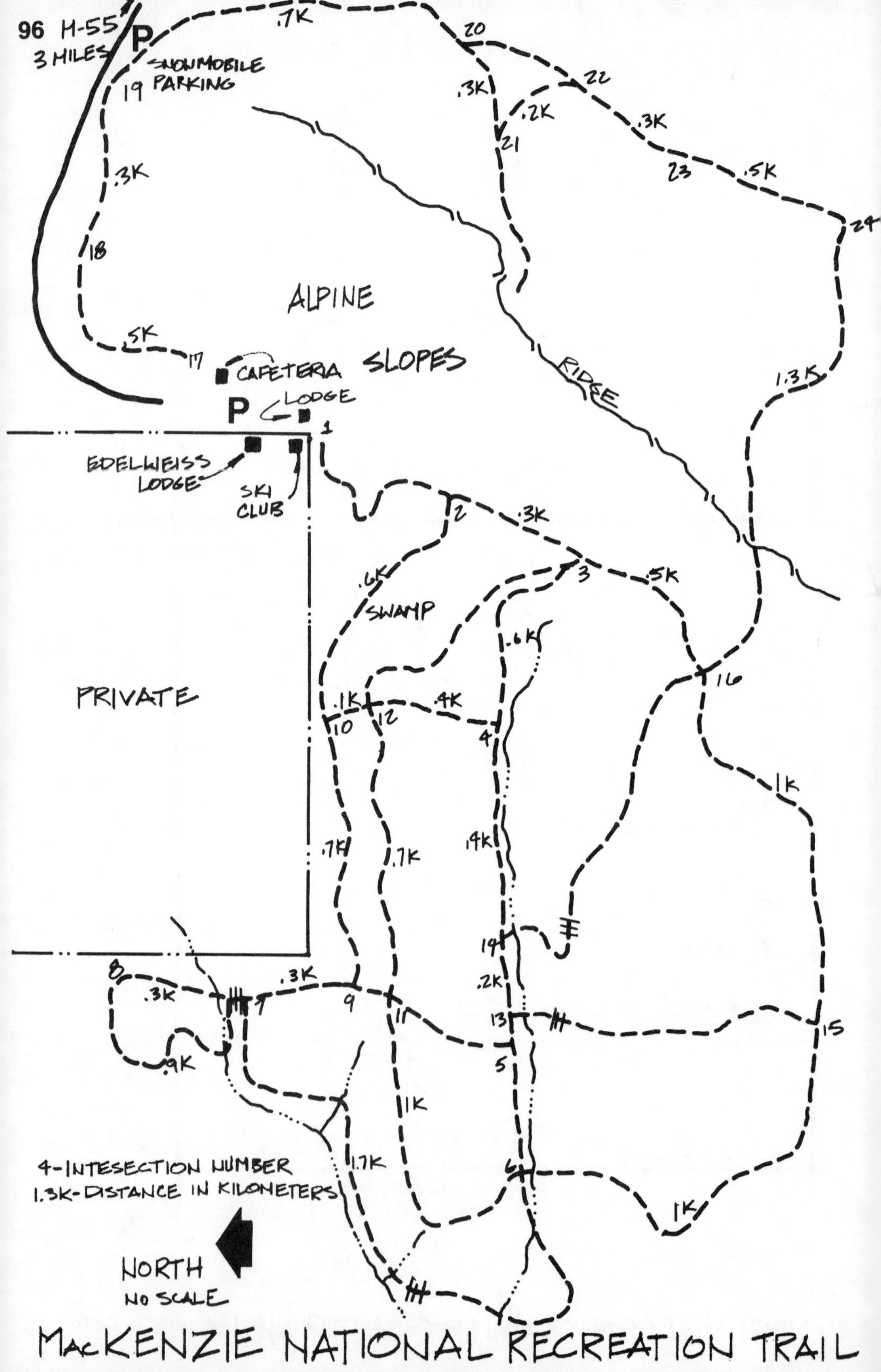

MacKENZIE NATIONAL RECREATION TRAIL

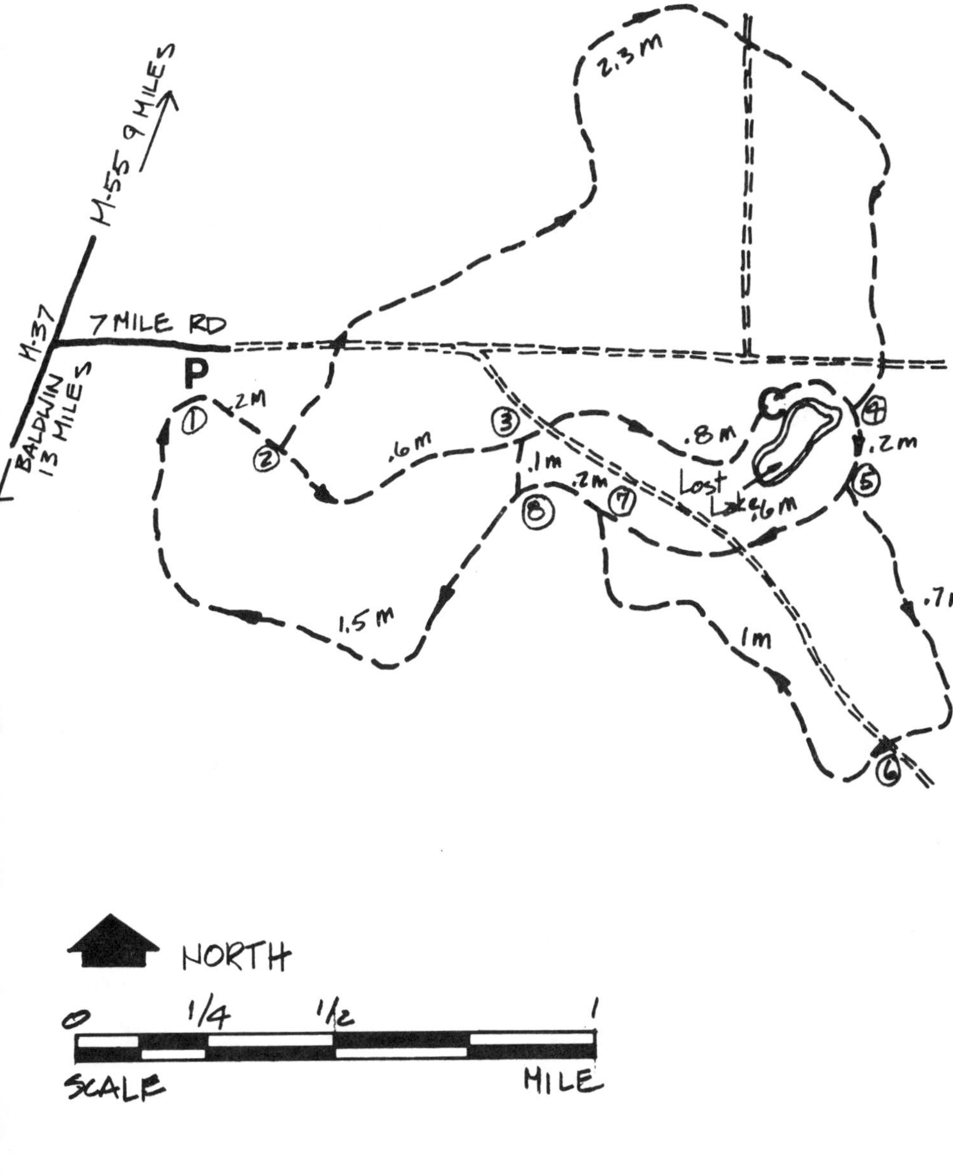

M-55 9 MILES
M-37
7 MILE RD
BALDWIN 13 MILES
P
1
.2M
2
.6m
3
.1m
.8m
Lost Lake
4
.2m
5
.6m
.7m
6
1m
7
.2m
8
1.5m
2.3m
NORTH
0
1/4
1/2
1
SCALE
MILE

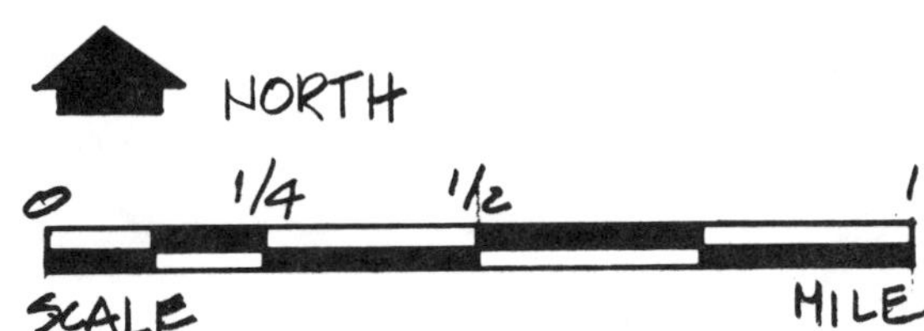

PINE VALLEYS PATHWAY

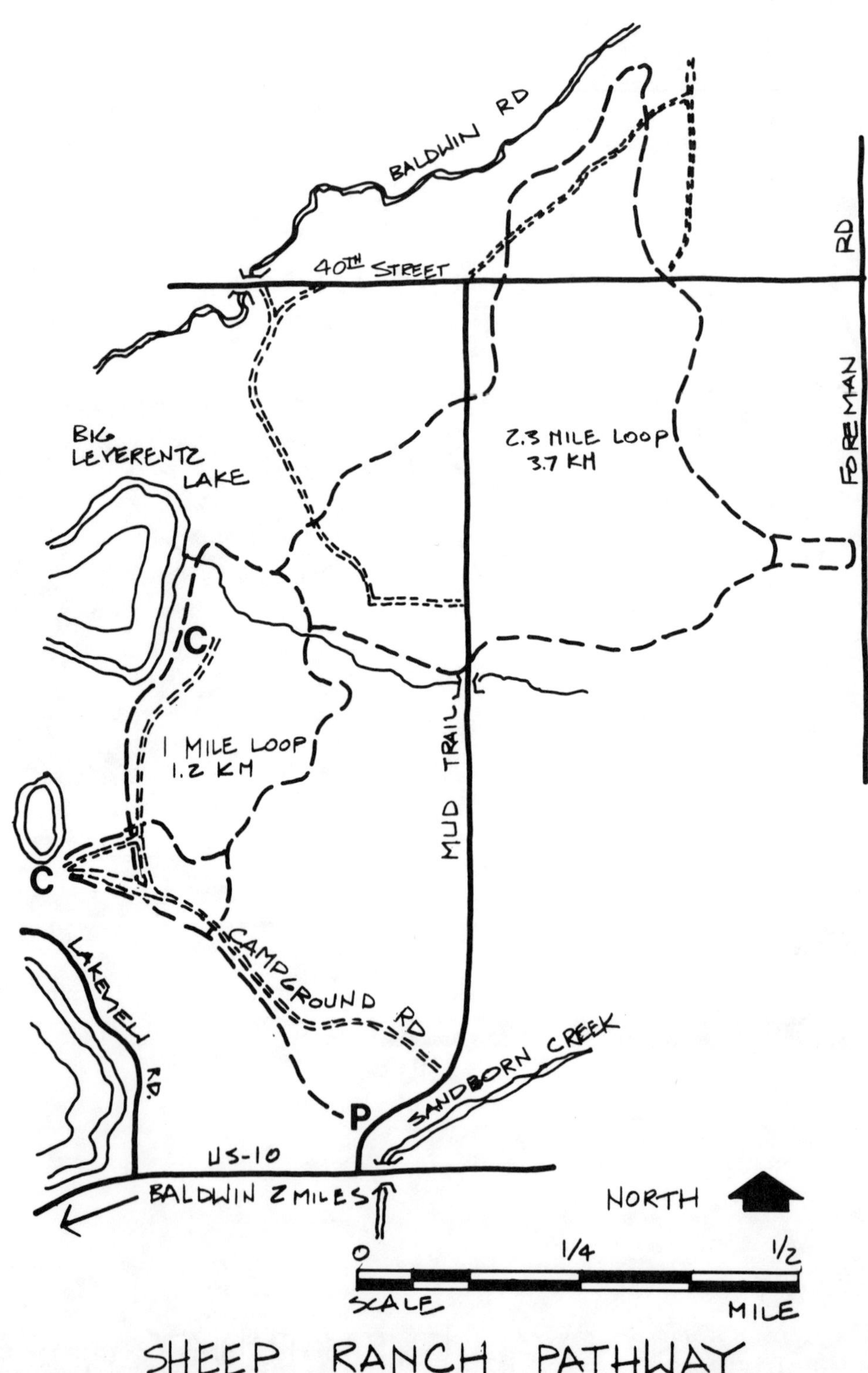

SHEEP RANCH PATHWAY

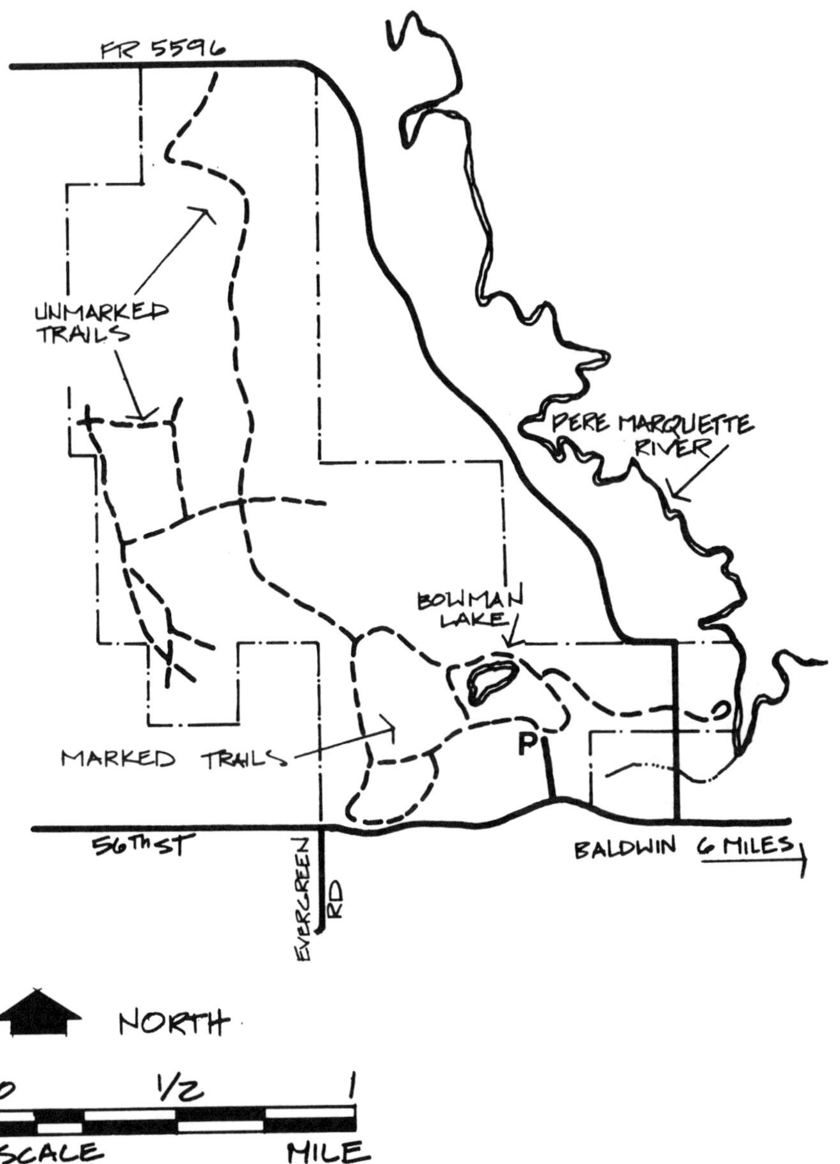

BOWMAN LAKE FOOT TRAVEL AREA

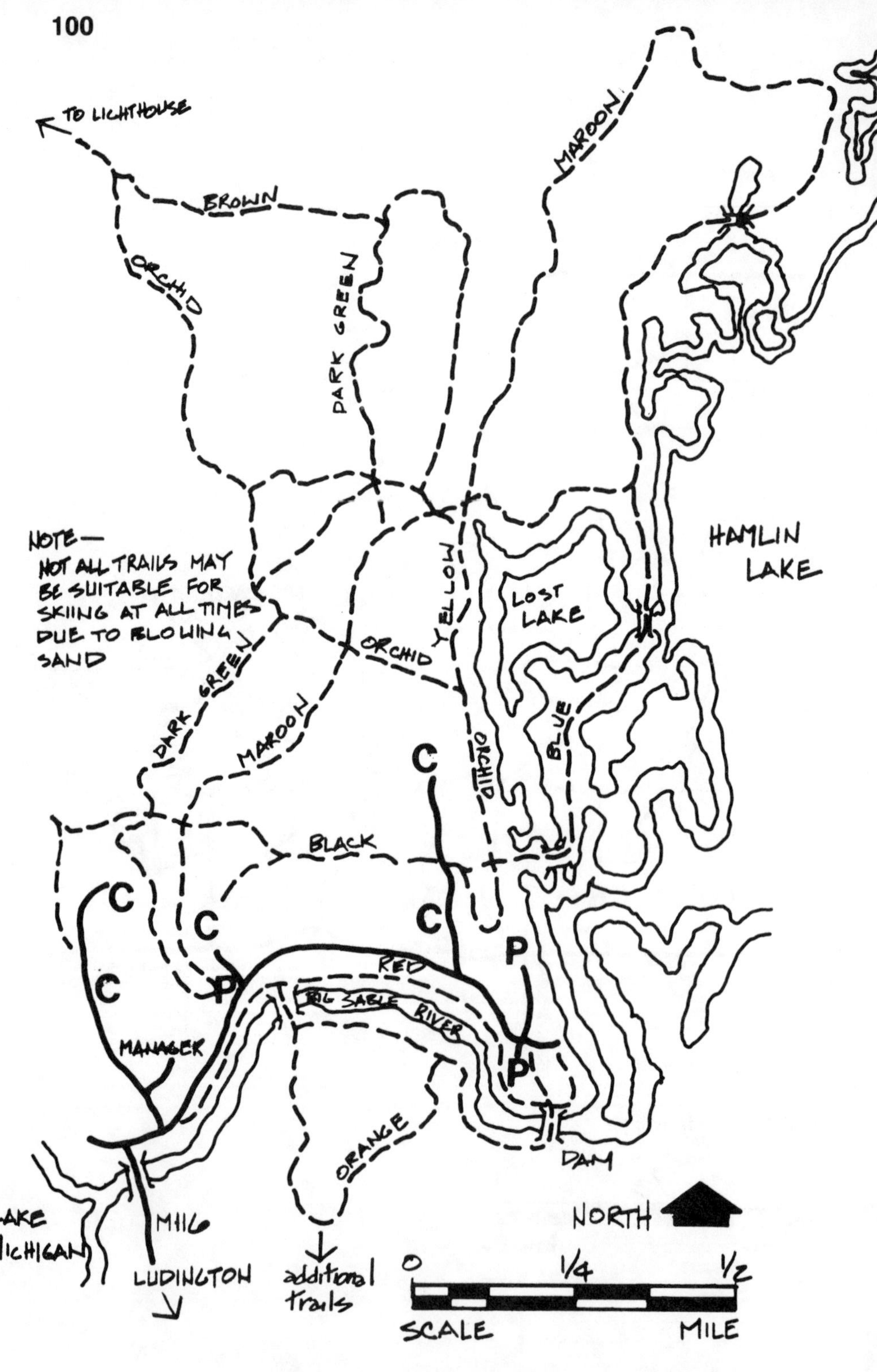

LUDINGTON STATE PARK

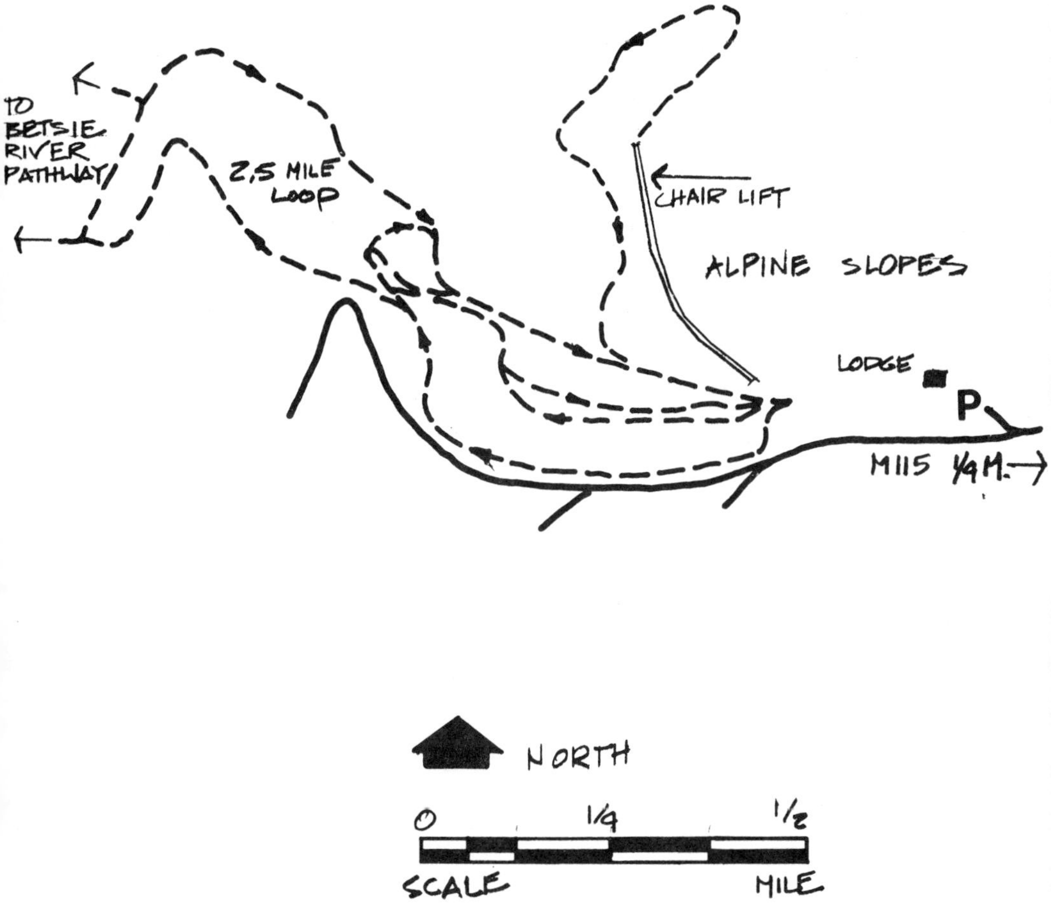

TO BETSIE RIVER PATHWAY

2.5 MILE LOOP

CHAIR LIFT

ALPINE SLOPES

LODGE

P

M115 1/4 M.

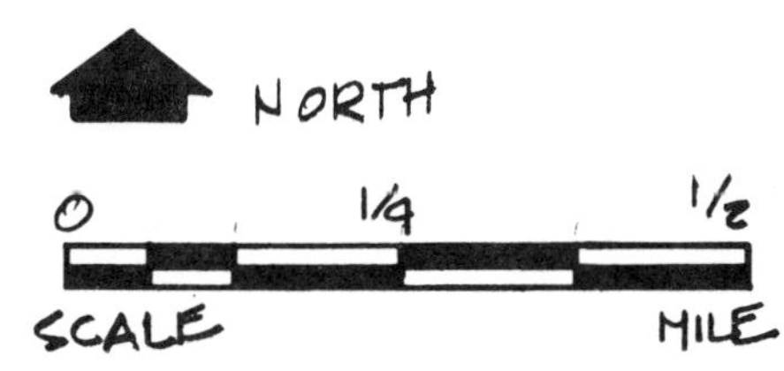

CRYSTAL MOUNTAIN

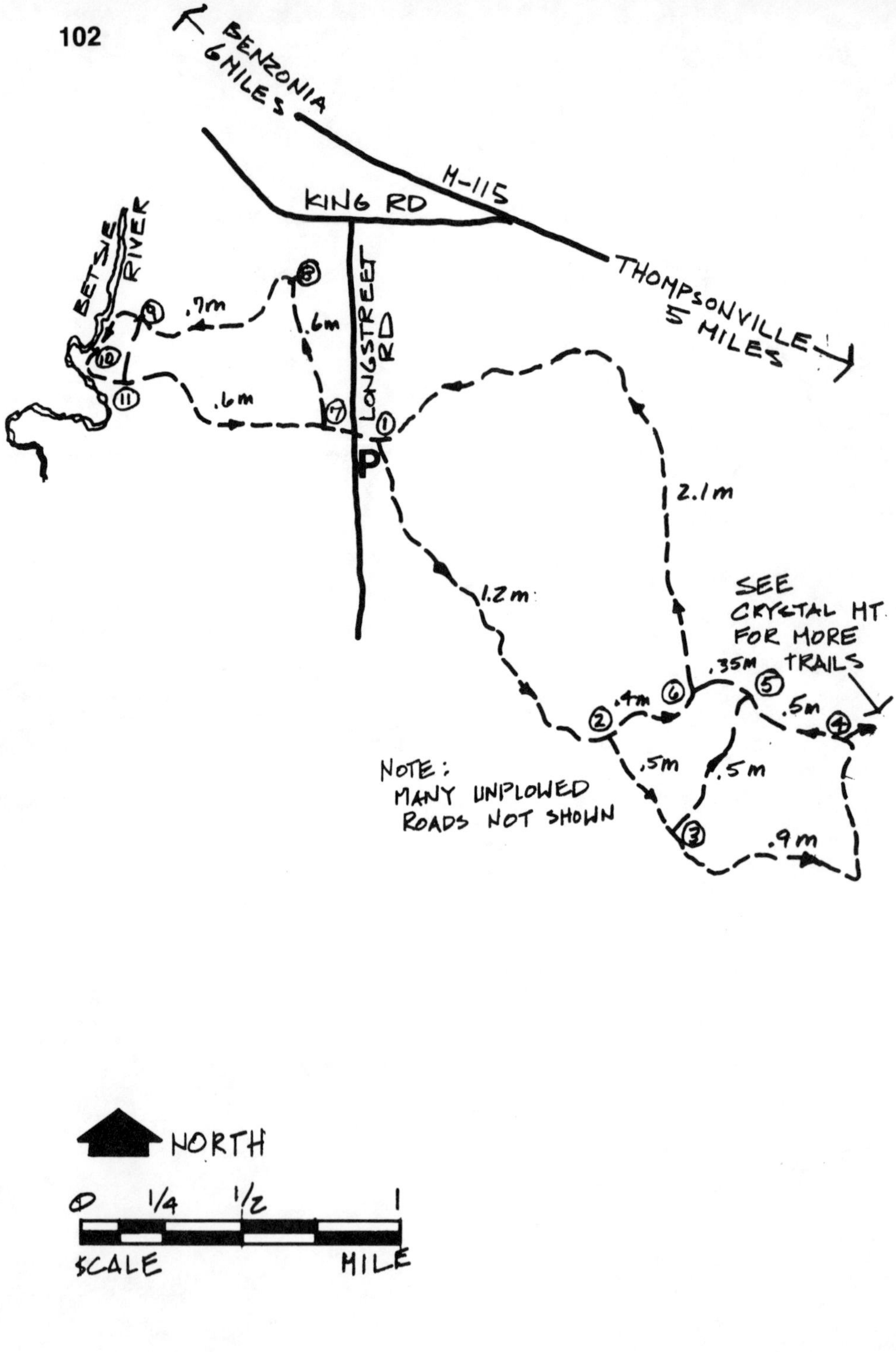

BENZONIA 6 MILES
M-115
KING RD
THOMPSONVILLE 5 MILES
BETSIE RIVER
LONGSTREET RD
.7m
.6m
.6m
P
1.2m
2.1m
.4m
.35m
.5m
.5m
.5m
.9m
SEE CRYSTAL MT FOR MORE TRAILS
NOTE: MANY UNPLOWED ROADS NOT SHOWN
NORTH
0 1/4 1/2 1
SCALE MILE

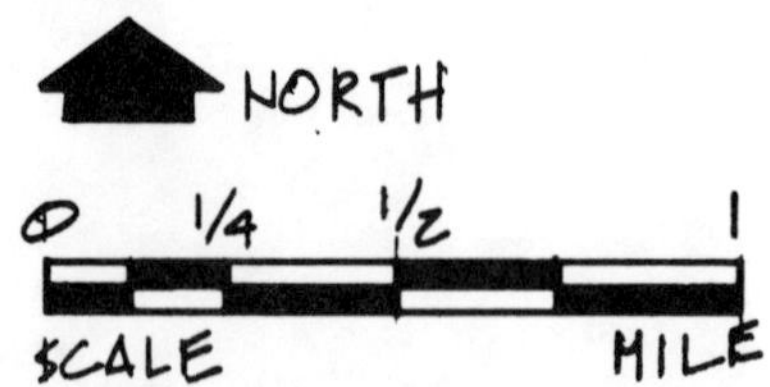

BETSIE RIVER PATHWAY

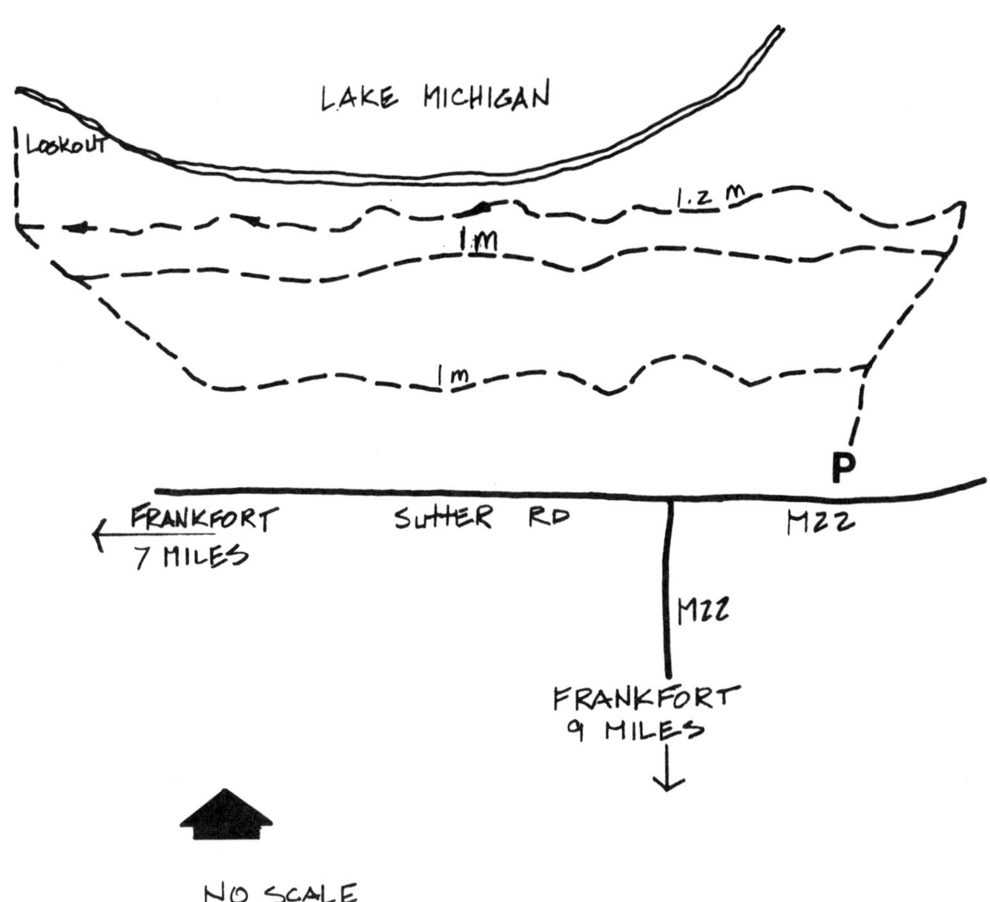

OLD INDIAN
CROSS COUNTRY SKI TRAIL

EMPIRE 14 MILES
ESCH ROAD
P
Otter Creek
LAKE MICHIGAN
Lookout
Lookout
LOOKOUT
C
OTTER LAKE
BASS LAKE
DEER LAKE
M-22
PLATTE RIVER
C P
M22
2.0 M
1.5 M
1.1 M
.5 M
1 M
.8 M
NORTH
0 1/2 1
SCALE MILE

PLATTE PLAINS CROSS COUNTRY SKI TRAIL

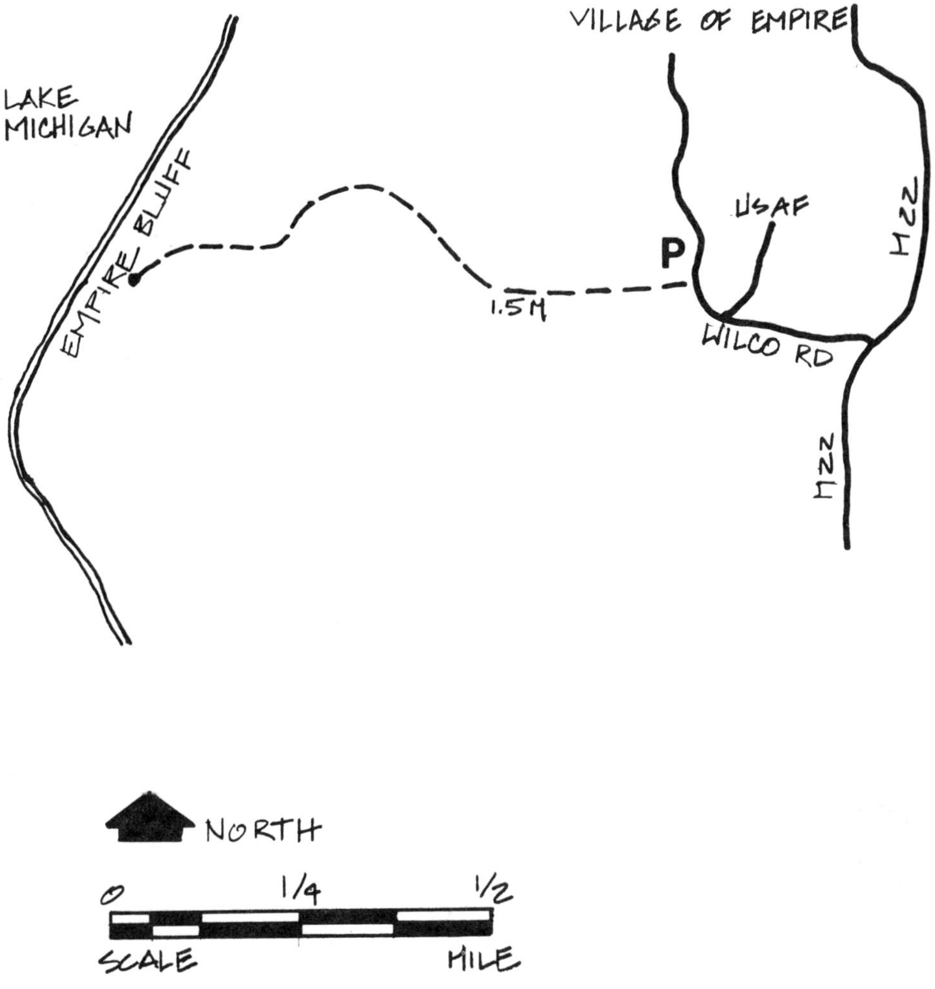

VILLAGE OF EMPIRE
LAKE MICHIGAN
EMPIRE BLUFF
USAF
P
M22
1.5M
WILCO RD
M22
NORTH
0
1/4
1/2
SCALE
MILE

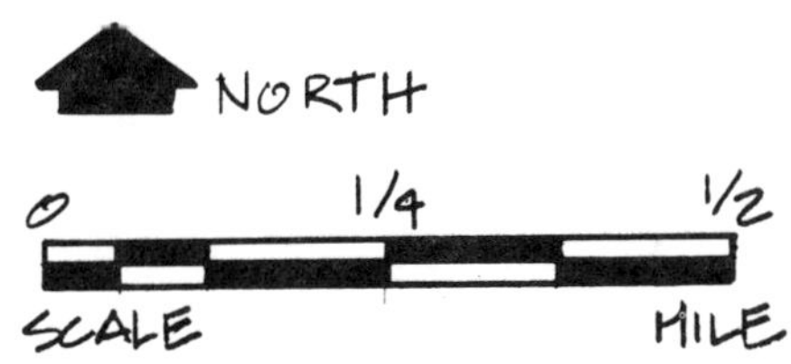

EMPIRE BLUFF
CROSS COUNTRY SKI TRAIL

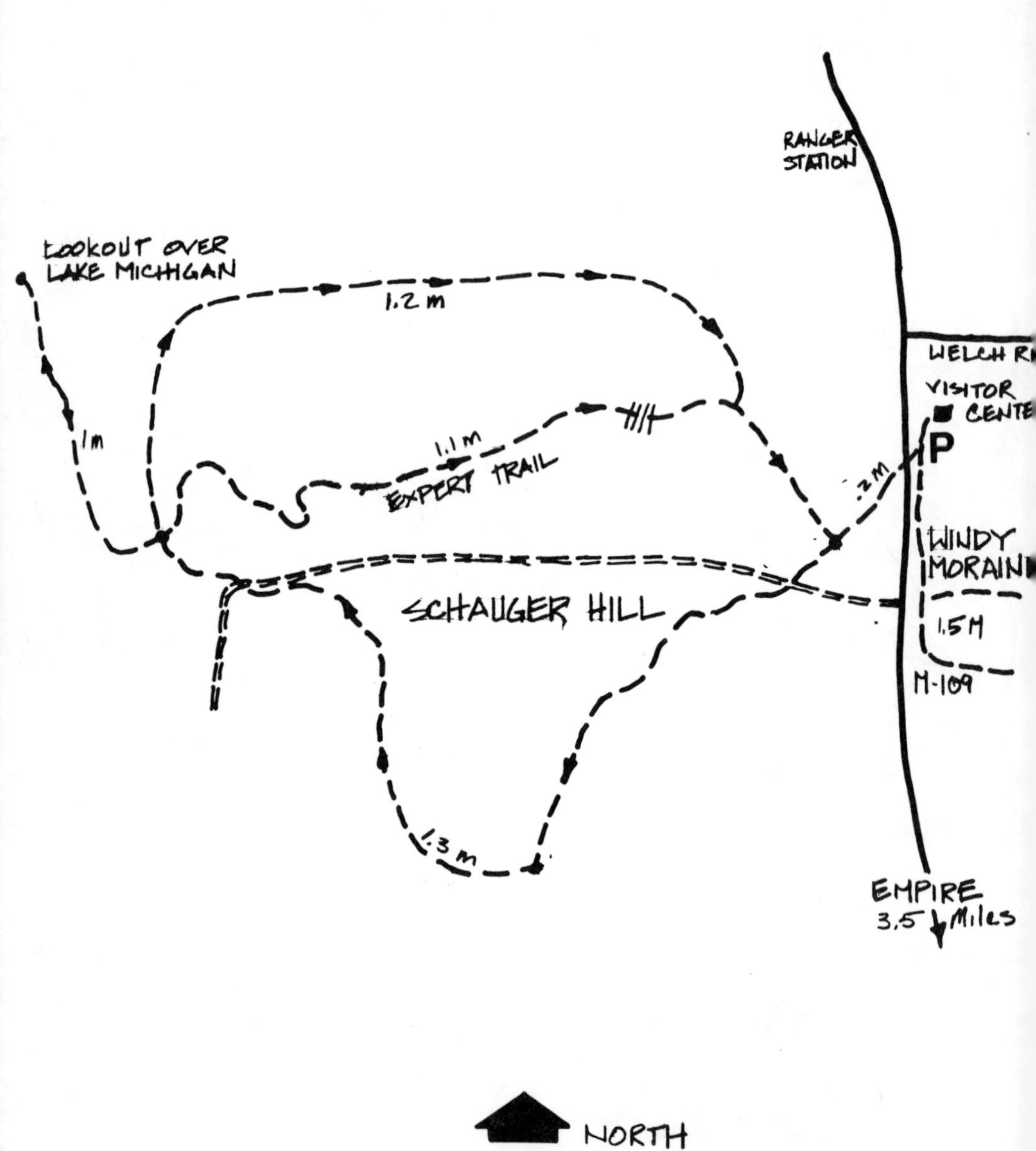

SCHAUGER HILL & WINDY MORAINE
CROSS COUNTRY SKI TRAILS

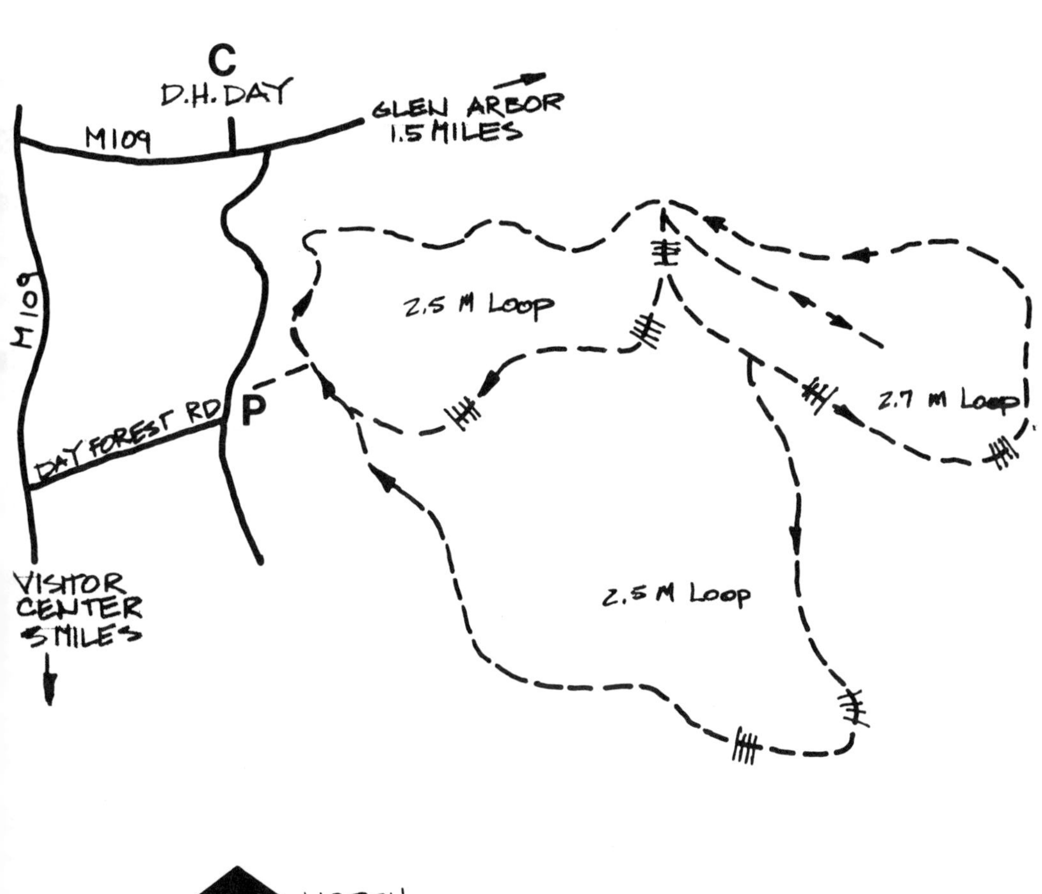

NORTH

NO SCALE

ALLIGATOR HILL
CROSS COUNTRY SKI TRAIL

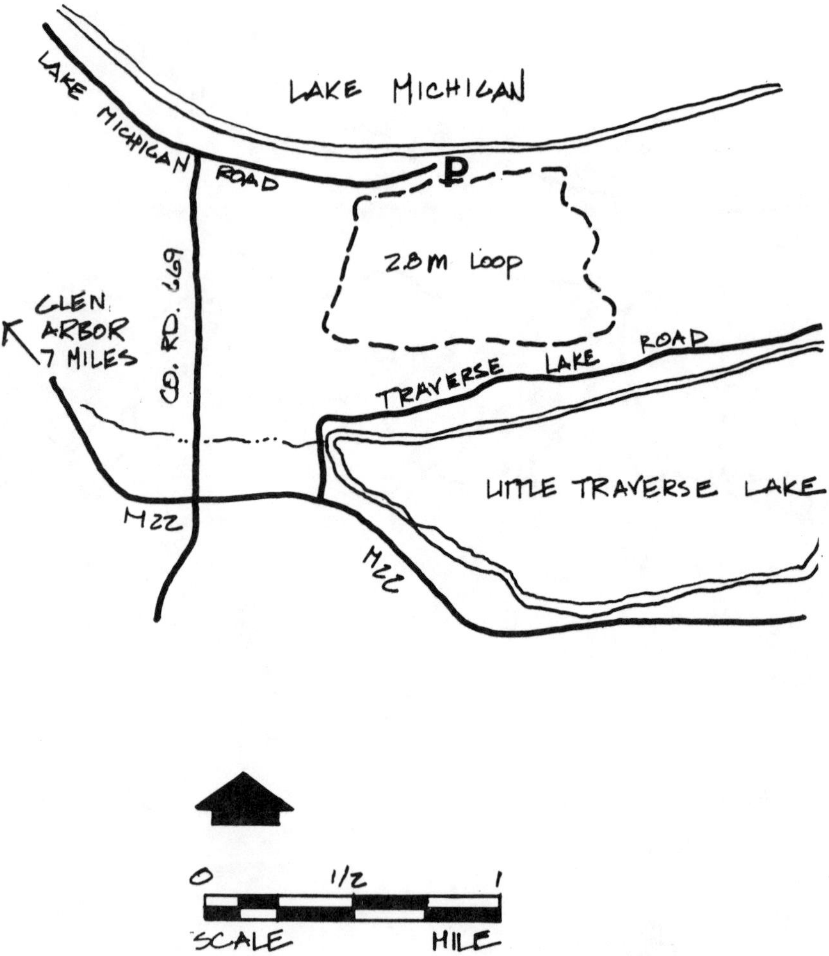

LAKE MICHIGAN
LAKE MICHIGAN ROAD
P
2.8M LOOP
CO. RD. 669
GLEN ARBOR 7 MILES
TRAVERSE LAKE ROAD
LITTLE TRAVERSE LAKE
M22
M22

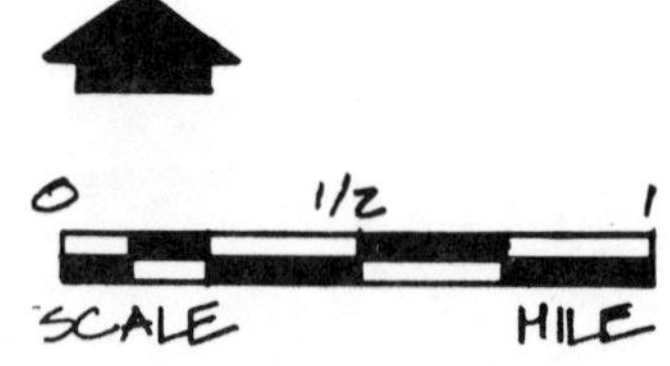

GOOD HARBOR BAY
CROSS COUNTRY SKI TRAIL

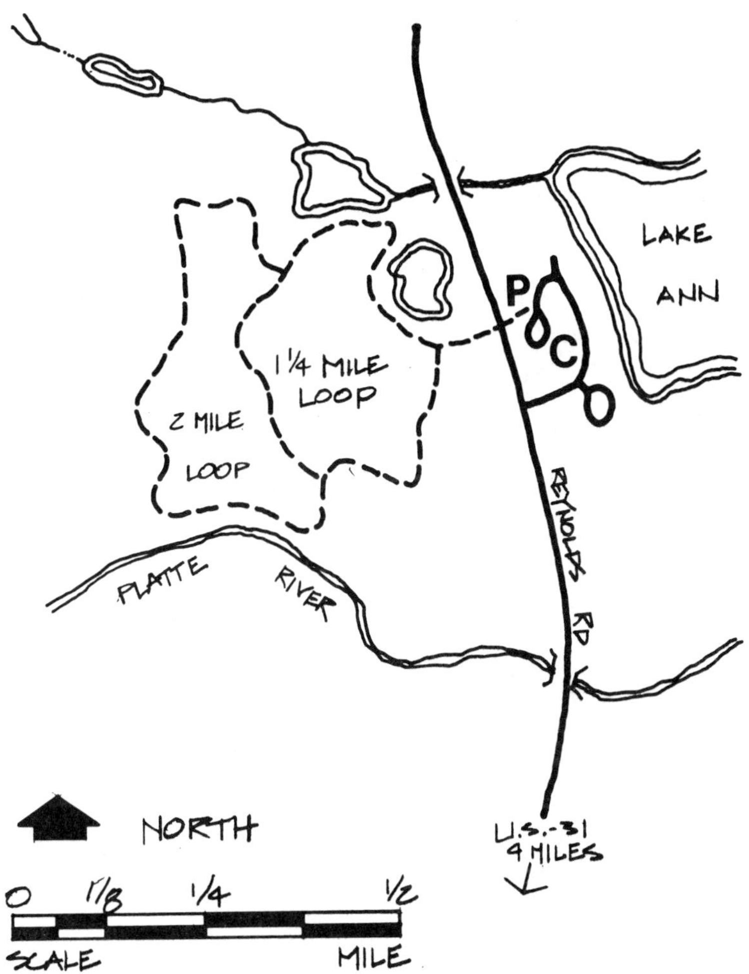

CHAIN O' LAKES PATHWAY

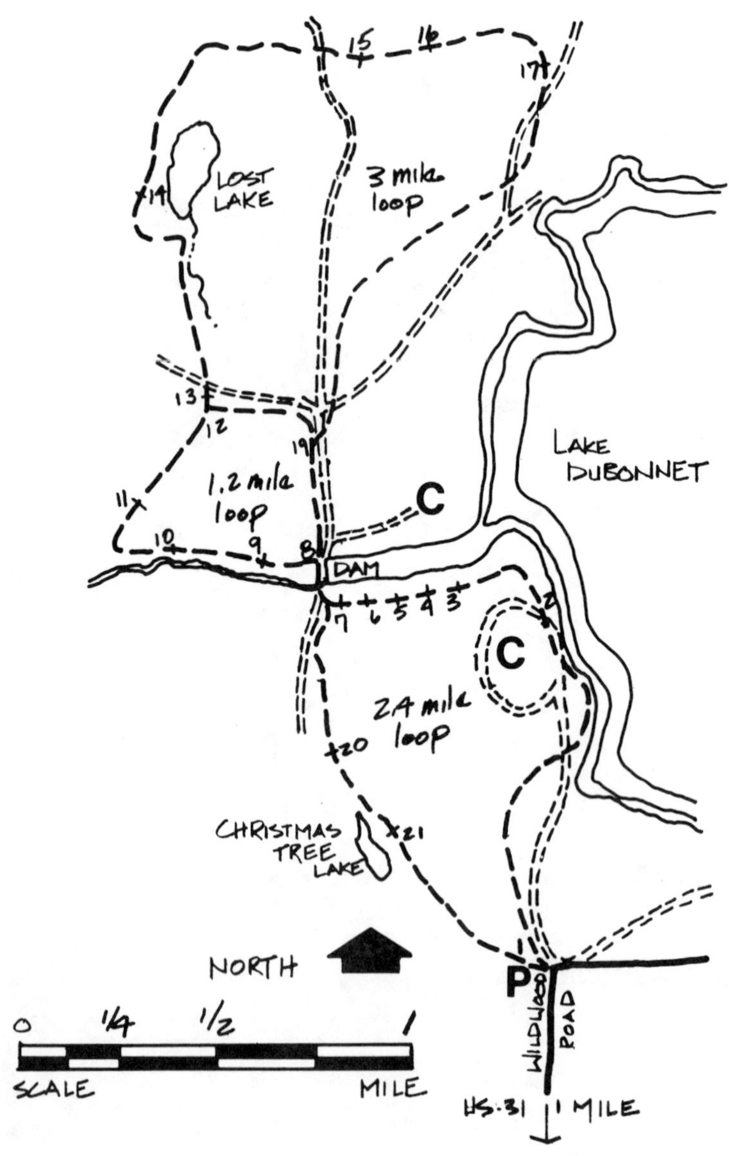

LOST LAKE NATURE PATHWAY

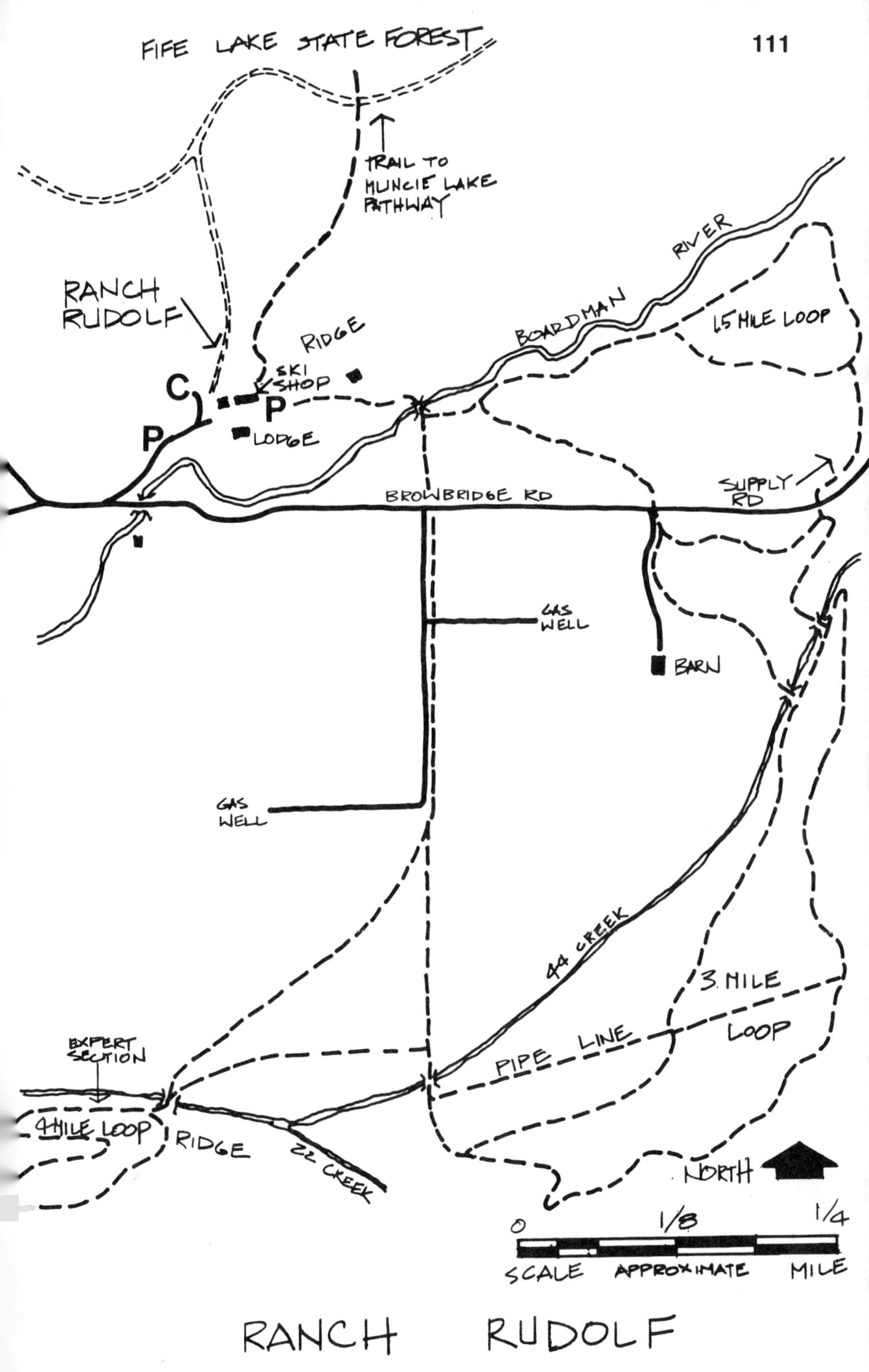

RANCH RUDOLF

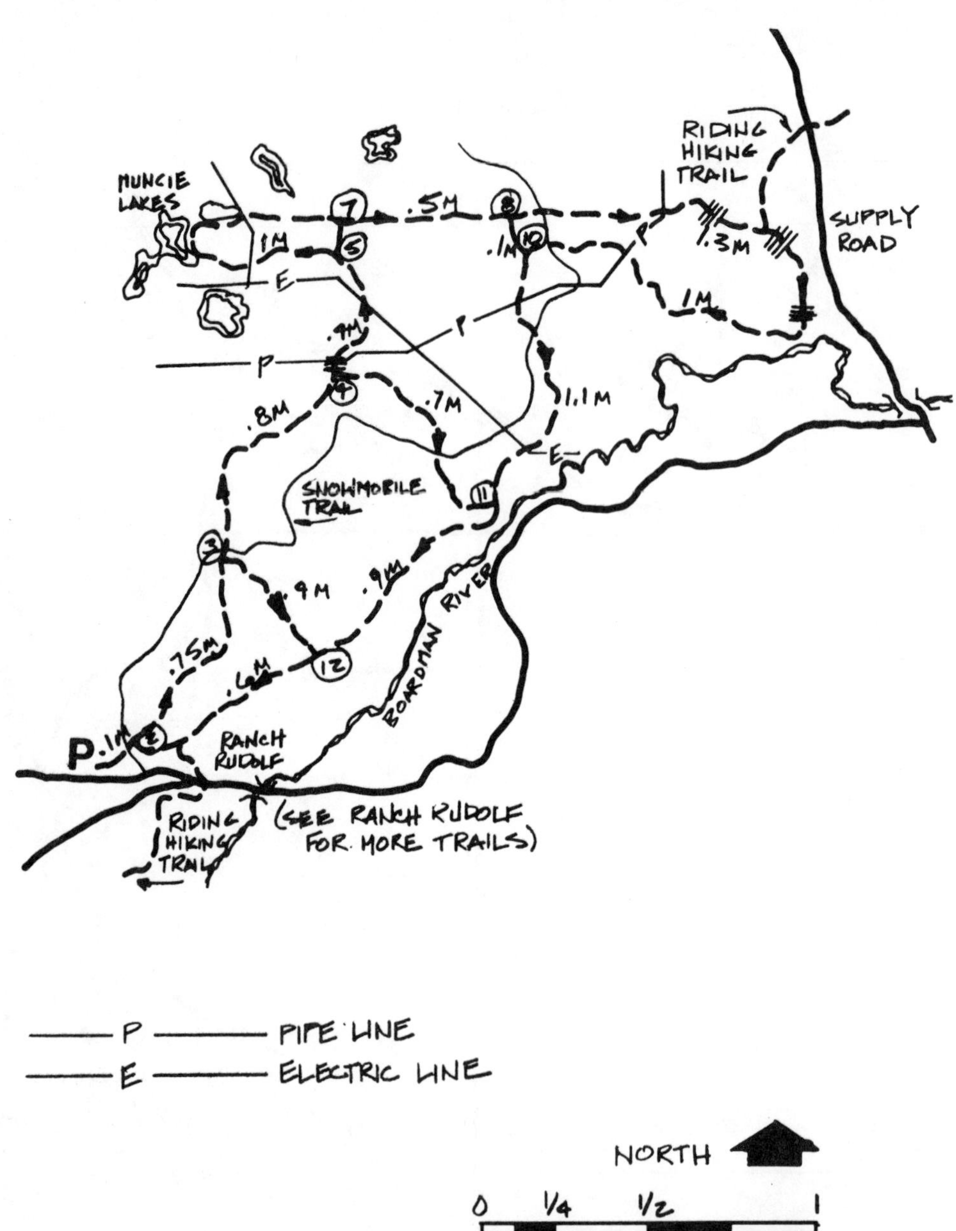

MUNCIE LAKE PATHWAY

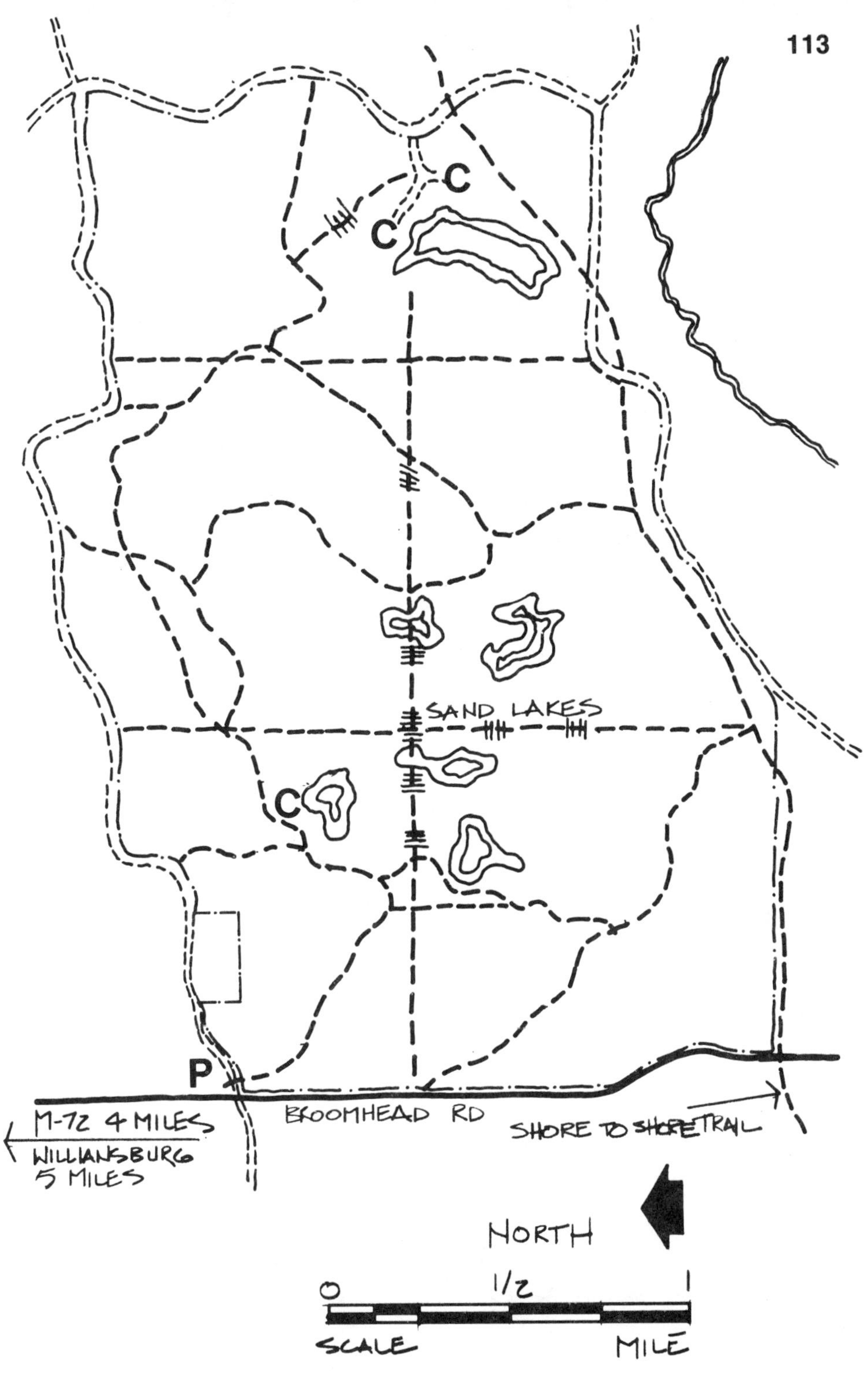

SAND LAKES QUIET AREA

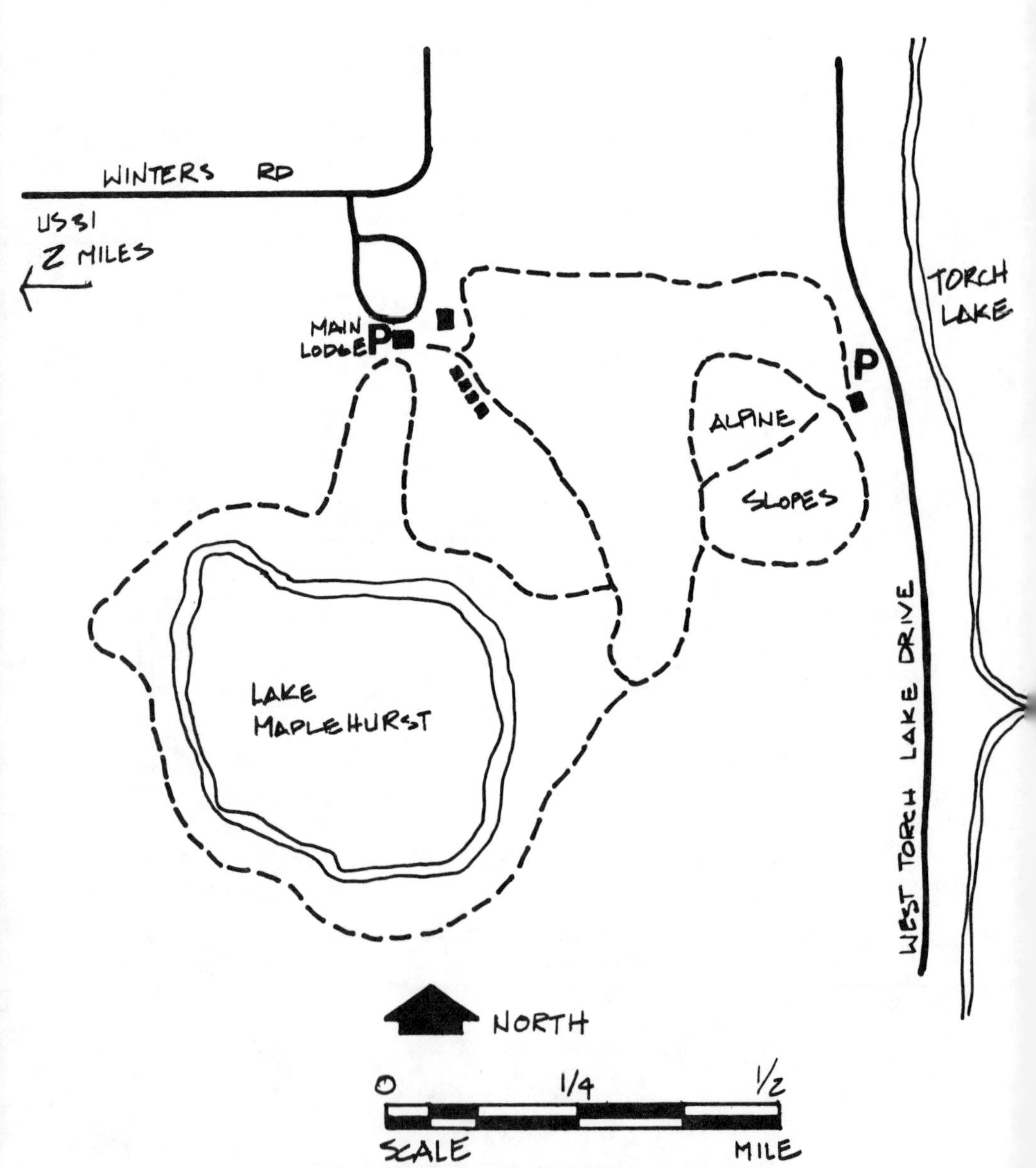
WINTERS RD
US 31
2 MILES
MAIN LODGE
P
P
ALPINE
SLOPES
TORCH LAKE
LAKE MAPLEHURST
WEST TORCH LAKE DRIVE
NORTH
0
1/4
1/2
SCALE
MILE

MAPLEHURST

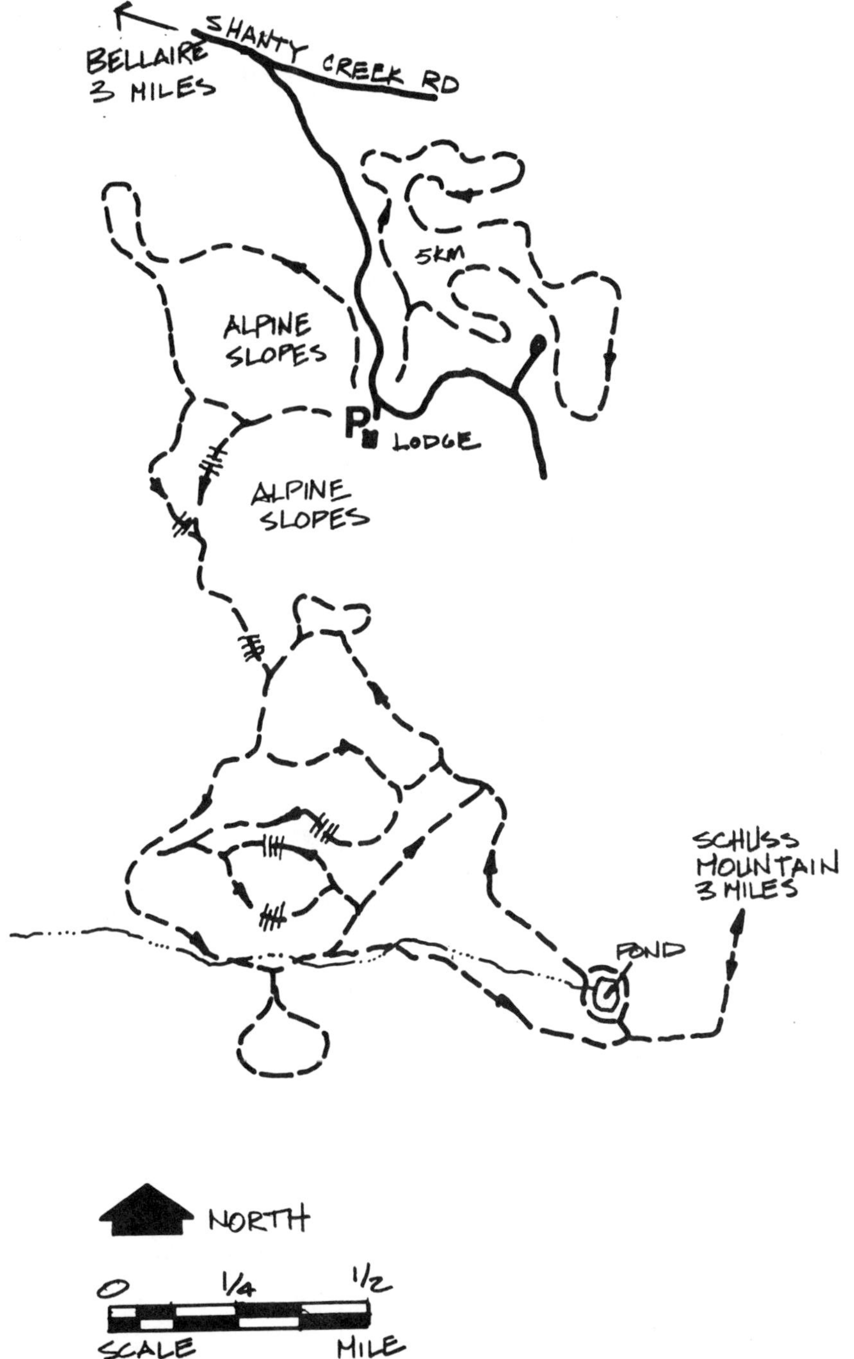

HILTON SHANTY CREEK
TOURING CENTER

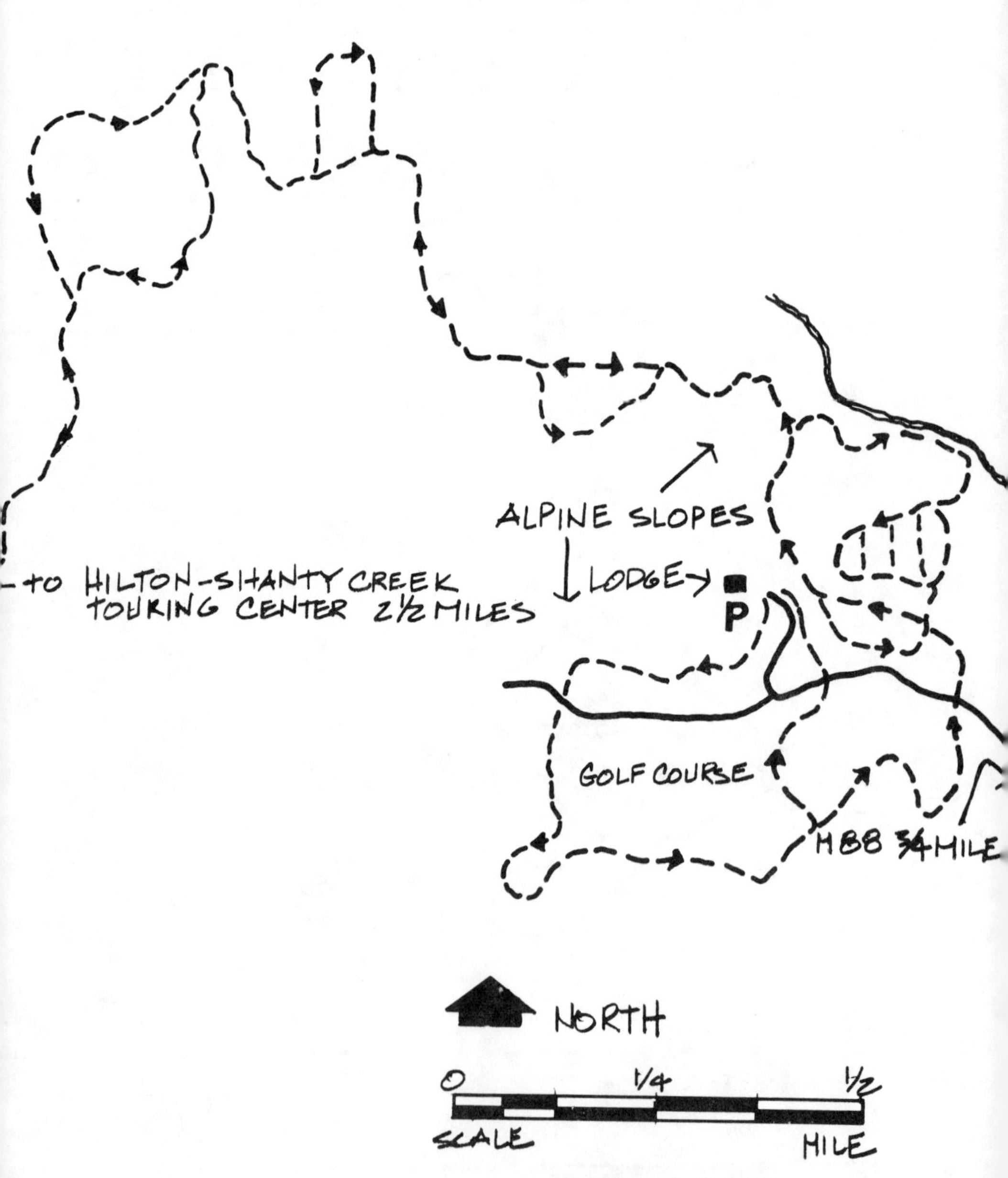

NORTH

0 1/4 1/2
SCALE MILE

SCHUSS MOUNTAIN

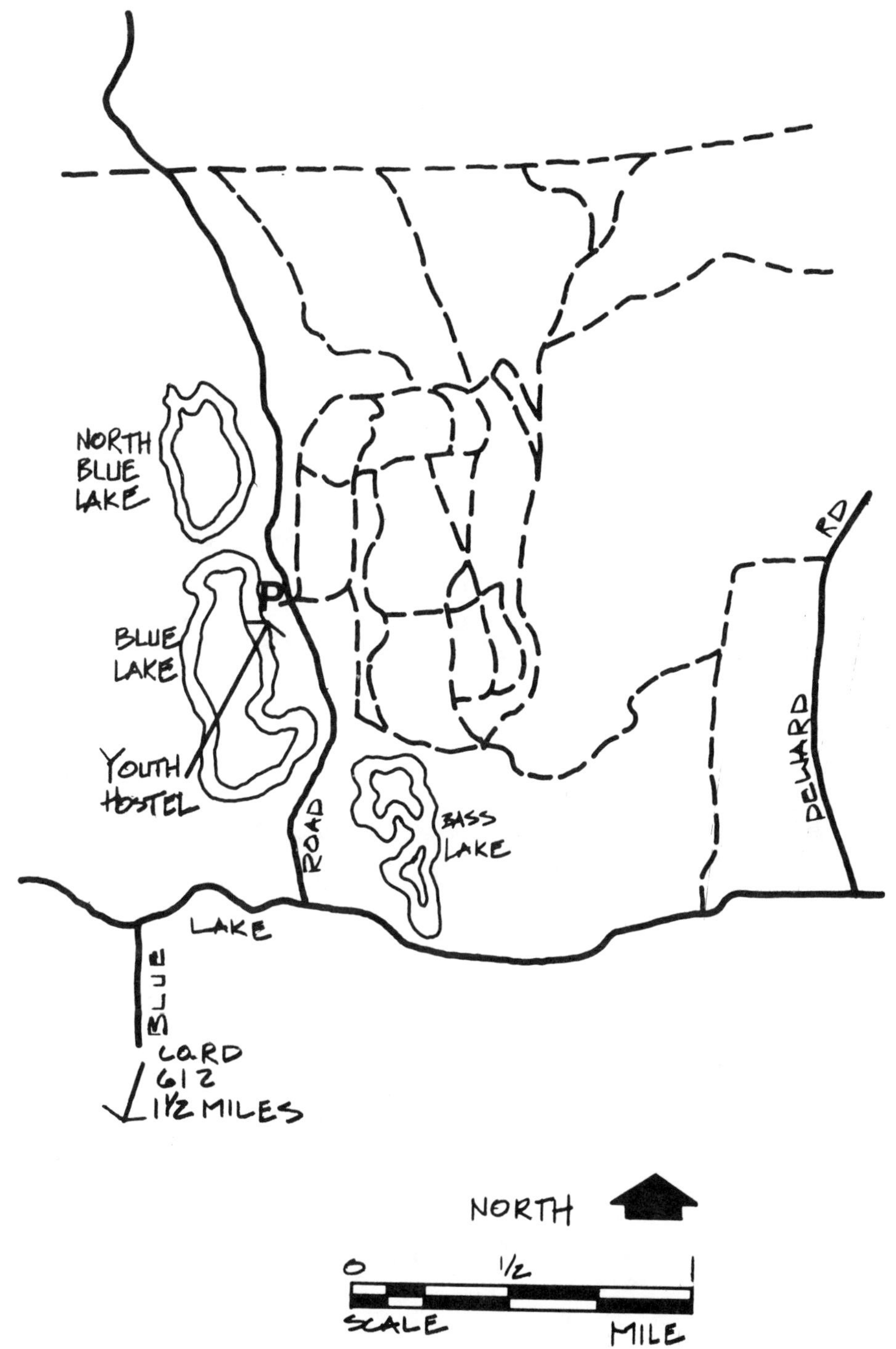

BLUE LAKE SKI AREA

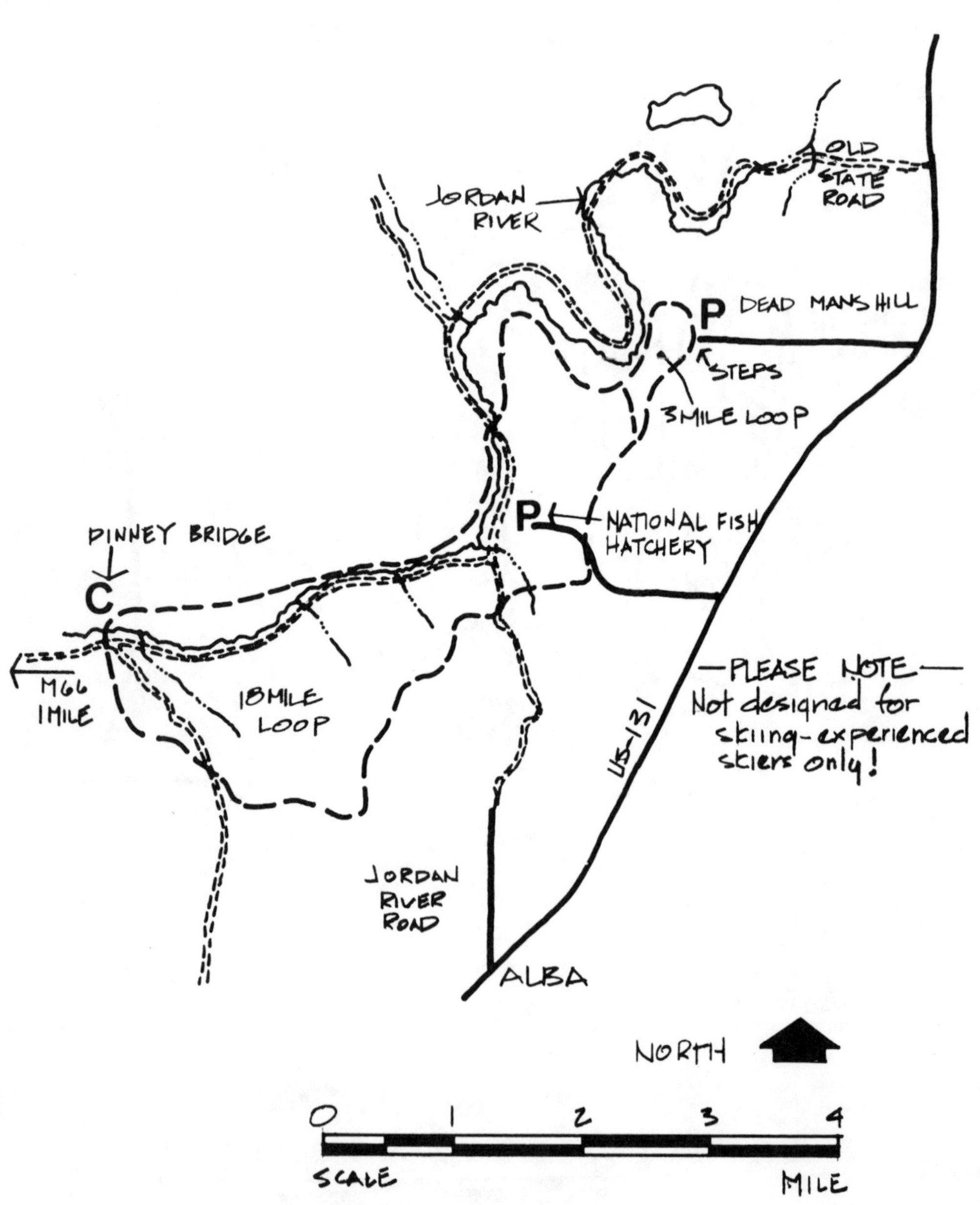

JORDAN RIVER PATHWAY

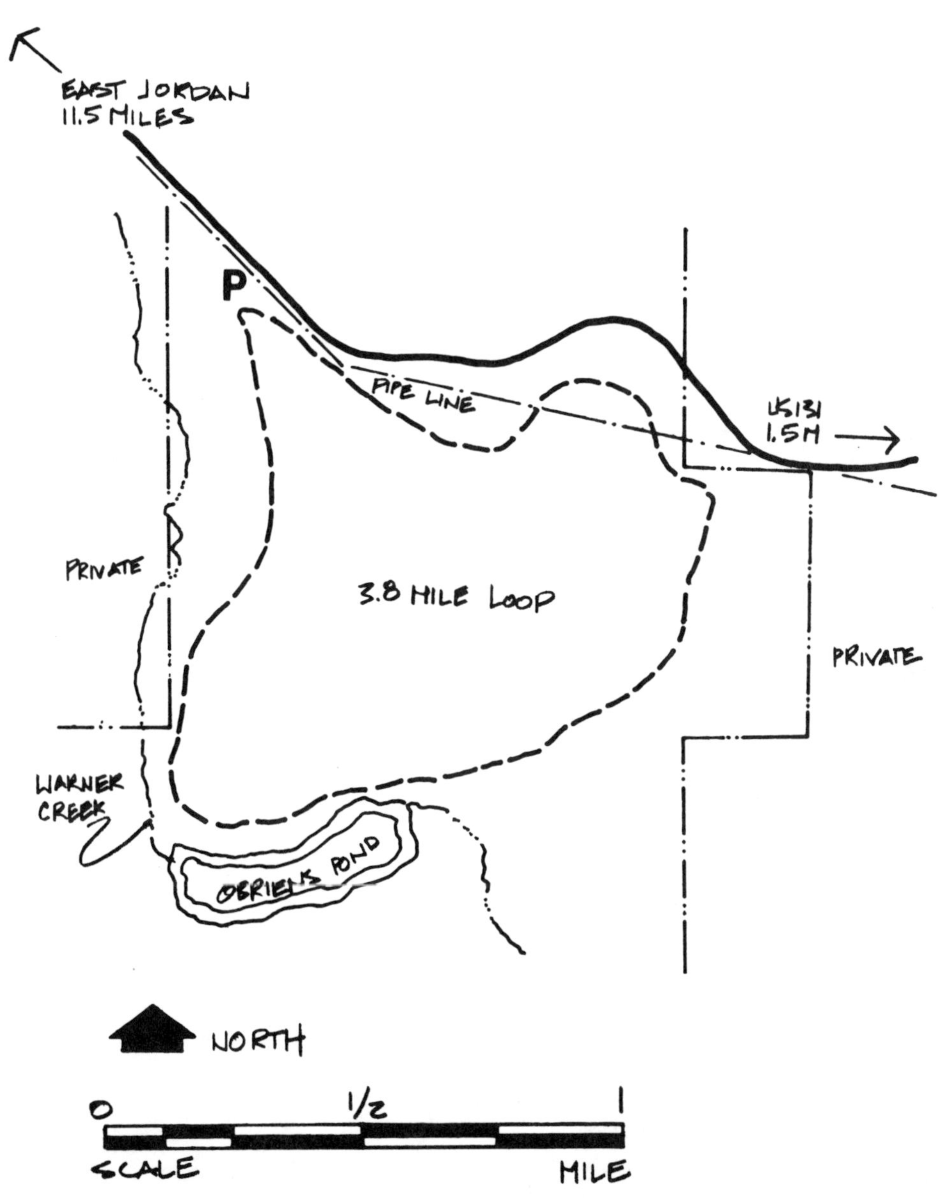

WARNER CREEK PATHWAY

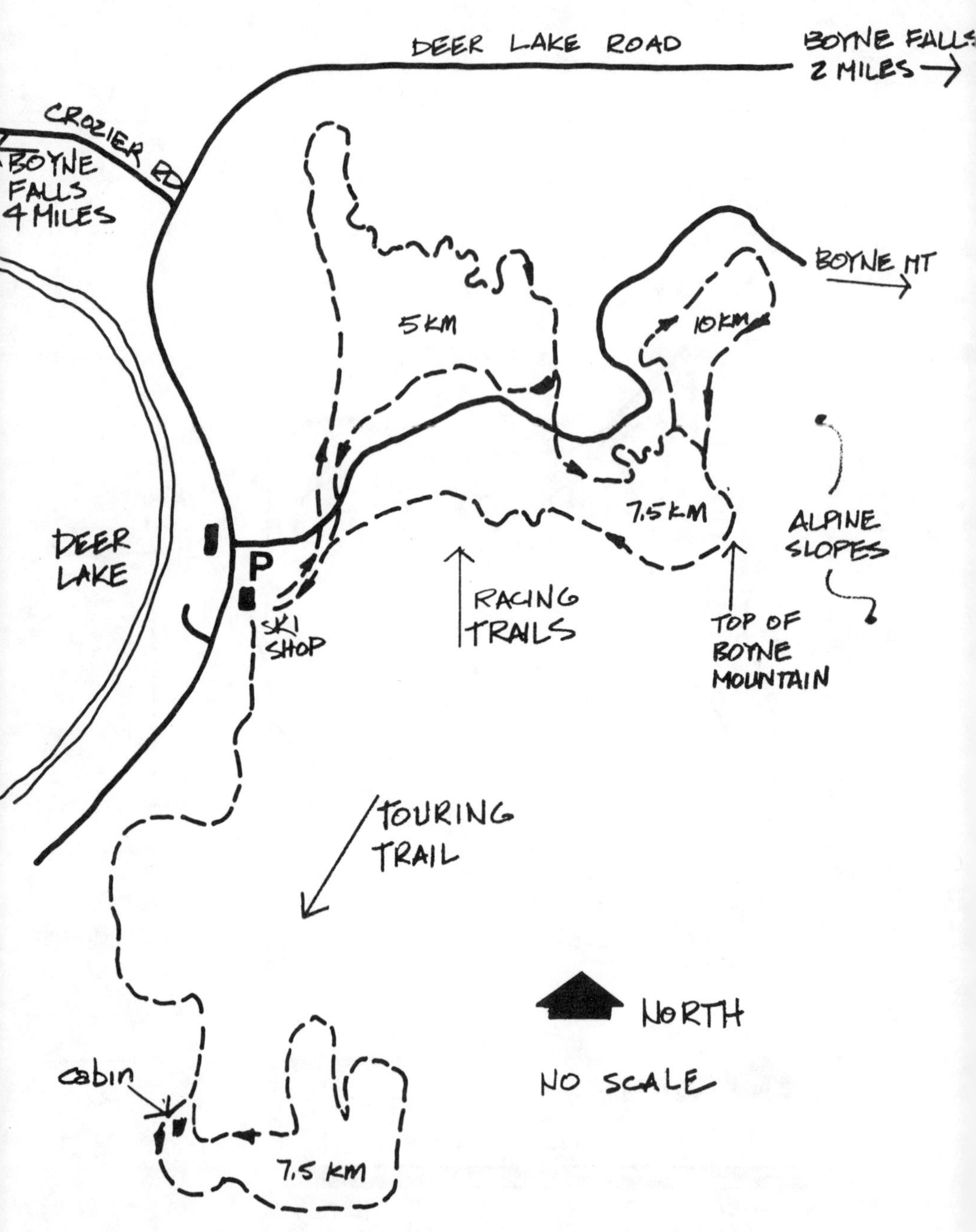

BOYNE NORDICAN

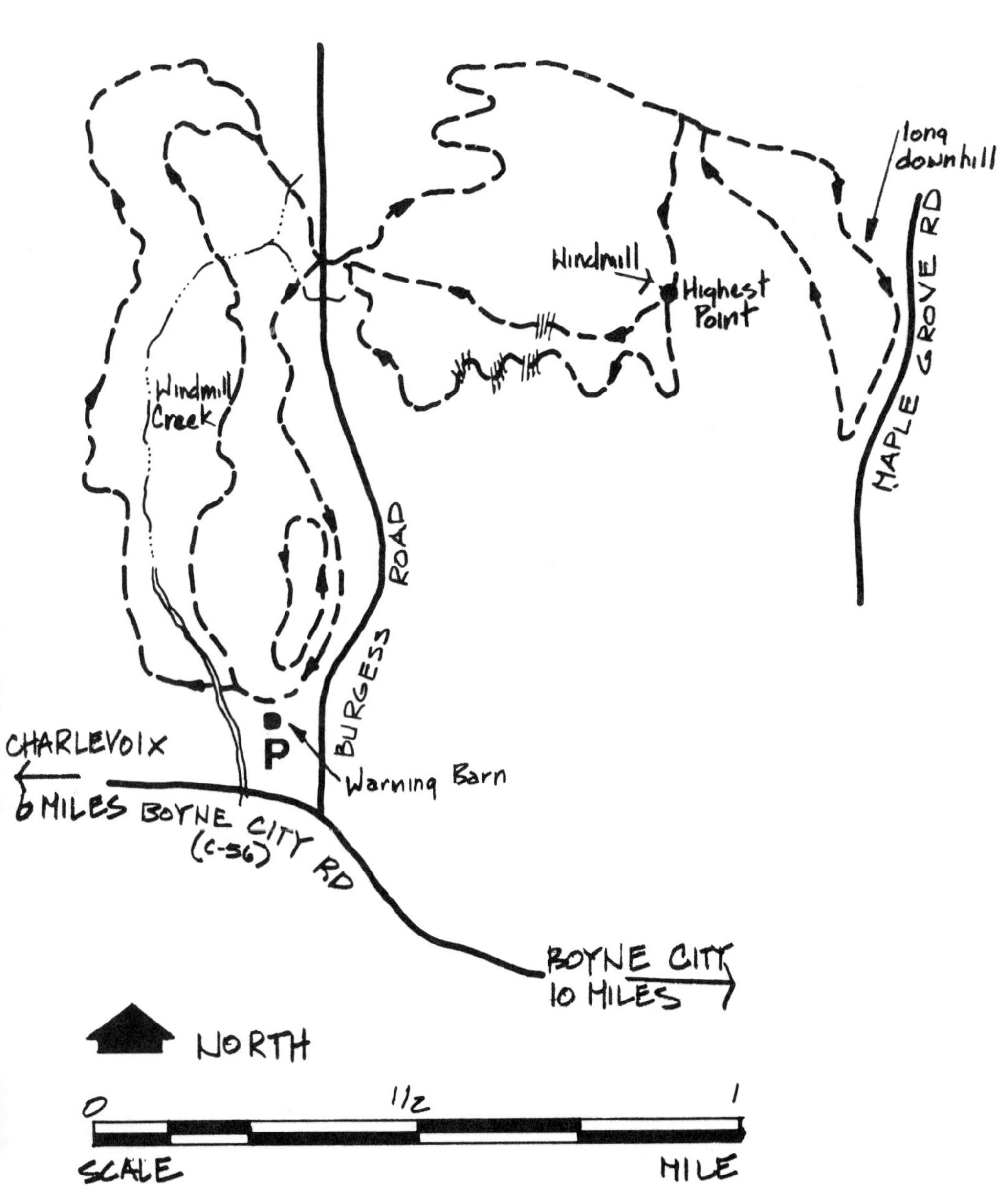

WINDMILL FARM
CROSS COUNTRY SKI AREA

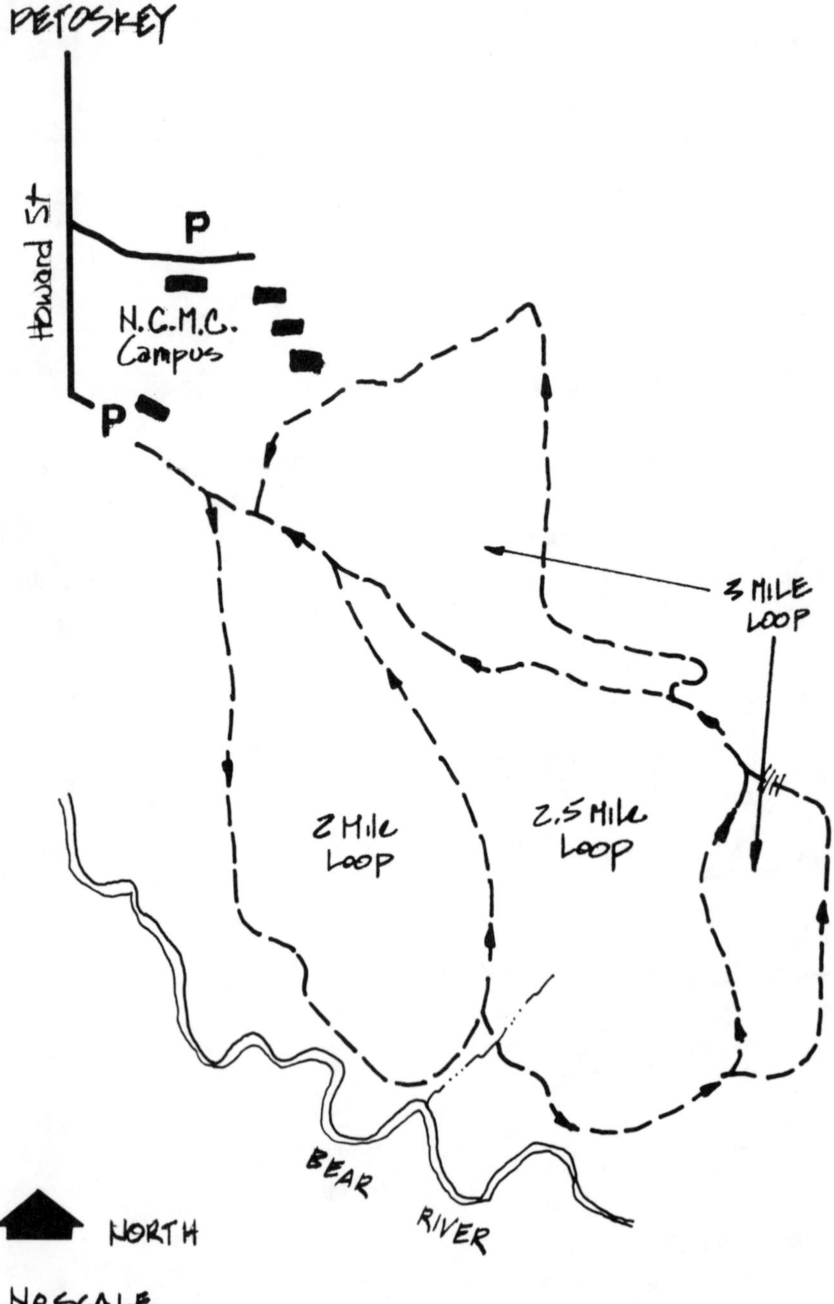

NORTH CENTRAL MICHIGAN COLLEGE
SKI TRAILS

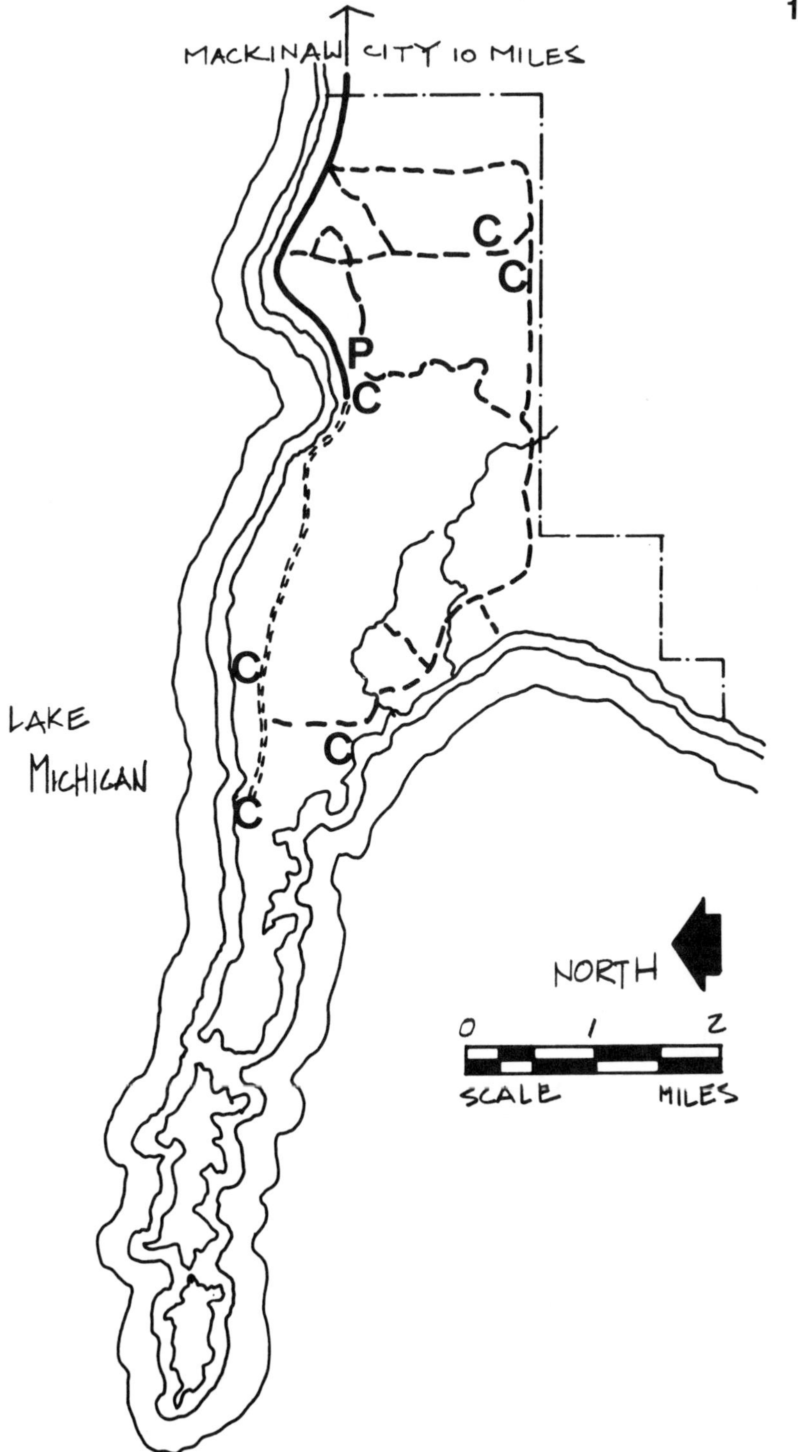

WILDERNESS STATE PARK

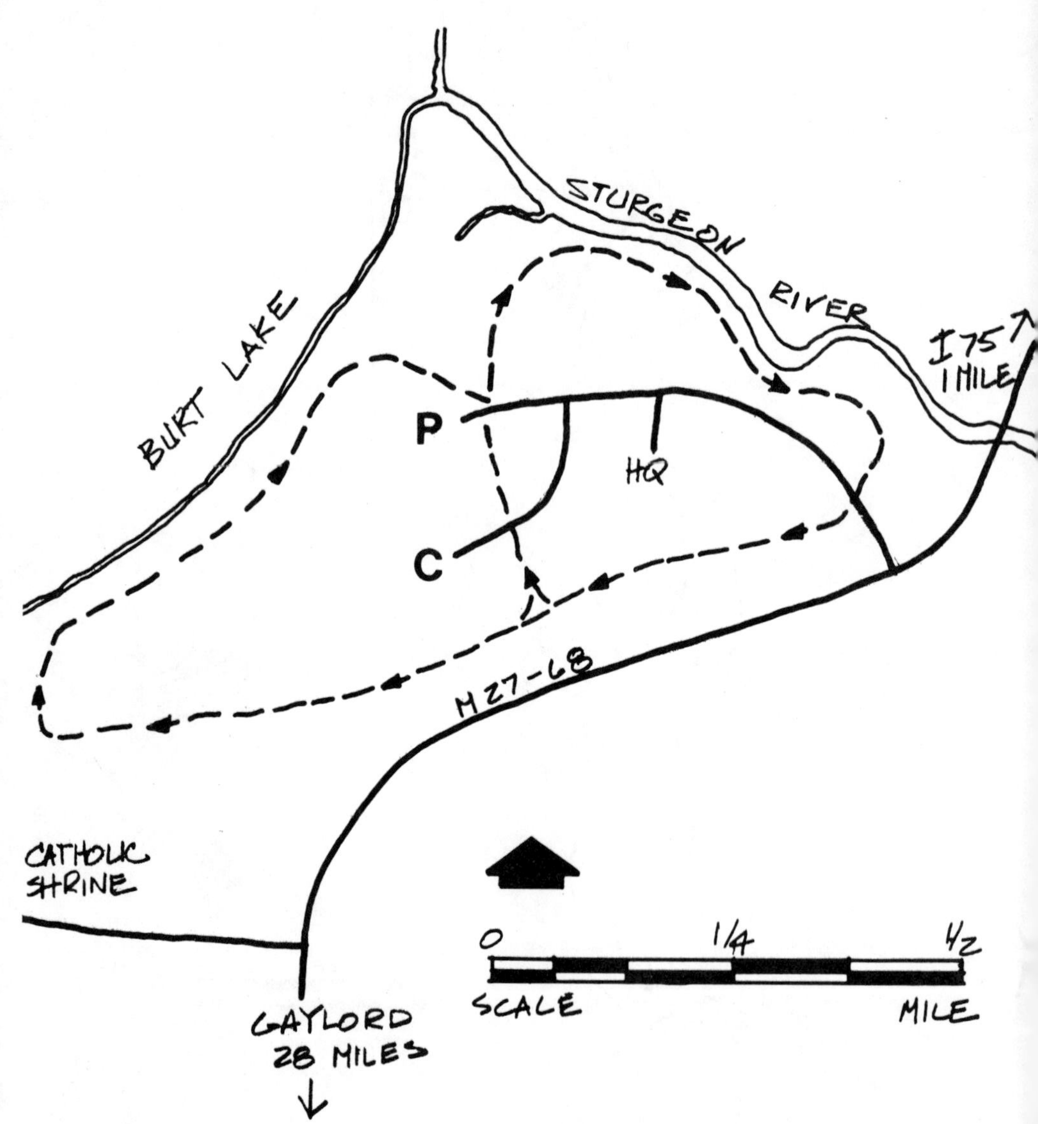

BURT LAKE STATE PARK

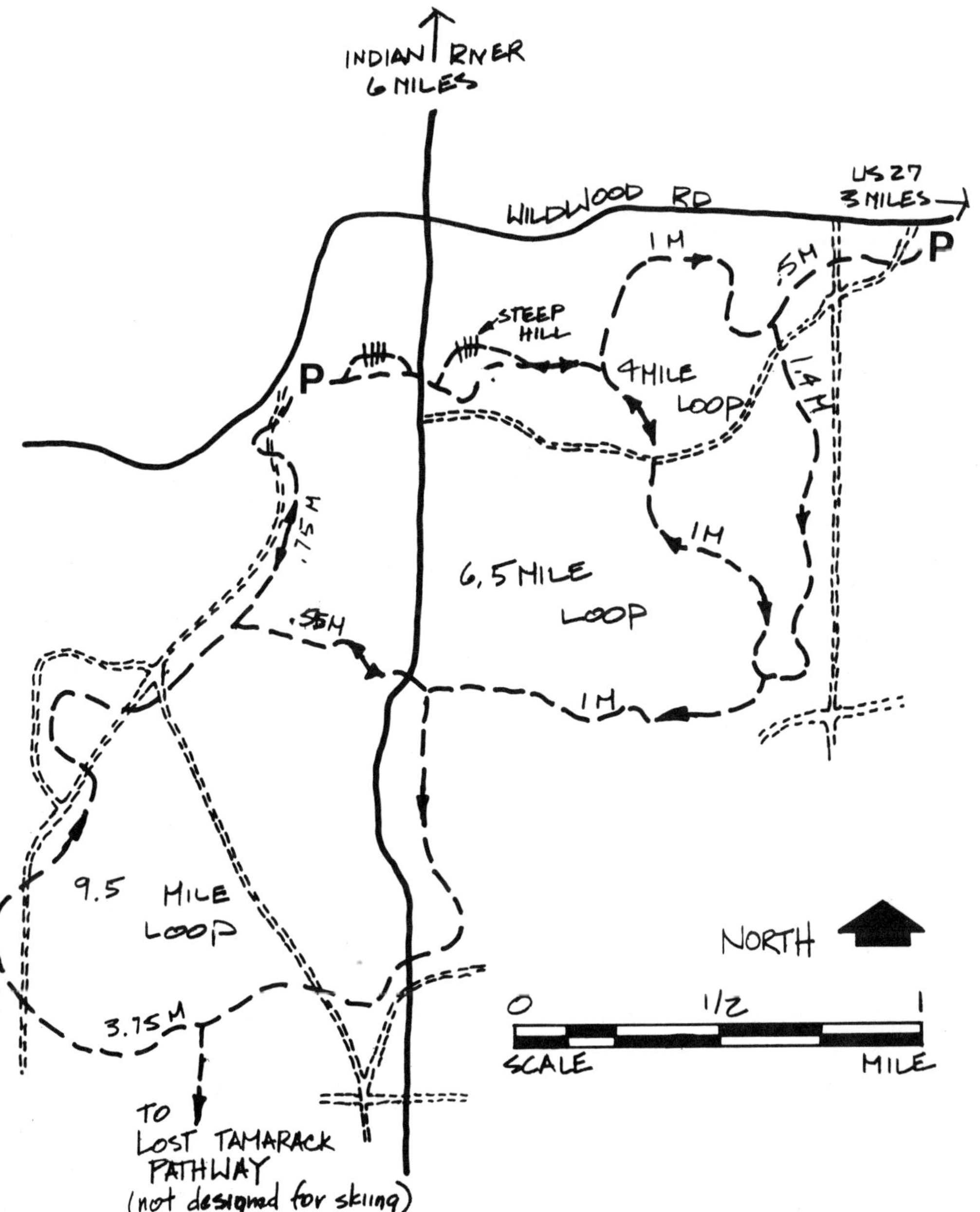

WILDWOOD HILLS PATHWAY

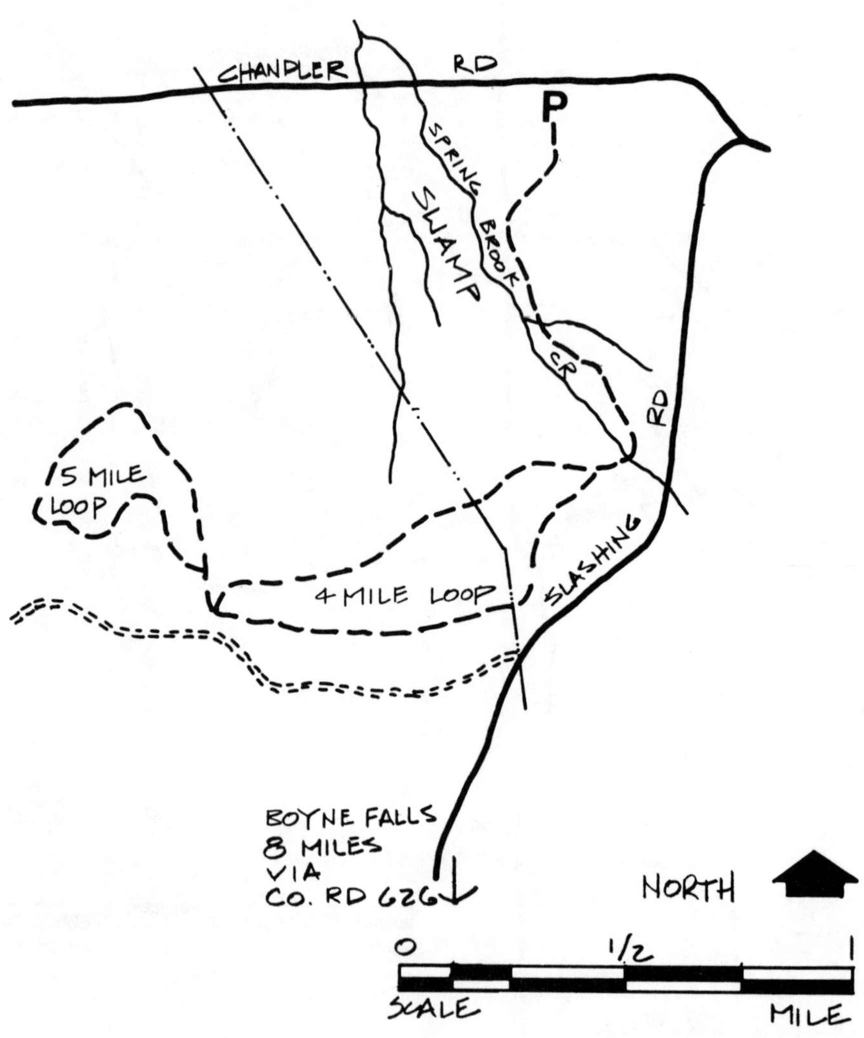

SPRING BROOK PATHWAY

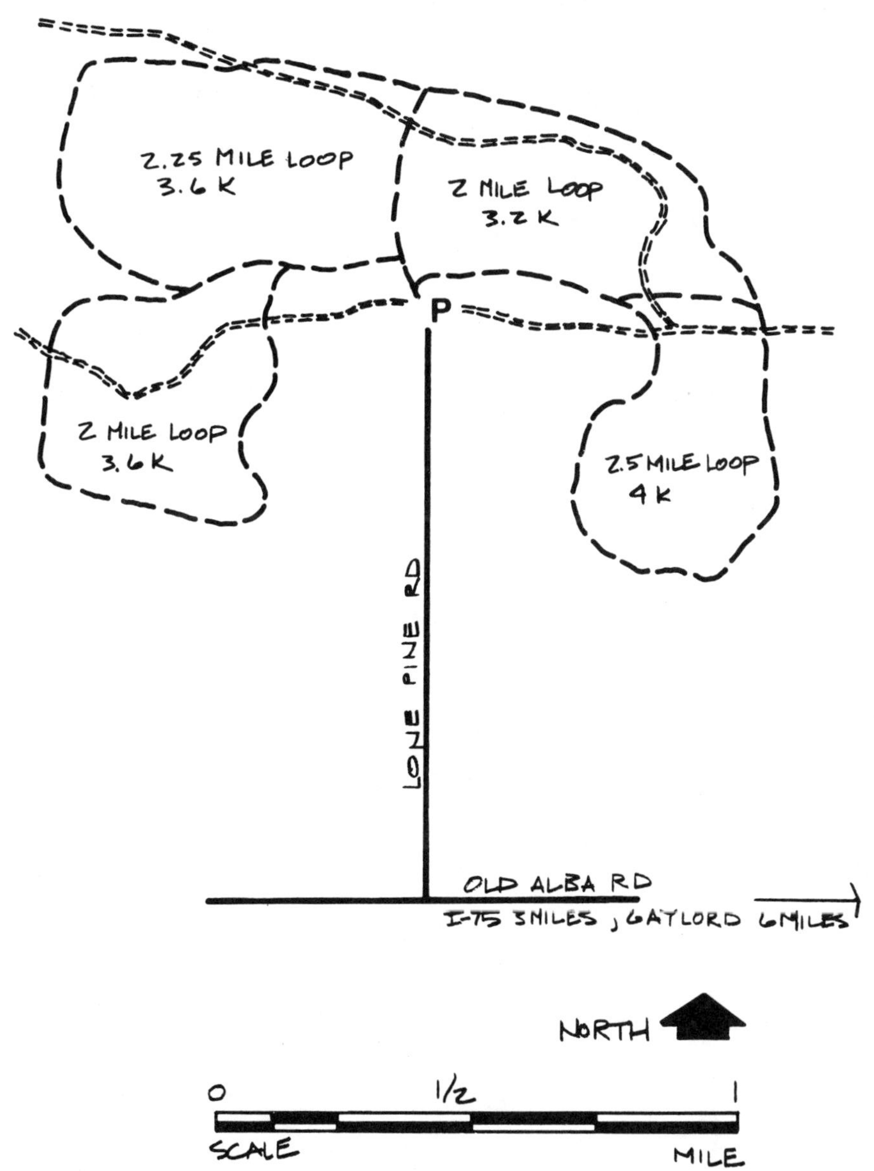

PINE BARON PATHWAY

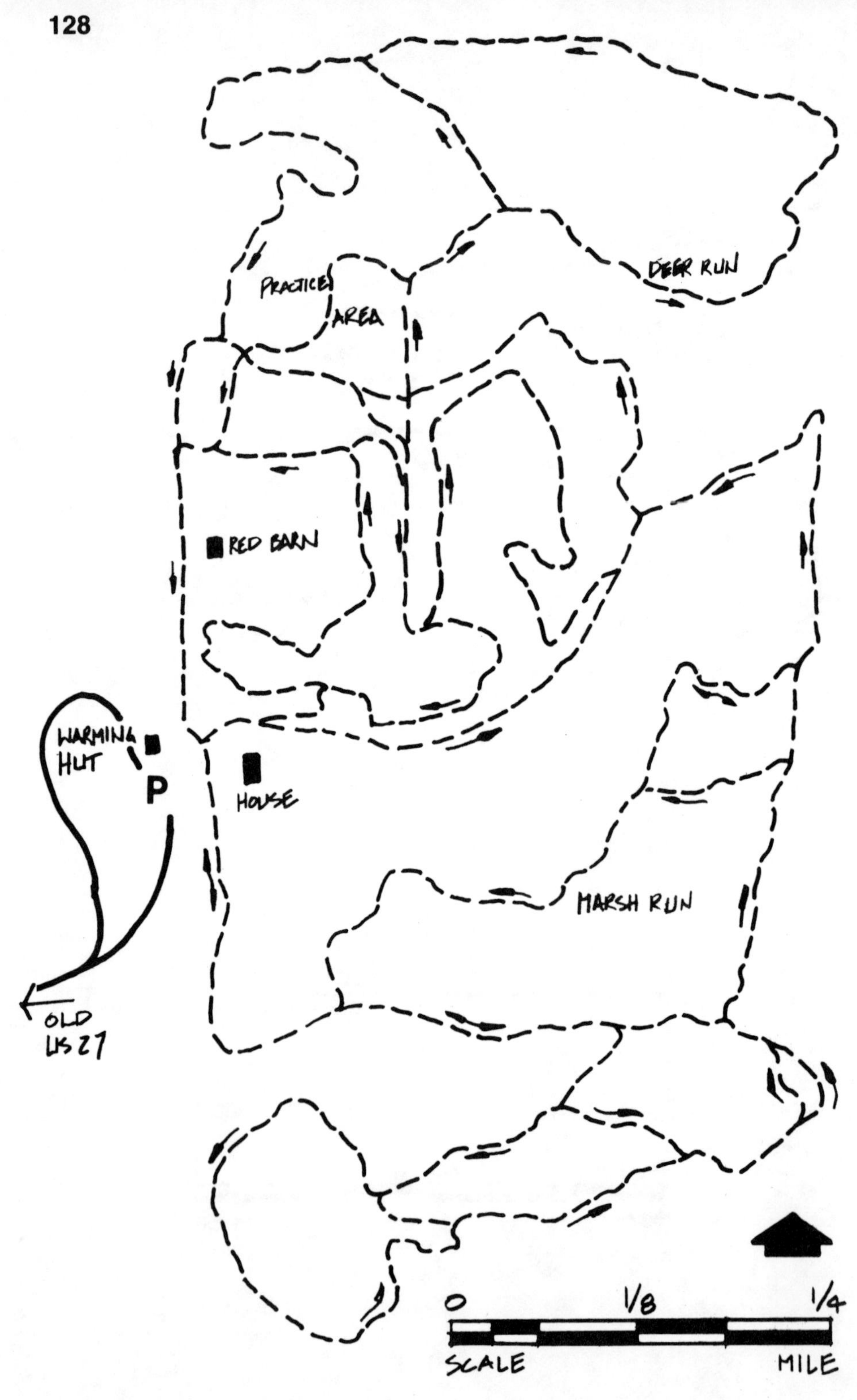

KEN MAR ON THE HILL

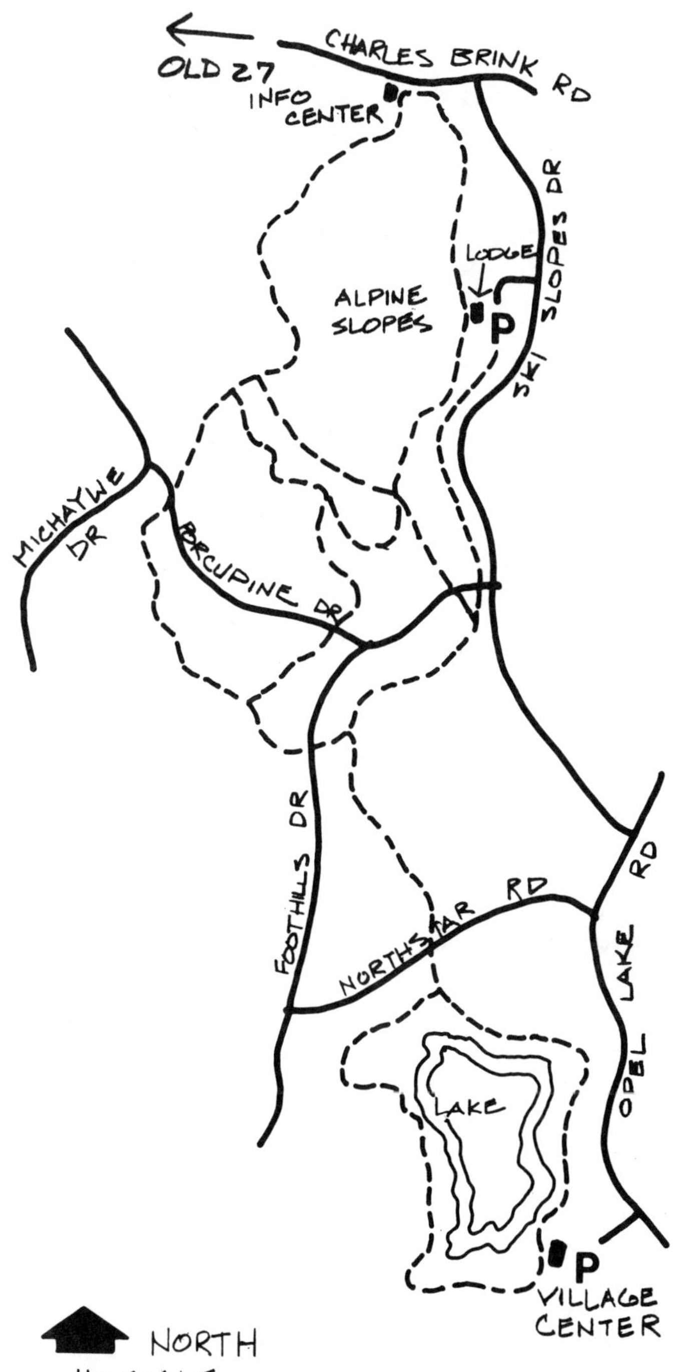
OLD 27
CHARLES BRINK RD
INFO CENTER
SKI SLOPES DR
LODGE
ALPINE SLOPES
P
MICHAYWE DR
PORCUPINE DR
FOOTHILLS DR
NORTHSTAR RD
LAKE
OPEL LAKE RD
P
VILLAGE CENTER
NORTH
NO SCALE

MICHAYWE

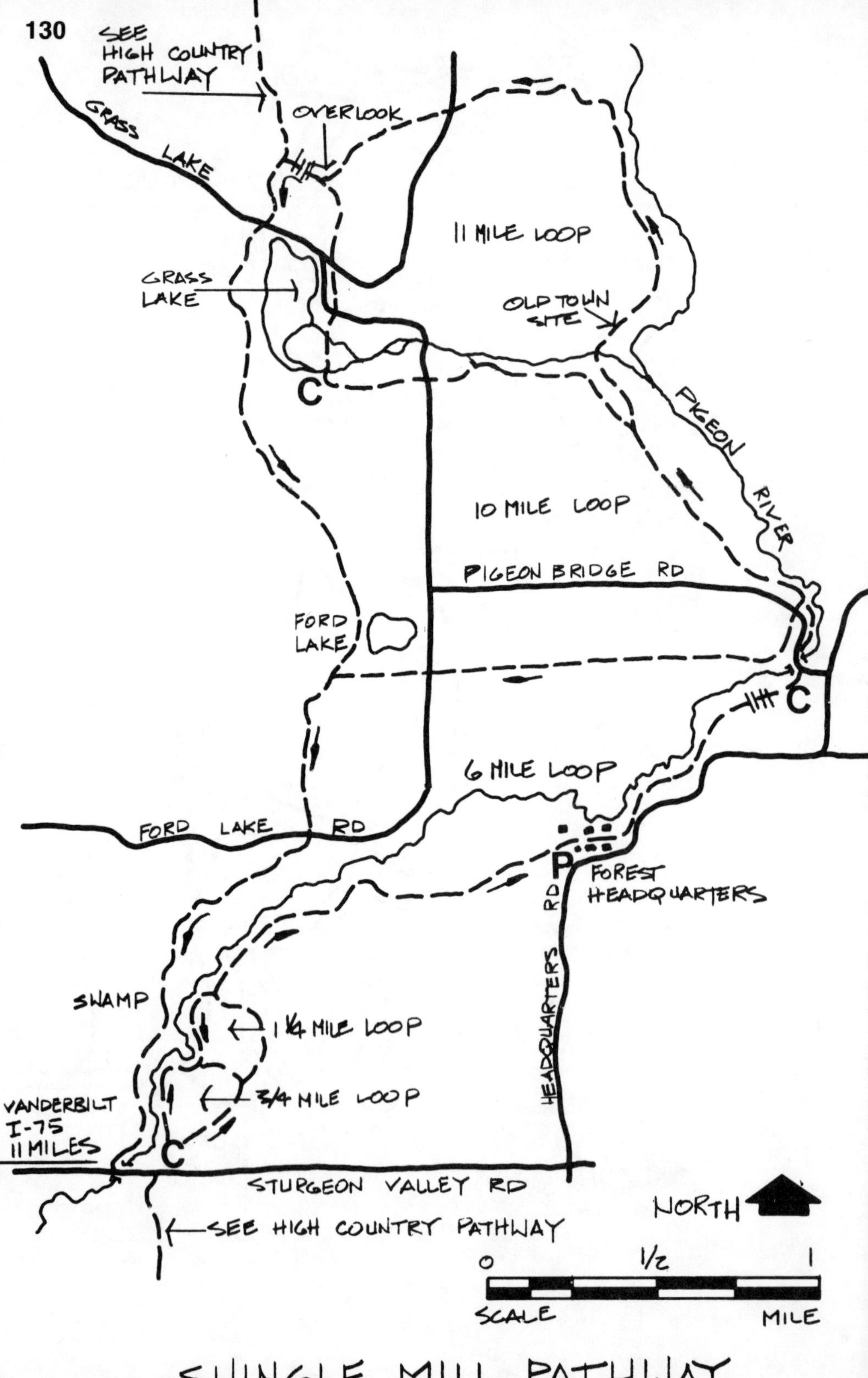

SHINGLE MILL PATHWAY

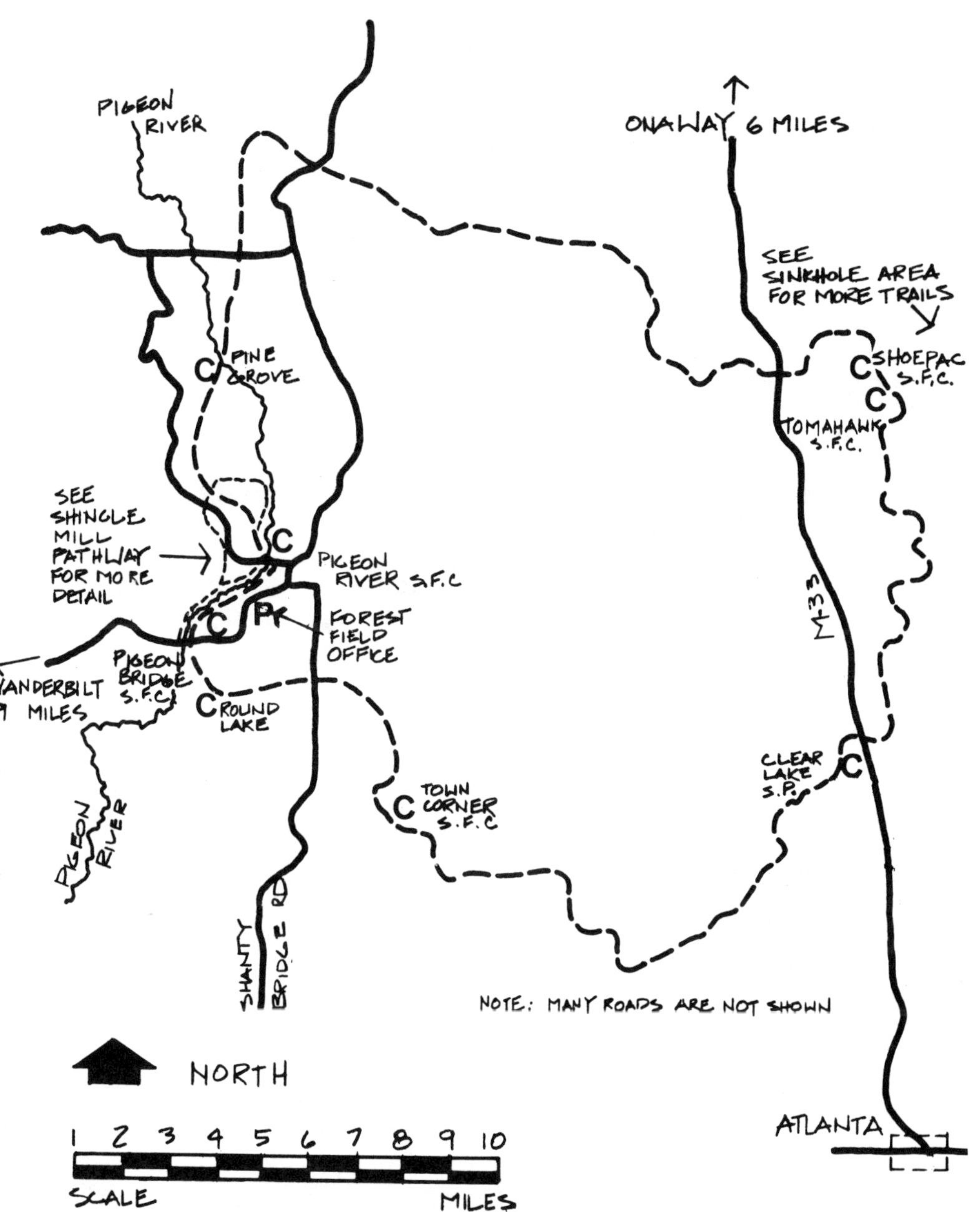

PLEASE NOTE:
PATHWAY NOT DESIGNED FOR SKIING - EXPERIENCED SKIERS ONLY

HIGH COUNTRY PATHWAY

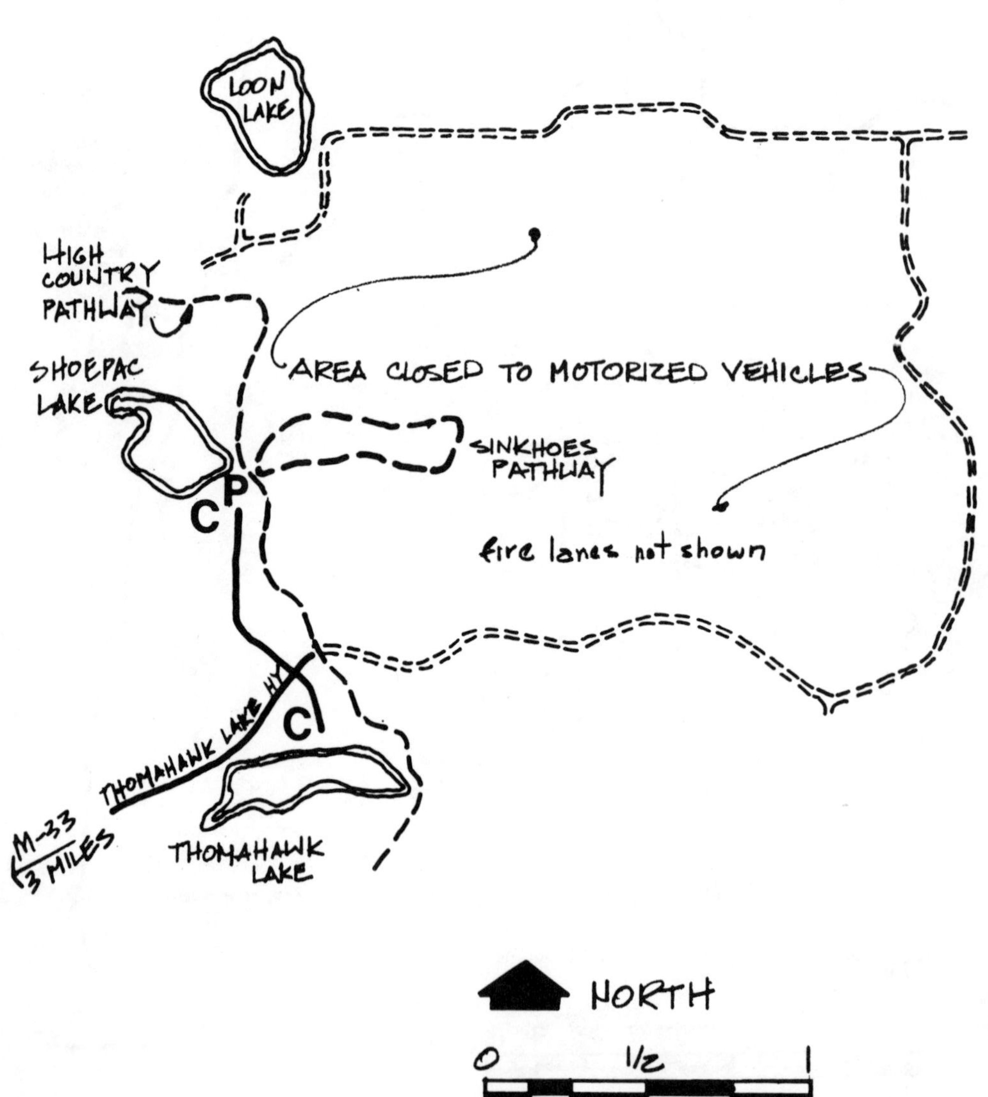

SINKHOLES AREA

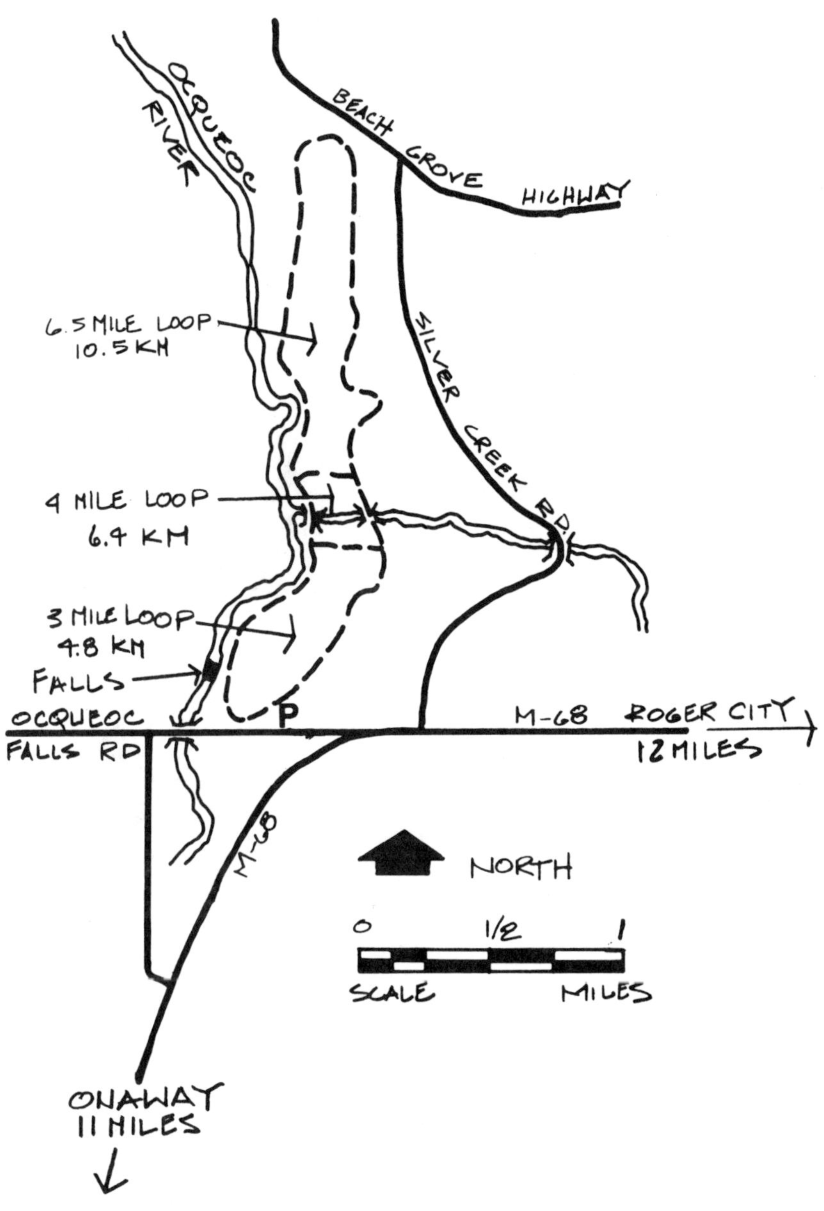

OCQUEOC FALLS BICENTENNIAL PATHWAY

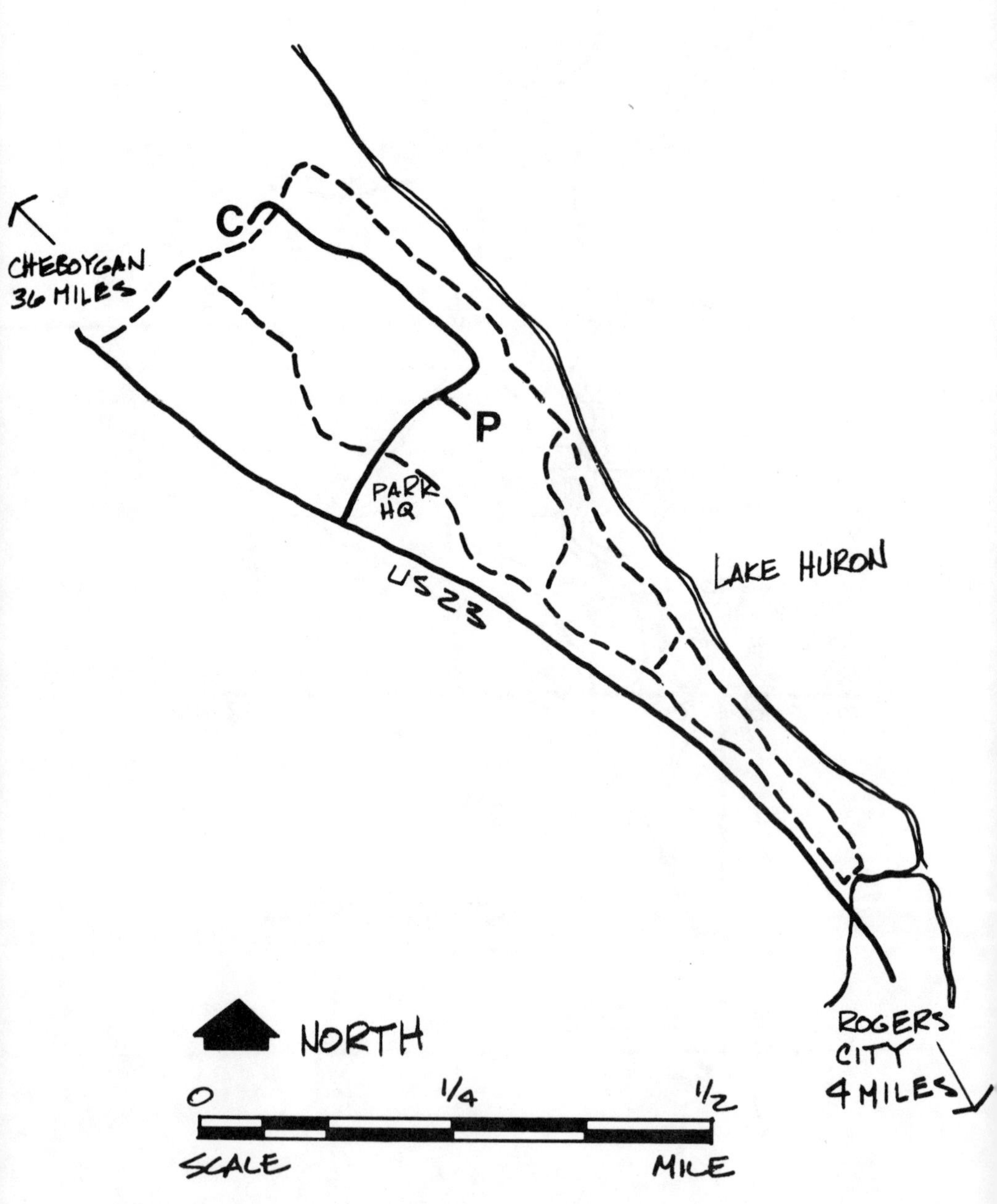

HOEFT STATE PARK

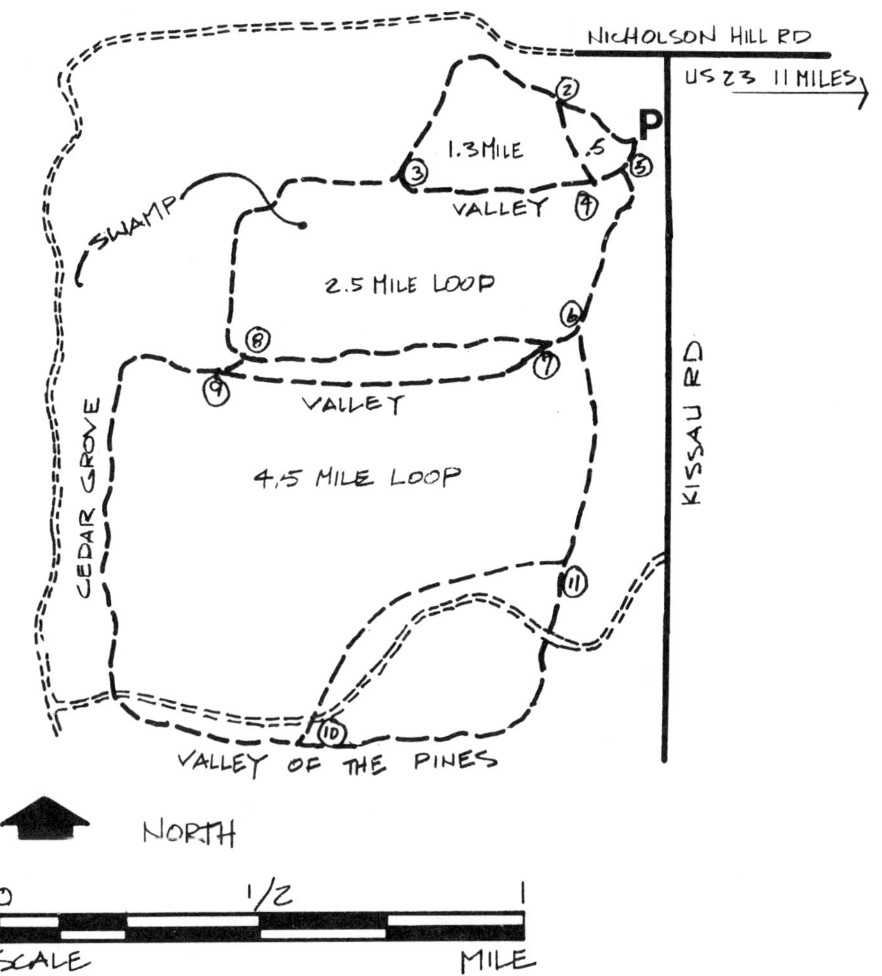

CHIPPEWA HILLS PATHWAY

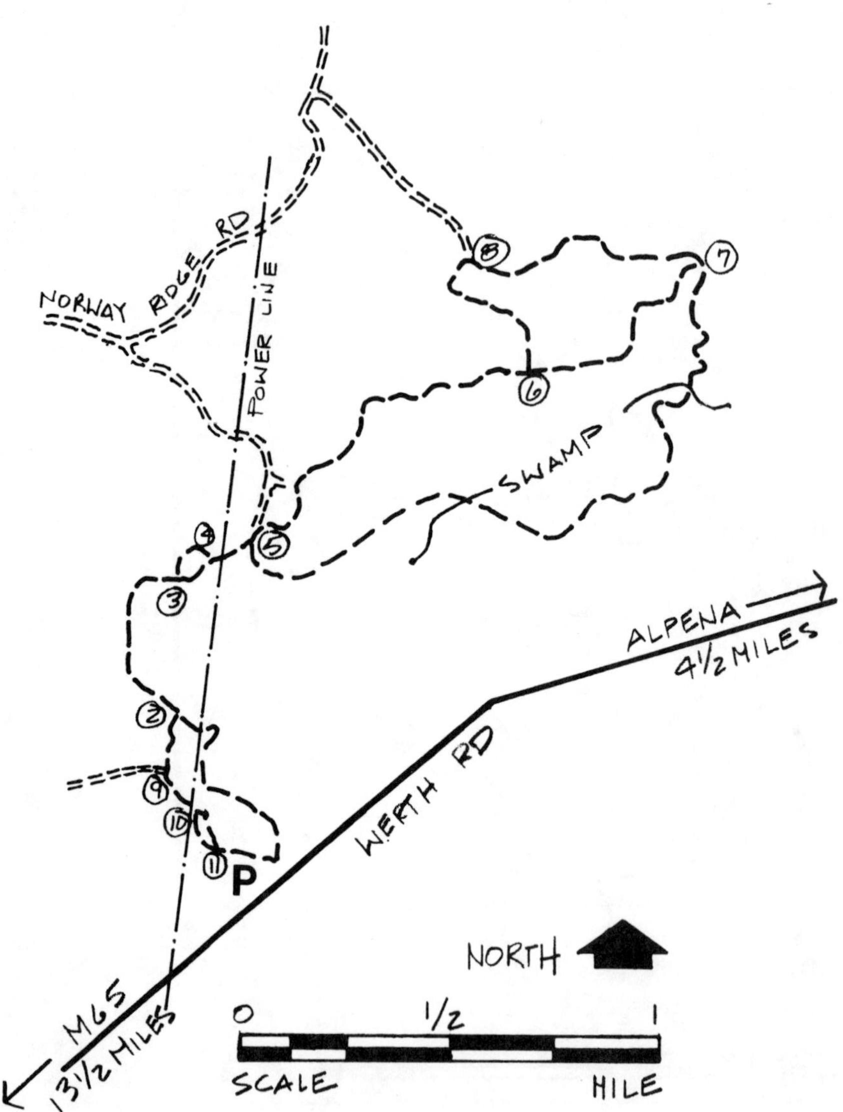

NORWAY RIDGE PATHWAY

Western Michigan Nordic Ski Patrol

Dear Fellow Cross Country Skier

For many years the National Ski Patrol System has been serving alpine skiers with first aid in cases of injury on the slopes. With the recent increase in cross country skiing it became apparent that a similar service was needed for nordic skiers. In 1976, the Western Michigan II section formed the first nordic ski patrol. It was formed for the threefold purpose of promoting nordic skiing safety, conducting winter search and rescue missions and providing first aid to injured skiers.

The patrol is comprised of volunteers who have completed the Red Cross advanced first aid and emergency care course. Following this, a written and practical first aid test is administered by the National Ski Patrol. Also required are demonstrated skiing ability and training in winter survival, winter search and rescue, orienteering and ski trip organization. An annual refresher course is also required.

At present there are only about 30 members in the nordic ski patrol for the entire state. With the growth of cross country skiing, many more are needed. If you are interested in helping us and your fellow skiers in this worthwhile endeavor, please contact the individual listed below.

Western Michigan Nordic Ski Patrol
c/o John Scott
119 North Church
Kalamazoo, MI 49007
(616) 349-6691

Have a safe and enjoyable winter.

NATIONAL SKI PATROL SYSTEM, INC.

LAKE SUPERIOR
160
161
GRAND MARAIS
158
M28
163
165
MUNISING
M77
M94
164
M28
SENEY
M41
M94
162
US 2
M35
166
M41
167
RAPID RIVER
MANISTIQUE
US 2
ESCANABA
M35
LAKE MICHIGAN

Region Three

REGION 3 EAST HALF OF THE UPPER PENINSULA

TRAIL MAP NUMBER	Name	Location	Number of Loops Distances (miles)	Total length of System (miles)	Maintained in the Winter	Total Acres
150	Pine Bowl Pathway 906-635-5281	16 miles south of Sault Saint Marie on M129, then west on Tone Rd for 3 miles, then south on Wilson Rd .75 miles	3 loops 2,5,4, 9.5	17	no	2000
151	Kincheloe Memorial Golf Course Cross Country Ski Area 906-495-5706	3 miles east of I75 at Exit 378	4 loops	12.7km	yes	2000
152	Sherman Park 906-635-5341	2 miles west of Sault Ste Marie via Easterday Ave and 4th Ave	2 loops	1.5	yes	37
153	Kinsmen Ski Trails 705-942-4001	4 miles NE of Sault Ste Marie, Canada via 17 North, Old Garden River Rd and Landslide Rd	7 loops 4,5,5,5, 7,10,10 km	50km	yes	1000
154	Stokley Creek Lodge 705-649-3421	17 miles north of Sault Ste Marie, Canada on 17 North at Goulais River	many 4 to 20km	90km	yes	unlimited
155	Paradise Pathway 906-293-5131	½ mile west of Paradise on M123	2 loops 3,6	6.5	yes	unlimited
156	Tahquamenon Falls State Park 906-492-3415	Between Newberry and Paradise on M123	not looped	12	no	22000
157	Natural Area Pathway 906-492-3415	14 miles west of Paradise at Tahquamenon Falls State Park	3 loops 3,8,11	13	no	unlimited
158	North Country Trail	Tahquamenon Falls State Park to Munising, generally along the shore of Lake Superior	not looped	70 +	no	unlimited

P —Pro Shop · R —Rentals · W—Warming Area · C —Certified Instruction · S —Snack Bar · D —Dining Room · B —Brown Bag · A —Accommodations

Novice	Intermediate	Expert	Terrain	Trail Use Fee	Campground	Remarks	TRAIL MAP PAGE
√	√		rolling				144
√	√		rolling	√		W,S Start at golf course club house	145
√			rolling				146
√	√	√	flat to hilly			W,C,S,D Operated jointly by the Sault Ste Marie Kinsmen and Soo Finish Ski Clubs and the Sault Ste Marie Region Conservation Authority 5 km lighted trail Adjoins downhill ski area	147
√	√	√	flat to hilly	√		R,W,C,S,D,B,A Privately operated nordic ski area A unique touring experience All trails groomed with a double track	148
√	√		rolling				149
√	√		flat to rolling	√	√	Part of the North Country Trail Trail extends from Whitefish Bay to the Lower Falls along the Tahquamenon River See Natural Area Pathway for trails on the north side of M123 KOA campground in Paradise, no camping in the park	150
√	√	√	flat to rolling	√	√	KOA campground in Paradise Part of the North Country Trail	151
	√	√	varied terrain		√	Trail not specifically designed for skiing Only experienced skiers with winter outdoor skills should use this trail See above two listings and Pictured Rocks National Lakeshore for more information and phone numbers Campgrounds along the trail are not plowed	152

REGION 3 EAST HALF OF THE UPPER PENINSULA

TRAIL MAP NUMBER	Name	Location	Number of Loops Distances (miles)	Total length of System (miles)	Maintained in the Winter	Total Acres
159	Canada Lakes Pathway 906-293-5131	4 miles east of Newberry on M28 then 1.5 miles south on Co Rd 403	4 loops 2,3.7,4.6, 6.6	7.7	no	un-limited
160	Grand Marais Ski Trails 906-494-2521	4.5 miles east of Grand Marais on H-58	5 loops	15	yes	1320
161	Pictured Rocks National Lake-shore-Grand Marais Ski Trail 906-387-2607	1 mile east of Grand Marais on H-58	1 loop	5km	no	un-limited
162	Ashford Lake Pathway 906-341-2518	16 miles north of Manistique on M49	3 loops 3,6,9	11	no	1000
163	Pictured Rocks National Lake-shore-Munising Ski Trail 906-387-2607	North of Munising on Lake Superior at the end of City Line Rd	1 loop	6km	no	un-limited
164	Valley Spur Cross Country Ski Trail 906-387-2512	6 miles SW of Munising on M94	3 loops 1,3,6km	7km	yes	152
165	Laughing Whitefish Falls State Park	2 miles north of M94 at Sundell	1 loop	2	no	NA
166	Rapid River Cross Country Ski Trail 906-474-6442	7 miles north of Rapid River on US41	3 loops 2.2,5,8.1	9	yes	693
167	Days River Pathway 906-786-2351	3 miles north of Gladstone on US2/41, then 1.5 miles west on Days River Rd	3 loops 2.2,6.5, 9.2	9.6	no	6000

Novice	Intermediate	Expert	Terrain	Trail Use Fee	Campground	Remarks P —Pro Shop, R —Rentals, W—Warming Area, C —Certified Instruction, S —Snack Bar, D —Dining Room, B —Brown Bag, A —Accommodations	TRAIL MAP PAGE
	√		rolling		√	KOA campground in Newberry	**153**
√	√	√	flat to rolling			Developed through the efforts of the Grand Marais Chamber of Commerce	**154**
√	√		flat to rolling			Managed by Pictured Rocks National Lakeshore Portion of trail follows Sable Creek	**155**
	√		level to gently rolling				**156**
√	√	√	flat to rolling			Managed by Pictured Rocks National Lakeshore	**157**
√	√		rolling to hilly			Managed by USFS-Munising District Trails are groomed after each significant snowfall or at least once each week	**158**
√	√		rolling to hilly			Falls are very scenic	**none**
√	√	√	flat to hilly			Managed by USFS-Munising District Trails are groomed after each significant snowfall or at least once each week	**159**
√	√	√	flat to hilly			Trail follows the Days River	**160**

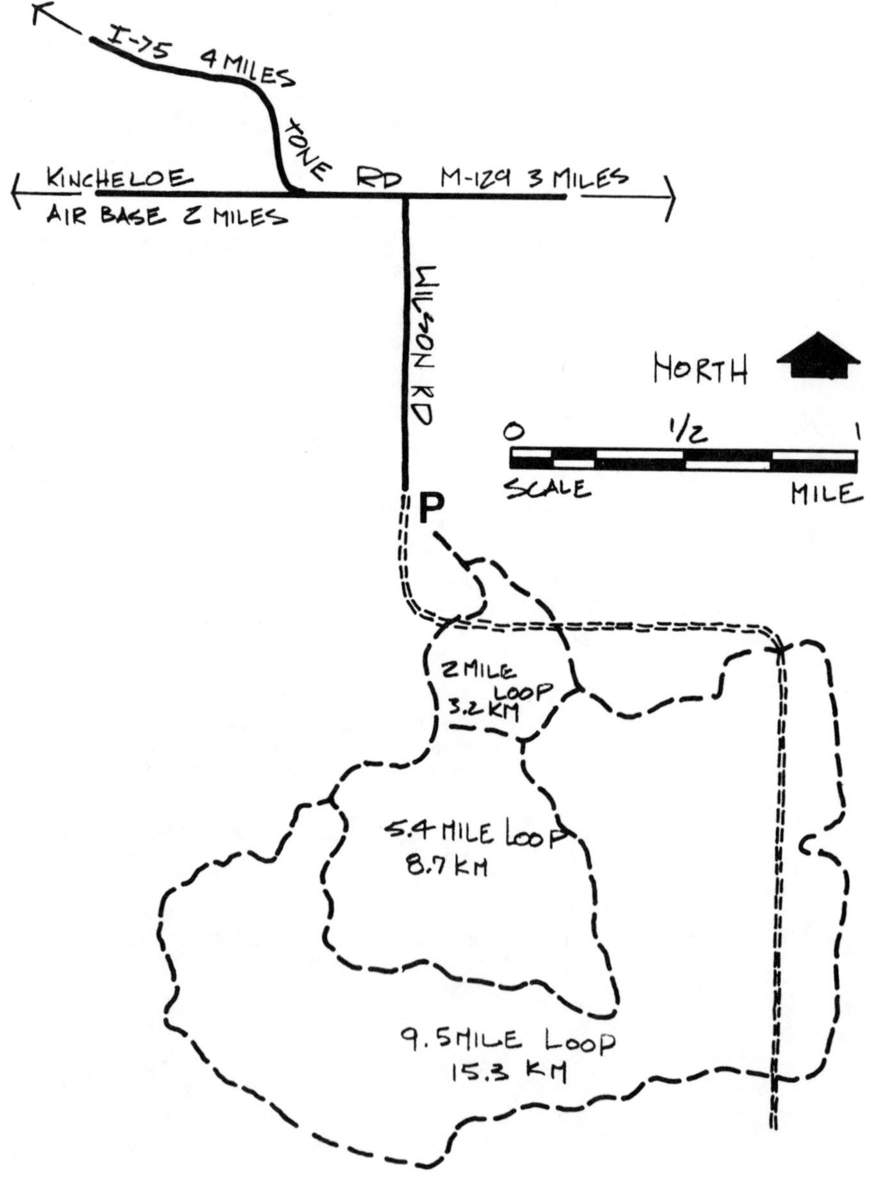

PINE BOWL PATHWAY

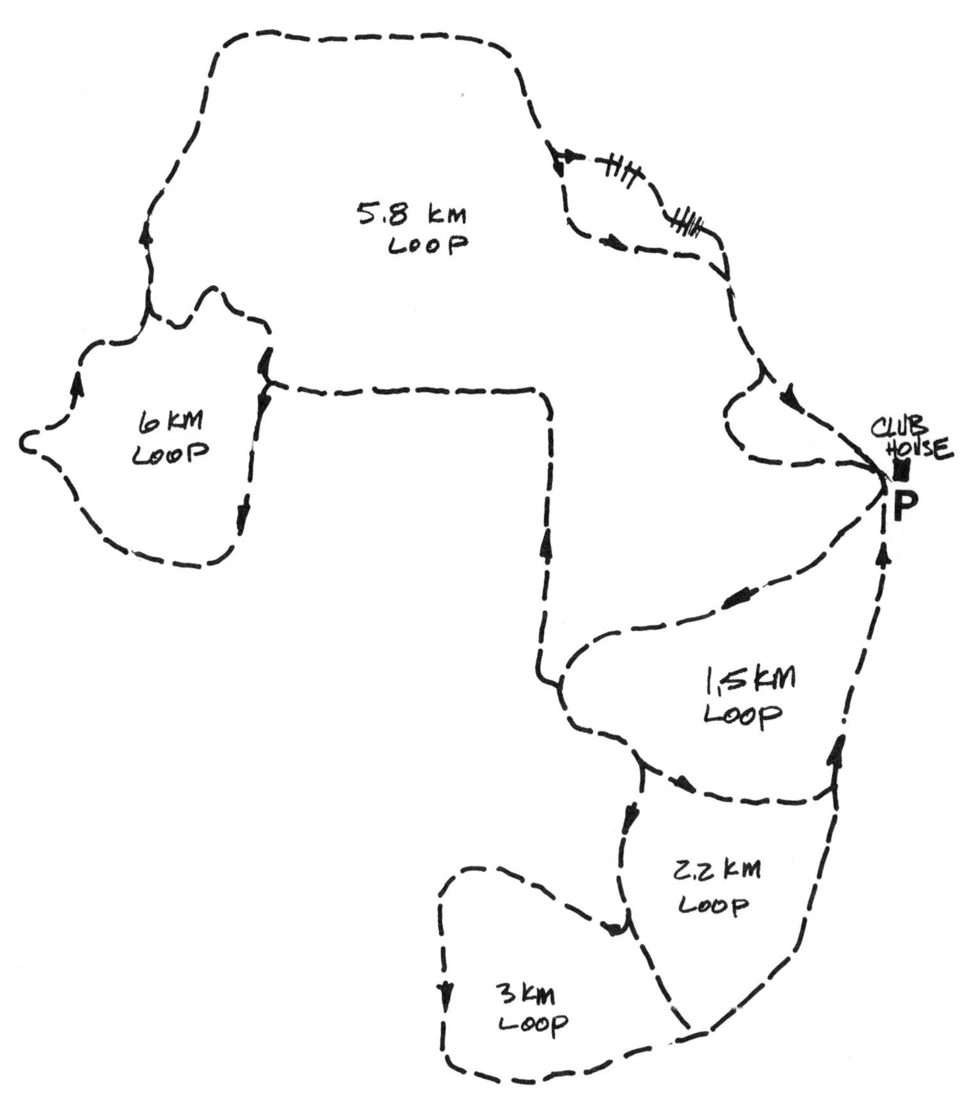

KINCHELOE MEMORIAL GOLF COURSE
CROSS COUNTRY SKI AREA

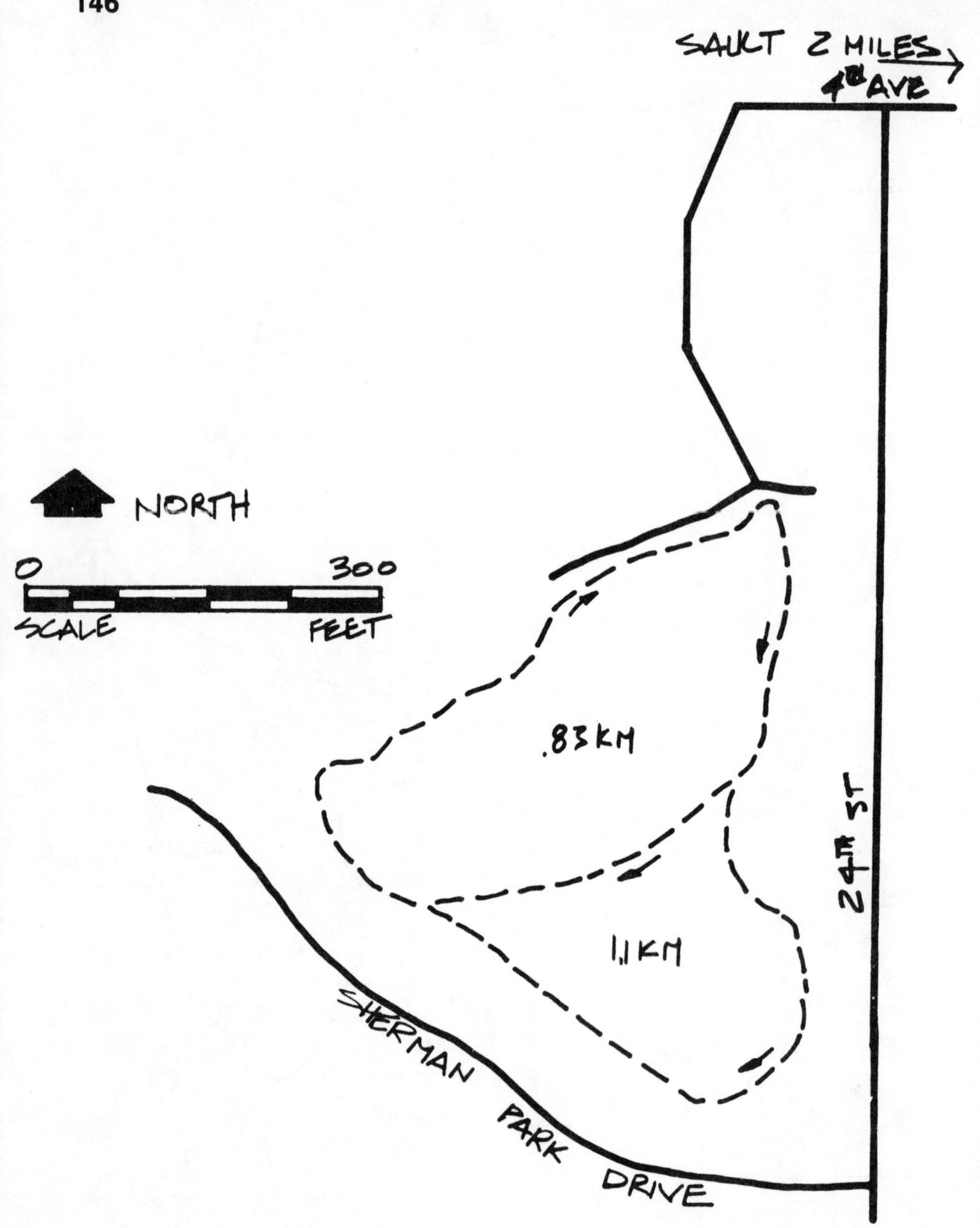

SHERMAN PARK SKI TRAIL

RANKIN 5KM

OLYMPIC 2.5KM

CRYSTAL CREEK 5K

HIAWATHA 7.5KM

KINSMEN 2K

HIAWATHA LODGE

LANDSIDE RD

P

SAULT STE MARIE

PINDER FARM 5KM

LOOKOUT 4KM

RED PINE 5KM

5th LINE RD

LOOKOUT

EXTENSION 10KM

NO SCALE

KINSMEN SKI TRAILS

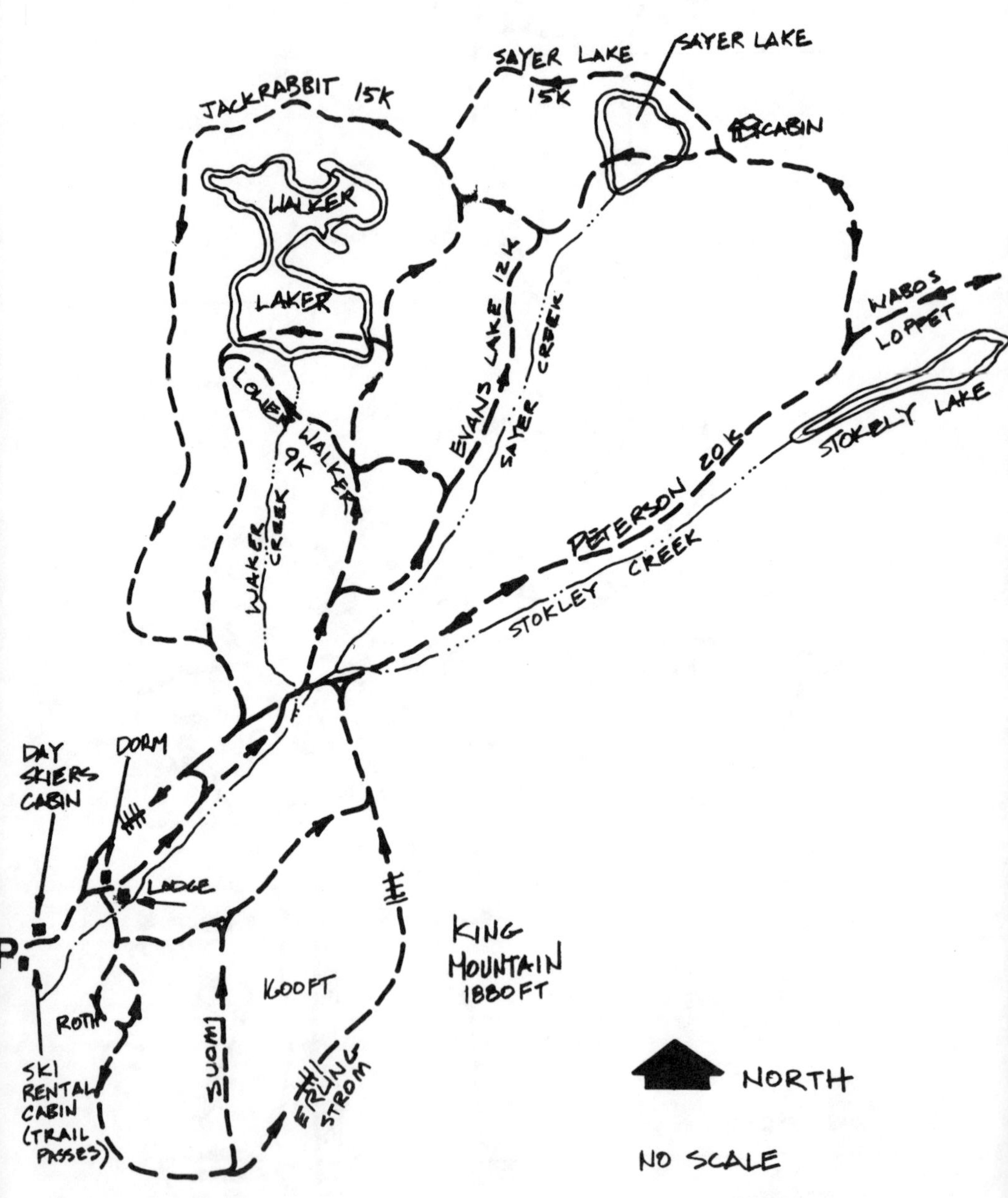

STOKELY CREEK LODGE

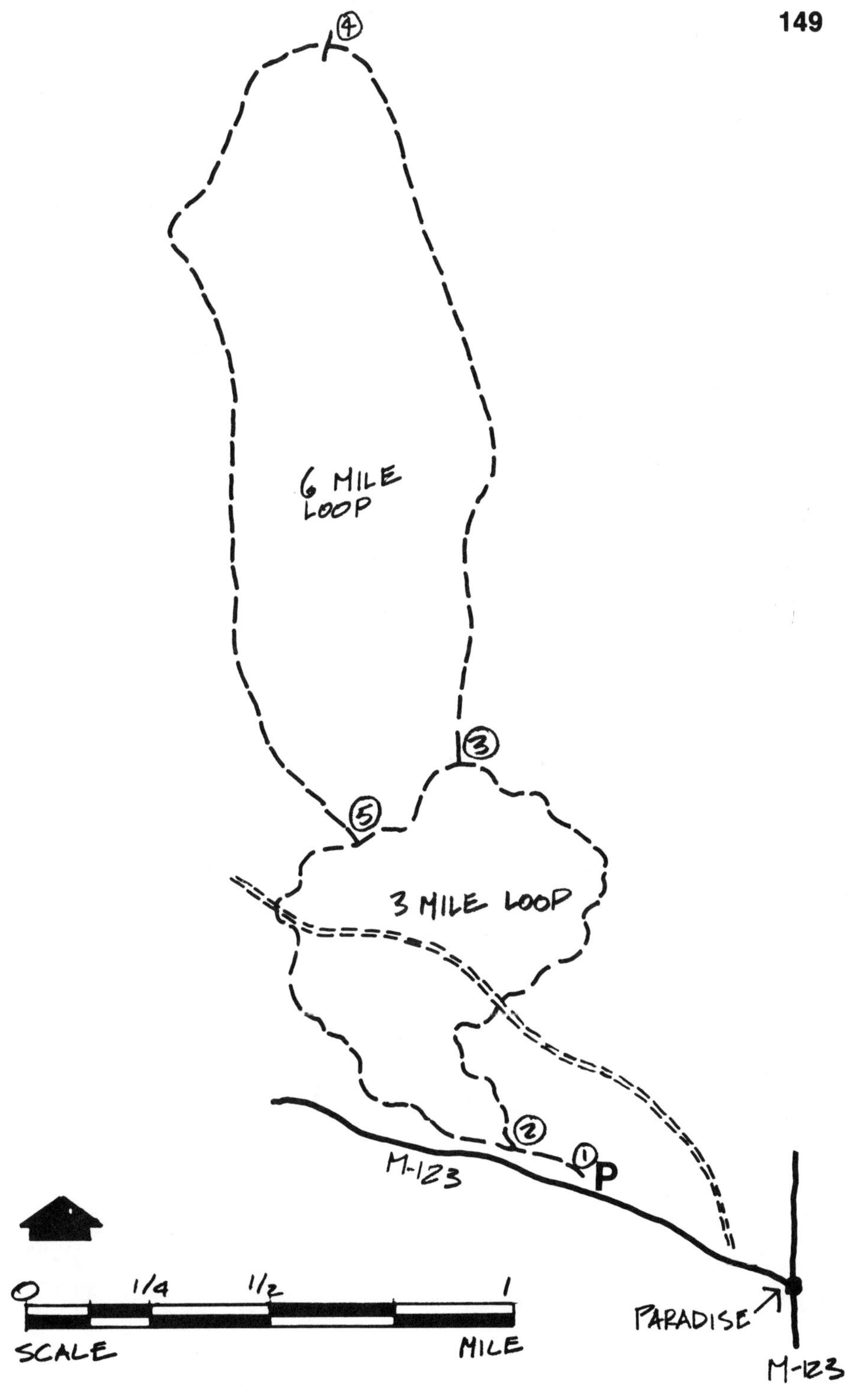

PARADISE PATHWAY

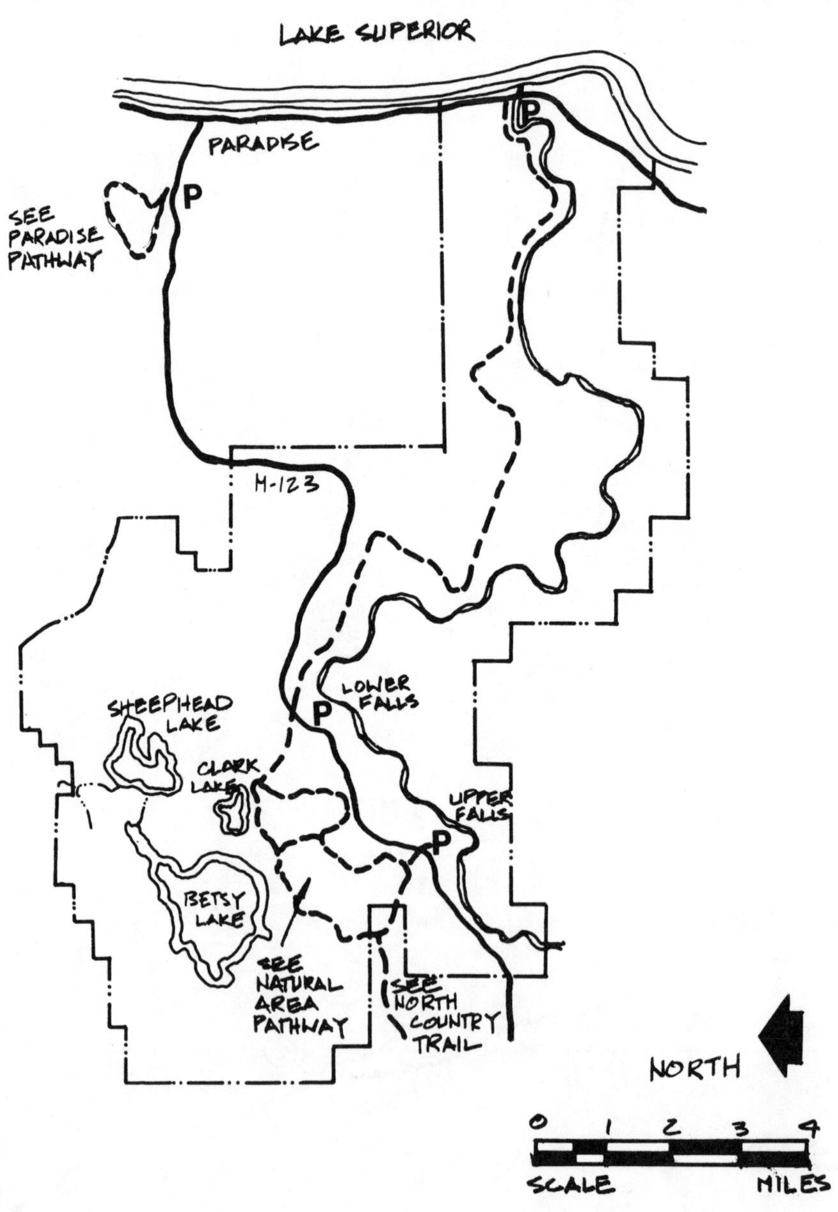

TAHQUAMENON FALLS STATE PARK

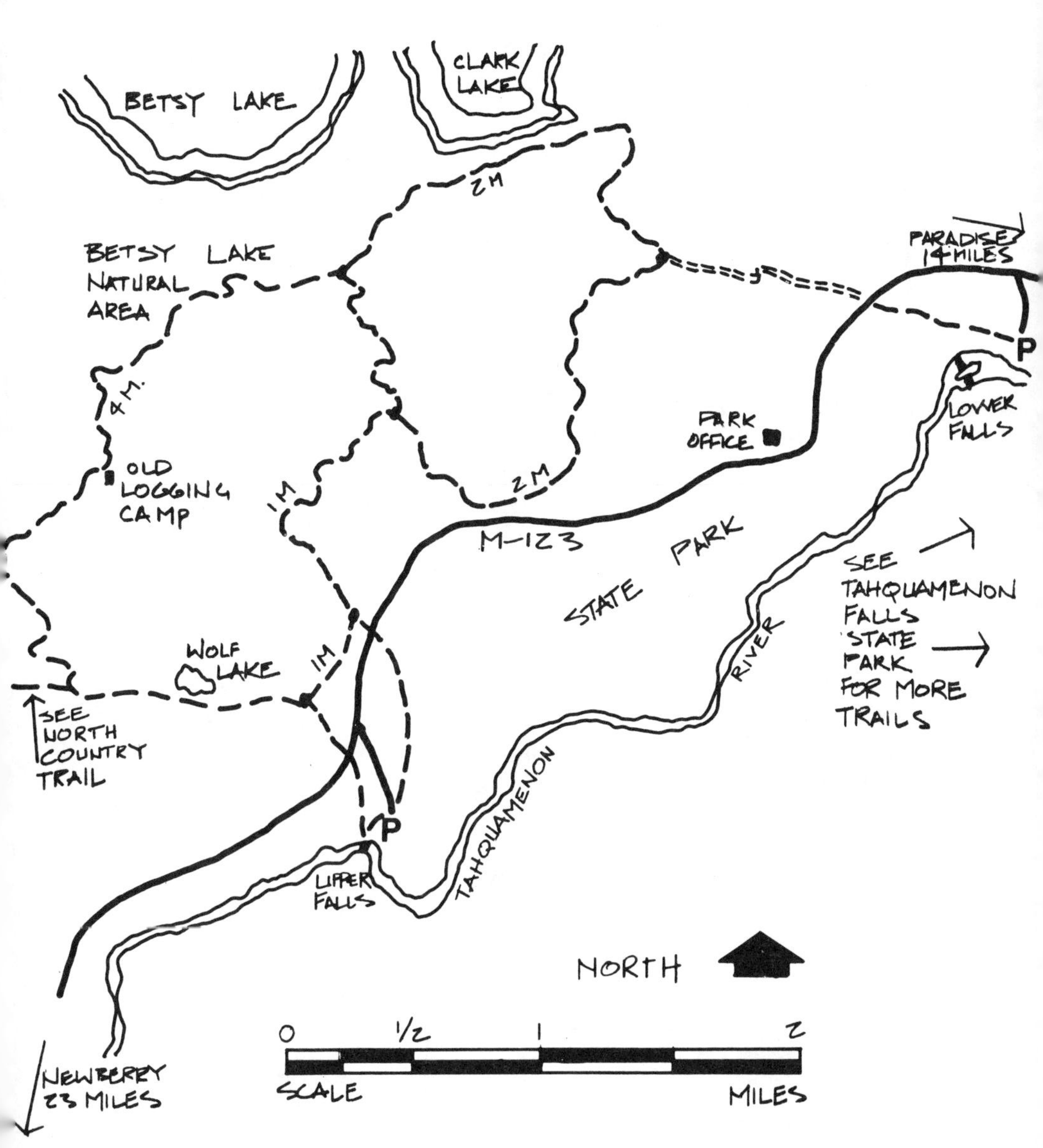

NATURAL AREA PATHWAY
TAHQUAMENON FALLS STATE PARK

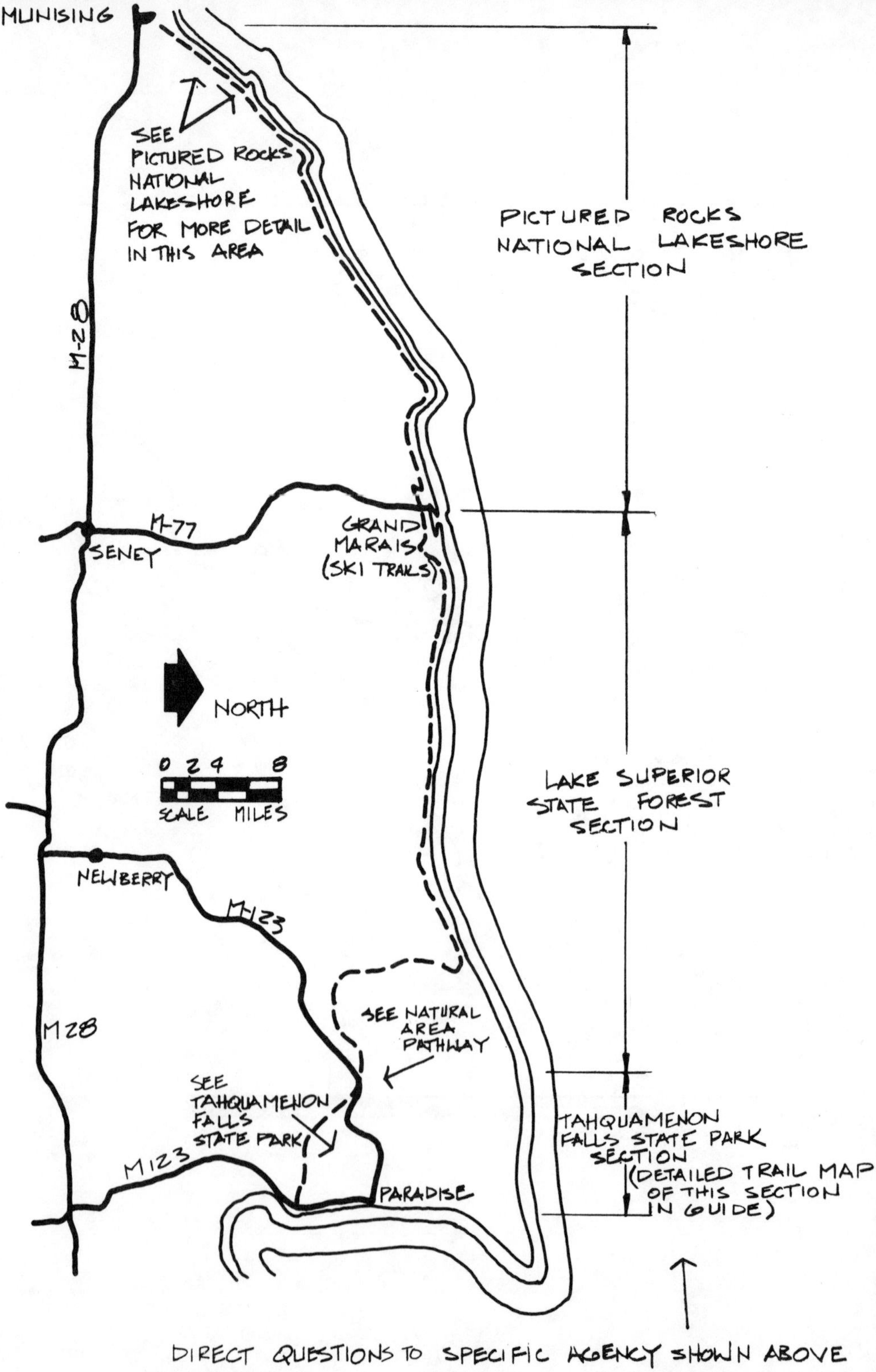

MUNISING

SEE PICTURED ROCKS NATIONAL LAKESHORE FOR MORE DETAIL IN THIS AREA

PICTURED ROCKS NATIONAL LAKESHORE SECTION

M-28

M-77

SENEY

GRAND MARAIS (SKI TRAILS)

NORTH

0 2 4 8

SCALE MILES

LAKE SUPERIOR STATE FOREST SECTION

NEWBERRY

M-123

M28

SEE NATURAL AREA PATHWAY

SEE TAHQUAMENON FALLS STATE PARK

M123

PARADISE

TAHQUAMENON FALLS STATE PARK SECTION (DETAILED TRAIL MAP OF THIS SECTION IN GUIDE)

DIRECT QUESTIONS TO SPECIFIC AGENCY SHOWN ABOVE

NORTH COUNTRY TRAIL

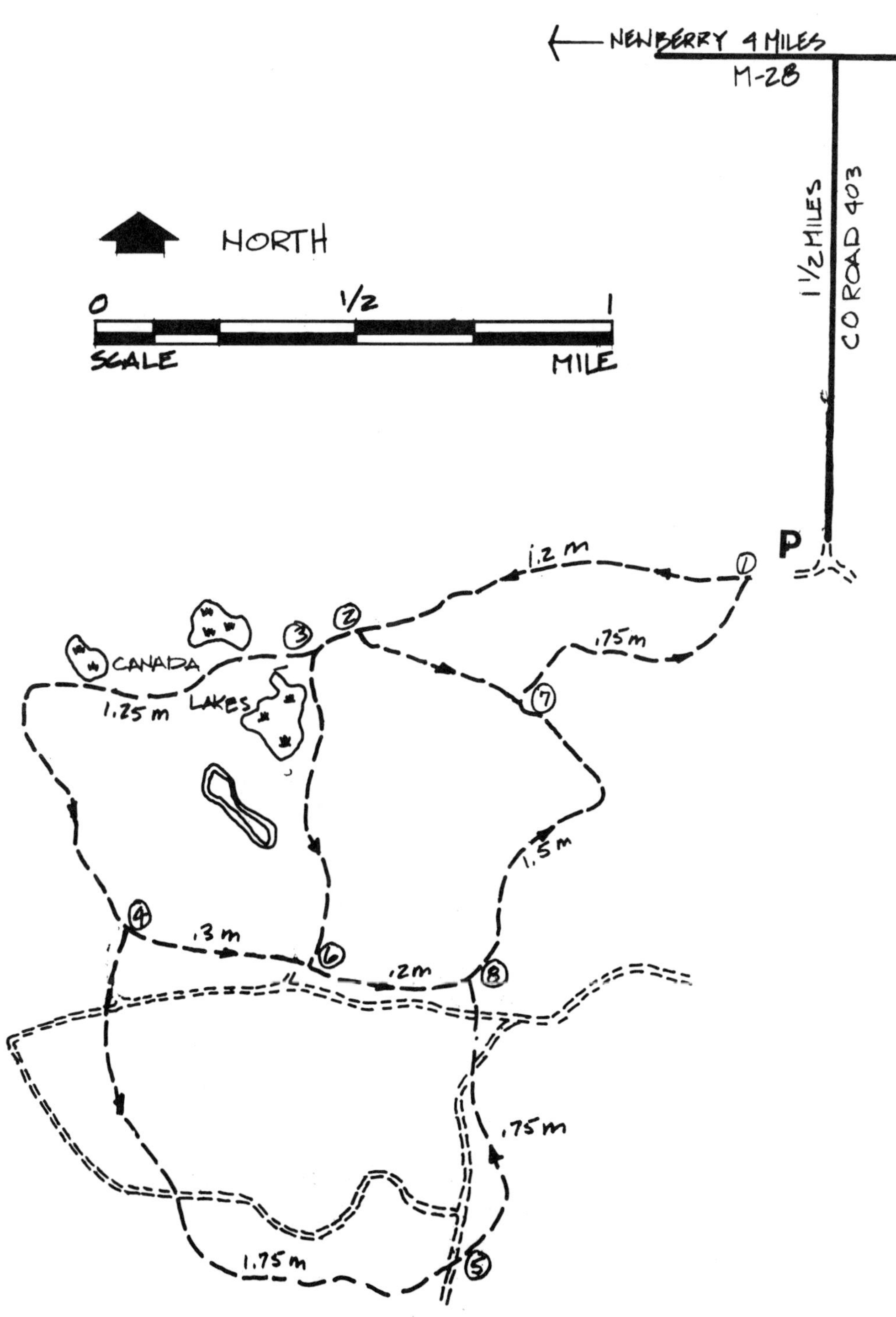

CANADA LAKES PATHWAY

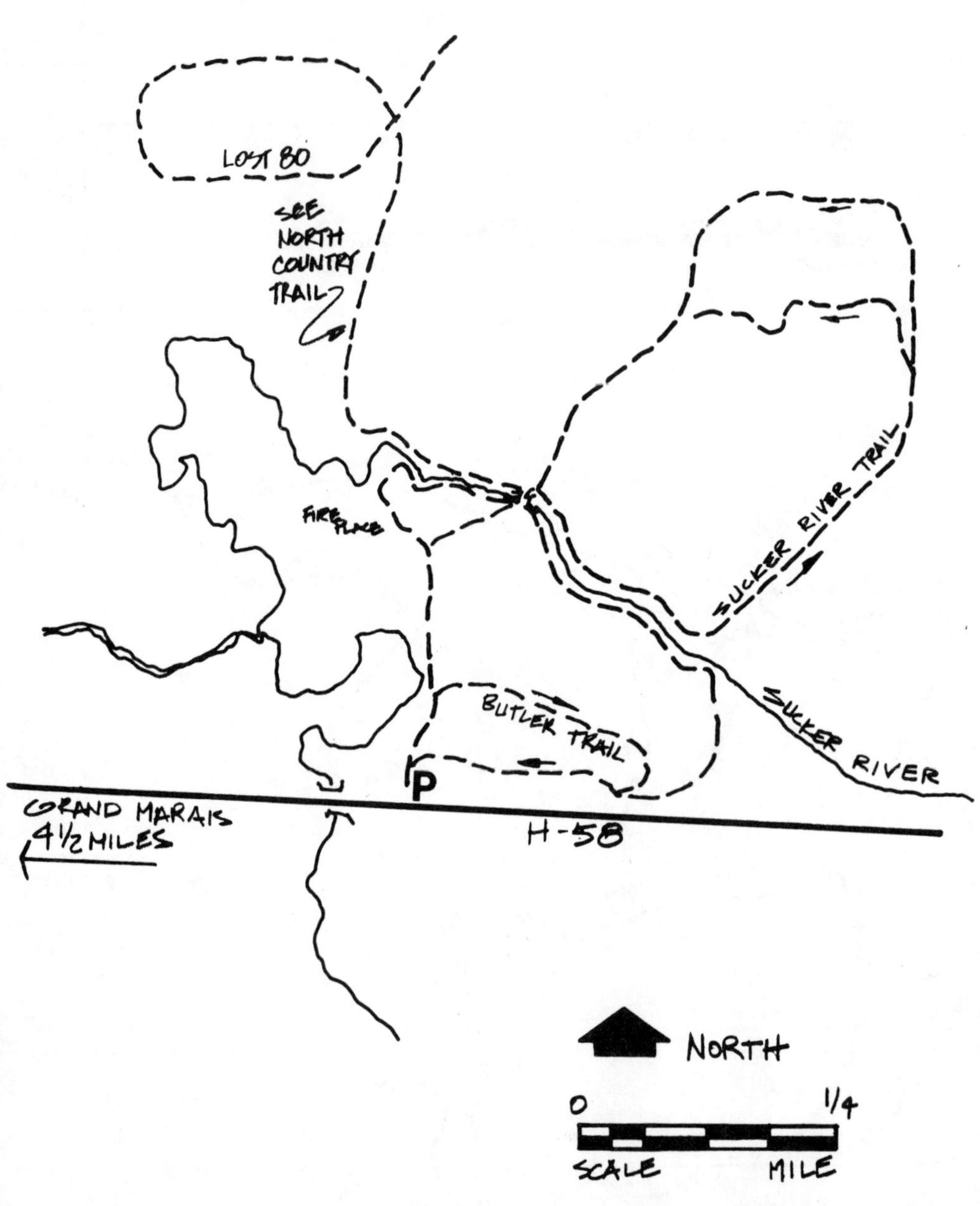

GRAND MARAIS SKI TRAILS

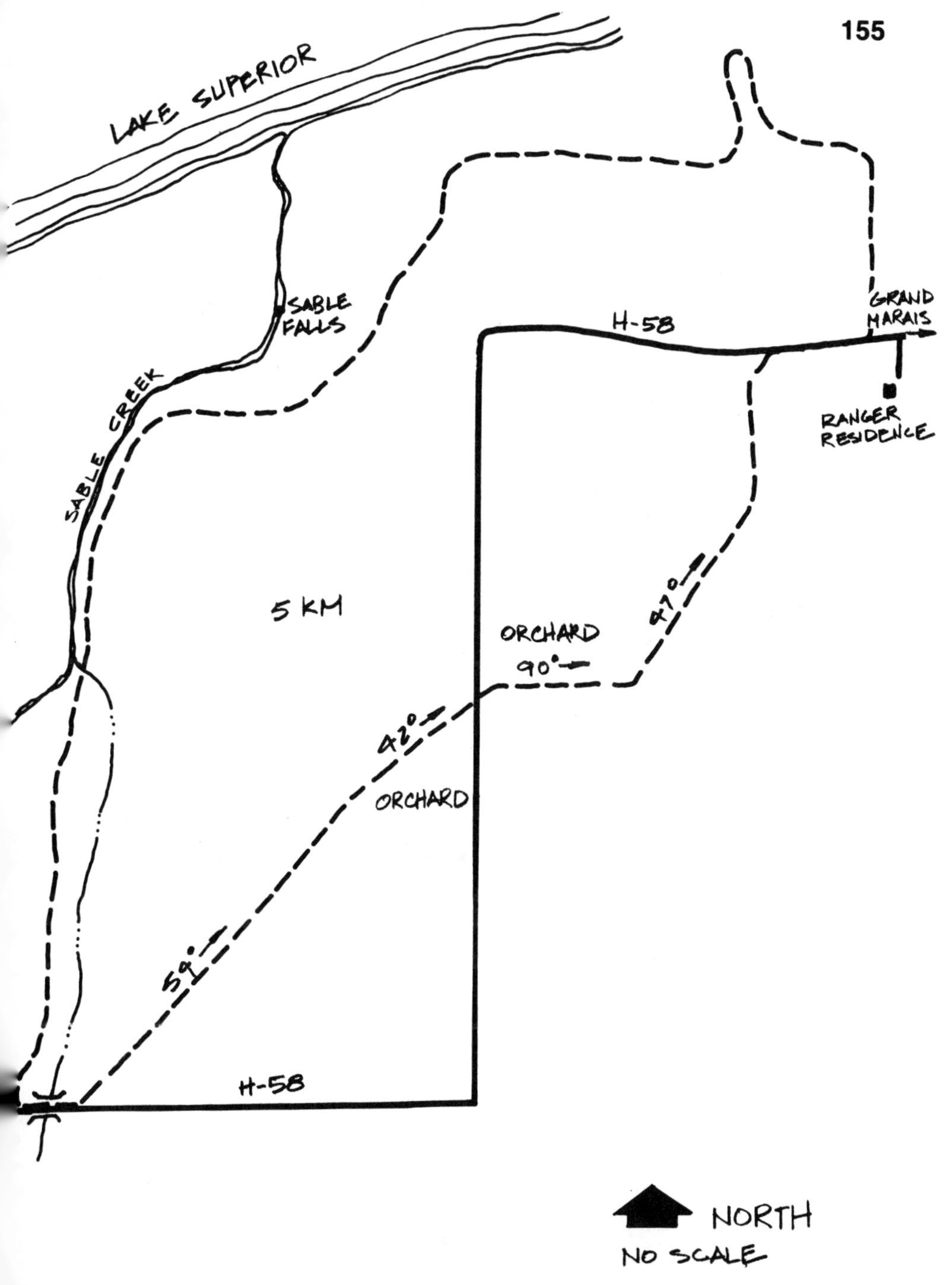

PICTURED ROCKS NATIONAL LAKESHOKE
GRAND MARAIS TRAIL

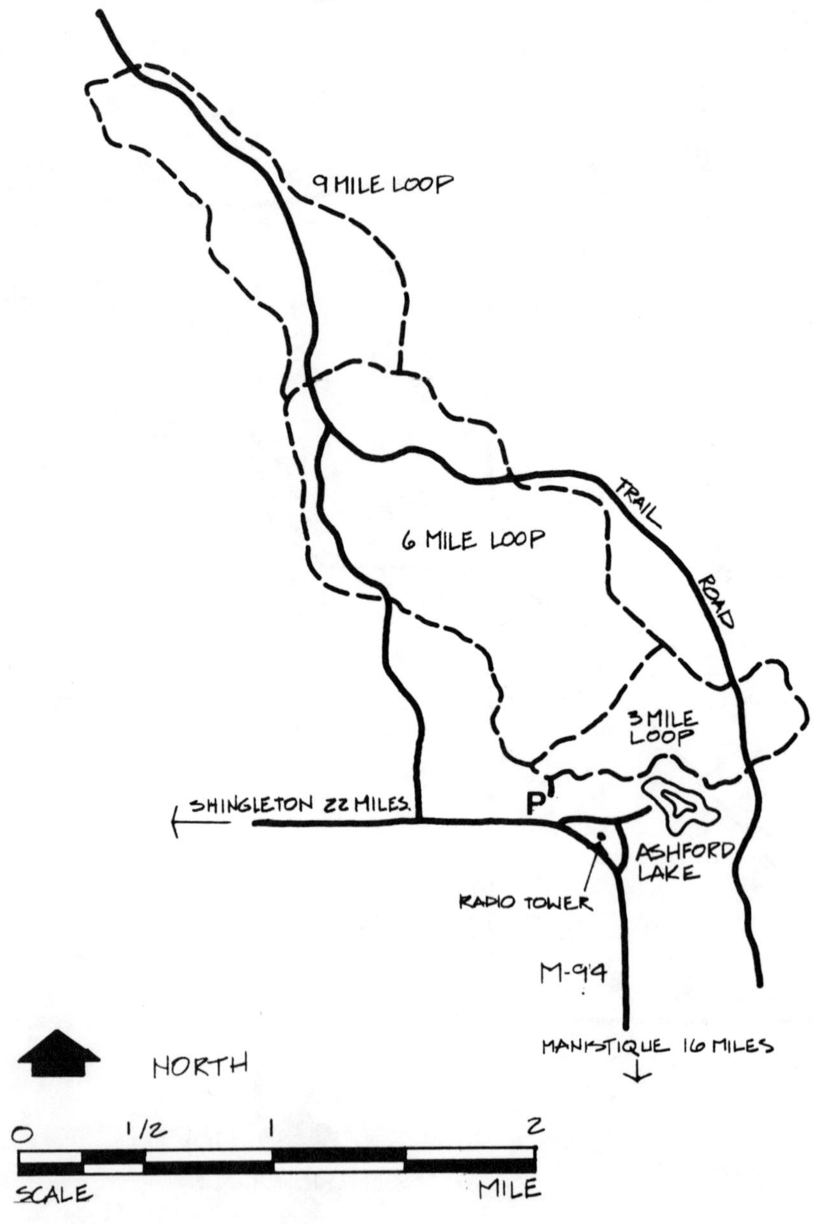

ASHFORD LAKE PATHWAY

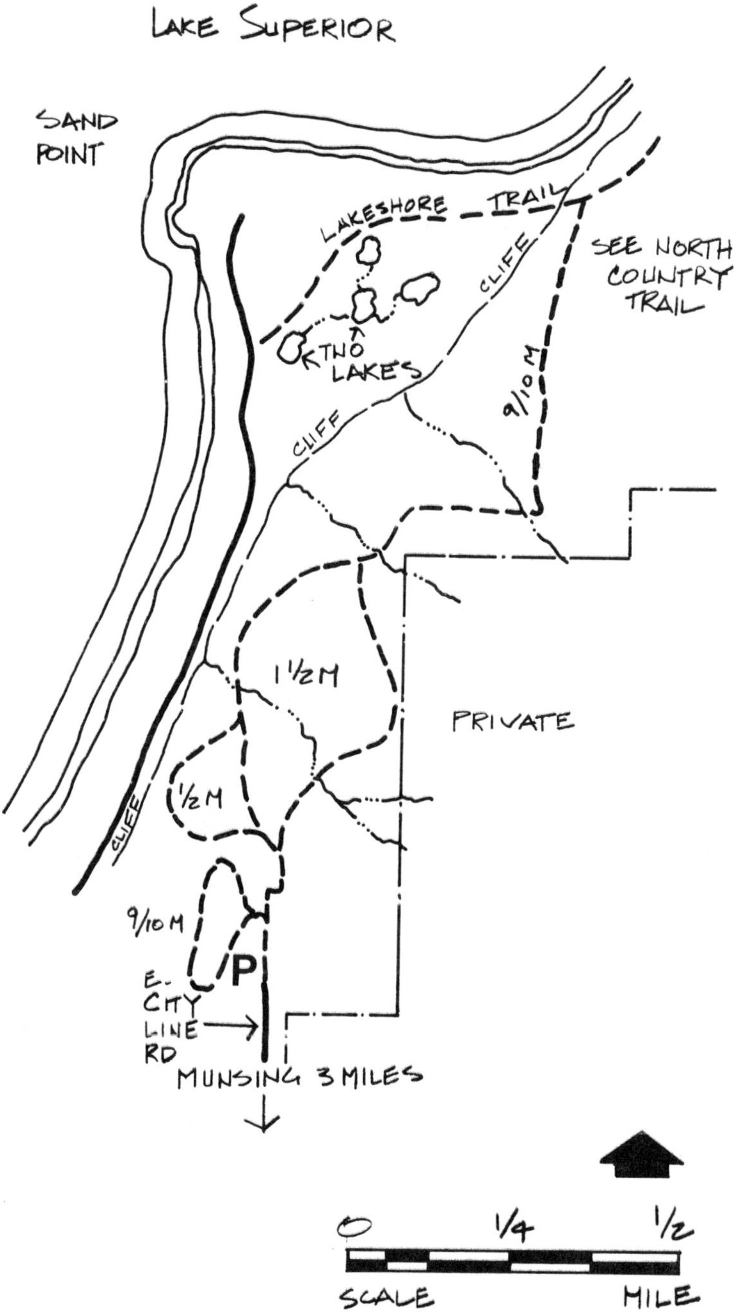
LAKE SUPERIOR
SAND POINT
LAKESHORE TRAIL
CLIFF
SEE NORTH COUNTRY TRAIL
TWO LAKES
9/10 M
CLIFF
1 1/2 M
PRIVATE
1/2 M
CLIFF
9/10 M
P
E. CITY LINE RD
MUNSING 3 MILES
0
1/4
1/2
SCALE
MILE

PICTURED ROCKS NATIONAL LAKESHORE
MUNISING TRAIL

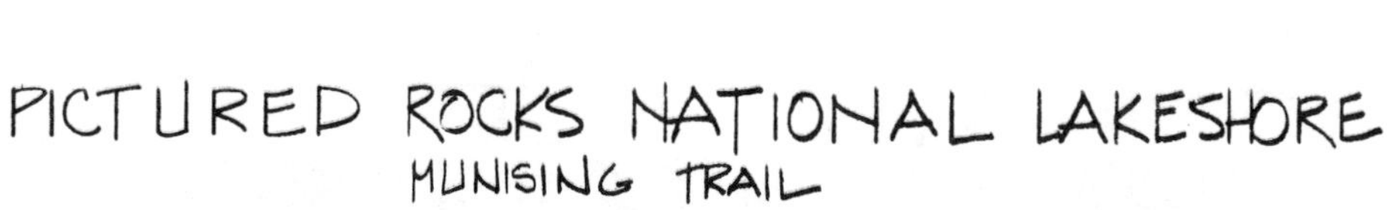

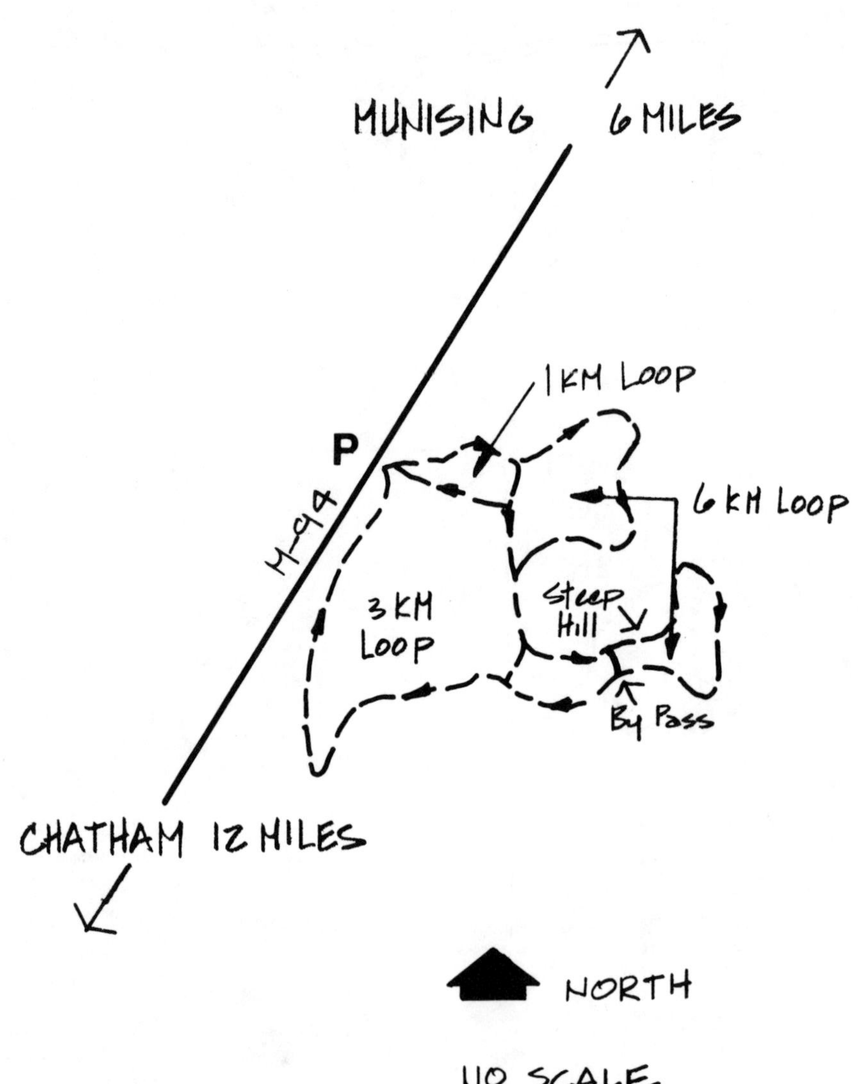

NO SCALE

VALLEY SPUR
CROSS COUNTRY SKI TRAIL

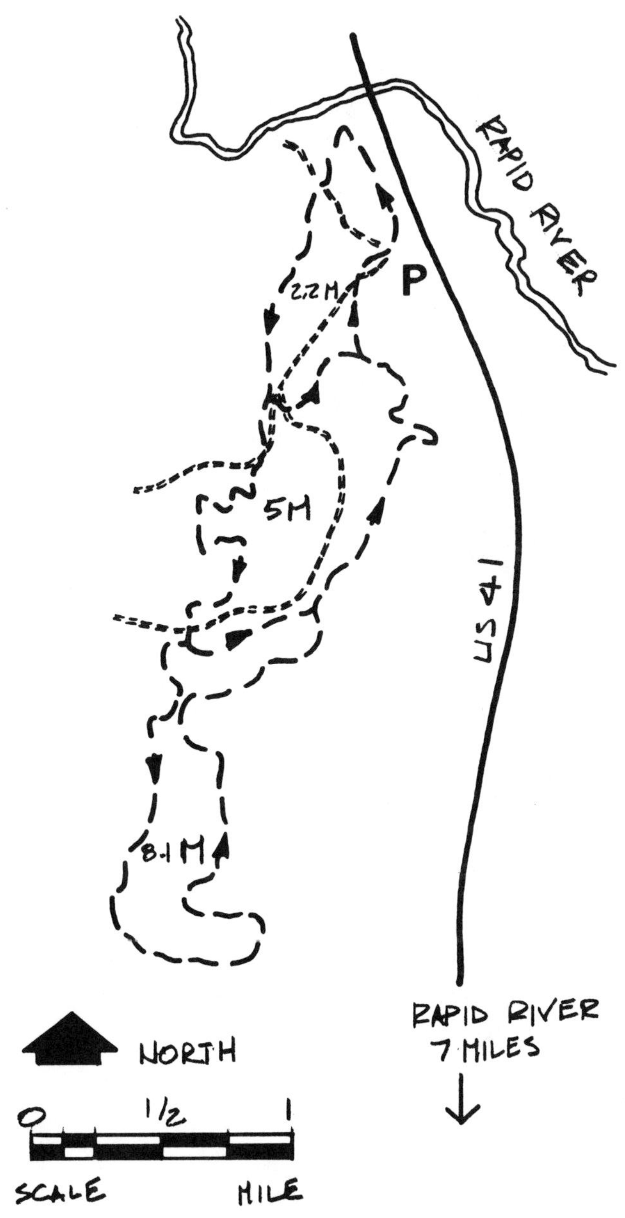

RAPID RIVER
CROSS COUNTRY SKI TRAIL

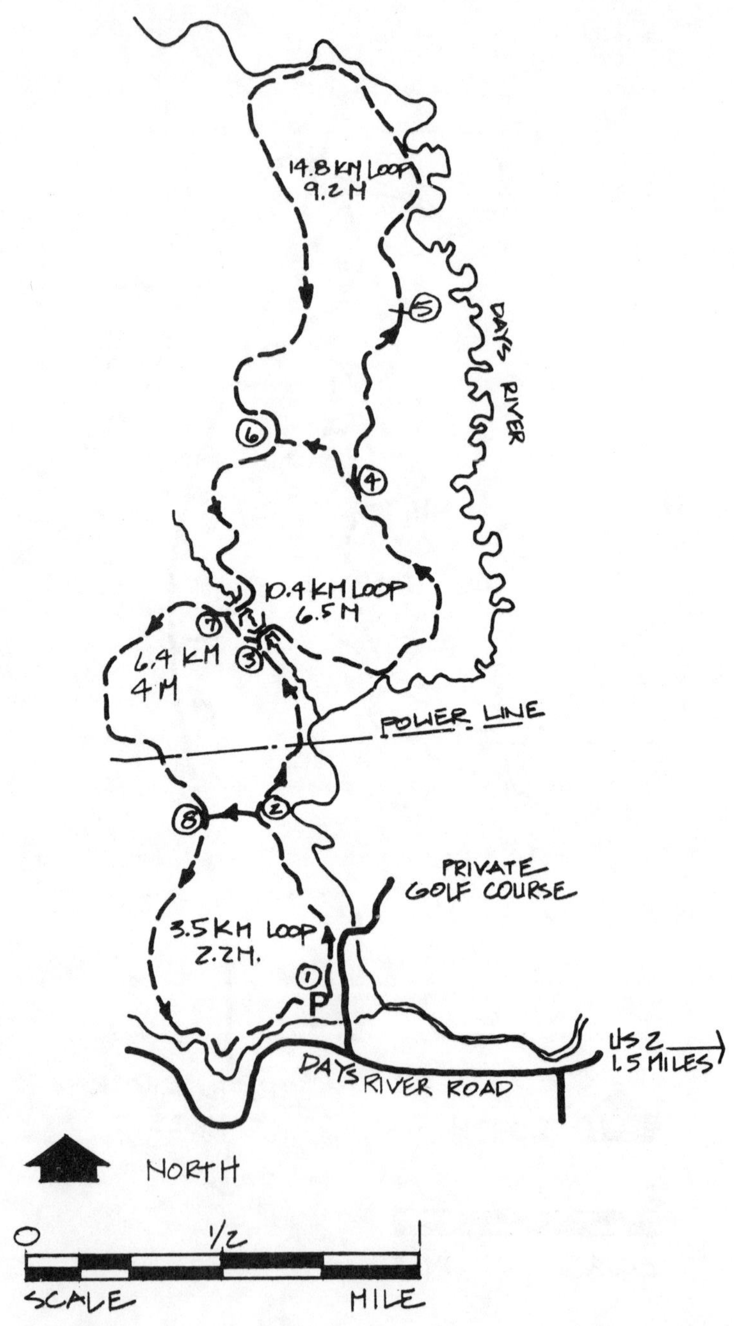

DAYS RIVER PATHWAY

Trail Notes

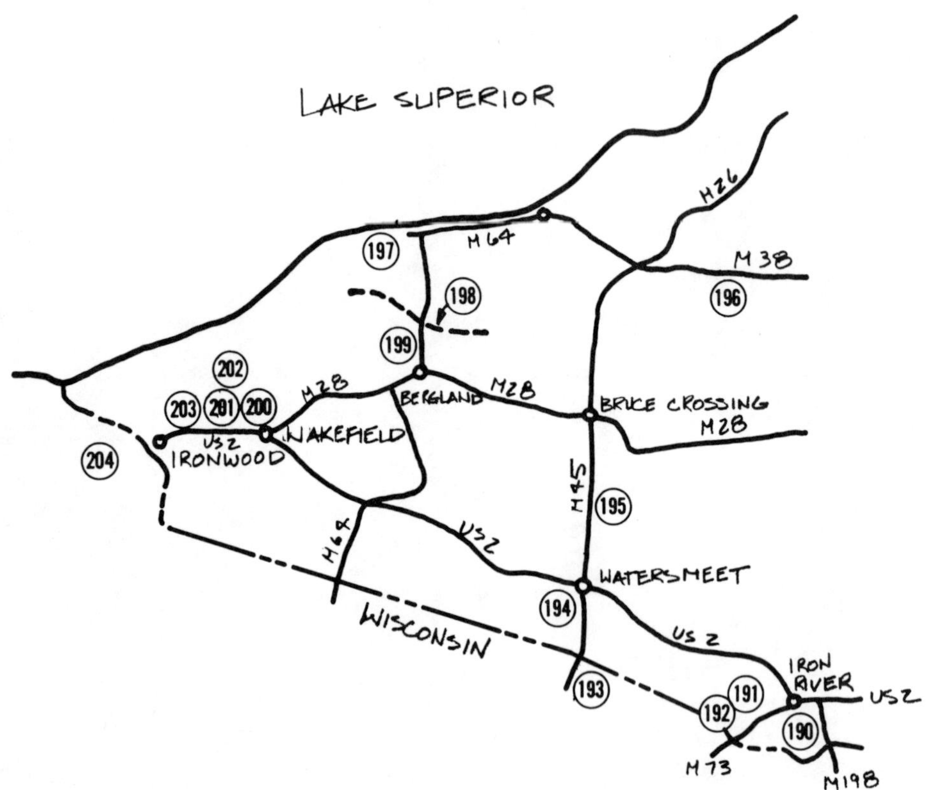
LAKE SUPERIOR
M26
M64
M38
197
198
196
199
202
M28
BERGLAND
M28
BRUCE CROSSING
M28
203
201
200
US2
WAKEFIELD
IRONWOOD
204
M45
195
M64
US2
WATERSMEET
194
WISCONSIN
US 2
193
IRON RIVER
191
192
US2
190
M73
M198

Region Four

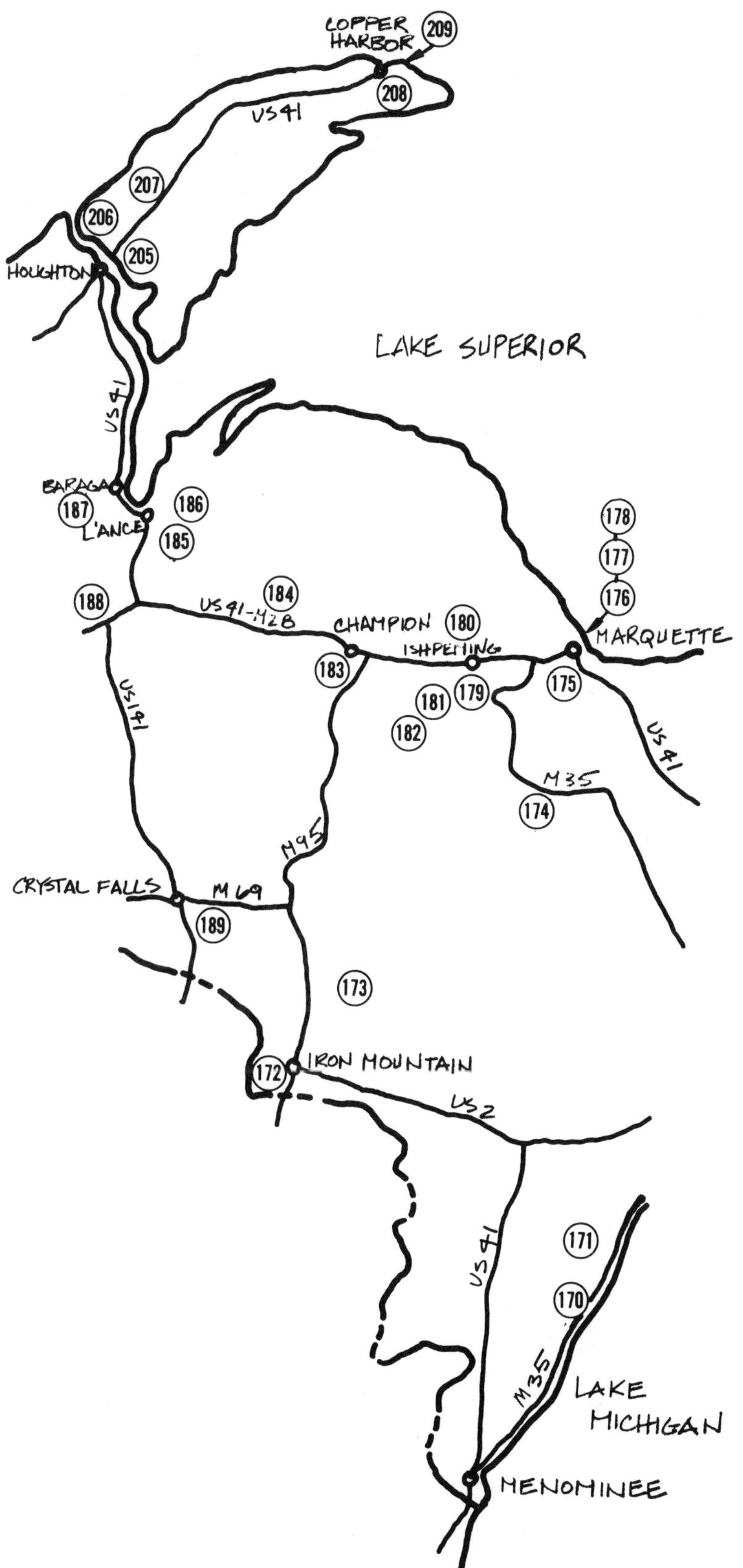

COPPER HARBOR
209
208
US41
207
206
205
HOUGHTON
LAKE SUPERIOR
US41
BARAGA
187
186
L'ANCE
185
178
177
176
188
184
US41-M28
CHAMPION
180
MARQUETTE
ISHPEMING
183
179
175
181
182
US191
US 41
M35
174
M95
CRYSTAL FALLS
M69
189
173
172
IRON MOUNTAIN
US2
US41
171
170
M35
LAKE MICHIGAN
MENOMINEE

REGION 4 WEST HALF OF THE UPPER PENINSULA

TRAIL MAP NUMBER	Name	Location	Number of Loops Distances (miles)	Total length of System (miles)	Maintained in the Winter	Total Acres
170	Wells State Park 906-863-9747	1 mile SW of Cedar River on M35	NA	4	no	300
171	Cedar River Pathway 906-753-6317	7.5 miles north of the town of Cedar River on River Rd (Co Rd 551)	4 loops 2,3.5,5,7	11	no	1000
172	Pine Mountain 906-774-2747	1.5 miles NW of Iron Mountain	2 loops 5, 5 km	10km	yes	40
173	Merriman East Pathway 906-353-6653	NE of Merriman 7 miles via M95 and Merriman East Truck Trail	2 loops 3.3,5.6	9	no	un-limited
174	Anderson Lake Pathway 906-346-0486	5 miles SW of Gwinn on Co Rd 557	4 loops	6	no	un-limited
175	Blueberry Ridge Pathway 906-485-4193	6 miles south of Marquette via Co Rd 553 at Co Rd 480	3 loops 2.5,5, 8.5	9	no	700
176	Cliffs Ridge Ski Area 906-225-0486	In the City of Marquette, 2 miles from Lake Superior on Co Rd 553	1 loop	4.5	no	NA
177	Park Cemetery City of Marquette 906-228-8200	In Marquette, north of Business US41 via Seymour Ave at Ridge St	2 loops	2.2km	yes	40
178	Presque Isle Park, City of Marquette 906-228-8200	3 miles north of downtown Marquette on Lakeshore Blvd	1 loop	3.2km	yes	60
179	Suicide Bowl 906-485-1746	Between Negaunee and Ishpeming on BR M28	4 loops 2.5,5,7.5, 10 km	NA	yes	NA
180	Al Quaal Recreation Area 906-486-6181 906-486-6581	Adjacent to the National Ski Hall of Fame on US41	4 loops 1 to 7	NA	NA	NA

P —Pro Shop S —Snack Bar
R —Rentals D —Dining Room
W—Warming Area B —Brown Bag
C —Certified Instruction A —Accommodations

Novice	Intermediate	Expert	Terrain	Trail Use Fee	Campground	Remarks	TRAIL MAP PAGE
	√	√	flat to rolling		√	Good trails for training	**none**
√	√	√	flat to rolling		√	Campground not plowed at trail Trail follows the Cedar River Wells State Park (1.5 miles south of Cedar River) has complete facilities	**174**
	√	√	rolling to hilly			P,R,W,S,D,B,A Privately operated alpine ski area with 90m ski jump Trail groomed with a double track weekly	**none**
√	√		rolling				**175**
√	√		flat to rolling			Interpretive trail around Flack Lakes	**176**
√	√		flat to slightly hilly			Snowmobile trail passes through area	**177**
	√	√	rolling	√	√	P,R,S,B,D Privately operated alpine ski area Campground nearby	**none**
√	√		rolling			Trail groomed 3 times each week Managed by Marquette Parks & Recreation Department	**178**
√			rolling			Trail groomed weekly Managed by Marquette Parks & Recreation Department	**179**
√	√	√	rolling to extremely difficult hills			Nordic training center and USSA race course Operated by the Ishpeming Ski Club Very demanding course—not for the beginner The 2.5 km trail is lighted	**180**
√	√		rolling to hilly			W,S Winter recreation area operated by the City of Ishpeming	**none**

REGION 4 WEST HALF OF THE UPPER PENINSULA

TRAIL MAP NUMBER	Name	Location	Number of Loops Distances (miles)	Total length of System (miles)	Maintained in the Winter	Total Acres
181	Cleveland Cross-Country Ski Trail 906-486-6273	At the end of Hill St in Ishpeming, 1 mile west of the Suicide Bowl	2 loops 3.5,5km	5.1km	yes	NA
182	Black River Falls Pathway 906-485-4193	8 miles south of Ishpeming via Co Rd 581	3 loops 2.5,5,8	9.5	no	1000
183	Champion Rossignol Ski Touring Center 906-339-2294	One block south of US 41 on M95	5 loops 1,1.5, 3.5,5, 5 km	16km	yes	200
184	McCormick Experimental Forest	10 miles north of US41 at Champion on the Huron Bay Grade (Co Rd 607)	not looped	3.5+	no	14000
184	Craig Lake State Park 906-339-4461	2 miles west of Michigamme on US 41 at Craig Lake Rd	not looped	15+	no	10000
185	Laws Lake Ski Trails 906-524-6518	4.5 miles SE of L'Anse via US41 on Herman Rd at Laws Lake Rd	2 loops 4,5 km	9km	yes	500
186	Indian Cemetery Ski Area 906-524-6518	4 miles NE of L'Anse via Indian Cemetery Rd	3 loops 2,3.5 4.5km	10	yes	1000
187	Six Mile Creek Pathway 906-353-6651	4.5 miles SW of Baraga (US41) on Six Mile Creek Rd (Baraga Plains Rd)	3 loops 4.8,11.1, 14.9 km	15km	yes	1500
188	P.A.C. Ski Trail 906-353-6651	2 miles NW of Covington at the Ponnistoos Athletic Club	1 loop	5km	yes	240

P —Pro Shop
R —Rentals
W—Warming Area
C —Certified Instruction
S —Snack Bar
D —Dining Room
B —Brown Bag
A —Accommodations

Novice	Intermediate	Expert	Terrain	Trail Use Fee	Campground	Remarks	TRAIL MAP PAGE
√	√		rolling to hilly			All trails maintained with a track setter Excellent trail built and maintained by Norman Juhola	**181**
√	√		gently rolling			Trail crosses Black River	**182**
√	√	√	flat to hilly		√	P,R,W,B,S Privately operated nordic ski area Camping available at Michigamme Shores private campground, 906-339-2216 Trails groomed 3 times weekly	**183**
	√	√	rolling			No development at this time For experienced skiers only Additional skiing possible to White Deer and Bull Dog Lakes Wilderness area of virgin forest with many lakes, streams and rock outcrops	**184**
	√	√	rolling		√	Unadministered state park No development at this time For experienced skiers only Camping at Michigamme Shores private campground, 906-339-2116 Contact Champion Nordic Ski Shop for complete pro shop service, 906-339-2294	**184**
	√		rolling			Developed by the Young Adult Conservation Corps. Trails groomed weekly Complete ski shop services available at Indian Country Sales in L'Anse, 906-524-6518	**185**
√	√	√	rolling to hilly			Developed by the Young Adult Conservation Corps Trail groomed weekly Complete ski shop services are available at Indian Country Sales in L'Anse	**186**
	√		rolling			Trail groomed weekly Complete ski shop services are available at Indian Country Sales in L'Anse Heavily wooded trail	**187**
	√		rolling			Trail groomed weekly Complete ski shop services are available at Indian Country Sales in L'Anse	**188**

REGION 4 — WEST HALF OF THE UPPER PENINSULA

TRAIL MAP NUMBER	Name	Location	Number of Loops Distances (miles)	Total length of System (miles)	Maintained in the Winter	Total Acres
189	Lake Mary Plains Pathway 906-875-6622	4 miles east of Crystal Falls on M69, then south one mile to Glidden Lake State Forest Campground	2 loops 3.4,6.2	9	no	unlimited
190	Brule Mountain 906-265-4957	6 miles SW of Iron River	5 loops 1.5,3,3, 3,5km	20km	yes	960
191	GE-CHE Trail 906-265-5139	West of Iron River on US2, then south on M73 for one mile, then west on USFS101	2 loops	8km	yes	unlimited
192	Hagerman-Brule Ski Trail 906-265-5139	8 miles SW of Iron River via M73 and USFS 102 (Hagerman Lake Rd) to trail head at Covenant Point	many	3km 14	yes	2000
193	Gateway Ski Area 715-547-3321	On US45 at the Wisconsin River, 2 miles south of Michigan in Wisconsin	many	30km	yes	NA
194	Sylvania Recreation Area and vicinity 906-358-4551	Between Watersmeet and Land-O-Lakes, WI west of US95	several some not looped	38 +	yes	unlimited
195	Limberlost Ski Area 906-827-3708	4 miles east of Paulding in Bond Falls Rd	3 loops	9	yes	2200

P —Pro Shop
R —Rentals
W—Warming Area
C —Certified Instruction

S —Snack Bar
D —Dining Room
B —Brown Bag
A —Accommodations

Novice	Intermediate	Expert	Terrain	Trail Use Fee	Campground	Remarks	TRAIL MAP PAGE
✓	✓		flat to rolling		✓		**189**
✓	✓		flat to rolling	✓		P,R,W,S,D,B,A Privately operated alpine ski area Campground at the ski area All trails are double tracked	**190**
✓	✓	✓	rolling to hilly		✓	Managed by the USFS Iron River District Trail connects with the Hagerman-Brule Ski Trail	**191**
✓	✓	✓	rolling to hilly			P,R,W,C,S,D,B,A Privately operated nordic ski area at the Covenant Point Bible Camp Group accommodations on weekends only Family accommodations on weekdays only Restaurant on weekends only The Institute holds cross-country ski clinics and ski expeditions. Write for brochure to Upper Peninsula Wilderness Institute, Covenant Point-Hagerman Lake, Iron River, Mi 49935, 906-265-2117 Trail system connects with the GE-CHE Trail Many logging trails available for skiing	**191**
✓	✓	✓	rolling	✓		P,R,W,C,S,A Privately operated alpine ski area with extensive nordic trails Gateway Lodge (800-472-7208) has in-door heated pool, saunas and ice skating rink Trails groomed weekly Site of the Gateway Cup Cross Country Race	**192**
✓	✓	✓	rolling to hilly		✓	P,R,W,C,B at Sylvania Outfitters, one mile west of Watersmeet on US2, 906-358-4766 W,S,D,A at Pineaire Lodge, south of Waters-meet on US45 9 mile trail connects Sylvania Outfitters with the Pineaire Lodge Campgrounds in the area are ski in only Citizen race at Sylvania Outfitters Guide service available at Sylvania Outfitters	**193**
✓	✓		rolling to hilly		✓	P,R,W,S,B at Limberlost Ski Shop on Bond Falls Rd Motel in Paulding, 4 miles Beautiful falls	**194**

REGION 4 WEST HALF OF THE UPPER PENINSULA

TRAIL MAP NUMBER	Name	Location	Number of Loops Distances (miles)	Total length of System (miles)	Maintained in the Winter	Total Acres
196	Old Grade Ski Trail 906-884-2411	7 miles west of Nisula on M38 at Courtney Lake Recreation Area access road	2 loops 1.8,3.9	4	no	500
197	Porcupine Mountains Wilderness State Park 906-885-5798	17 miles west of Ontonagon via M64 and M107 at the alpine ski slopes	3 loops 4,7,9	16 +	yes	unlimited
198	Trapp Falls Section—North Country Trail 906-575-3441		point to point	74km	no	unlimited
199	Gogebic Ridge Trail 906-575-3441	North of Bergland on M64	point to point	14km	no	unlimited
200	Indianhead Mountain 906-229-5181	1.5 miles west of Wakefield via US2	6 loops .5,.8,1.2, 2,3.2,3.5	10km	yes	NA
201	Snowcrest-Blackjack 906-667-0587	Blackjack alpine ski area or Snowcrest Lodge, between Wakefield and Bessemer north of US2	5 loops 2,3,4,8, 13 km	32km	yes	480
202	Circle Hills Resort 906-932-3857	4 miles east of Ironwood via US2, then north on Big Powderhorn Rd 5 miles	6 loops	11km	yes	150
203	Wolverine Ski Trail 906-932-4465 906-932-4470	West of Iron Mountain on US2 1 mile, then north 1.25 miles then east .5 mile to Wolverine Ski Jumping Hill	several	11.5km	yes	NA
204	Whitecap Mountain 715-561-2227	15 miles west of Ironwood in Wisconsin, Rte 77	6 loops 1,3,5,10, 15,25km	40km	yes	NA
205	Mont Ripley 906-487-2340	½ mile east of Hancock on M26	1 loop	5km	yes	NA
206	McLain State Park 906-482-0278	7 miles west of Calumet on M203	1 loop	3	yes	400

P —Pro Shop
R —Rentals
W—Warming Area
C —Certified Instruction
S —Snack Bar
D —Dining Room
B —Brown Bag
A —Accommodations

Novice	Intermediate	Expert	Terrain	Trail Use Fee	Campground	Remarks	TRAIL MAP PAGE
√			gently rolling			Additional unmarked trails in area Managed by the USFS Ontonagon District	**195**
√	√	√	flat to hilly		√	P,R,W,S at the alpine ski lodge Plowed campsites available on request Unplowed campsites along the trail	**196**
		√	hilly			Managed by USFS Bergland District Trail designed for hiking but can be skied by experienced skiers	**197**
	√	√	ridge with some steep hills			Managed by USFS Bergland District Trail follows old Lake Gogebic Iron River Indian Trail to North Country Trail	**198**
√	√	√	flat to hilly			P,R,W,C,S,D,B,A Privately operated alpine ski area Trails groomed after each snowfall	**199**
√	√	√	flat to hilly			P,R,W,C,S,D,B,A Privately operated lodge and alpine ski area	**200**
√	√		flat to hilly		√	P,R,W,C,S,D,A Privately operated resort Complete resort facilities including an in-door pool and sauna	**none**
√	√	√	rolling to hilly			Built and maintained by the Wolverine Ski Jumping Hill Committee Excellent training trail	**201**
√	√	√	flat to hilly		√	P,R,W,C,S,D,B,A Privately operated alpine ski area with major nordic trail system Trails designed by Swen Wiik	**202**
√	√		flat to rolling			P,R,W,S Privately operated alpine ski area by Michigan Technological University	**none**
√	√		flat to gently roliing		√	Trail designed for cross country skiing	**203**

REGION 4 WEST HALF OF THE UPPER PENINSULA

TRAIL MAP NUMBER	Name	Location	Number of Loops Distances (miles)	Total length of System (miles)	Maintained in the Winter	Total Acres
207	Swedetown Ski Trails 906-337-4520	One mile west of US41 at Calumet. Follow signs	5 loops 2,3,5, 5,7.5	20km	yes	NA
208	Copper Harbor Pathway 906-353-6653	West end of Lake Fanny Hooe on Clark Mine Rd	3 loops	11.9km	yes	NA
209	Fort Wilkins State Park 906-289-4215	On US41 east of Copper Harbor	2 loops	2	yes	200

P —Pro Shop　S —Snack Bar
R —Rentals　D —Dining Room
W—Warming Area　B —Brown Bag
C —Certified Instruction　A —Accommodations

Novice	Intermediate	Expert	Terrain	Trail Use Fee	Campground	Remarks	TRAIL MAP PAGE
√	√		flat to rolling			P,R,C at the TV Sport Center, 507 Oak St, Calumet, 337-4520 Trail system built and maintained by Copper Island X-C Ski Club All trails groomed with a track setter Shelter available at trail head	**204**
	√	√	rolling to hilly	√		Trails groomed with a track setter	**205**
√			flat	√		R,W,S,B,A At Lake Fanny Hooe Resort and Campground 906-289-4451 Trail is along Lake Fanny Hooe and through the fort area	**206**

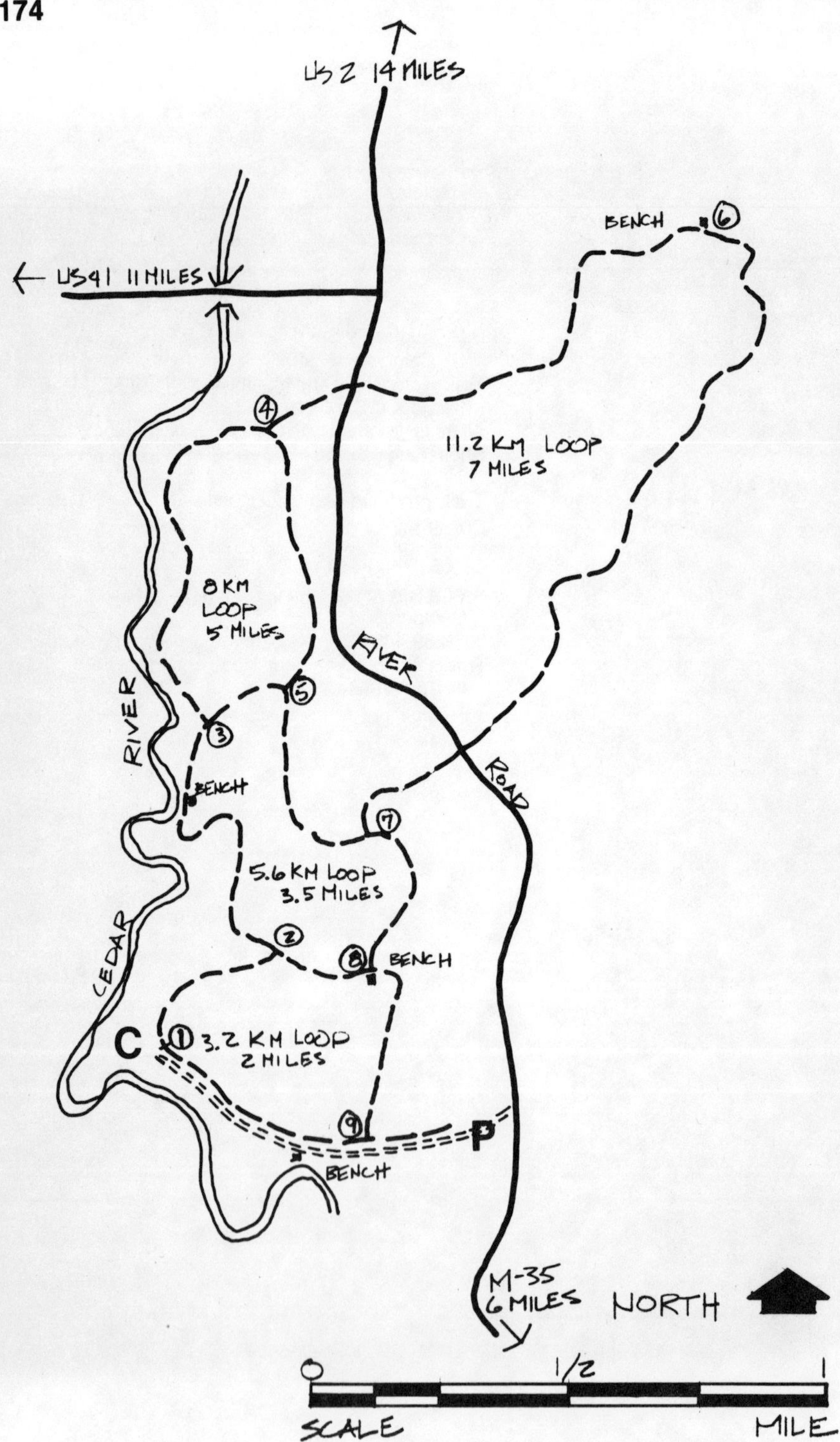

CEDAR RIVER PATHWAY

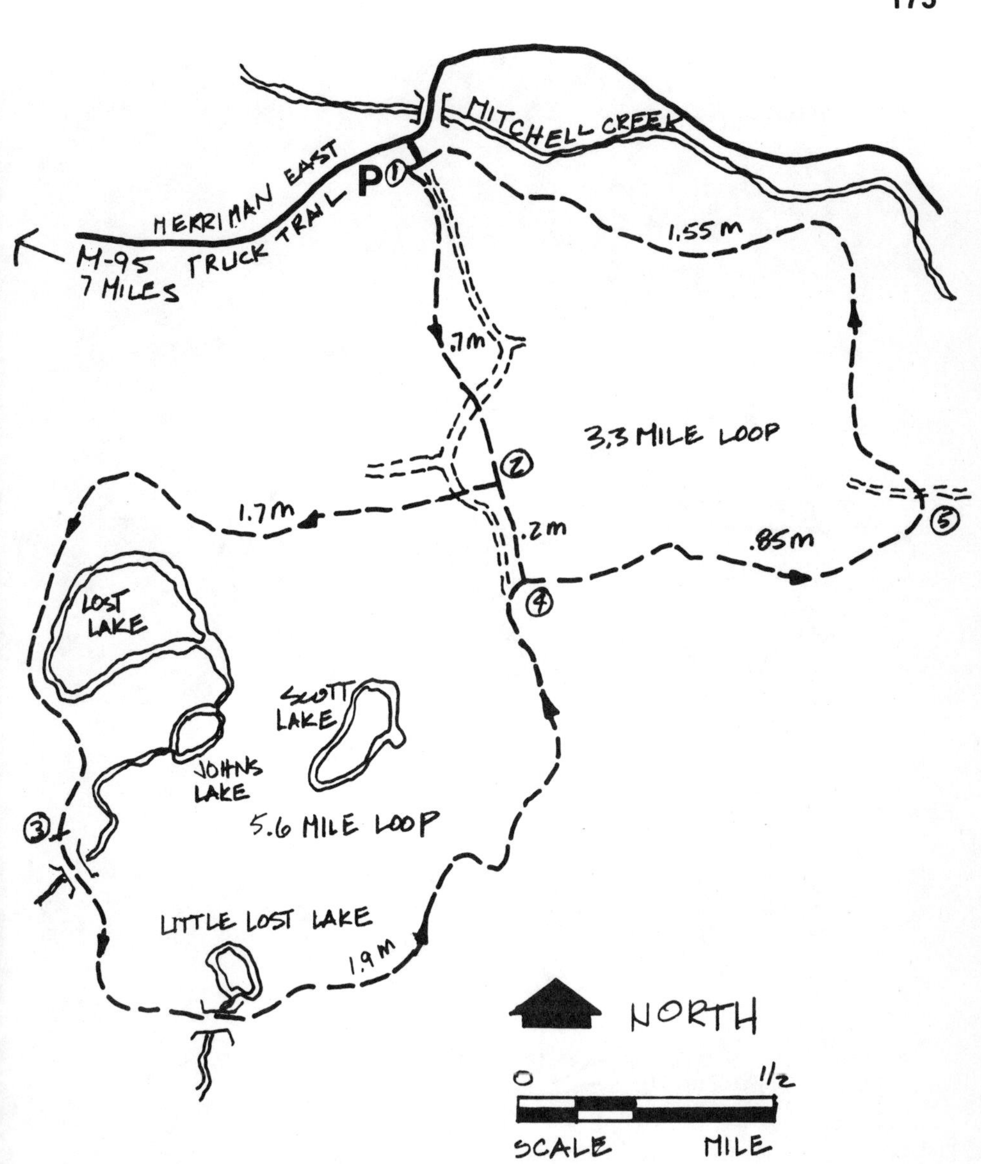

MERRIMAN EAST PATHWAY

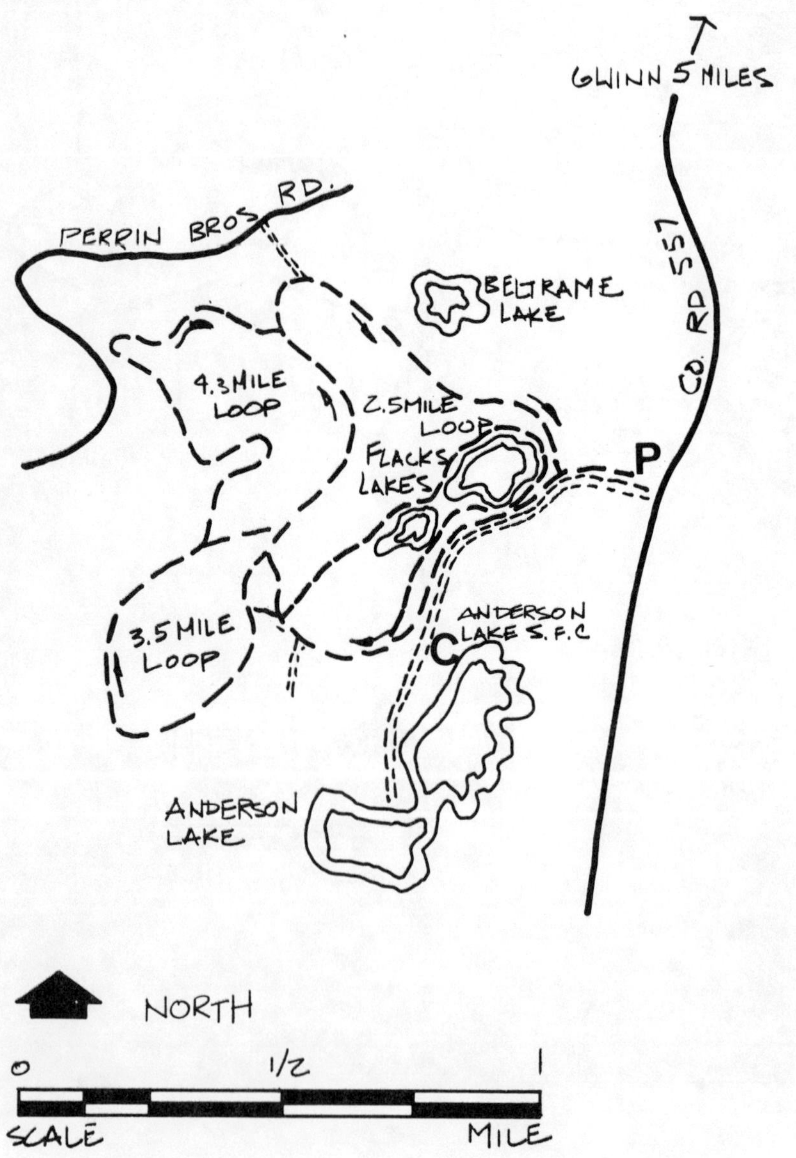

ANDERSON LAKE PATHWAY

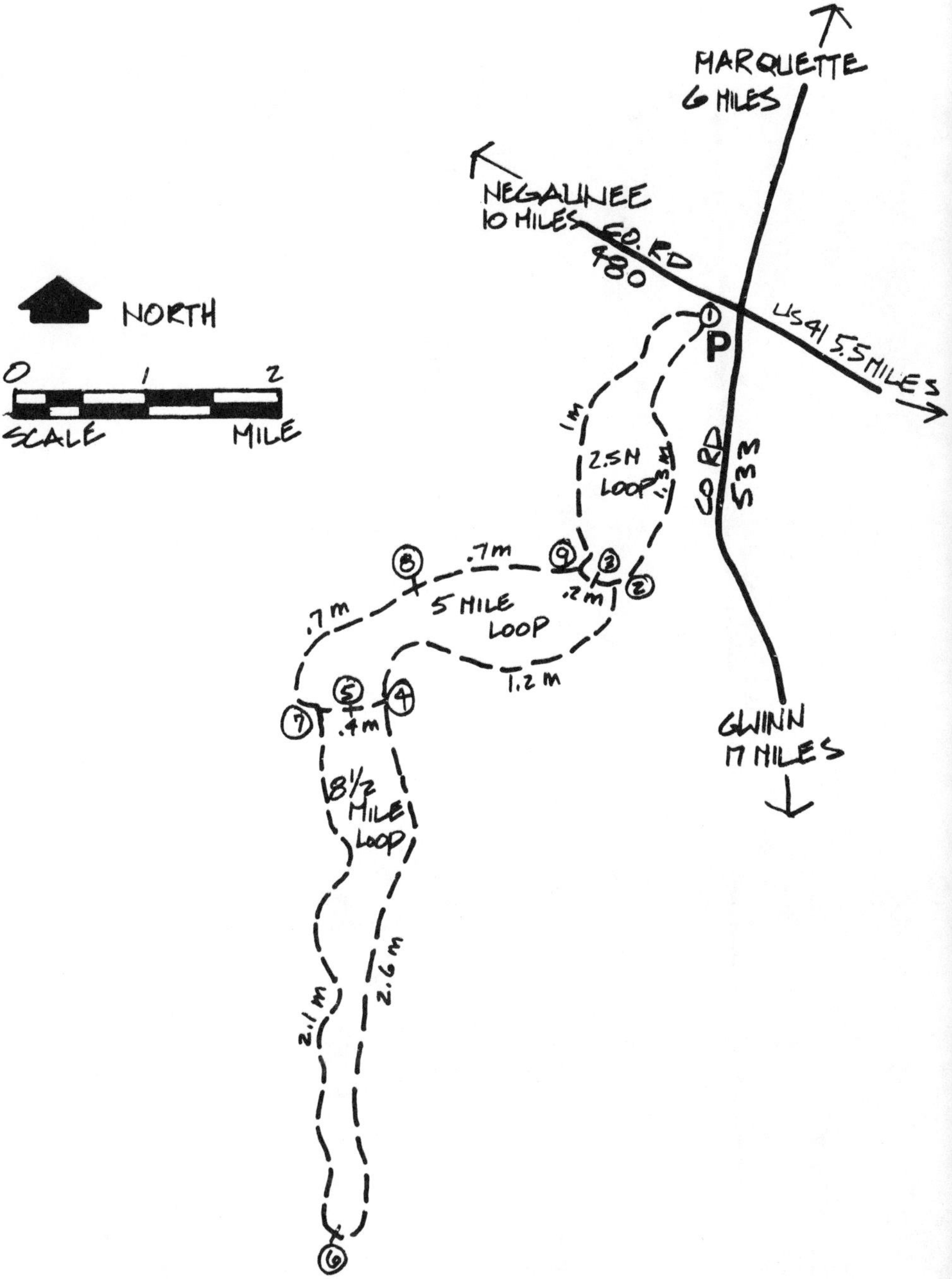

MARQUETTE
6 MILES

NEGAUNEE
10 MILES

CO. RD
480

US41 5.5 MILES

NORTH

0 1 2
SCALE MILE

P

1M
2.5M
LOOP

5 MILE
LOOP

.7m
.7m
.2m
1.2m
.4m

8 1/2
MILE
LOOP

2.1m
2.6m

GWINN
17 MILES

BLUEBERRY RIDGE PATHWAY

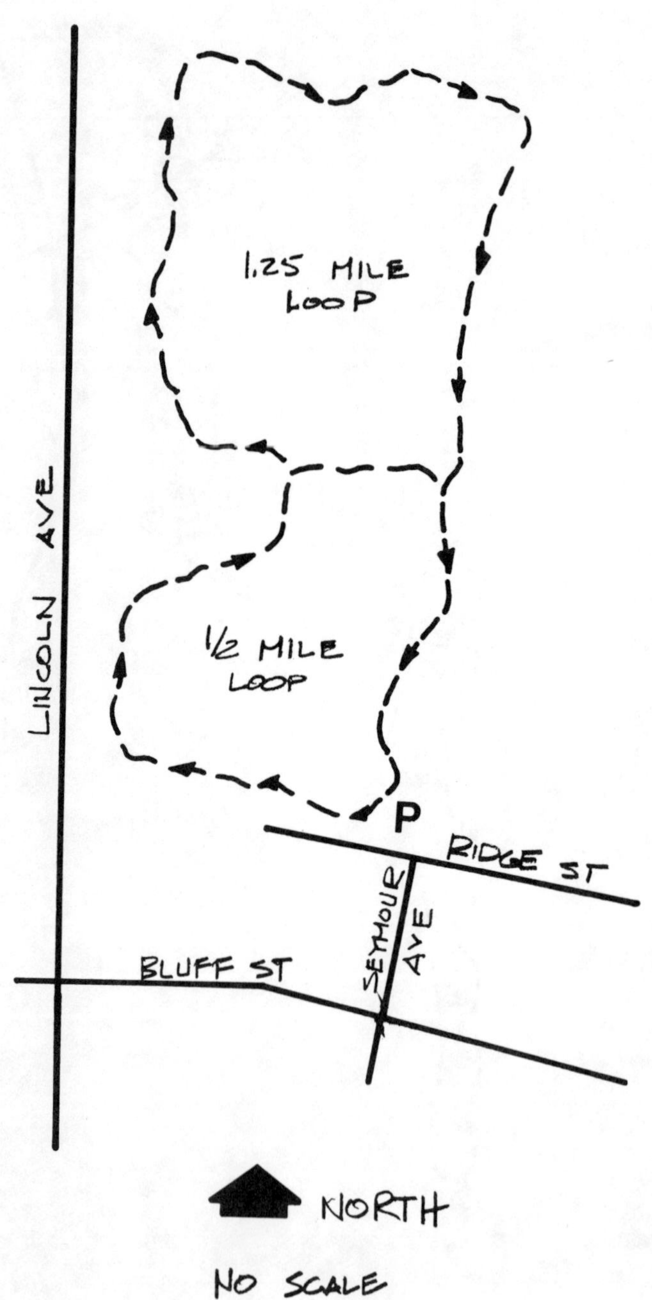

PARK CEMETERY
CITY OF MARQUETTE

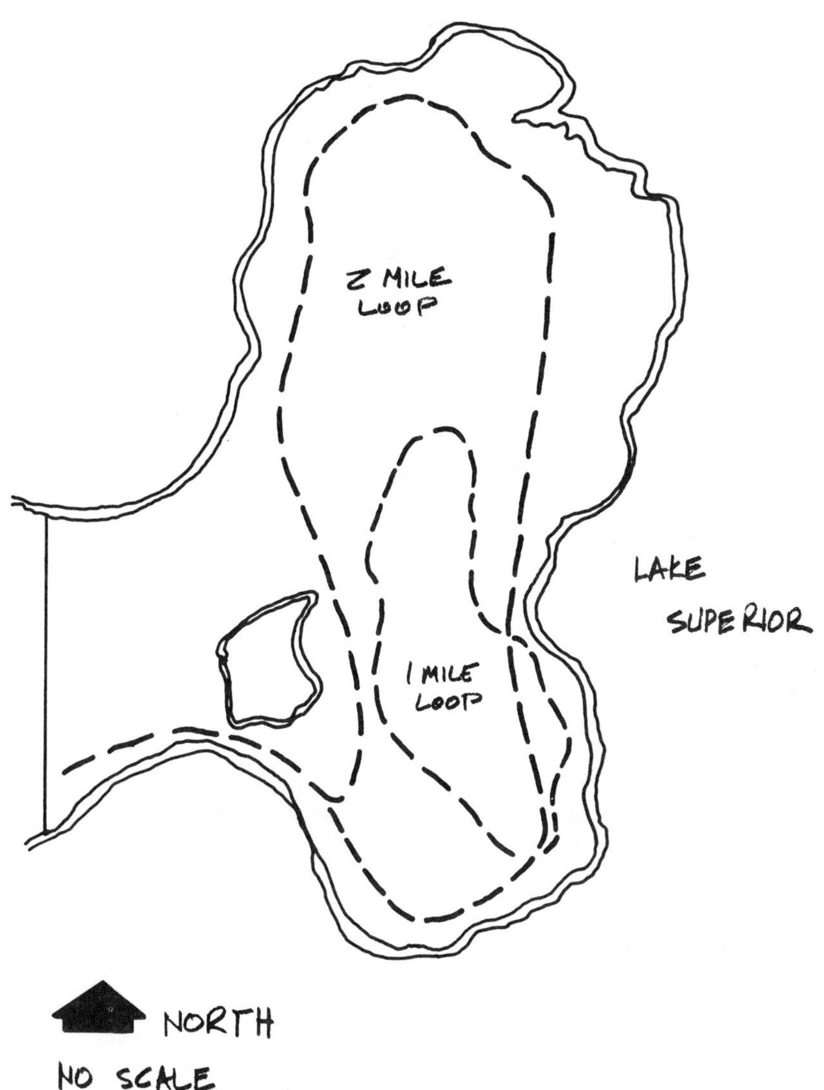

NORTH

NO SCALE

PRESQUE ISLE PARK
CITY OF MARQUETTE

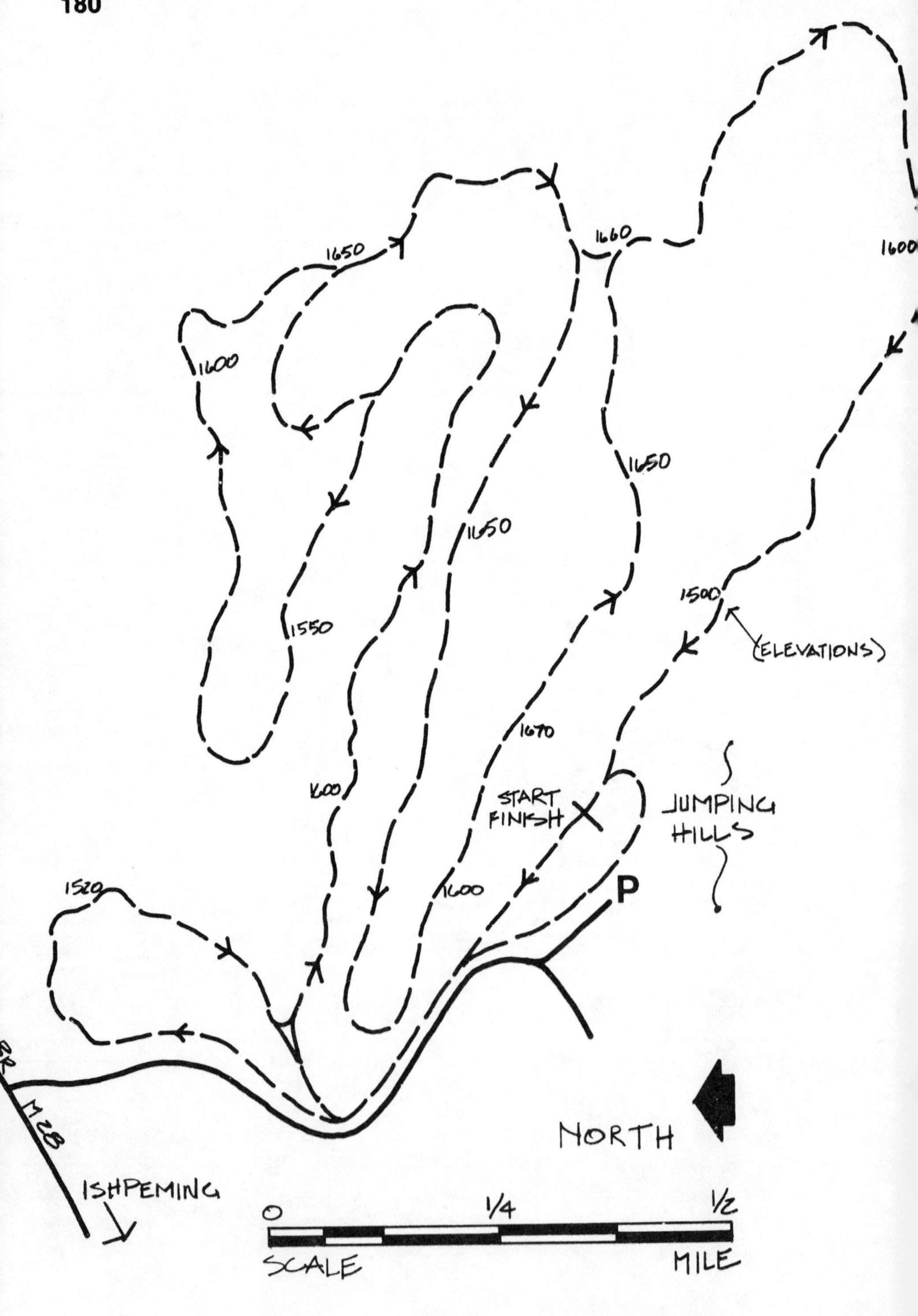

SUICIDE BOWL

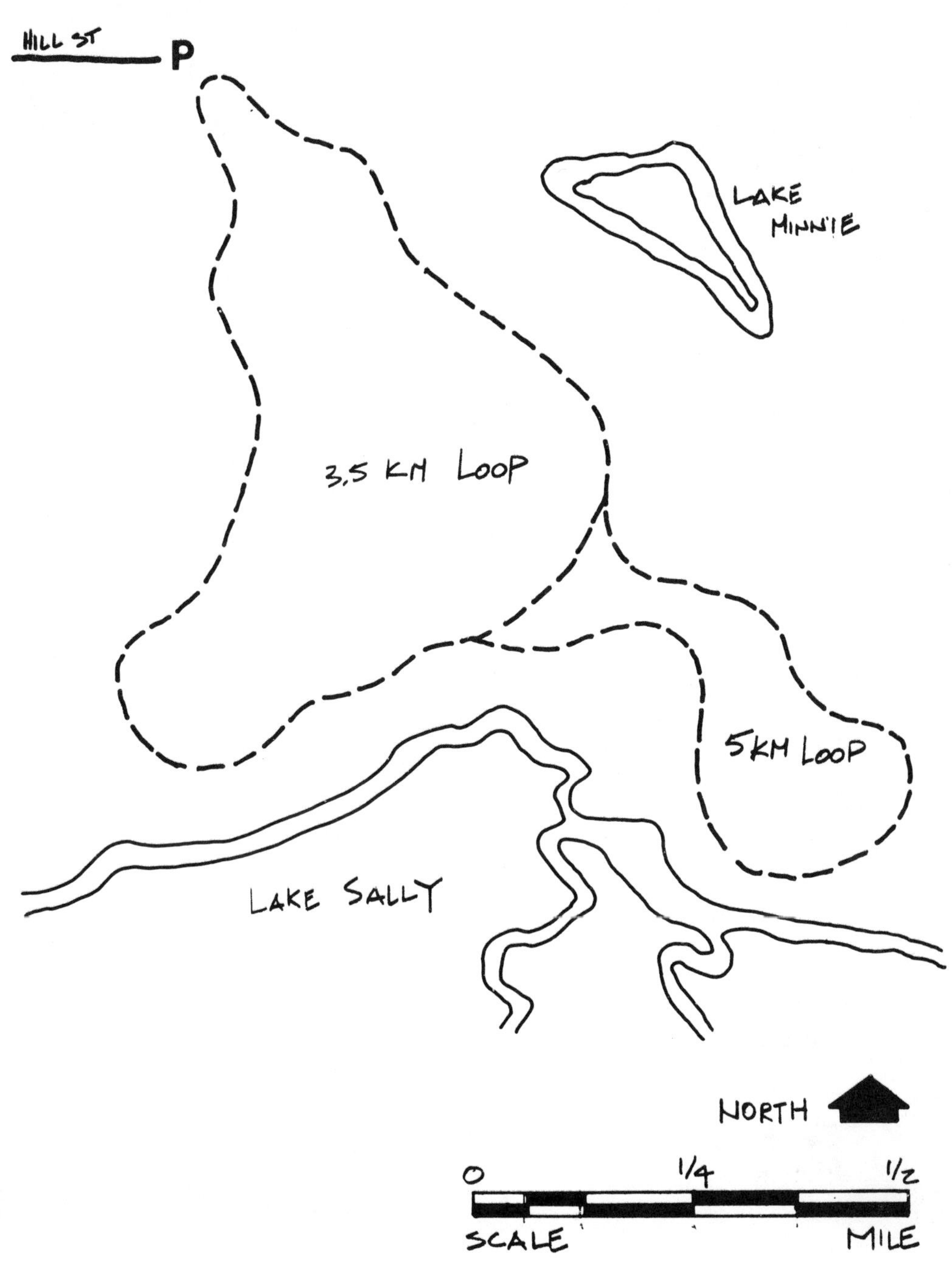

CLEVELAND CROSS COUNTY SKI TRAIL

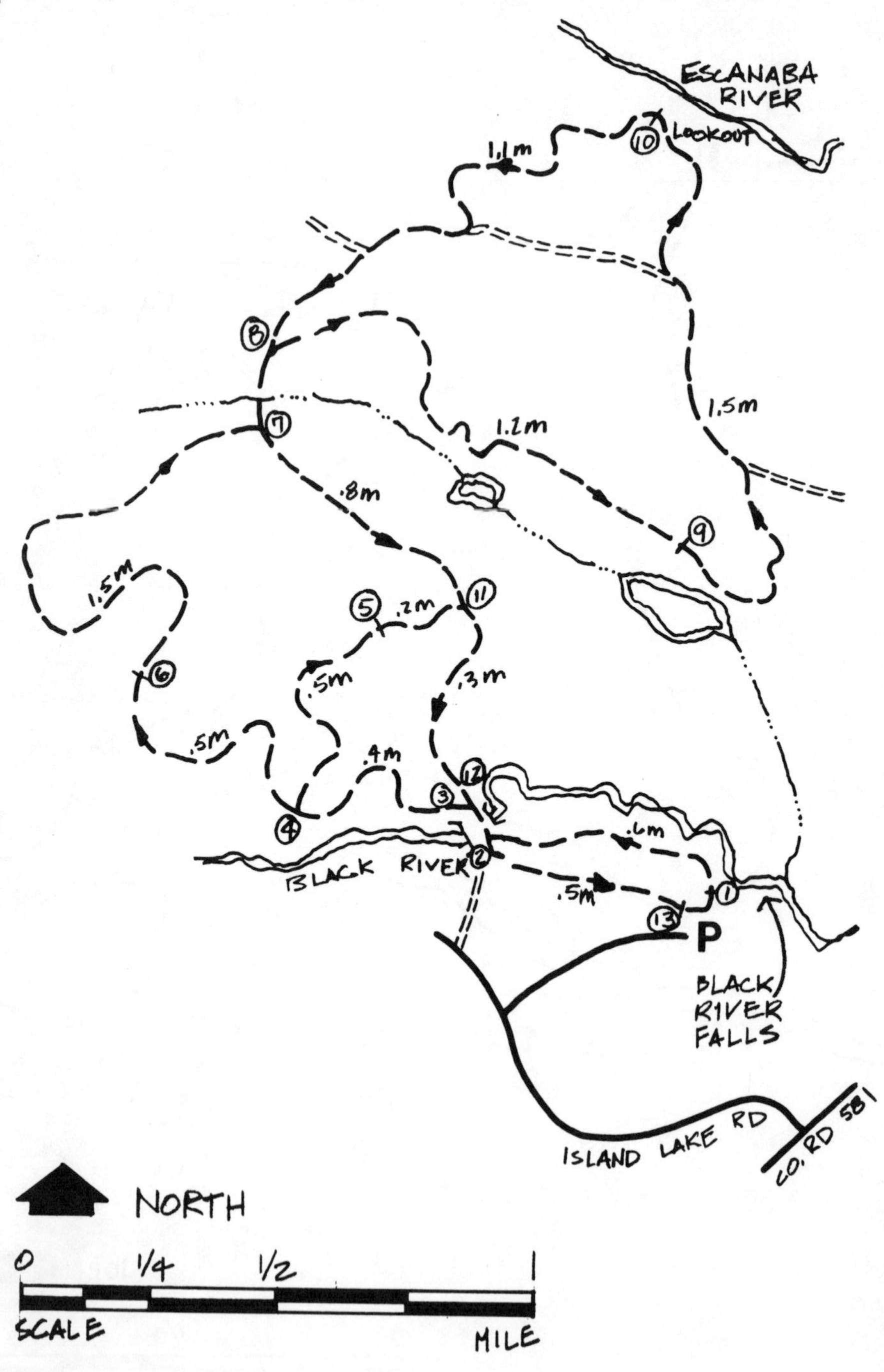

BLACK RIVER PATHWAY

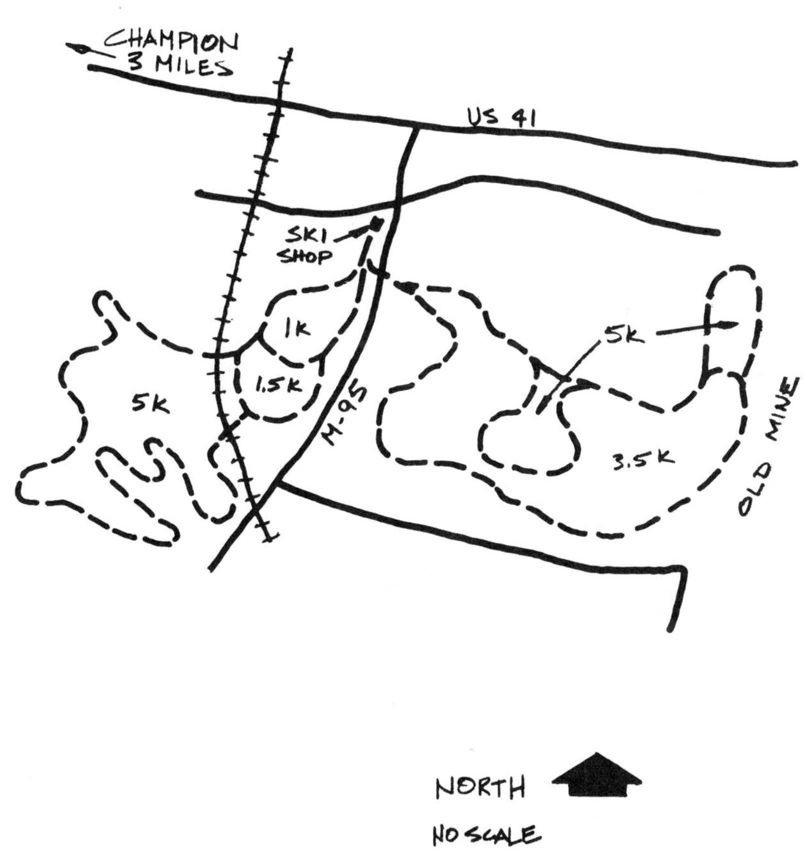

CHAMPION ROSSIGNOL SKI TOURING CENTER

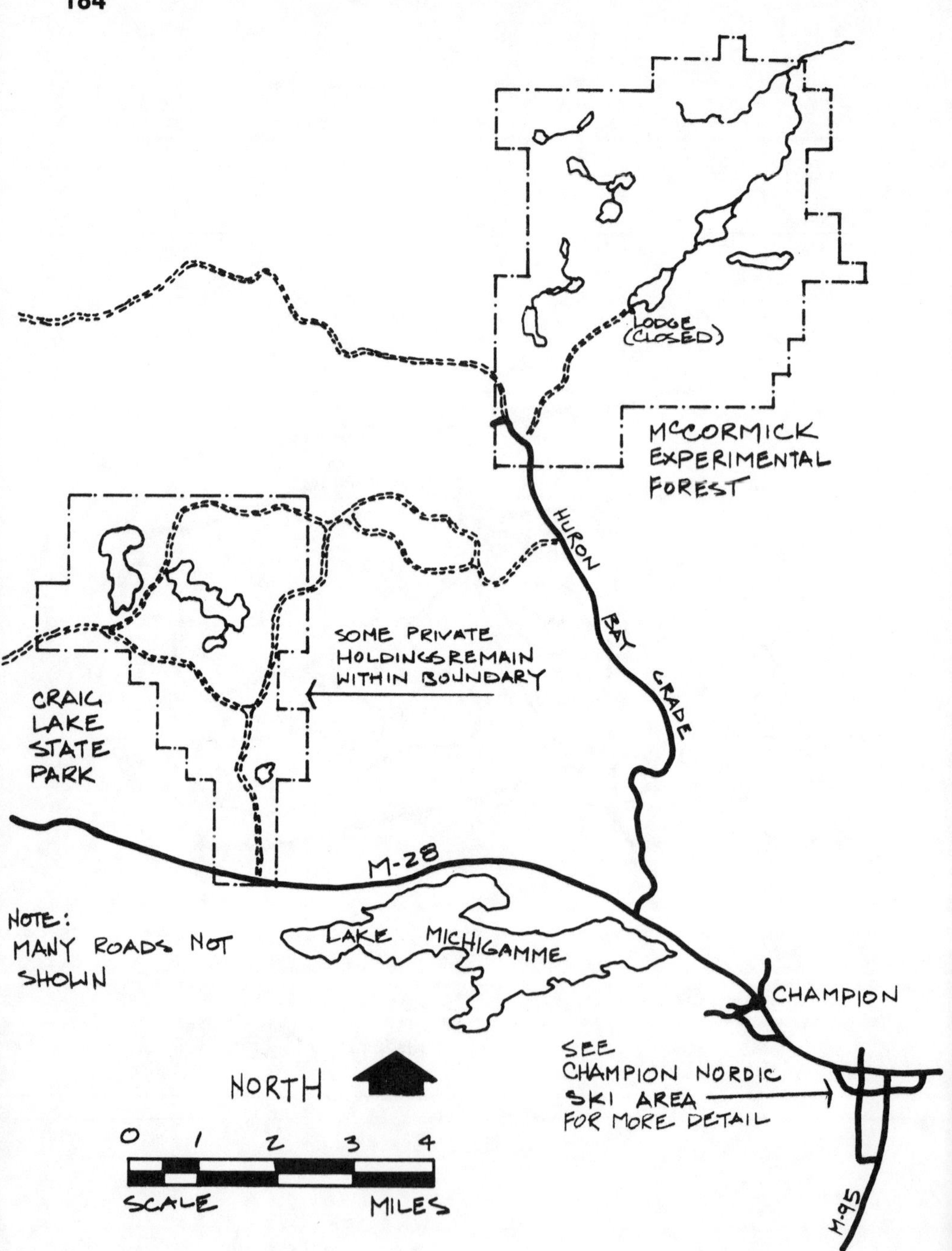

McCORMICK EXPERIMENTAL FOREST
CRAIG LAKE STATE PARK

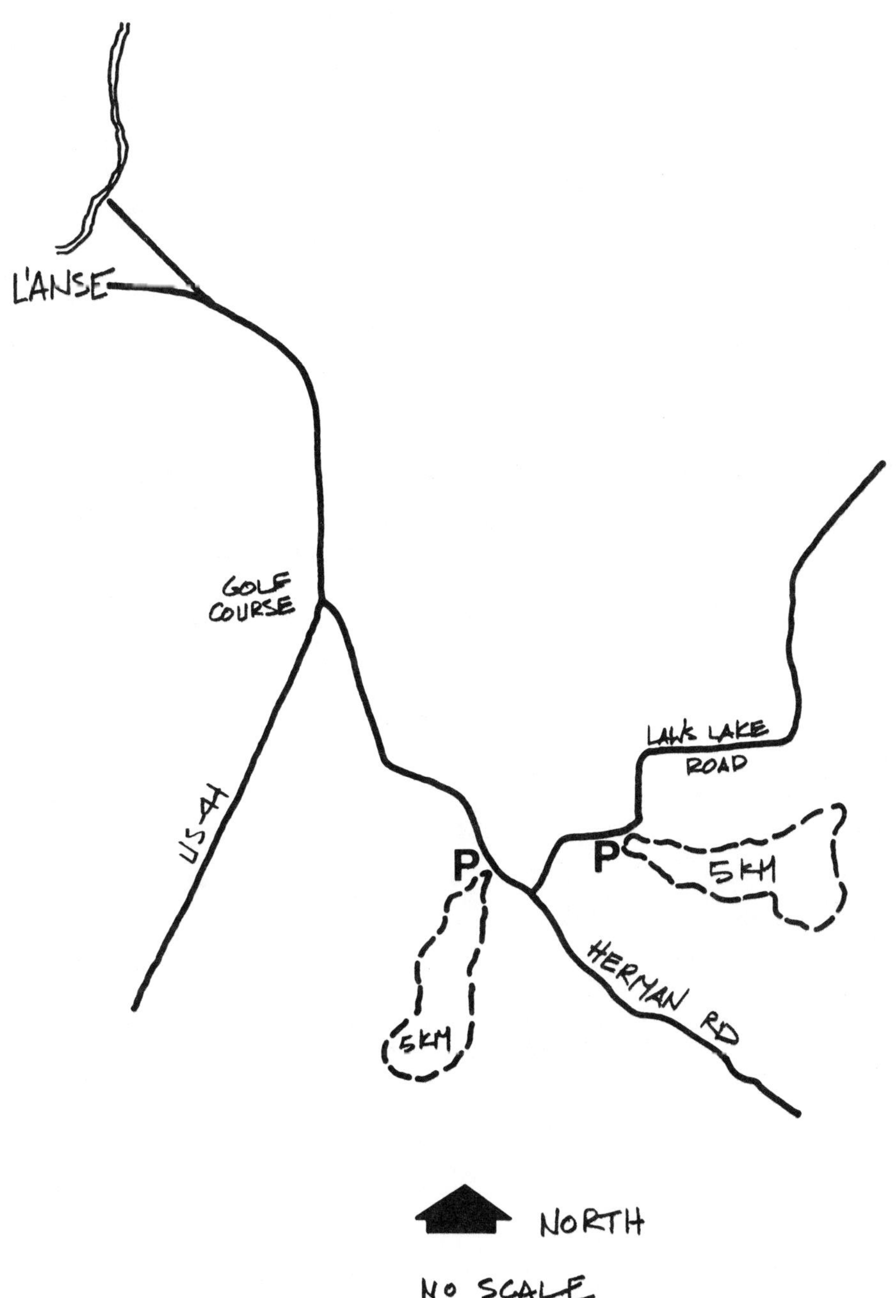

LAWS LAKE SKI TRAILS

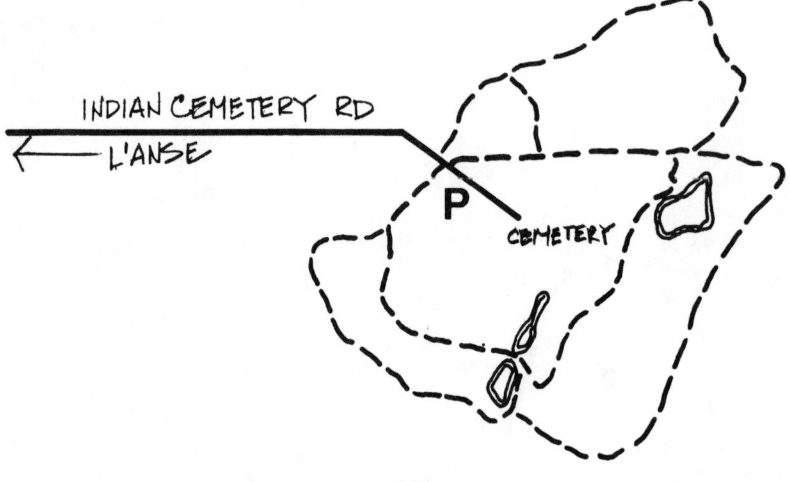

NO SCALE

INDIAN CEMETERY SKI AREA

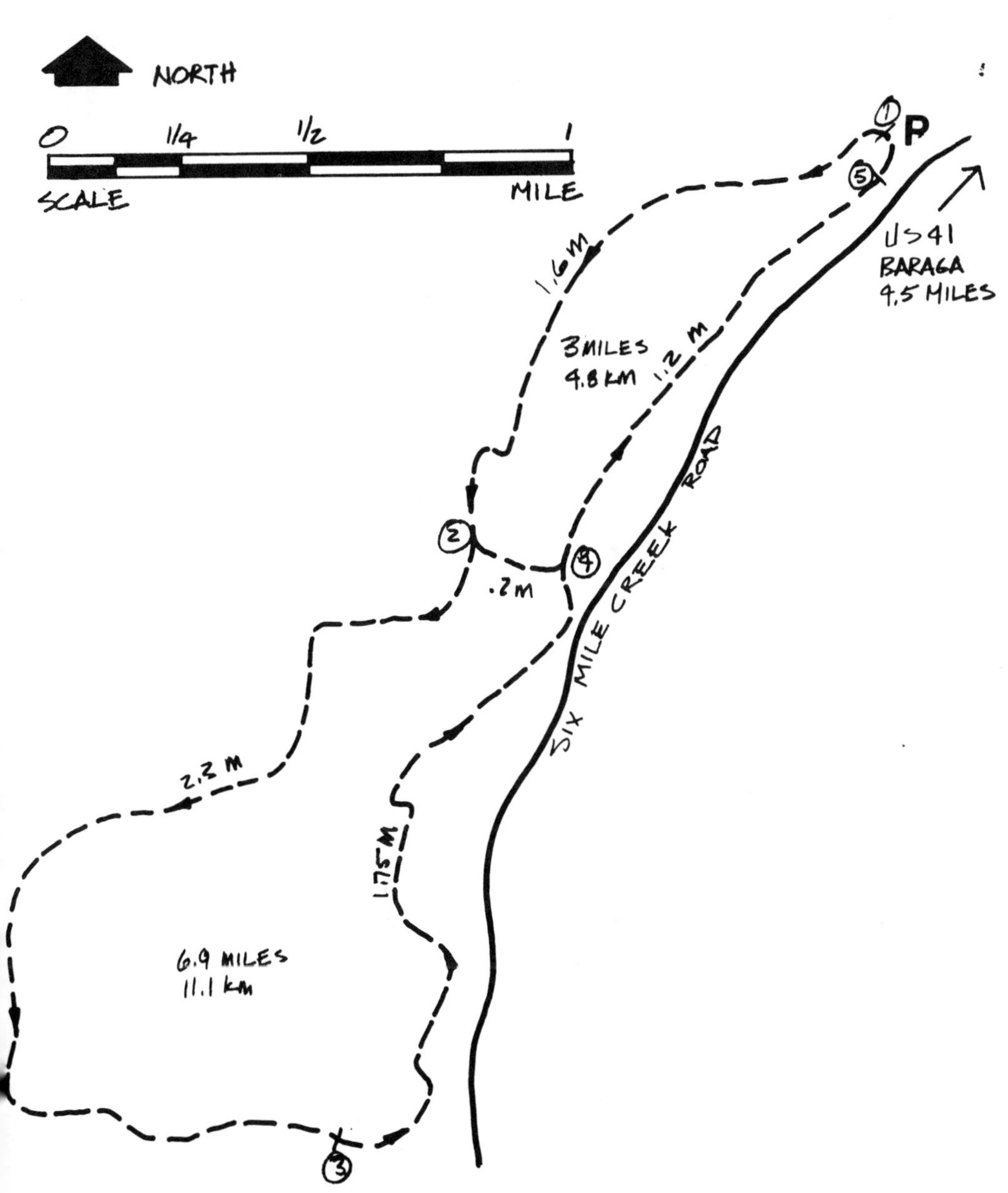

SIX MILE CREEK PATHWAY

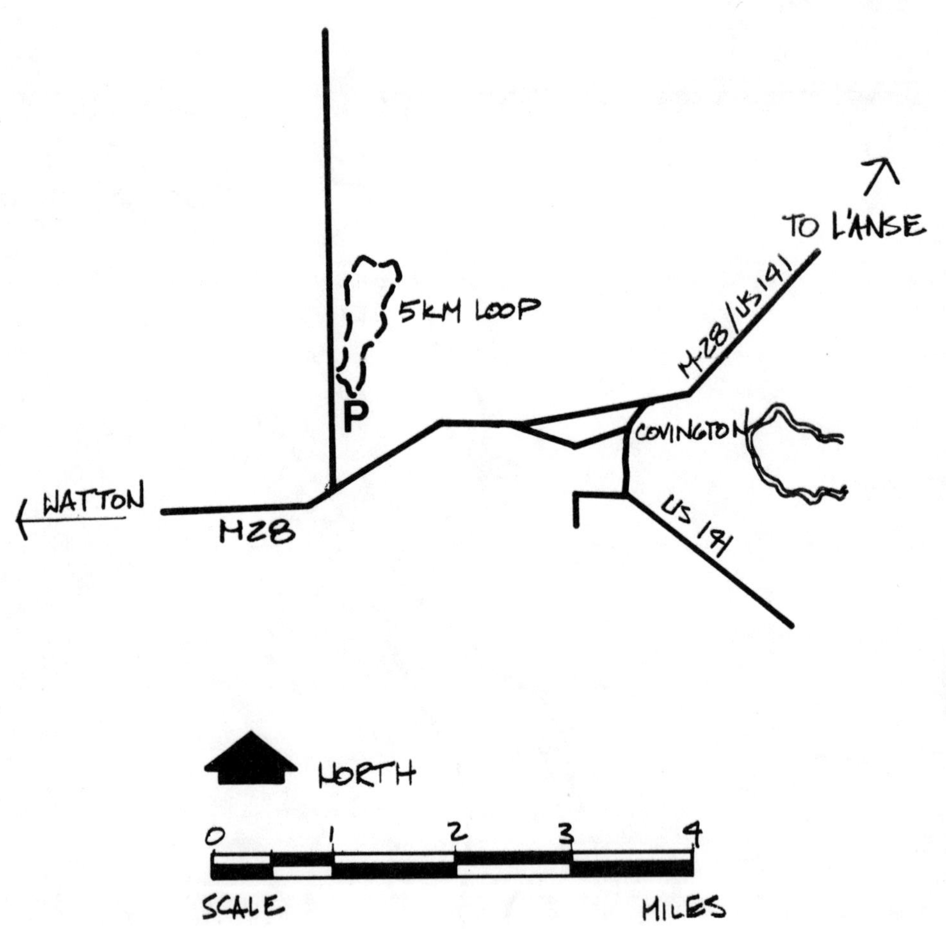

PAC SKI TRAIL

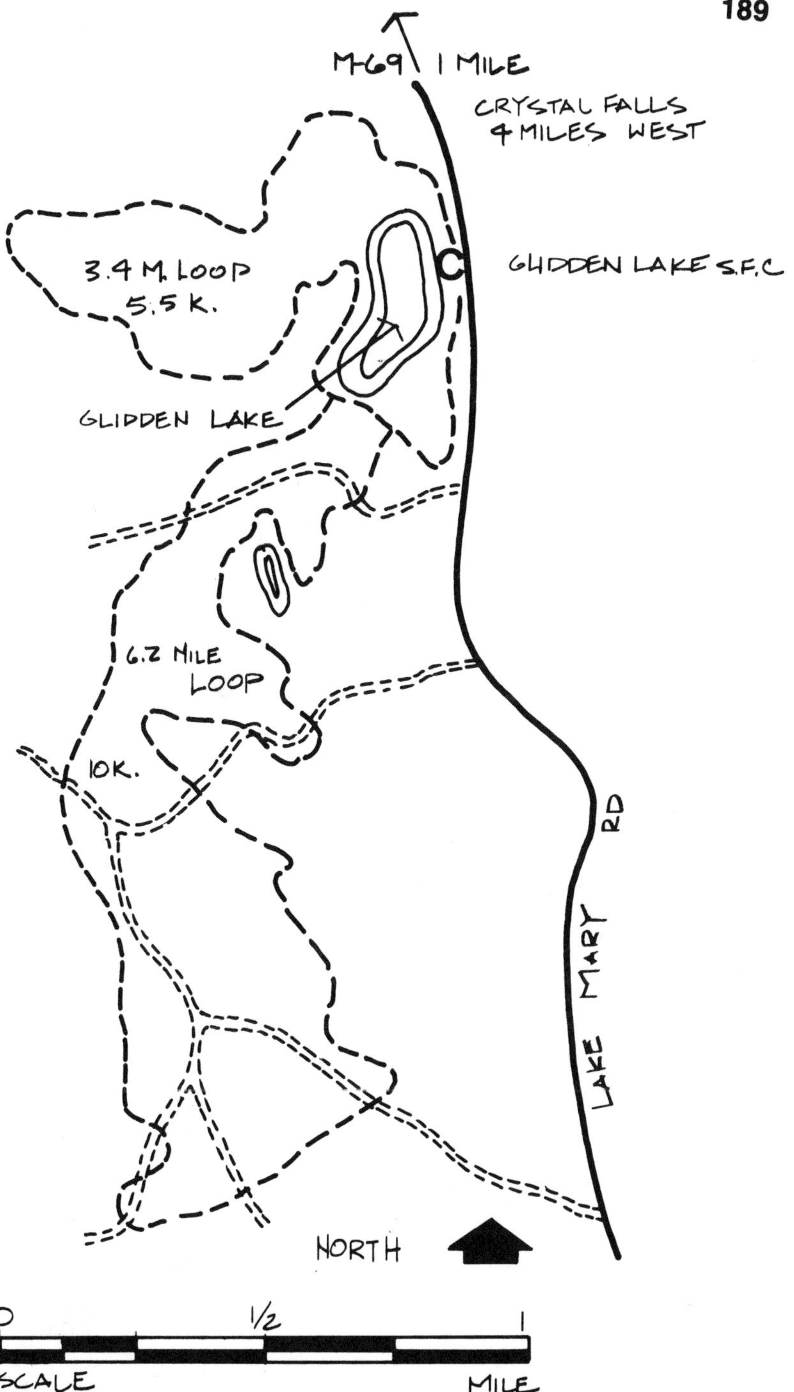

LAKE MARY PLAINS PATHWAY

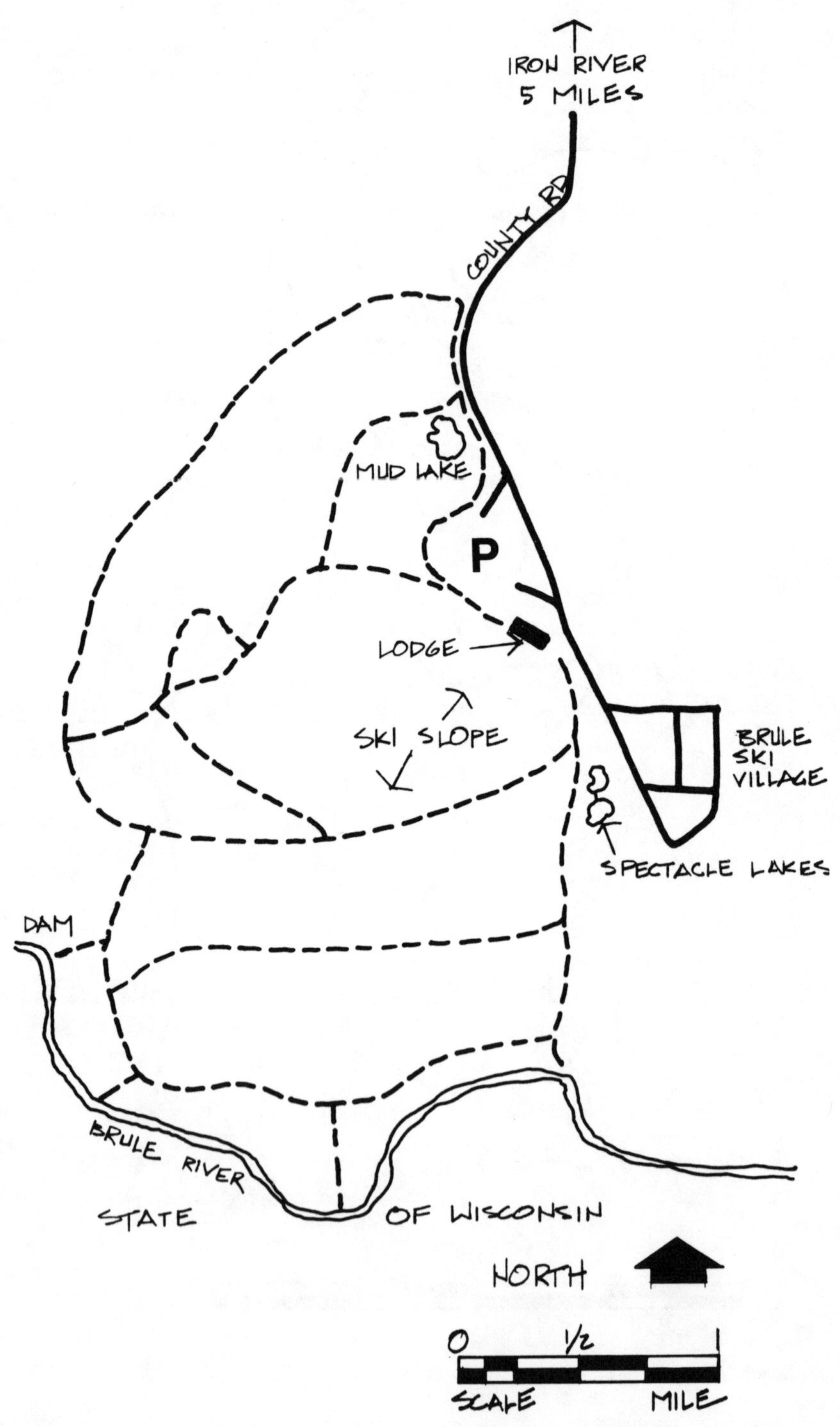

BRULE MOUNTAIN

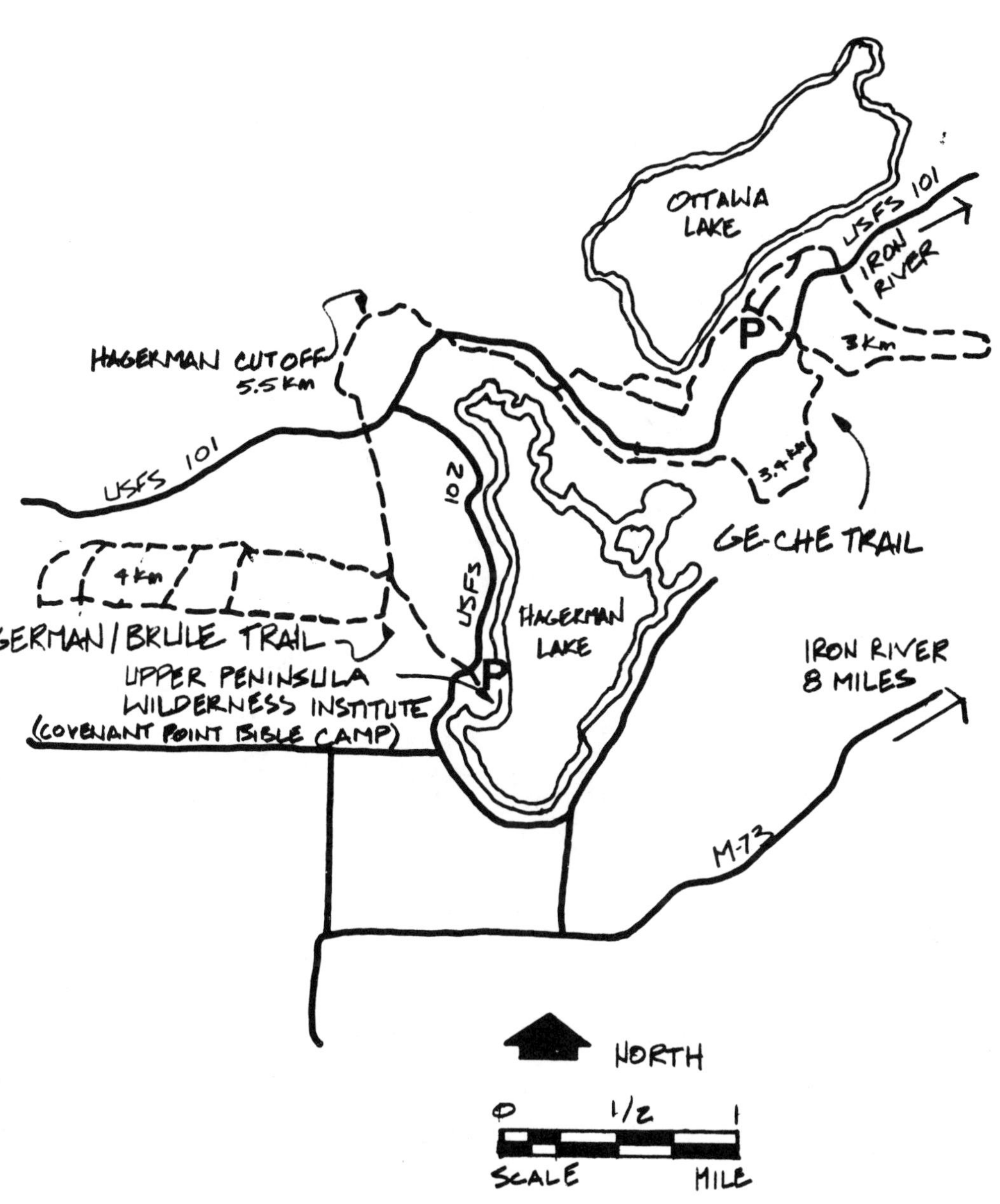

HAGERMAN - BRULE & GE-CHE SKI TRAILS

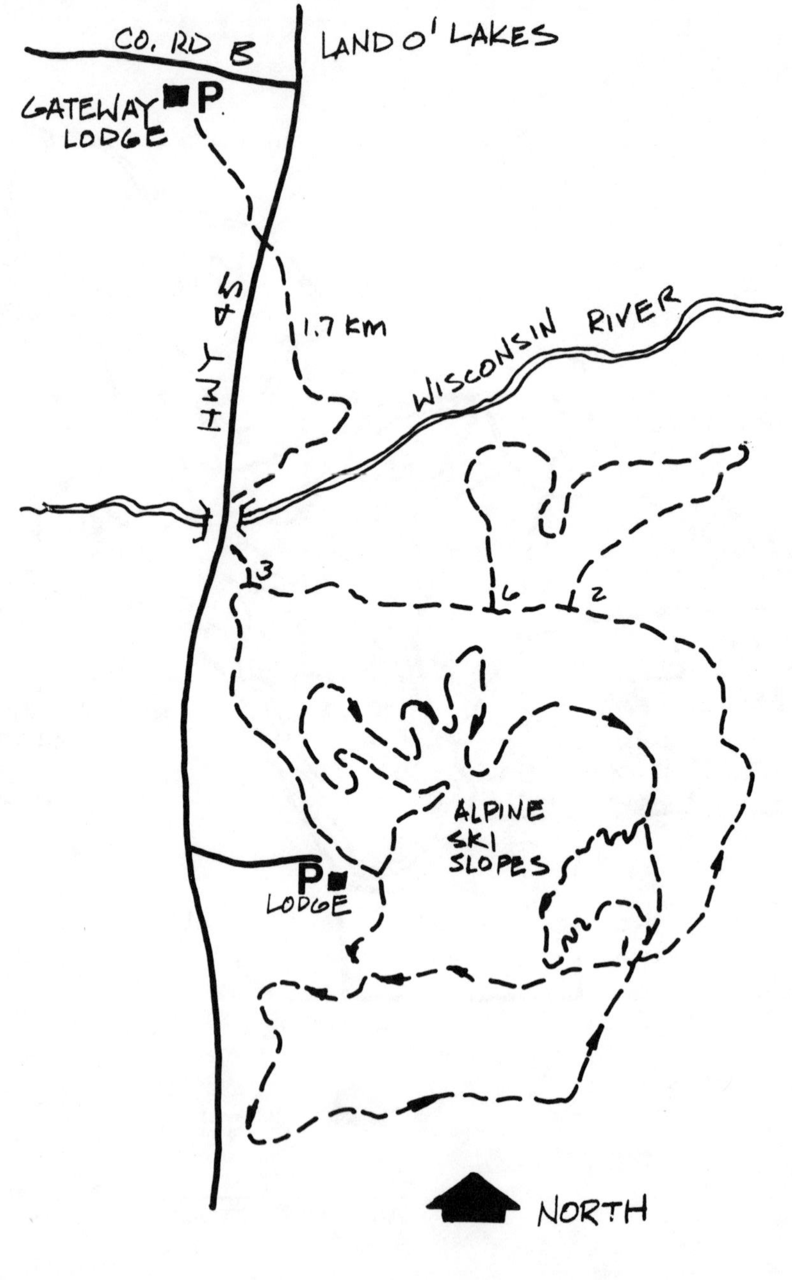

GATEWAY SKI AREA

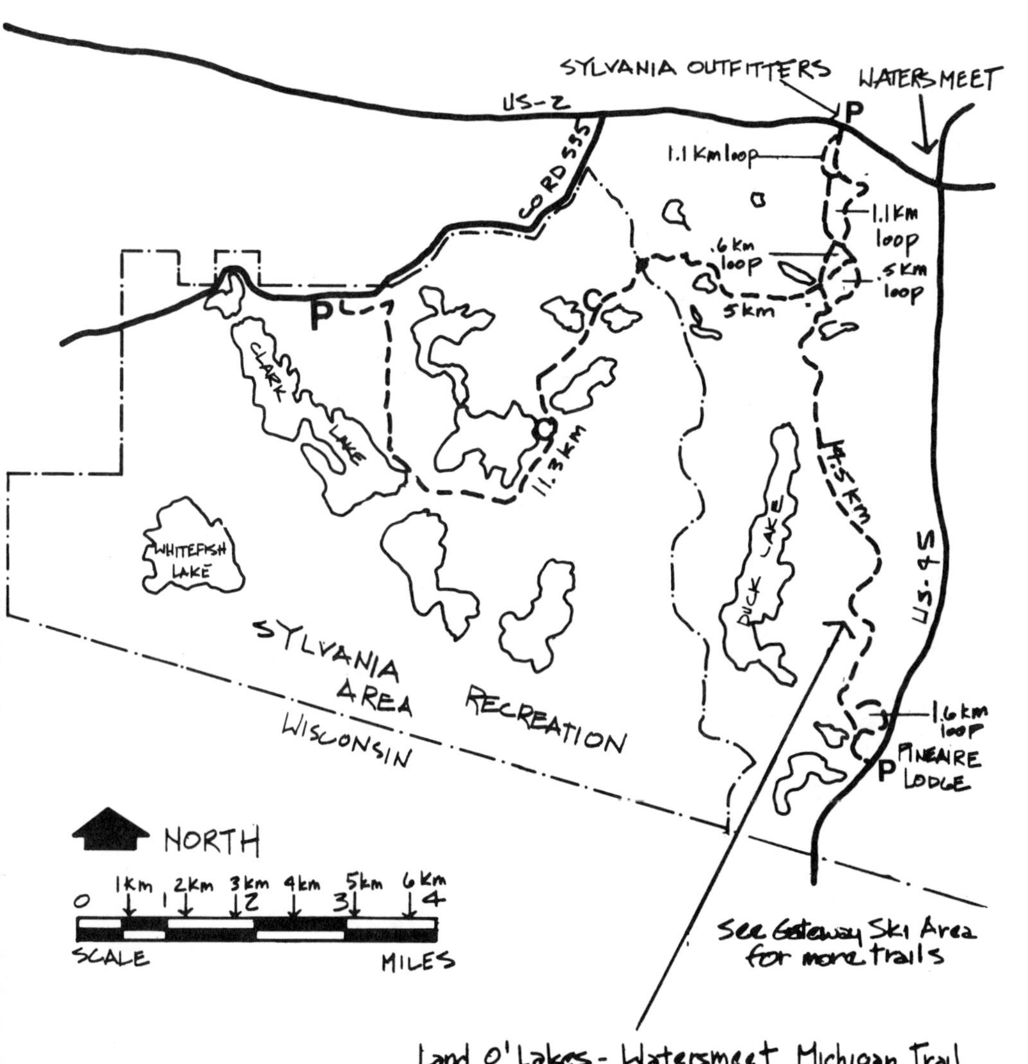

SYLVANIA RECREATION AREA AND VICINITY

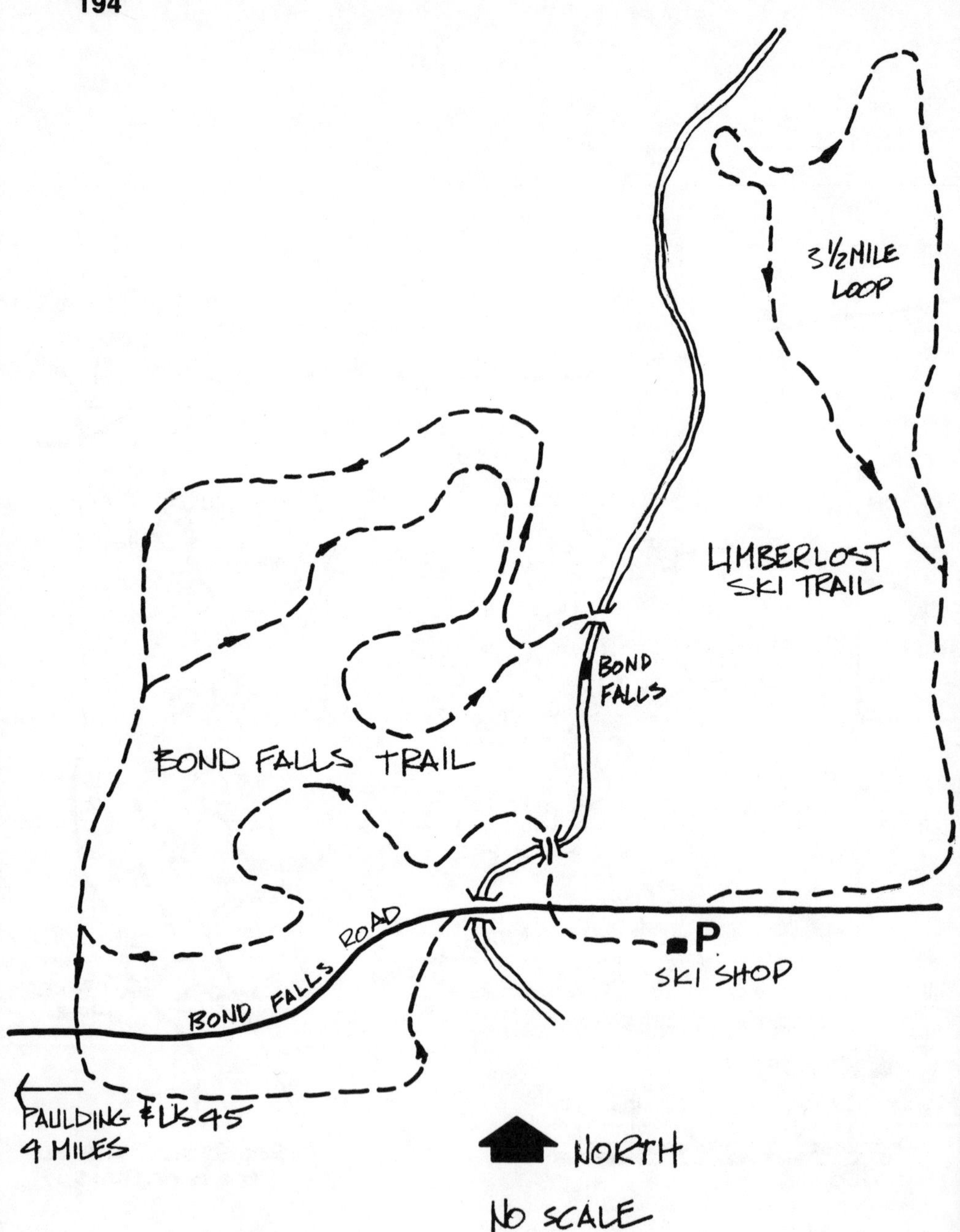

LIMBERLOST SKI AREA

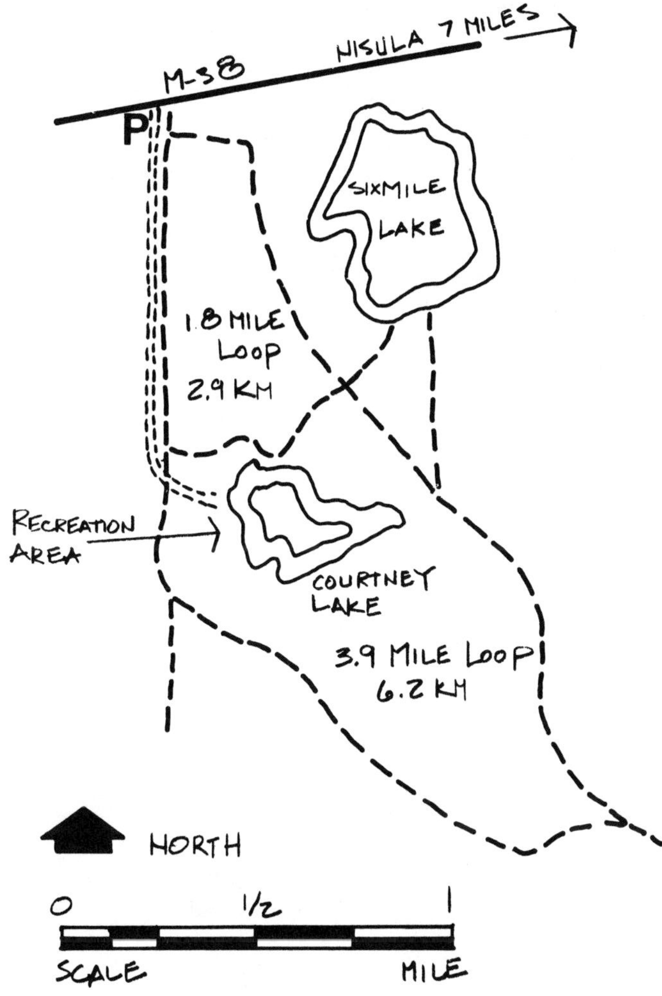

OLD GRADE SKI TRAIL

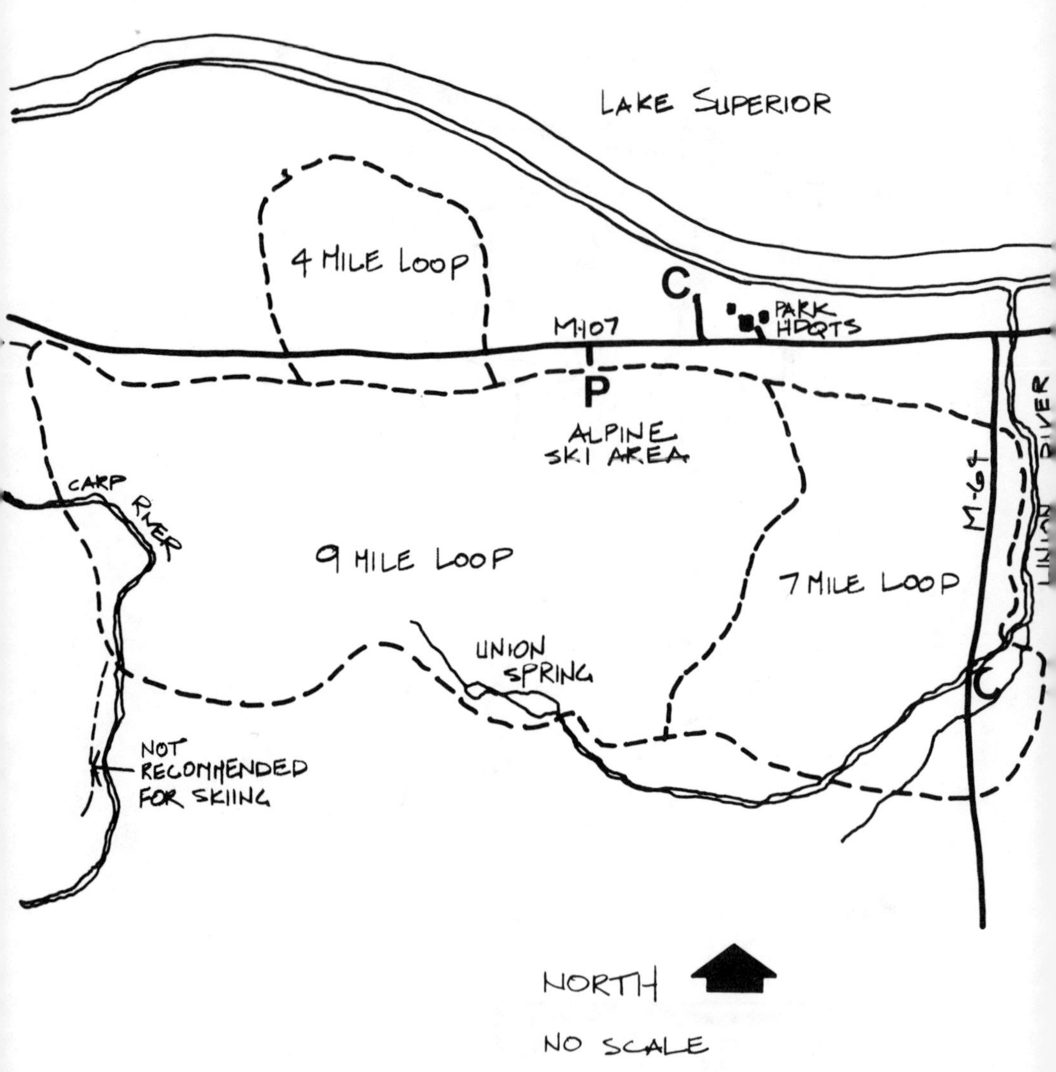

PORCUPINE MOUNTAINS
WILDERNESS STATE PARK

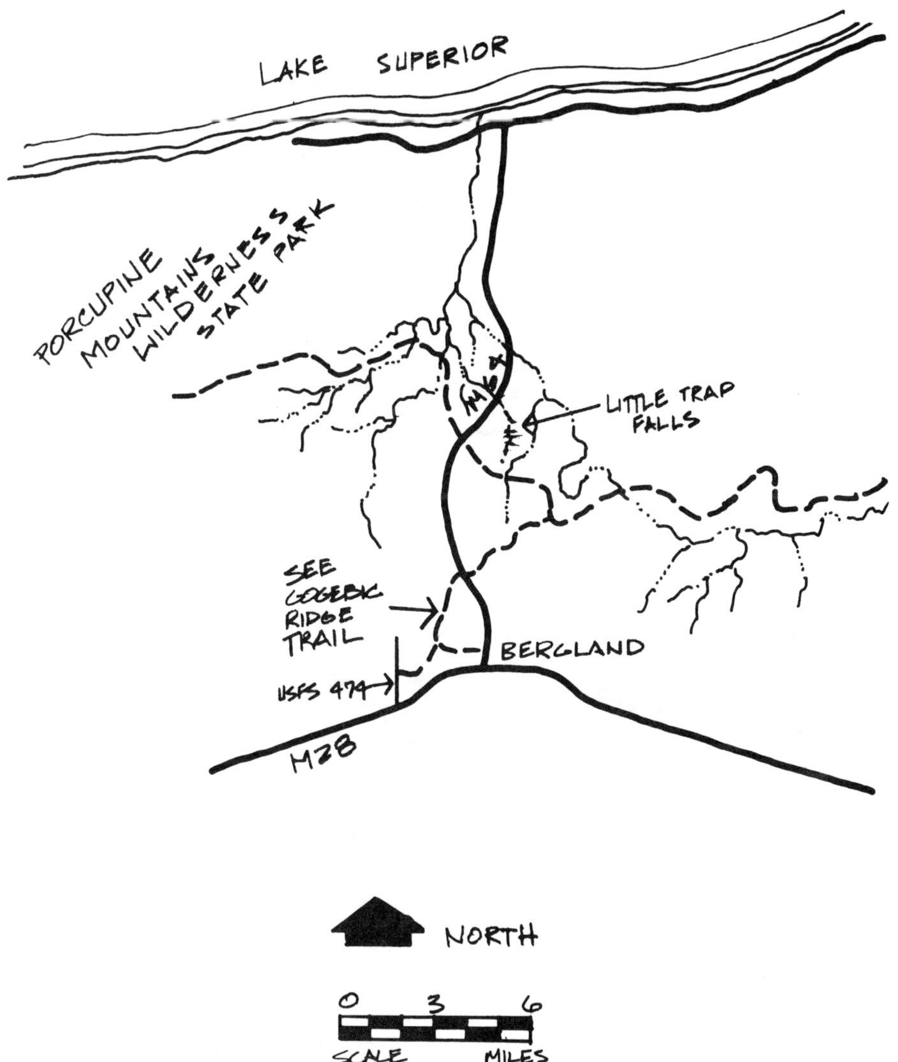

TRAPP FALLS SECTION
NORTH COUNTRY TRAIL

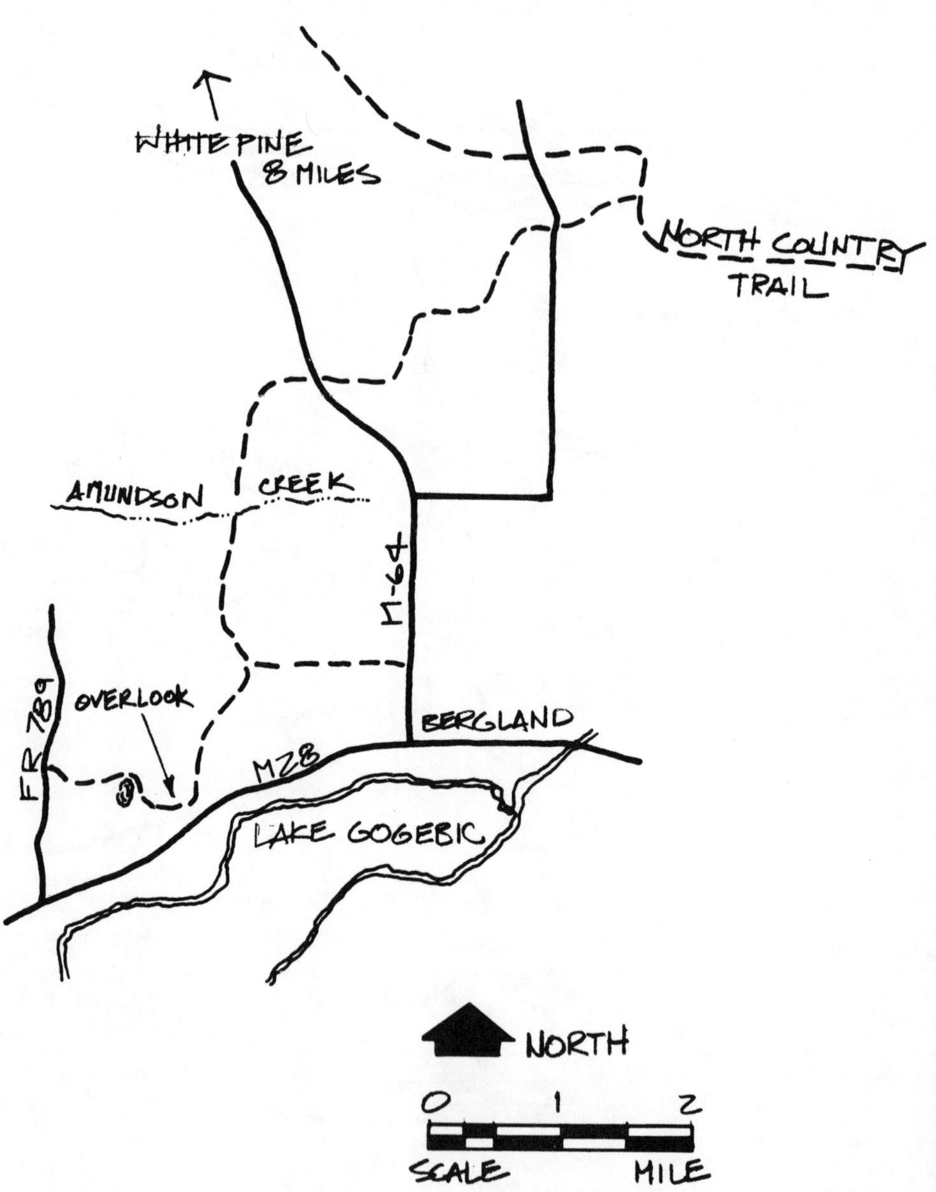

GOGEBIC RIDGE TRAIL

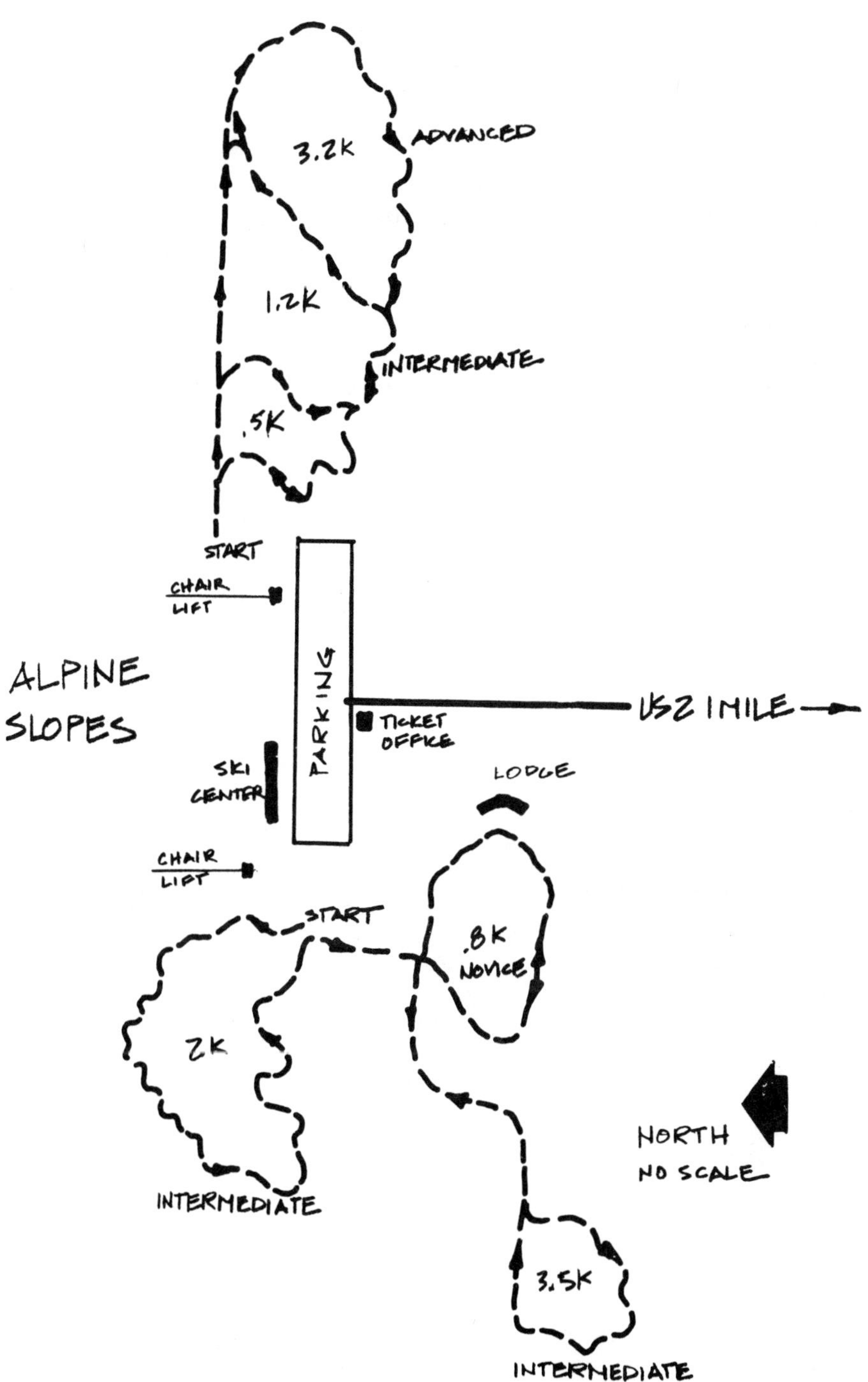

INDIANHEAD MOUNTAIN

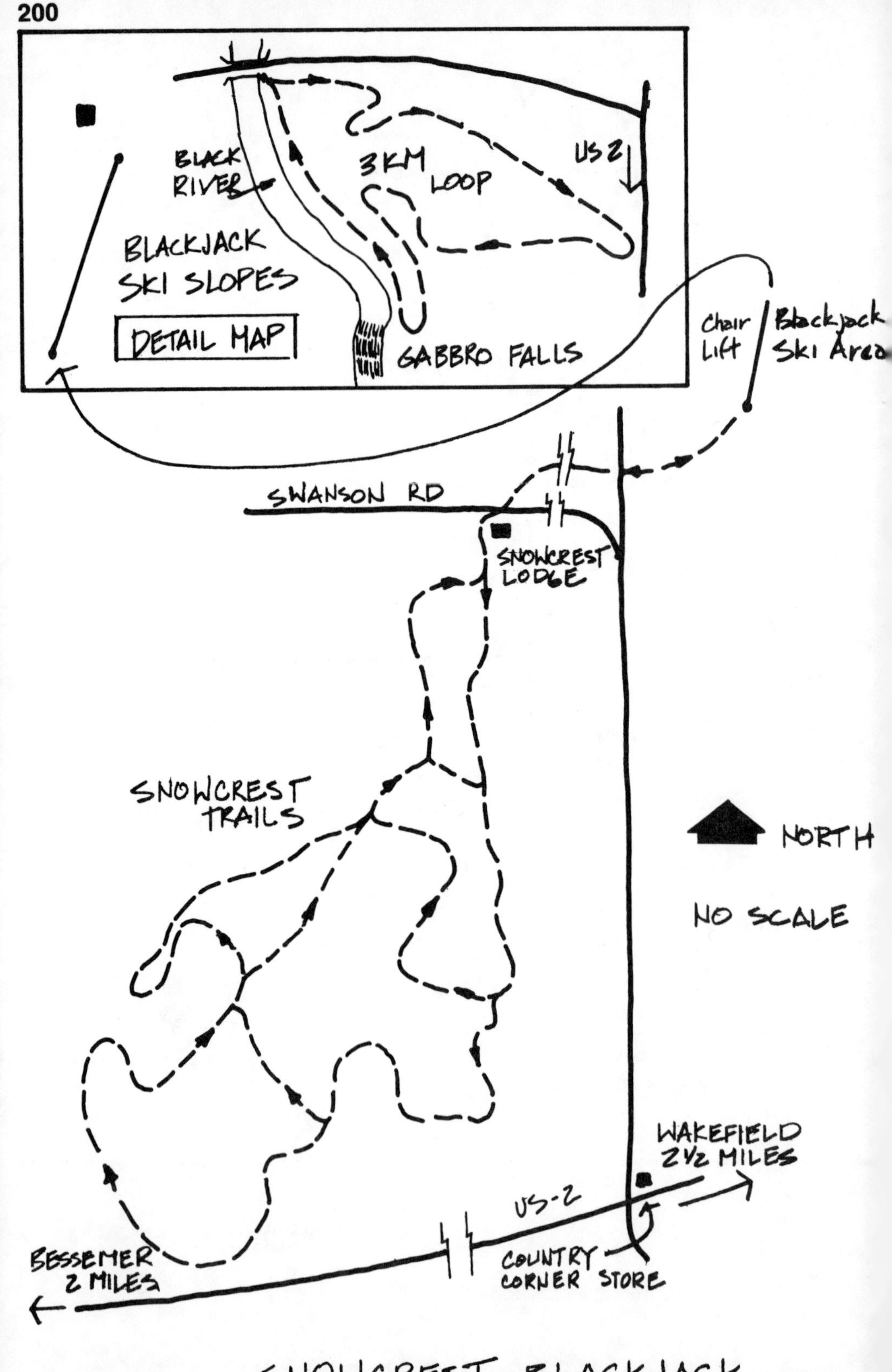
BLACK RIVER
3KM LOOP
US 2
BLACKJACK SKI SLOPES
DETAIL MAP
GABBRO FALLS
Chair Lift
Blackjack Ski Area
SWANSON RD
SNOWCREST LODGE
SNOWCREST TRAILS
NORTH
NO SCALE
WAKEFIELD 2½ MILES
US-2
BESSEMER 2 MILES
COUNTRY CORNER STORE
SNOWCREST-BLACKJACK

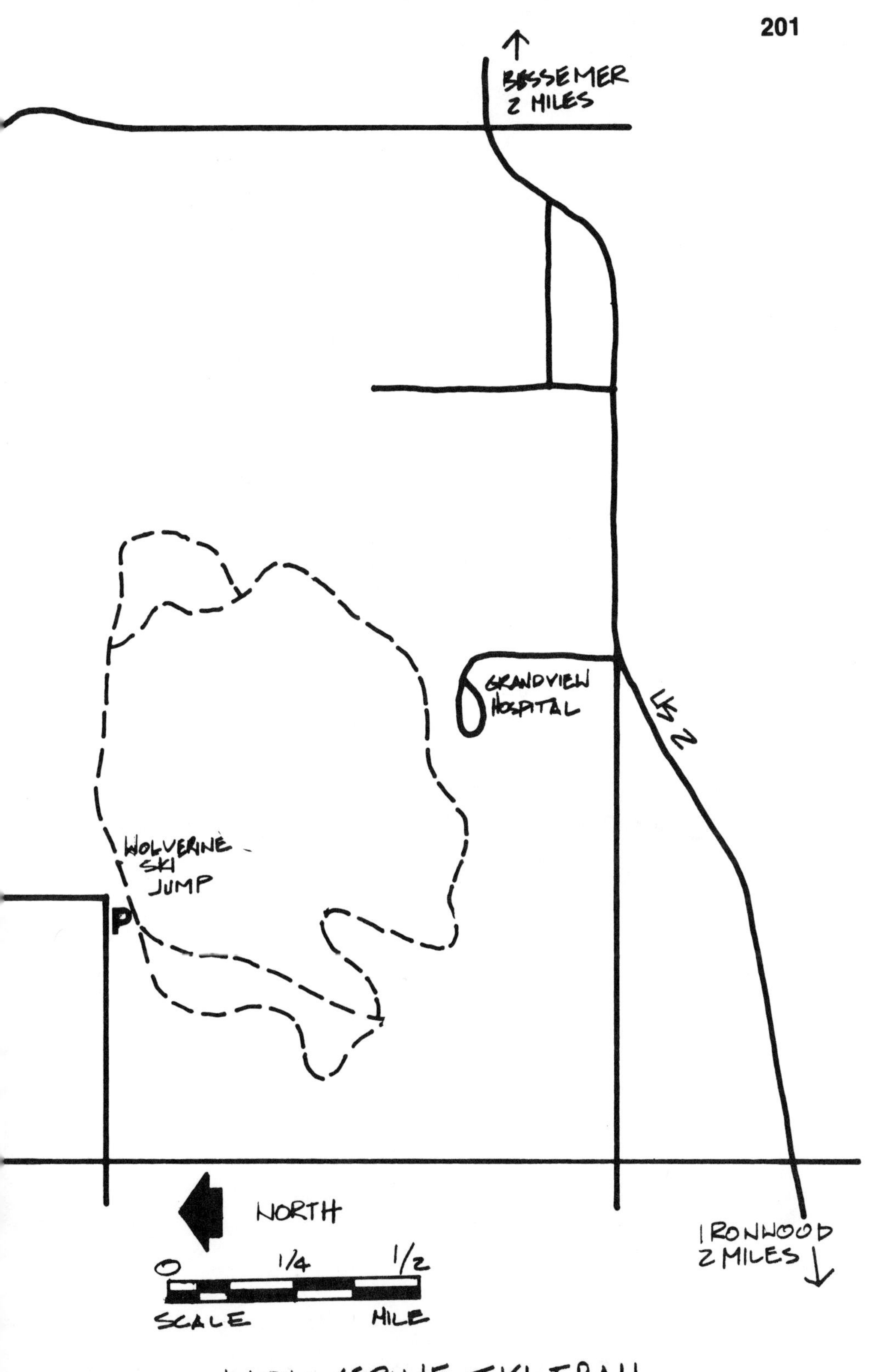

WOLVERINE SKI TRAIL

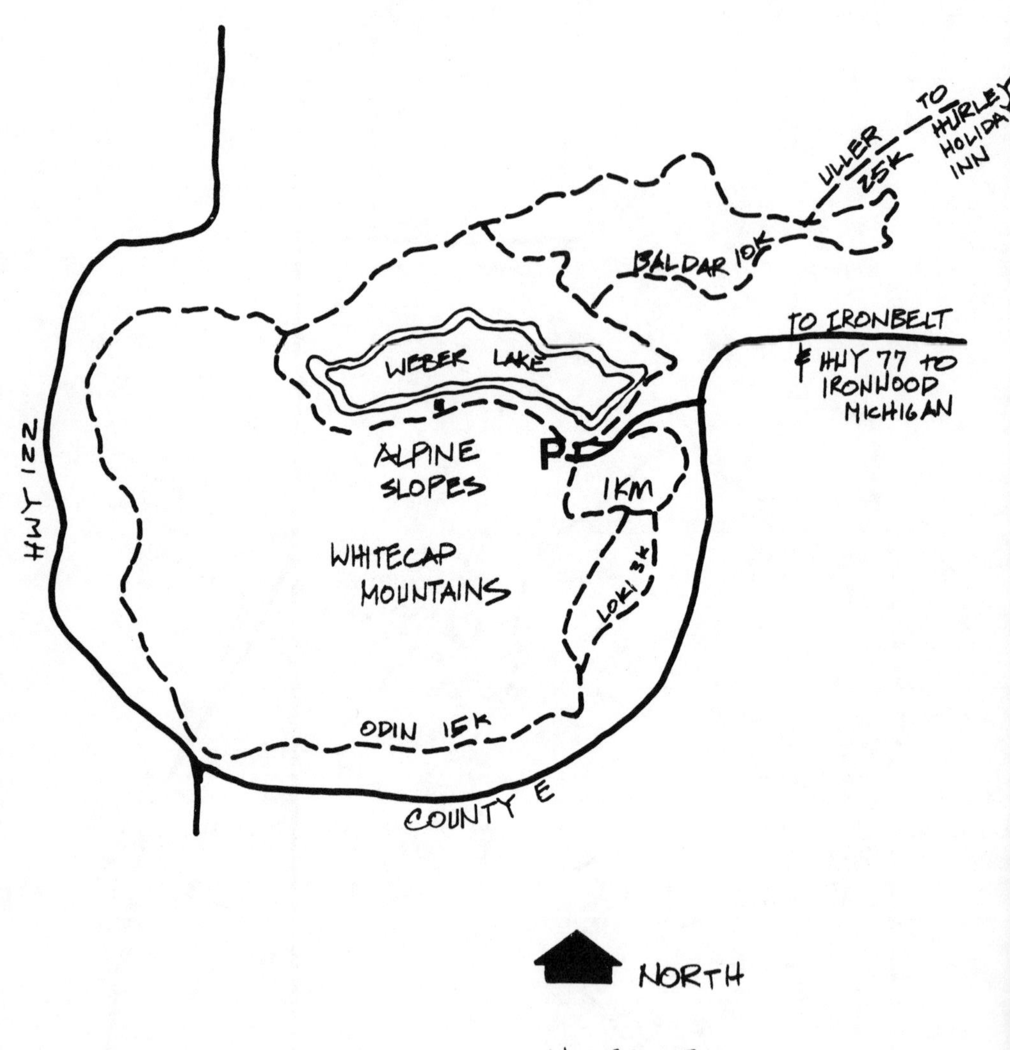

NO SCALE

WHITECAP MOUNTAIN

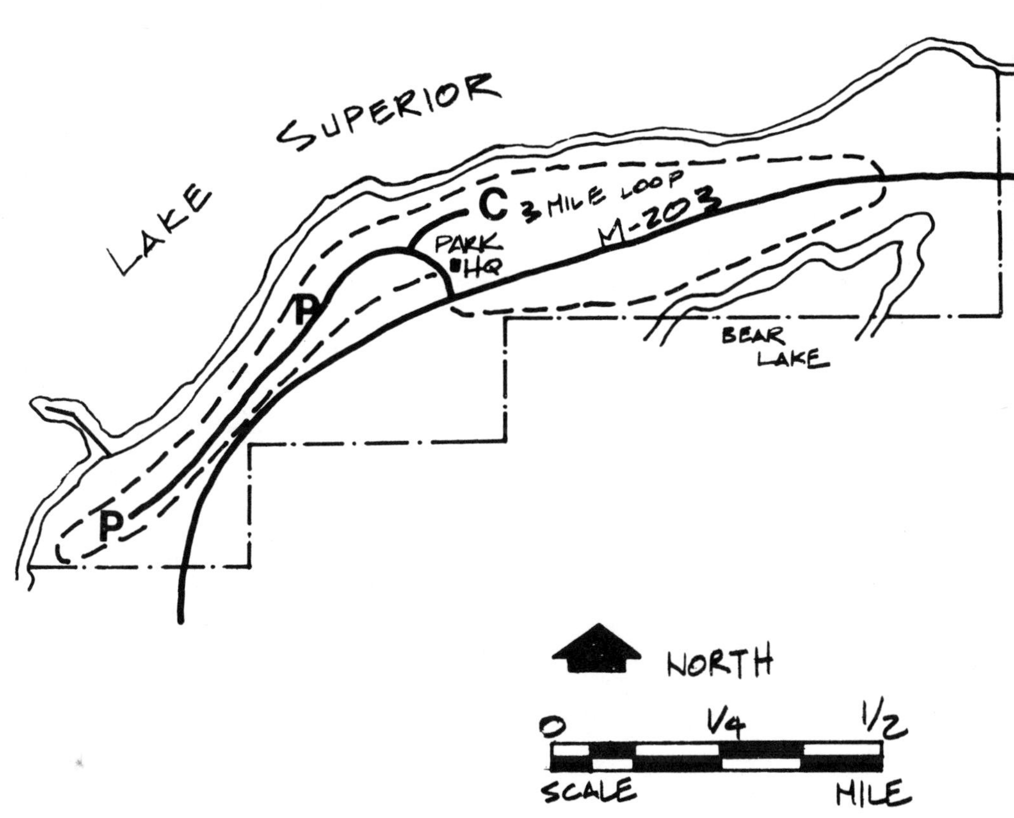

McLAIN STATE PARK

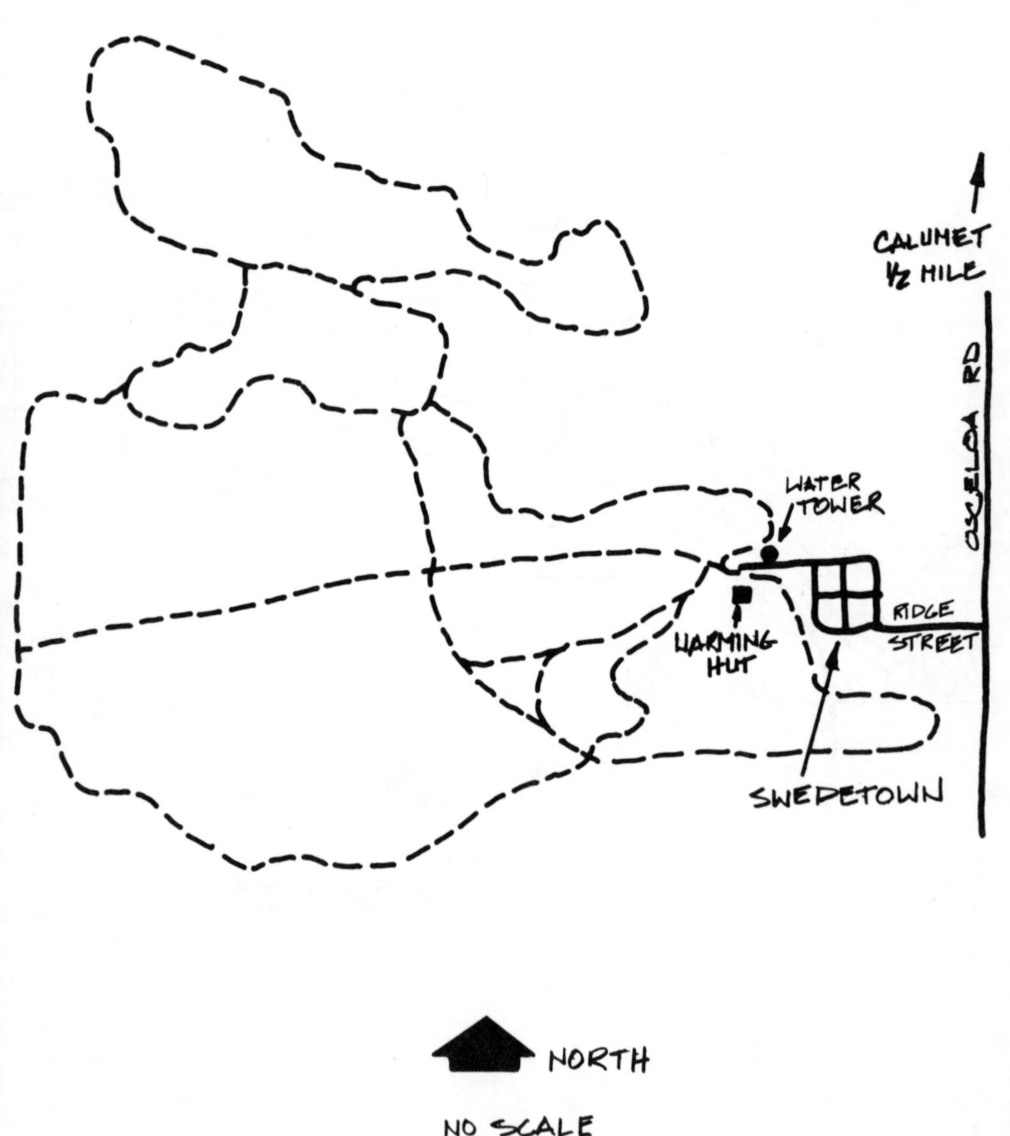

SWEDETOWN SKI TRAILS

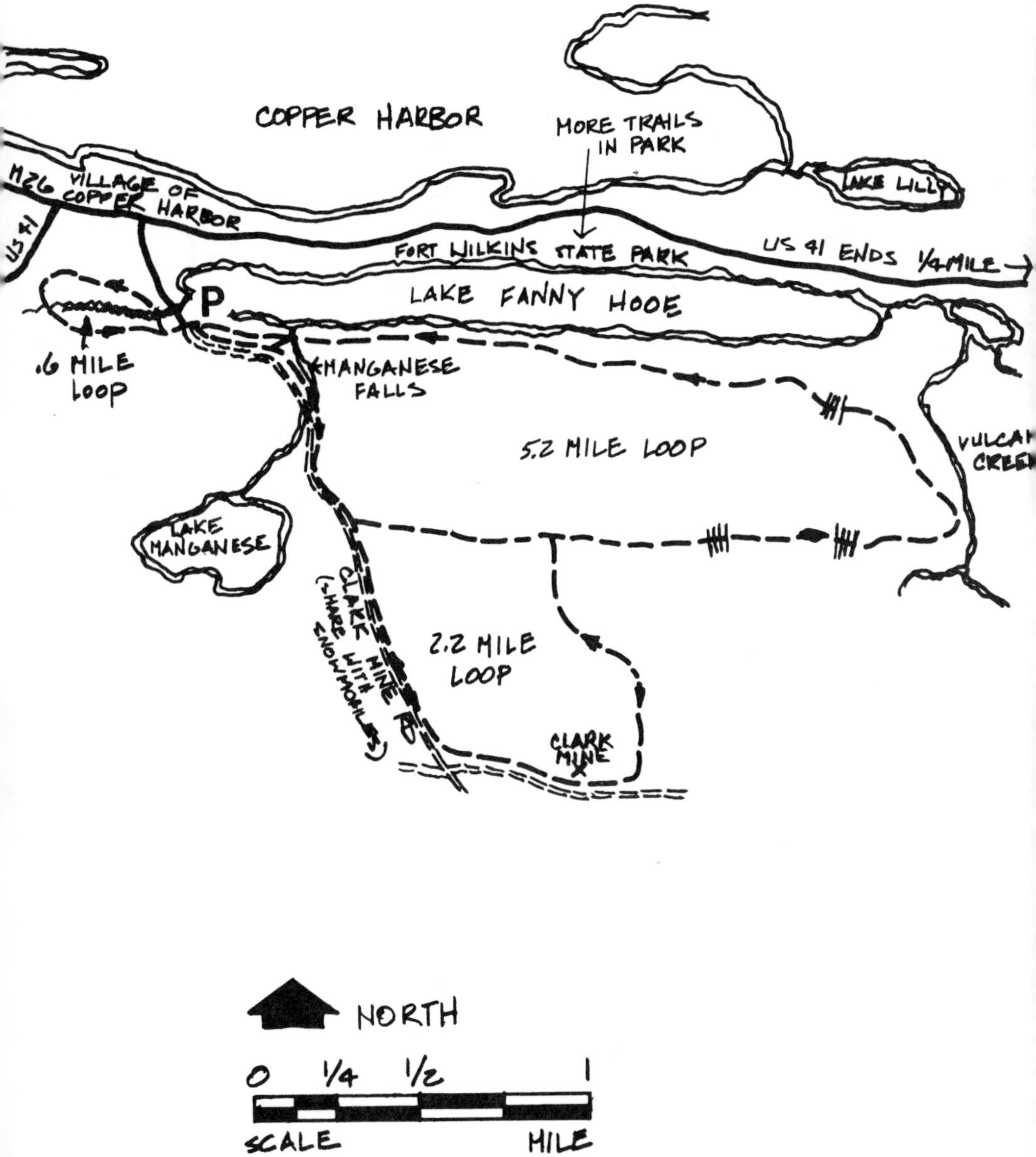

COPPER HARBOR
MORE TRAILS IN PARK
LAKE LILLY
M26 VILLAGE OF COPPER HARBOR
US 41
FORT WILKINS STATE PARK
US 41 ENDS 1/4 MILE →
LAKE FANNY HOOE
P
.6 MILE LOOP
MANGANESE FALLS
5.2 MILE LOOP
LAKE MANGANESE
CLARK MINE RD (SHARE WITH SNOWMOBILES)
2.2 MILE LOOP
CLARK MINE

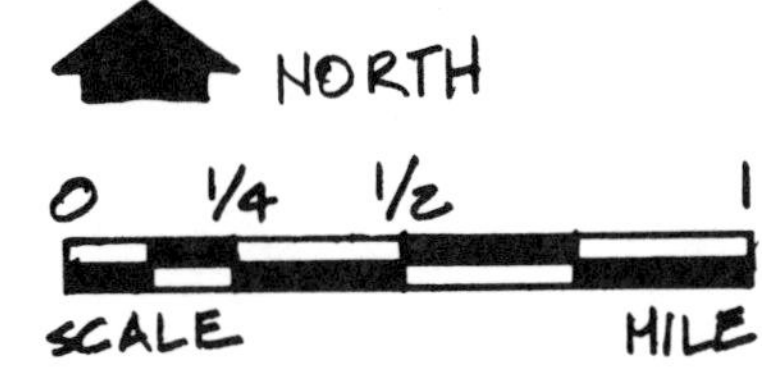

COPPER HARBOR PATHWAY

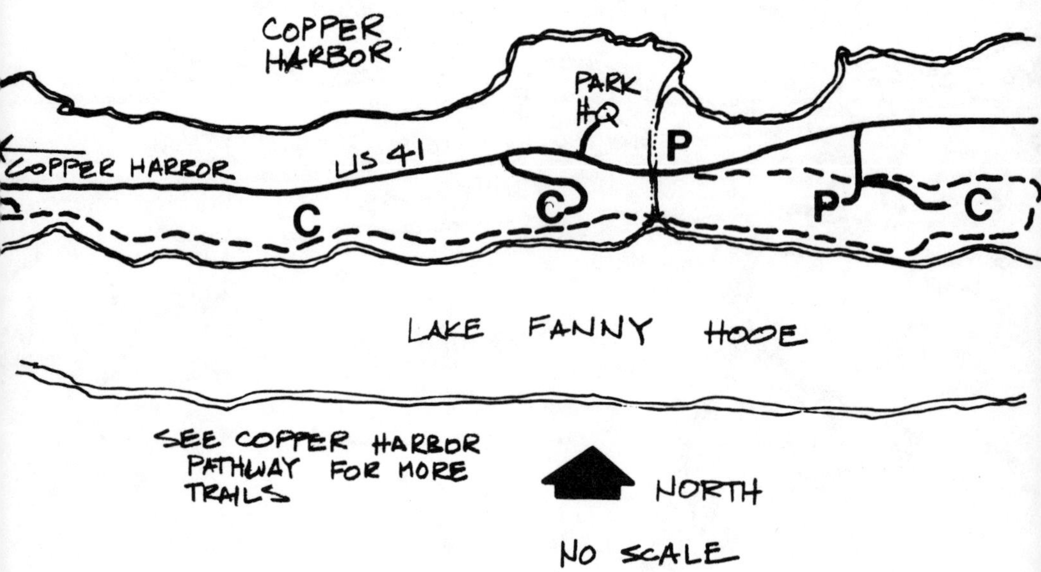

FORT WILKINS STATE PARK

Trail Notes

Technique Fundamentals

by Danforth Holley
Certified Professional Ski Instructor of America (Nordic)

This chapter is not intended to provide you with complete and comprehensive instruction. Rather, it is intended in this book to give the beginner an idea of the basic movements in the sport of cross country skiing. Many of the movements illustrated on the following pages appear quite easy to execute. However, if you have never had a pair of skis attached to your feet before, you will notice from the first moment, a degree of clumsiness that can only be eliminated by practice and instruction. Instruction is critically important to achieve maximum enjoyment from the sport. This chapter is not intended to be a substitute for instruction, but rather an aid to it. These following pages cannot and should not replace the personal instructor who will be able to recognize a flaw and correct the problem, an aspect that no amount of reading and practice can replace.

Good technique is not difficult or complex, but rather the natural and effortless way to propel yourself on skis. The basic movement, the diagonal stride is directly related to normal walking, but is refined and adapted for use with skis. Good technique does not require the beginner to ski fast or for long distances. That will come with the experience and desire to do so, if you choose. It does, however, result in the same efficiency that the racers have when they ski. The key word here is efficiency. Regardless if you are 15 or 50, a citizen racer to be or just a Sunday afternoon tourer, good technique will allow you to get the maximum enjoyment out of the sport while expending the least amount of energy. This is especially important if you are not, athletically oriented. Without good technique, regardless of how strong you may be, you will struggle, plod along and most likely become frustrated. But this need not happen if you learn the basic cross country technique.

As a beginner, the easiest place to learn to ski is at a nordic ski area which has a prepared ski track that is mechanically made. This might seem at first totally contradictory to the whole idea of cross country skiing, which is supposed to promote the idea of making your own trail wherever you choose, but like a lot of things, that will come later. Good tracks will not only reduce your apprehension, but will also speed your progress and mastery of the technique. If a prepared track is not available, get some of your skiing friends to make a track a few hundred yards long for you. Practice on it before tackling the trail.

But first things first. . . . Before you get on the snow, you must first learn how to get in your ski equipment. Usually the skis are put on first, since hands must be free to secure the ski boot to the binding. The only difficulty with putting on skis is to make sure that the correct ski goes on the proper foot. This might seem trite, but I have seen many beginners 2 miles from the parking lot, having great difficulty skiing, not realizing that the skis are reversed!!! For 75mm bindings there is a small symbol of a foot or words stamped on the binding to help you determine which ski is for what foot. An easier way to make this determination is by the shape of the binding. These bindings are not symmetrical. The binding will protrude further out one side of the ski than the other. The side that occurs on will be the ski for that foot.

On the newer 50mm bindings, should you have a pair, the bindings *are* symmetrical so the skis can be interchanged, though that is not recommended. I suggest placing a small piece of tape on the right ski, to make proper identification easy.

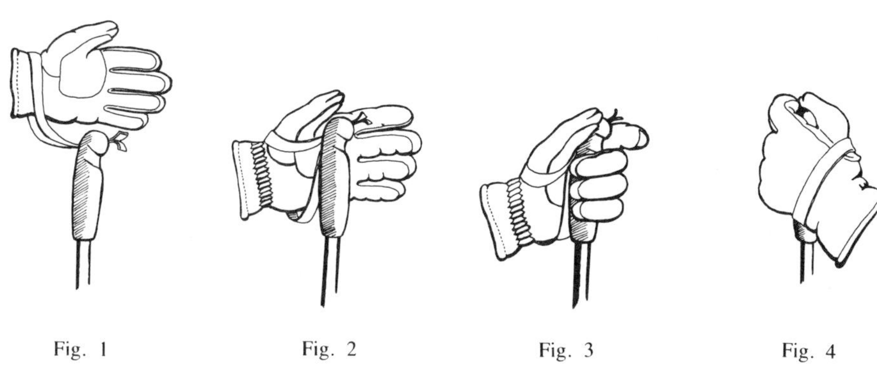

Fig. 1 Fig. 2 Fig. 3 Fig. 4

Properly grasping the poles is also very important, for safety as well as for enjoyment. First, place your hand through the strap when the strap is *above* the pole as shown in figure 1. The most common error is to do this with the strap hanging down. Then lower your hand as shown in figure 2 so that the strap is in your palm. Next grip the pole as shown in figures 3 and 4. The index finger should fit snugly just below the top of the pole. If this does not occur, adjust the strap accordingly. Unlike downhill poles that have straps, the cross country ski pole strap is intended to take most of the force of poling without the need for a tight grip of your hand. This eliminates considerable strain and allows blood to flow freely through your fingers to keep them warm. In addition, with this configuration, if the pole basket gets snagged on a branch, the strap and pole will have the tendency to slide off your hand rather than bind to it. A very important safety feature.

Fig. 1 Fig. 2 Fig. 3

Diagonal Stride

The diagonal stride, the basic technique of cross country skiing is somewhat similar to walking in that opposite arm and leg move together. To learn the stride, begin walking on skis in a ski track on level ground. Do not use poles at first since this will only hinder natural arm movement. Like walking, do not shuffle your feet in the track. When bringing the rear foot forward, lift the foot completely so that body weight is completely transferred to the opposite foot. As the rear foot moves forward and passes the other one, it should begin to glide as the foot that was passed begins to push to propel you forward. After this begins to feel comfortable, poles can be added to increase glide. They are not intended to be balancing devices, for this will only push your body from side to side with little effect on forward glide. They should be placed in the snow only a few inches outside the edge of the track for maximum effect.

In figure 1, the skier has just planted the left pole. The left ski has just completed the kick and the weighted right ski is about to complete the forward glide. Notice the fingers on the right hand are not gripping the pole. The proper pole strap position discussed earlier, will allow the fingers to relax in order to

Fig. 4

Fig. 5

promote good blood circulation to reduce cold fingers and frostbite. As the hand moves forward, the pole will naturally move back into the hand ready to be gripped loosely as shown in figure 2. In figure 2, the left leg and right arm are swinging forward in unison, while the left pole is pushing. In figure 3, as the left foot passes the right, the right ski begins to kick. The right arm continues to swing forward.

In figure 4, the right ski continues to the end of the kick while the left pole finishes the push. The left ski is still gliding forward. Figure 5 is opposite figure 1 with the left ski nearing the end of its glide and the right pole is relaxed and open. A tight grip will greatly reduce arm swing tiring you quickly. The pole, instead of trailing out behind you will end almost straight up in the air, reducing glide distance and balance.

The objective of the diagonal stride is to develop maximum glide. But, don't try to force natural movements of your body. First keep the stride short to maintain balance and maximum body weight shift to the kicking leg. Do not try to imitate others. As your balance improves, the glide will become longer.

Fig. 1 Fig. 2 Fig. 3

Double Pole Stride

The double pole stride is a modification of the diagonal stride where both poles are used in unison to increase glide. The leg movements are identical; however, when one leg kicks, both arms swing forward in a natural opposing movement as illustrated in figures 1 through 3. As the kicking leg comes forward, both poles are planted firmly into the snow (figure 4). As both feet come side by side, the poles are pushed backward, with both feet gliding, as shown in figure 5.

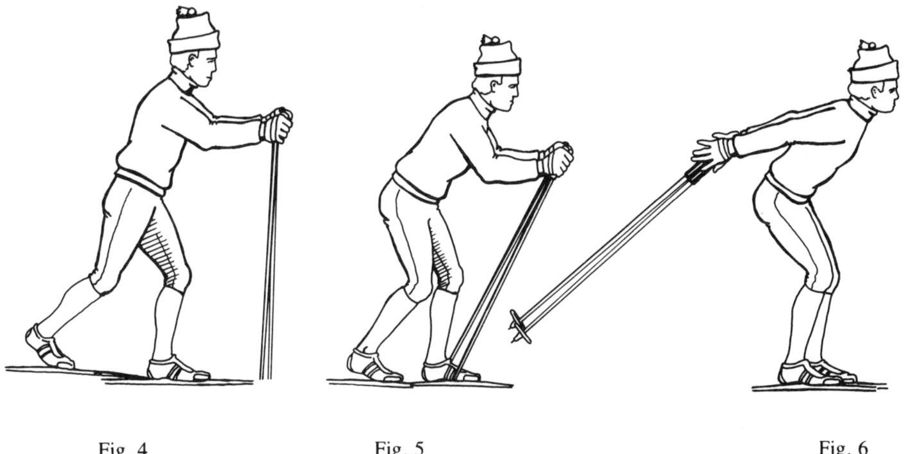

Fig. 4 Fig. 5 Fig. 6

Without the leg movement, another technique is available to you, which is the double pole. With legs side by side, just swing both arms in unison, planting both poles together and pushing off together. Using this technique on any downhill grade, no matter how gradual, will dramatically increase glide much more than by using the diagonal stride.

Kick Turn

The kick turn is very useful when a 180-degree turn is desired in a very confined location where a star turn can't be executed. This turn is also quicker than a star turn.

Fig. 1.

Figure 1 shows the skier intending to turn left. The left pole is planted at the tail of the skis, while the right pole is to the right of the skis near the tips of the skis.

Fig. 2

Figure 2 shows the skier with the left ski raised and the tail in the snow at the *midpoint* of the right ski.

Fig. 3

In figure 3, the left ski has been placed down in the snow in the opposite direction, parallel to the right ski.

Fig. 4

And finally, in figure 4 the right ski is brought around behind the left ski to be positioned parallel to the left ski. The new opposite direction has been achieved.

Pole position may vary somewhat; however, you will quickly realize that a pole in a slightly incorrect position will make it impossible to execute this turn.

Star Turn

For the beginner, the least difficult way to change direction when not moving is by executing the star turn. Starting with parallel skis, lift the ski in the direction you wish to turn (lift is shown here). Angle that ski slightly, while making sure not to let the ski tails overlap each other. The skier then lifts the right ski and repositions it parallel to the left one. Repeat the process until the desired direction is reached.

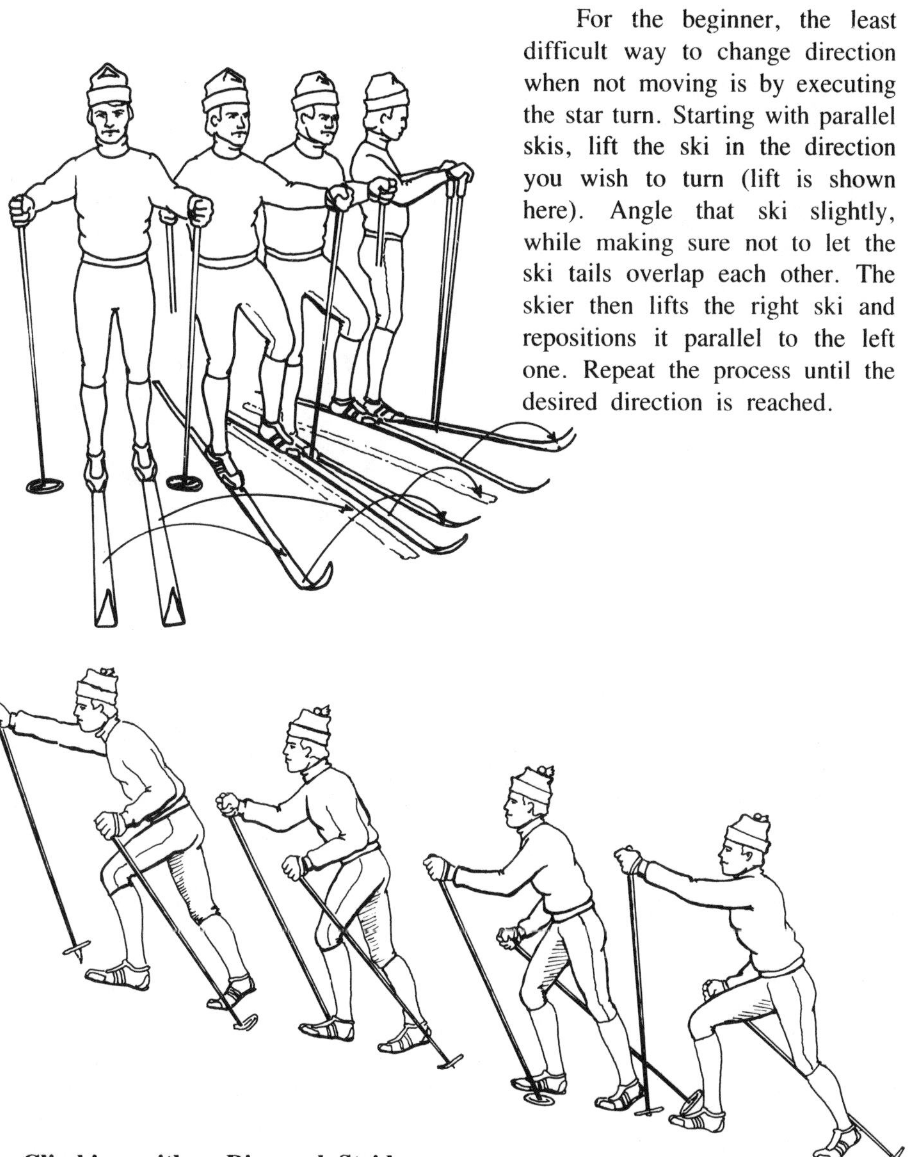

Climbing with a Diagonal Stride

When climbing gradual hills it is important for you to maintain glide and momentum for as long as possible; hopefully until you reach the top. By using a shortened version of the diagonal stride, maintain upper body position directly over the forward leg to maximize weight on the kicking leg. To increase this weight as the slope becomes steeper, separate your skis a few inches if possible to force total body weight shift to the kicking leg.

Herringbone

This step is most commonly used for steep uphill climbs where the diagonal stride cannot be maintained. It is best accomplished by pivoting the skis down to the inside. This will assure firm footing. The skis should form a 45-degree angle to each other. If the hill is very steep, place the pole grips in the palms of your hands so that the poles act as a brake in case the skis lose sufficient grip. If the hill becomes steeper, separate the tips of the skis even farther.

Modified Sidestep

This technique is used as a means to climb steel slopes as an alternative to the herringbone. It is faster and much easier than the standard sidestep. This technique is demonstrated by the skier on the left who is keeping his skis parallel to one another and stepping uphill with the uphill ski being placed slightly forward each time. This step is especially helpful in deep powder snow.

Recovering from a Fall

Undoubtedly, the first technique that you will become most proficient in will be how to get up from a fall. Even with a well-groomed track and the best of instruction, the first fall will occur much sooner than you wish. With a little common sense, getting up is not hard or difficult, regardless of how tangled your skis, legs, arms and poles may be.

For a simple fall to the side this technique is not necessary, but when you really take a spill. . . . you must take the weight off your skis and poles before repositioning them will be possible.

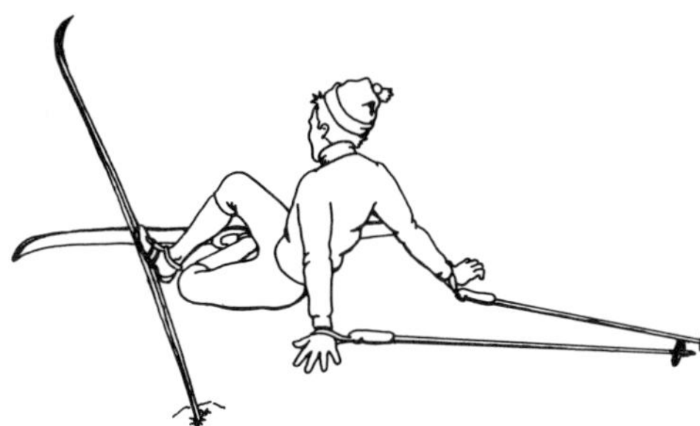

Fig. 1

In figure 1 the skier is shown immediately after a fall. Though the poles are clear of the tangled skis, many times you will not find this the situation.

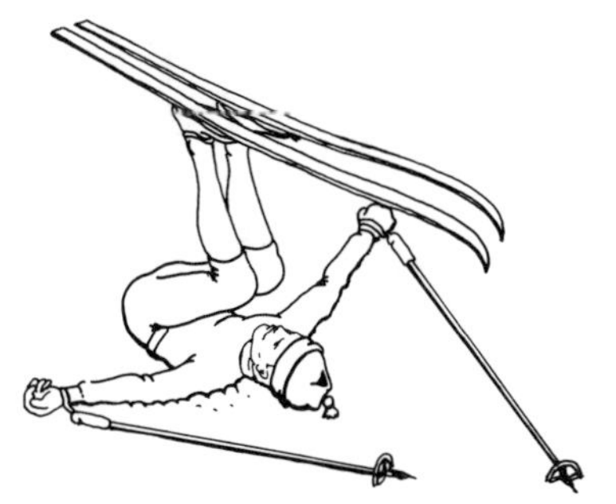

Fig. 2

Figure 2 shows the skier has taken his weight off the back skis by rolling onto his back and raising the skis above his head. This will also free any poles that are tangled.

Next, in figure 3 the skier has brought both skis down next to his body with his feet tucked under him as closely as possible. This is important so that the skis will not slide out from under him when attempting to stand. When falling on a slope, reposition the skis perpendicular to the slope to keep them and you from sliding down the slope before you are ready.

Fig. 3

Figure 4 shows the skier using the poles as an aid in getting up on his feet. Though this is not absolutely necessary, if they are used, be sure to grasp them together before putting weight on them, so they will not break.

Fig. 4

Regardless of how tangled you may be, if you are in deep snow resist the temptation to remove your skis. They are an excellent floatation device. And remember, how do you expect to get into your bindings if you can't even see them!

Snowplow

The skier below is executing the most common method of controlling speed. With his skis pivoted inward, to increase resistance, all he has to do to reduce speed is to increase the angle between the skis. Poles can be dragged to increase resistance but this is not usually necessary. To steer when using the snowplow, just shift more weight to the opposite ski in the direction you wish to turn.

Snowplowing in a Track

When it is necessary to reduce speed in a track, the snowplow can be used, but only one ski at a time. On the straight this will reduce speed substantially without damage to the track or loss of control. The skier above, is controlling speed in a curve by placing the ski on the outside of the curve in the snowplow position. This will assist him in offsetting the outward force that occurs in a curve. With only one ski out of the track at a time, it will be much easier to place it back in the track than if both skis were out simultaneously.

The two skiers below show additional methods for controlling downhill speed, especially in deep powder snow. Poles *must* be put into the positions shown prior to the start of the downhill run. Do not attempt to reposition poles once the downhill run has begun.

Skate Turn

This technique is a very efficient method of turning, since it is very quick, resulting in an increase in speed. To execute this turn, the skier in figure 1 has unweighted the ski in the direction he wishes to turn (right shown here), while pushing off with the left ski that has been slightly pivoted to increase bite. In figure 2 the unweighted ski has been repositioned in the direction of travel, which then is quickly followed by the left ski (not shown). If the turn is large, these steps may have to be repeated in quick succession.

Crouch or Racing Tuck

This position is used to increase speed (by reducing air resistance) on downhill runs. Keep body weight balanced with legs relaxed and one ski slightly forward to improve stability.

Parallel Turn

The parallel turn involves weight shift from side to side and up and down and the pivoting of skis to properly execute this downhill technique. Begin by planting the pole that is on the inside of the turn (not shown). The skier then positions himself in a more erect stance to unweight the skis. This will then allow the skis to turn. Once in the turn the skier then weights the outside ski to push against the snow. Now in the new direction, the skier then evenly distributes his weight between both skis.

Telemark Turn

This is the classic nordic turn that was developed in the province of Telemark, Norway when cross country skis were much larger and more difficult to control. While using poles for balance, figure 1 shows the skier with the inside ski in a position where the tip of the inside ski is even with the boot of the outside ski. At this point, the inside lower leg should be just about parallel with the ski. Continue this position until the new direction is

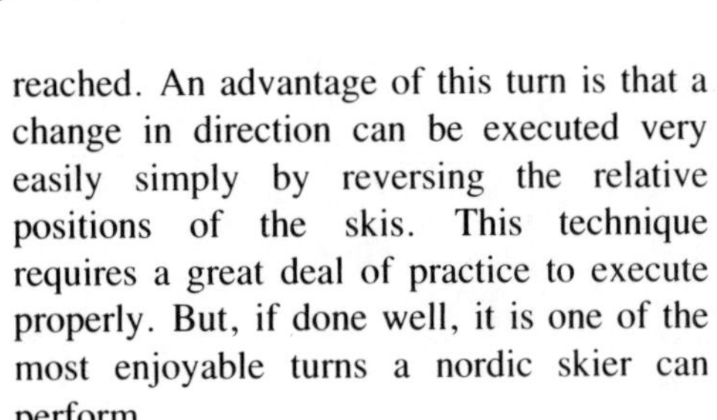

Fig. 1

reached. An advantage of this turn is that a change in direction can be executed very easily simply by reversing the relative positions of the skis. This technique requires a great deal of practice to execute properly. But, if done well, it is one of the most enjoyable turns a nordic skier can perform.

Waxing for Recreational X-C Skiers

by Danforth Holley
Certified Professional Cross Country Ski Instructor (Nordic)

Proper waxing is one of the key elements for the maximum enjoyment of the sport. Contrary to public opinion, the skills needed to properly wax skis is very overrated. The method for waxing is simple and with some practice only takes a few minutes before each tour and not the long time that is often thought.

Definitions to Understand for Proper Waxing

Camber—The curve of the ski. This allows for more uniform body weight distribution throughout the length of the ski in order to permit the ski to glide across the snow farther.

Glide Zone—Actually there are two zones. The front 1/3 of the ski and the rear 1/3 of the ski.

Glide Wax—Special waxes, some color coded, some not, applied to the Glide Zones of the ski for the sole purpose of creating maximum glide across the snow.

Kick Zone—Approximately the center 1/3 of the ski extending forward from a point directly under the rear of the heel plate.

Kick Wax—Special color coded hard and soft waxes corresponding to the various temperature and snow conditions applied to the kick zone of the ski.

Klister—A special soft kick wax used when snow is wet or ski tracks are icy.

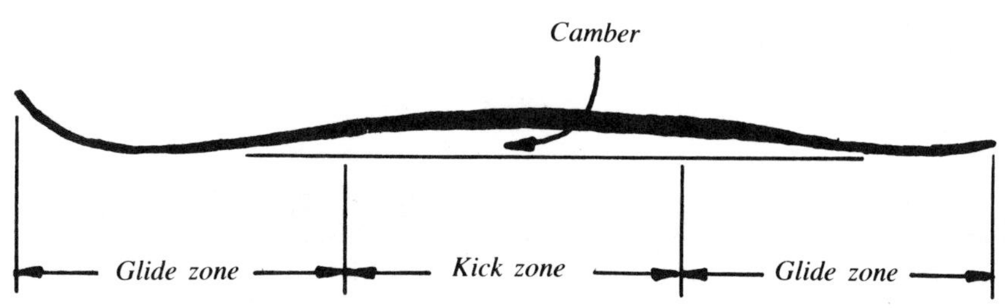

Characteristics of Snow

The only aspect that makes waxing appear difficult is trying to wax skis when there is almost unlimited combinations of snow and temperature conditions. This problem can be simplified if you are aware of what snow is actually made. Though snow often appears soft and velvety, it is actually made of tiny crystals of frozen water. The hardness and sharpness of these crystals determines the snow characteristics and; therefore, the proper wax to be used. The colder the temperature, the sharper the crystals and the warmer the temperature, the duller the crystals. The variety of waxes available are designed to match the characteristics of snow so that the crystals will only penetrate a given depth of the wax. This limited penetration of the wax permits you to push against the snow and be released by it at almost the same time. Therefore, harder wax is generally for colder temperatures (sharp crystals) and softer wax is for warmer temperatures (dull crystals). The exception to this occurs when there is ice on the ski track, in which case a klister (soft wax) is required.

Ski Preparation

Now we begin. . . . If the skis are brand new, they should be given some pre-wax preparation. Starting with clean, dry skis, the first step is to prepare the running surface or base. Sand the base with very fine sandpaper (#120 to #180) to get the base as smooth as possible and to remove any hairs that remain from the manufacturing process, should you have that type of ski. Then, thoroughly flush with water several times and completely dry the ski with a lint free towel. This step is not absolutely necessary but will make for more effortless skiing and better performance on the trail.

Update

Since most skis that are now sold are of fiberglass construction with synthetic bases, this chapter will deal with these skis, however, the same method can be used with the fading wooden skis by applying a pine tar to the wooden bases for moisture proofing and adhering purposes and then putting kick wax over the entire length of the ski and vary its thickness, with more wax on the center of the ski than at either end. All of this is best done by hand not hot iron.

Another most important updating is that most fiberglass skis with synthetic soles are so-called waxless skis but never the less, there is a new concept and great trend toward waxing or technically it could be termed lubricating or a combination of both of these so-called waxless skis. This can be accomplished by use of a fluorinated silicone over the entire ski which greatly enhances the glide and also protects the pattern or kick area from excessive wear and icing, or the glide area may be waxed with a universal wax (preferably hot waxed) and the pattern area (fish scales, diamonds, steps, etc.) can be lubricated with a fluorinated silicone or liquid wax and silicone for reasons mentioned above.

General Waxing Information on Waxable Skis

The first step is to wax the glide zones of the ski. For best results, the glider wax will work the best and remain longest on the skis when it is melted and penetrates into the pores of the base. The type of wax needed is not critical for the beginner, since the wrong selection will only result in a very minimal reduction in glide length, a problem you should not find annoying. Many manufacturers provide a wide range and also "universal" glide zone waxes which are very suitable for recreational skiers, and should be chosen initially. In fact, there is one universal glider wax that can also be used in the kick area by applying thicker layers.

To apply the glide wax, position the ski horizontally on a work bench, between two saw horses or anywhere so that the ski will not see-saw on the ski binding. With the use of an old clothes iron (don't plan to use it for clothes again), press the chosen wax against the iron so that the resulting liquid wax drips off the point of the iron onto the ski base to form a long thin ribbon. Once the wax starts melting, you must work fast or it will end up in a big puddle on the ski. Be sure not to allow the wax to smoke since this will change the character of the wax. Next heat the wax into the base by rubbing the iron on the base. This action will not only spread the wax, but also melt a portion of the wax zone. The wax has been sufficiently heated when the top of the ski (the side of the ski away from the snow) near the tip and tail feels warm to the touch. Then place the ski outside to cool completely. Once cooled, repeat the process several times to get maximum penetration of the wax into the pores of the base. If at any time the iron appears to drag on the ski when ironing in the wax, additional wax should be added to that portion of the ski. Caution: If when ironing, the base turns white, STOP IRONING IMMEDIATELY. The base has gotten too hot. It should cool before proceeding. Next, scrape off the ridged glider wax to produce a smooth uniform surface. The best tool for this is a plastic scraper, available at most ski shops. Unlike metal, plastic will not gouge the ski base. Be sure to also remove all the wax out of the groove. Keeping the groove to its full depth is very important because it helps you to control the skis.

Up to this point, all the work can be done most anytime, even well in advance of the ski tour, however, the remaining steps can only be completed when the conditions of the snow that is to be skied on are known.

The following step involves applying the correct kick wax on the remaining center 1/3 of the ski. The proper application of this wax is very important since it allows you not to slip backward when you put weight on your ski to kick backwards. To select the correct wax to apply, you must first know the type of snow that you are going to ski. If you are at the ski area this can easily be done by grasping a handful of snow and then opening your hand. If the snow remains powdery, then a hard kick wax is needed. On the other hand, if it turns into a ball of wet snow, or ice is in the tracks of the ski trail, then a soft wax is required. Remember to always crayon the wax on evenly in short, rapid strokes covering the entire ski bottom. What you then do depends on the snow temperature. If it is very cold, say less than 20°F., rub the wax out to a gloss with a waxing cork. Nearer freezing, smooth the wax surface slightly with a cork but leave it a bit rough.

For the Intermediate Skier

Many wax manufacturers have developed "two wax" systems designed especially for beginners that eliminate the rainbow of colored waxes that are on the market. One wax is for above 32°F. and one is for below 32°F. They are commonly known as Red/Blue, Plus/Minus and Gold/Silver. I would highly suggest starting out with one of these systems. They all work reasonably well except in some icy conditions, where klister is still required. After some experience is gained in waxing with these waxes you may want to graduate to the multi-colored wax system.

To apply the wax, choose the correct wax as mentioned above or by using a reliable weather report the night before the tour. By knowing what condition the snow is at that time, you can put on the first layer in your home. Though not absolutely necessary but to make the kick wax more durable, a thin layer of green (for cold weather) and blue (for warmer weather) can be ironed into the base as a first or binder layer. If the two wax system is used, select the proper one of the two and proceed accordingly. To iron on the wax, first crayon a uniform layer of the chosen wax onto the kick zone. Then with an iron, smooth out the wax the same way as done for the glider wax application. After the ski has cooled, scrape off excess wax to produce a uniform layer. If the conditions you anticipate will require additional wax, use a cork instead of a scraper to smooth out the wax. If you don't know what the conditions will be, just leave the wax on and wait until the next day. It is much faster to scrape off wax than to add it. Not only will this method eliminate, for the most part, the need to purchase special binder wax (not worth the money for the beginning skier) but you will reduce the time normally needed to wax once you arrive at the skiing site.

For the Serious Tourer

If you have not melted in any kick wax, wait until you are at the trail head to choose the correct wax to apply. Refer to a wax chart and do not hesitate to ask a few people who have skied the trail. With that information, you should have a good idea with which wax to start. If there is a choice between two colors, choose the colder of the two, since it is much easier to add a warmer (softer) wax over a colder (harder) wax than the reverse. Ever try to spread peanut butter over jelly? That is what it is like. Once the wax is evenly crayoned over the entire kick zone, buff the wax out with a cork to make a smooth uniform layer. Add another layer or two and then try out the skis on the snow. Be sure to ski at least 300 feet, so the wax will have an opportunity to set up properly on the skis. If slipping still occurs when attempting to kick backward, the next question is should I add more wax of the same color or go on to the next warmer (softer) wax? Adding more thin layers of the same wax is much safer than using the next softer wax, since that may result in using a wax that is too soft which will cause ice to form on the skis. The ice will cause poor kick and glide. However, later in the day if the temperature increases, a softer wax may be needed. But don't confuse lack of kick after skiing a while with warmer weather conditions. It may be a result of loss of kick wax which is causing the slipping. When waxing the kick zone, remember it does not extend beyond the heel of the boot. In most cases kick wax added back of that point will only reduce glide and have little effect on improving kick.

If the conditions are very warm (above 40°F.) or the ski track is icy, klister will most likely be needed. In wet conditions where red hard wax is not quite enough, yellow klister in the tin can be used with good success. However, if the track is icy, usually only tube klister will be effective. Spray on klisters are not recomended.

To apply klister try to do it in a warm room. That will make the job much easier. If the tube of klister you have selected from that wax chart is cold, warm the tube with a propane torch. With a clean ski free of wax, apply a thin ribbon of klister along each side of the groove for about two-thirds the length of the normal kick zone starting with the heel end. Klister does not require as much contact with the ice to be equally effective as hard wax does on powder snow. While still warm, and using your finger or the stick provided with the klister, evenly smooth it out, covering the width of the ski. This will take some practice to do it well. If the klister becomes hard before you finish, warm up the klister with the torch using quick long swings so that the flame will not damage the base. Once the klister is spread, let the ski cool *completely* outdoors before skiing on them. It is a good idea to take along a small tube of waterless hand soap (available at most ski shops) to clean your hands. After skiing, remove all of the klister with a scraper and wax remover before packing up, since warm klister tends to get on everything.

For waxable skis, that is about it, with one important exception. It is always necessary to remove all waxes including sticky klister and by far, the best method is to use the very best wax remover sold in bulk cans with a dauber and in spray cans. It will save much time and produces a clean ski. Remember, for best results of waxing it is absolutely necessary to apply the new wax on thoroughly cleaned bottoms.

This chapter is, I believe, the first material written on waxing that categorizes for the x-c skier in a crystal clear way the methods for the beginner, intermediate and serious recreational skier.

Also, it is a first writing in a general way and not mentioning any brand names. You do not have to stick to any one brand as mentioned in most ski books. In all honesty, there are a number of good waxes or lubricants available to the skiing public.

Most Important, Good Tour

Ski Tour Planning Guide

by Dennis R. Hansen

A Word of Caution

Planning a ski tour whether it is only a few hours long or will involve the entire day, requires serious planning. Outdoor recreation in the winter can be extremely rewarding, but proper precautions should be taken because of the hazardous weather conditions that you may encounter.

The effect of wind during the winter is very critical since it accentuates the low temperatures on the human body. Commonly called the Wind Chill Factor, the temperature is usually well below the actual air temperature reading. When combined with moisture on your body, this problem is greatly compounded. Since wet clothing draws off body heat, it is extremely important to stay as dry as possible and adequately protected from the wind with proper clothing. If care is not taken, you could become affected by hypothermia, frostbite or both. Either condition is dangerous but can be avoided, if care is taken.

Wind Speed Cooling Power of Wind

Expressed as "Equivalent Chill Temperature"

mph	**Local Temperature (°F)**											
calm	40	30	20	10	5	0	-10	-20	-30	-40	-50	-60
	Equivalent Chill Temperature											
5	35	25	15	5	0	-5	-15	-25	-35	-45	-55	-70
10	30	15	5	-10	-15	-20	-35	-45	-60	-70	-80	-95
15	25	10	-5	-20	-25	-30	-45	-60	-70	-85	-100	-110
20	20	5	-10	-25	-30	-35	-50	-65	-80	-95	-110	-120
25	15	0	-15	-30	-35	-45	-60	-75	-90	-105	-120	-135
30	10	0	-20	-30	-40	-50	-65	-80	-95	-110	-125	-140
35	10	-5	-20	-35	-40	-50	-65	-80	-100	-115	-130	-145
40	10	-5	-20	-35	-45	-55	-70	-85	-100	-115	-130	-150
Danger				Higher Danger (flesh may freeze in 1 min.)				Great Danger (flesh may freeze in 30 seconds)				

Frostbite is the freezing of skin and/or appendages as the result of inadequate protection from cold temperatures. Hands, feet, face and ears are especially vulnerable to this condition. The first danger signal is a tingling or numb sensation. If treated early, usually by improving blood circulation, warming the effected area and adding dry clothing (being sure to remove wet clothing first) should correct the problem. In the case of the face, your companions should check each other often for any signs of visible frostbite, in the form of white or gray patches of skin. If for some reason frostbite does occur, warm the affected area gradually and protect it from any additional exposure while continuing to improve blood circulation. Under no circumstances should you massage, rub, apply high heat or break blisters, for this will only aggravate the condition. Your most important concerns should be to prevent additional frostbite and keep the effected area as clean as possible. In the case of fingers and toes, keep them separated with sterile gauze.

Hypothermia is another condition that you should guard against. This condition is harder to recognize and often affects its victims without their knowledge. Only constant vigilance on the part of all your companions will keep this problem from affecting your group.

Hypothermia is caused by the drastic lowering of the body core temperature resulting from exposure to cool or cold temperature, wind, moisture and coupled with fatigue. It's not necessary to have extremely low temperatures for this condition to occur. It can happen very rapidly and may in extreme cases result in death if not treated promptly. Symptoms include uncontrolled shivering, heavy speech, fumbling, extreme fatigue, stiff joints, irrationality, bluish lips, dilated pupils and breathing difficulties. In mild cases, treatment involves replacing wet clothing with dry, then rewarming the entire body by wrapping the victim in blankets, clothing or placing them in a sleeping bag to allow their own remaining body heat to rewarm themselves. If possible, give the victim warm liquids and food to warm them internally. In more severe cases, it may be necessary to provide additional heat by sharing the body heat of another through direct skin to skin contact. Of course, the victim should be taken to a medical facility when possible. If you guard against the possibility of contracting hypothermia by staying dry, warm and do not become overly tired, this problem should not occur.

Both hypothermia and frostbite can be prevented through the proper selection and use of clothing. The following section should be helpful in that regard.

Clothing Suggestions

Thoughtful choice and proper use of clothing is the single most important consideration that will make your tour an enjoyable experience. Clothing selection is a very individual matter since the conditions under which it is worn are unique to you alone. The speed you ski, your technique, the length of the tour, your perspiration rate, weather conditions and your tolerance of cold temperatures will all affect the type of clothing you should wear. An outfit that is perfect for someone else may be very uncomfortable for you. For those reasons, the only accurate way to determine what is correct for you, especially in different weather conditions is by experimentation. It is not necessary to buy special cross country outfits to be properly dressed. In most cases your existing wardrobe should contain clothing that is very suitable for cross country skiing. The following suggestions you may find useful as a starting point to determine what is correct for you.

More than anything else, the clothing you choose should accomplish three objectives. It should keep you WARM, regardless of the temperature or how much it changes; DRY, regardless of the amount of moisture your body produces or falls on you in the form of snow or sleet; and your clothing should allow for the MAXIMUM AMOUNT OF BODY MOVEMENT WITHOUT DISCOMFORT.

The easiest way to keep warm is to wear several layers of lightweight clothing rather than a single heavy garment. Not only does this permit you to adjust the amount of clothing to the activity level or change in weather conditions but the layers of clothing develop air space between them which add to the insulating value of the clothing without adding weight. If you rely on one heavy garment, you will likely be either too warm or too cold most of the time, not to mention the bulkiness of such clothing.

Even with the proper number of layers, some perspiration will develop. It is therefore essential that it be evaporated as rapidly as possible in order to stay dry. To accomplish this, I have found "fishnet" and polypropylene underwear to be quite effective. When dry, it creates a thin layer of warm air, and when wet it promotes evaporation. Another source of moisture that should be prevented from collecting is caused by external sources, either from falling snow or sleet or by snow being picked up on clothing as a result of falls or normal skiing. If the snow is dry it should be removed, being careful not to push it into the fabric. The exception is on knee socks, where small amounts of dry snow should be left untouched since this adds insulating quality. Obviously in moist snow or sleet conditions, a water repellent outer garment is the order of the day.

The third requirement of cross country ski clothing is that it should provide competely unrestricted movement of all parts of the body. Snug or tight fitting clothing will soon chafe skin and may restrict blood circulation, not to mention the general uncomfortable feeling. For maximum comfort, any garment that may bind in the shoulders, waist, knees or thighs should be avoided. This is why much of the new cross country clothing is made of stretch fabric.

Since the head radiates about 40% of body heat, it is the single most important part of your anatomy in controlling the overall body temperature. With proper use of head gear, total perspiration can be kept to a minimum, making the job of staying dry much easier. Depending on the weather conditions you may choose anything from not wearing any head protection in very warm weather, to a full knit ski mask or balaclava for maximum protection from wind and snow. In between these two extremes, a headband and light knit ski cap are very useful for most situations. When planning a day tour, it might be a good idea to put a knit ski mask or balaclava in your pack in case the weather turns windy or cold.

Hand protection is another very individual matter. Control of the poles vs. the warmth of mittens will be the major decision you will have to make. In most situations gloves should be suitable for most everyone. But for cold weather, mittens are very useful regardless of the loss of control of the poles that may result (another good item to carry in your day pack).

As mentioned in the first part of this section, staying dry is a major objective of the clothing you wear. This becomes of prime importance when choosing upper body clothing. Next to your skin you should consider "fishnet," polypropylene or Duofold underwear. The next layers should be of fabric that breathes such as a turtle neck seater, flannel shirt or wool sweater. The weight of the garment you choose will depend on personal need and weather conditions you expect to encounter. A third layer similar to the second but a little heavier, and that should be enough. I do recommend that you take along a wind breaker, down sweater or vest in your pack to put on when you stop for a break to eat or rest. Without this extra garment you could become chilled, especially if it's windy.

Freedom of movement is the most important consideration when choosing lower body garments. Most any loose fitting trousers will do just fine. Corduroy, poplin, wool or the stretch "warm ups" are excellent. Stay away from jeans because they usually are cut too tight and become very uncomfortable when wet. Trousers used with gaitors are an excellent combination for bushwacking and general skiing. They keep snow off the lower leg and out of the boots, not to mention the extra layer for warmth.

Of course, knickers are the customary pants for the cross country skier. Not only do they give the maximum freedom of movement but they also are the most comfortable since they don't bind in the crotch or rub at the ankles. They are available in many different fabrics and styles to suit anyone's taste. Combined with the knee sox, I think they are well worth the investment if you ski very much. Many people have made knickers from a pair of pants and some elastic. But don't cut them off too short. Leave plenty of room in the knees.

Proper protection of the feet is very important because of their susceptibility to frostbite. Generally, two layers are the norm. An inner layer of light wool or cotton and the outer layer of wool seem to work well. But experiment on your own. I personally use just one pair of wool soxs and find that to be very satisfactory. If the weather becomes very cold, try an old pair of soxs OVER your boots. You will be surprised how warm they can keep your feet. Don't forget an extra pair for your day pack. Wet feet are no fun.

Equipment and Food Checklist

The amount of gear you need to take with you will depend on the length, location and trail or area you intend to ski. Nevertheless, it's very important that you take along a few items to make your tour safe and enjoyable.

Since it is very uncomfortable to carry things in your pocket, a "fanny pack" is convenient for most short tours. Not only is it just the right size, but unlike a day pack nothing is covering your back to restrict evaporation. Of course, for the day long tour, a larger day pack that allows complete freedom of movement for your arms is essential. Both types of packs come in many different shapes and sizes to suit your specific needs.

1. Spare ski tip—Too many times I've seen people having to walk miles in deep snow for the sake of this $7 item.
2. Trail or area map—Just take this book along.
3. Wax/cork/scraper—Usually one wax warmer and one colder should be enough.
4. Compass.
5. Waterproof matches.
6. Knife—Handy to have at lunch, if nothing else.
7. Chap stick.
8. Sunglasses with elastic strap.
9. Extra mittens or gloves and soxs.
10. Plastic trash bag—Can be used as emergency clothing.
11. Food and liquid—The amount will depend on the length of your tour. But always take something. You will be surprized how hungry you can get. It should taste good, repenish body fluids and be high in calories. Oranges, apples, Gatorade mixed with orange juice, raisins, candy, cheese, dried fruit, salami, cookies, hot chocolate, honey and tea are good on the trail.
12. Whistle—Blowing a whistle when lost or disabled is much more efficient than yelling in order to attract attention.
13. First aid kit.

Holley International Company markets many of the items listed above including a spare ski tip, Holley Solar-Air Emergency Kit (emergency plastic shelter) and the Holley Universal X-C Trail Kit which contains universal ski wax, lubricant for waxless skis, compass and a cork/scraper tool. These products are available at your local ski shop.

Two valuable emergency kits are available directly from the Holley International Company's special order department. One called "HELP" contains 70 essential items for wilderness survival in a container only 4½" X 3½" in diameter. The other is the "HIKER" first aid kit. This kit contains 25 items in a plastic contoured case only 3¾" X 3¼" X 1". Write Holley International Company, 63 Kercheval Suite 204A, Grosse Pointe Farms, MI 48236 for prices and order information.

Ski Tour Checklist

When planning a ski tour the following list should help you make the tour a safe trip.

1. Check skis and poles for breaks and loose screws.
2. Choose companions carefully. Their skill and strength will determine the length of your tour. Never ski faster than the slowest skier in your group.
3. Check you map and decide on the route or area you intend to ski.
4. Be sure you have all necessary equipment and food.
5. Choose clothing for anticipated weather conditions. At least one member of the group should take additional clothing for unexpected problems that might occur.
6. Leave your trip schedule with a responsible person and contact them on your return.

One Last Comment

This section is only intended as a brief summary of the topics covered and not as a conclusive reference. For detailed information on subjects such as winter camping, orienteering, skiing technique, regional trail guides and racing, I suggest that you refer to the Recommended Reading section of this book. It lists over 80 books, pamphlets and magazines covering every aspect of cross country skiing.

Competition Calendar

DECEMBER

COPPER ISLAND SEASON OPENER—2.5, 5, 10 and 15 kms

Contact—Copper Island X-C Ski Club, 507 Oak St., Calumet, MI 49913 (906) 337-1726

SHANTY CREEK STAMPEDE—5, 10 and 15 kms

Contact—Hilton-Shanty Creek Lodge, PO Box 355, Bellaire, MI 49615 (616) 533-8621

ISHPEMING OPENER—5 and 10 kms

Contact—Knut Strom, 484 Ready St., Ishpeming, MI 49849 (906) 485-1747

COOL X-C LEROY LOPPET—12 kms

Contact—Cool X-C Ski Touring Center, 4571 210th Ave., LeRoy, MI 49655 (616) 768-4624

JANUARY

NORDICAN CUP—5, 7.5 and 10 kms

Contact—Le Cycliste, 726 Spring St., Petoskey, MI 49770 (616) 347-2261

COOL X-C 15 KILO—5, 7.5, 10 and 15 kms

Contact—Cool X-C Ski Touring Center, 4571 210th Ave., LeRoy, MI 49655 (616) 768-4624

BUCHANAN WINTER FESTIVAL RACE—10 kms

Contact—Robert Ramsey, 1314 Crescent Lane, Niles, MI 49120 (616) 683-2371

PENTWATER VANN LÖP—10 kms

Contact—Rek-n-Reef, 347 S. Hancock St., Pentwater, MI 49449 (616) 869-6811

NORDICA—1.5 to 8 kms

Contact—Robert Fox, 297 Prospect, Romeo, MI 48065 (313)752-4616

LANSING WINTERFEST—Various

Contact—Lansing Park and Recreation Department, City Hall, Lansing, MI 48933 (517) 487-1270

CITY OF TROY NORDIC CLASSIC—Various

Contact—Troy Park and Recreation Department, 500 W. Big Beaver Rd., Troy, MI 48084 (313) 524-3484

BAHNHOF-HILTON SHANTY CREEK OPEN—10 and 15 kms

Contact—Hilton-Shanty Creek Lodge, PO Box 355, Bellaire, MI 49615 (616) 533-8621

NORTH AMERICAN VASA RACE—25 and 50 kms

Contact—Park Place Motor Inn, 300 State St., Traverse City, MI 49684 (616) 946-5410

COPPER COUNTRY CHAMPIONSHIP—Various

Contact—Copper Island X-C Ski Club, 507 Oak St., Calumet, MI 49913 (906) 337-1726

SNOW RUSH—Various

Contact—Oakland County Park and Recreation Department, 2800 Watkins Lake Rd., Pontiac, MI 48054 (313) 858-0906

FEBRUARY

MID-CANADA WILDERNESS LOPPET—20 and 40 kms

Contact—Mid-Canada Wilderness Loppet, 158 LaRonde Ave., Sault Ste. Marie, Ontario, Canada P6B 5R6

WHITE PINE STAMPEDE—20 and 50 kms

Contact—White Pine Stampede, PO Box 429, Mancelona, MI 49659 (616) 587-8351

AVALANCHE SKI CLASSIC—5 and 10 kms

Contact—Avalanche Ski Classic, PO Box 232, Boyne City, MI 49712

SILVER CREEK CHALLENGE—18 kms

Contact—Francie Szymanski, 1029 Ottawas Lane, East Tawas, MI 48730 (517) 362-8139

APPLE ISLAND SNOW CHASE—3 kms

Contact—West Bloomfield Park and Recreation Department, 6485 W. Maple Rd., West Bloomfield, MI 48033 (313) 661-2240

MERIDIAN CLASSIC—3 to 6 kms

Contact—The Freestyle Shop, 2682 E. Grand River Ave., East Lansing, MI 48823 (517) 351-9026

FARMINGTON HILLS NORDIC CLASSIC—Various

Contact—Farmington Hills Park and Recreation Department, 31555 11 Mile Rd., Farmington Hills, MI 48018 (313) 474-6115

GRAND RAPIDS LANGLAUF—3, 5, 10 and 15 kms

Contact—G. R. Langlauf, 1324 Lake Drive, Grand Rapids, MI 49503 (616) 451-3054

TURSKIREE RACE FESTIVAL—5, 10 and 15 kms

Contact—Hugh Acton, 7801 North 46th St., Augusta, MI 49012 (616) 731-5266

HOWELL CROSS COUNTRY SKI RACE—Various

Contact—Howell Park and Recreation Department, 925 W. Grand River Ave., Howell, MI 48843 (517) 546-0693

CHARLEVOIX WINTER CUP—4, 10, 20 kms

Contact—Charlevoix Chamber of Commerce, 408 Bridge St., Charlevoix, MI 49720 (616) 547-2101

LIVONIA NORDIC RACE—2 to 8 kms

Contact—Livonia Park and Recreation Department, 32025 Lyndon, Livonia, MI 48154 (313) 421-2000

KEN MAR CLASSIC—2, 3, 5, 10 and 15 kms

Contact—Ken Mar, Rte 3, Box 790, Gaylord, MI 49735 (517) 732-4950

SAINT URHO DAY CITIZEN RACE—5 and 10 kms

Contact—Champion Ski Touring Center, Champion, MI 49814 (906) 339-2294

MARCH

COOL X-C MICHIGAN RELAYS—3x5 kms and 3x7.5 kms

Contact—Cool X-C Ski Touring Center, 4571 210th Ave., LeRoy, MI 49655 (616) 768-4624

WOOD SKI CLASSIC—10 kms

Contact—Greg Sweval, RR1, Box 128A, Bessemer, MI 49911 (906) 663-4791/229-5420

BROCKWAY MOUNTAIN RACE—10 and 20 kms

Contact—Copper Island X-C Ski Club, 507 Oak St., Calumet, MI 49913 (906) 337-1726

ULLR DAG RACE—10 and 20 kms

Contact—Hilton-Shanty Creek Lodge, PO Box 355, Bellaire, MI 49615 (616) 533-8621

SLUSH RUSH—20 kms

Contact—Greg Swevel, RR1 Box 128A, Bessemer, MI 49911 (906) 663-4791/229-5420

Recommended Reading

General

Cross Country Skiing Today by John Caldwell. Stephen Greene Press, Brattleboro, VT 05301.

Ski Touring by Osgood and Hurley. Charles E. Tuttle Co., Inc., Rutland, VT 05701.

Complete Cross Country Skiing and Touring by Lederer and Wilson. W. W. Norton and Co. 55-5th Ave., New York, NY 10008.

Skiing with Kids by Northrop. The Chatham Press, Old Greenwich, CT 06870.

Wintering in Snow Country by Osgood. Stephen Greene Press, Brattleboro, VT 05301.

The Regnery Guide to Ski Touring by Wilk and Sumner. Henry Regnery Co., 180 N. Michigan Ave., Chicago, IL 60601.

Ski Touring—A Winter Affair by Bigglestone and Strait. Kendall/Hunt Publishing Co., 2460 Kerper Blvd., Dubuque, IA 52001.

Ski Cross Country, From Touring to Racing by Brady and Skienstad. Dial Press, New York, NY.

The Cross Country Skiing Handbook by Baldwin. Charles Scribner's Sons, 597-5th Ave., New York, NY.

Nordic Touring and Cross Country Skiing by Brady. Holubar Inc., Box 7, Boulder, CO 80302.

Manual of Ski Mountaineering by Brower. Sierra Club Books, 597 5th Ave., New York, NY 10017.

Wilderness Skiing by Steck and Tejada-Flores. Sierra Club Books, 597 5th Ave., New York, NY 10017.

The Family Wilderness Handbook by Welch. Ballantine Books, 101 5th Ave., New York, NY 10003.

Winter Hiking and Camping by Adirondack Mountain Club Inc., Ridge Road, Glen Falls, NY 12801.

The Complete Guide to Cross Country Skiing and Touring by Tokle and Luray. Holt, Rinehart and Winston Inc., 383 Madison Ave., New York, NY 10017.

Ski Orienteering by Kjellstrom. Silva Inc., Highway 39, North LaPorte, IN 46350.

Steve Rieschl's Ski Touring For the Fun of It by Freeman. Little, Brown & Company, Boston, MA.

Snow Camping by Nordic World Editors. Nordic World, PO Box 366, Mountain View, CA 94042.

Discover Cross Country Skiing by Nordic World Editors. Nordic World, PO Box 366, Mountain View, CA 94042.

Winter Safety Handbook Nordic World, PO Box 366, Mountain View, CA 94042.

Training for Nordic Skiing Nordic World, PO Box 366, Mountain View, CA 94042.

Cross Country Downhill by Pacific Search Press, 715 Harrison St., Seattle, WA 98109.

Ski Touring Schedule by The Ski Touring Council Inc., Troy, VT 05868. This is a schedule of events held in the northeastern United States, published each year.

Skiing Cross Country by Baldwin. McGraw-Hill Book Company, 1221 Ave. of the Americas, New York, NY 10020.

The Pleasures of Cross-Country Skiing by Lund. Avon Books, 959 8th Ave., New York, NY 10019.

Cross Country Ski the Natural Way by Odmark. Contemporary Books Inc., 180 North Michigan Ave., Chicago, IL 60601.

The Complete Book of Cross Country Skiing and Ski Touring by Liebers, Barnes & Noble Books c/o Coward, McCann & Geoghegan, 200 Madison Ave., New York, NY 10016.

Holley X-C Waxing Chart by Holley. Holley International Co., 63 Kercheval Ave., Suite 204A, Grosse Pointe Farms, MI 48236.

Cross Country Ski Waxing and Maintenance by Williams. Contemporary Books Inc., 180 North Michigan Ave., Chicago, IL 60601.

Waxing for Cross Country Skiing by Brady and Skiemstad. Wilderness Press, 2440 Bancroft, Berkeley, CA 94704.

Cross Country Skiing for Everybody by Collins and Faulkner. Great Lakes Living Press, Ltd., 21750 Main St., Matteson, IL 60443.

Be Expert with Map and Compass by Kjellstrom. Honey Hollow Rd., Pound Ridge, NY 10576.

Ski Touring Guides

Ski Touring in New England by Tapley. Stone Wall Press, 19 Mussey St., Lexington, MA 02173.

25 Ski Tours in the White Mountains by Ford and Ford. New Hampshire Publishing Co., Box 70, Somersworth, NY 03878.

The Guide to Ski Touring in Jackson Hole by La Vake and Horn. Allumette Studio, Box 1550, Jackson, WY 83001.

Ski Touring Guide to New England by Bass. Eastern Mountain Sports Inc., 1041 Commonwealth Ave., Boston, MA 02215.

Ski Touring Trails in Colorado Front Range by Suddith. The Touchstone Press, PO Box 81, Beaverton, OR 97005.

25 Ski Tours in Western Massachusetts by Frado, Lawson and Coy. New Hampshire Publishing Company, 9 Orange St., Sommersworth, NH 03878.

25 Ski Tours in Connecticut by Wass and Alvord. New Hampshire Publishing Company, 9 Orange St., Sommersworth, NH 03878.

25 Ski Tours in the Green Mountains by Ford and Ford. New Hampshire Publishing Company, 9 Orange St., Sommersworth, NH 03878.

Yellowstone Ski Tours by Barber. The Rocky Mountain Trading Co., PO Box 512, Yellowstone National Park, WO 82190

Snow Tours in Washington by Cameron. Signpost Books, 8912 192nd SW, Edmonds, WA 98020.

Ski Touring in Northern New Mexico by Beard. Adobe Press, PO Box 12334, Albuquerque, NM 87105.

Northern Colorado Ski Tours by Sudduth. Touchstone Press, PO Box 81, Beaverton, OR 97005.

Central Colorado Ski Tours by Sudduth. Pruett Publishing Co., 3235 Prairie Ave., Boulder, CO 80301.

Ski Tours in California by Beck. Wilderness, 2440 Bancroft Way, Berkeley, CA 94704.

Ski Touring Guide by Ski Touring Council Inc., Troy, VT 05868.

Cross Country Skee by John and Midge Schweitzer. 638 S. Mayflower Dr., Appleton, WI 54911 (Wisconsin Trail guide).

Washington Nordic Tours by Bradley. Signpost, 16812 36th Ave. West, Lynwood, WA 98036.

Aspen Tourskiing & Cross-Country by Auger. Columbine Books, PO Box 2842, Aspen, CO 81611.

Oregon Ski Tours by Sharrad. Touchstone Press, PO Box 81, Beaverton, OR 97005.

A Guide to Ski Touring Covering Colorado, Southern Wyoming and New Mexico by Queal. Rocky Mountain Division USSA.

Favorite Vermont Ski Inns and Lodging Guide by Janet and Rudyard Colter, McGraw-Hill Book Company, 1221 Avenue of the Americas, New York, NY 10020.

Cross-Country Canada by Keating. Van Nostrand Reinhold, 7625 Empire Drive, Florence, KY 41042.

Ski Tours in California by Beck. c/o Federation of Western Outdoor Clubs, 4534½ University Way, NE, Seattle, WA 98115.

Ski Trail Construction Guide

Ski Touring Planner by Knopp and Maloney. North Star Ski Touring Club of Minnesota, PO Box 15059, Commerce Station, Minneapolis, MN 55415.

Cross Country Ski Trails—A Guide to Their Design and Management by Paul Rasmussen. Northeastern Illinois Planning Commission, 400 West Madison St., Chicago, IL 60606.

Magazines

Nordic Skiing. PO Box 106, W. Brattleboro, VT 05301.

Cross Country Skiing. Ski Magazine, 380 Madison Ave., New York, NY 10017. Published once a year in the fall.

Ski X-C. 1597 Union St., Schenectady, NY 12309. Published once a year in the fall.

Backpacker (including Wilderness Camping). Ziff-Davis Publishing Co., One Park Ave., New York, NY 10016

INDEX